Practicing Texas Politics

A BRIEF SURVEY

Practicing Texas Politics

A BRIEF SURVEY/Sixth Edition

Lyle C. Brown
Baylor University

Joe E. Ericson
Stephen F. Austin State University

Robert S. Trotter, Jr.
*El Centro College of the Dallas County
Community College District*

Joyce A. Langenegger
San Jacinto College

Ted Lewis
Collin County Community College

HOUGHTON MIFFLIN COMPANY   BOSTON   NEW YORK

Editor-in-Chief: Jean Woy
Sponsoring Editor: Melissa Mashburn
Associate Editor: Katherine Meisenheimer
Editorial Associate: Vikram Mukhija
Associate Project Editor: Gabrielle Stone
Senior Production/Design Coordinator: Jill Haber
Senior Manufacturing Coordinator: Priscilla Abreu
Senior Marketing Manager: Sandra McGuire
Associate Marketing Manager: Beth Foohey

Cover Design: Len Massiglia
Cover Image: Olin Travis, *The Shower*.

Printed in the U.S.A.
Library of Congress Catalog Card Number: 98-72003
Student Text ISBN: 0-395-90608-3

4 5 6 7 8 9-DOC-05 04 03 02 01

Contents

Preface

The Sixth Edition of *Practicing Texas Politics: A Brief Survey* describes and analyzes state and local politics as practiced in the Lone Star State. It is intended for use in political science courses offered by colleges and universities. To provide timely information, coverage of subject matter is as current as possible.

This concisely written survey is designed for instructors who prefer a shorter textbook and the option to supplement it with outside reading assignments and Internet research projects. The brief edition also meets the needs of a course that combines the study of Texas government and American national government.

Important Features of This Edition

New material in the Sixth Edition of *Practicing Texas Politics: A Brief Survey* focuses on important political events and governmental developments in the 1990s. It includes: up-to-date descriptions and analyses of the primaries and general election of 1998, actions of the 75th regular session of the Texas Legislature, performance of Governor George W. Bush during his first term in office, significant changes in the comparative strength of the Texas Democratic and Republican parties, influence of the Christian Coalition and other interest groups; new developments in public education, reform of the state's juvenile justice system, administration of Texas's prisons and jails, supervision of released offenders, and legislative decisions on state taxing and spending for fiscal years 1998 and 1999.

To give readers a wider range of political views, we have included one reading for each chapter. For example, Joe E. Ericson discusses the "patchwork quilt" arrangement of the much-amended Texas Constitution; Bob Sablatura explains why Harris County commissioners award no-bid contracts to politically connected contractors and law firms; Steve Scheibal tells how hundreds of college students and recent graduates fill state-government staff jobs and serve internships in Austin; Bruce Hight provides a profile of the Texas Department of Economic Development and its executive director; and Glenn Castlebury describes what life is like for inmates of Texas prisons.

In addition to approximately 60,000 words of text, students are provided with charts, tables, photos, cartoons, and readings. Key terms and concepts appear in boldface and are listed at the end of each chapter. In addition, terms that the authors believe are of particular importance are listed and defined in a glossary at the end of the book. The Selected Sources for Research and Reading are divided according to chapter and features useful web sites and approximately 300 titles of books and articles, most of which have been printed in the 1990s. A detailed index covering chapters and readings is included at the end of the book.

The Complete Teaching Package

As with earlier editions of *Practicing Texas Politics: A Brief Survey*, teaching ancillaries designed to help instructors and students are available separately.

The *Instructor's Resource Manual with Test Items,* prepared by Robert K. Peters of Tyler Junior College, offers learning objective files, complete lecture outlines for each chapter, lists of audio-visual and Internet resources, multiple choice questions, and essay questions with answer notes.

Additional ancillaries include a Windows-compatible computerized Test Bank that contains questions found in the *Instructor's Resource Manual* and a set of twenty overhead transparencies presenting tables, maps, and figures from the text.

Practicing Texas Politics Web Site

For the first time, a web site will support this text. The site includes chapter outlines, links to Texas government and politics sites, student self-testing material including multiple-choice and true/false questions, an updated bibliography of books and articles for further reading and research, and an Ask the Author feature. Also, updates will be posted when major events affect the content of the text. The site is accessible through the Political Science home page located at **http://www.hmco.com/college**.

Acknowledgments

Changes in the author team for the Sixth Edition of *Practicing Texas Politics: A Brief Survey* feature the retirement of Eugene W. Jones, a valued collaborator for nearly three decades and professor emeritus at Angelo State University; the addition of Joyce A. Langenegger; and the replacement of Eileen M. Lynch by Ted Lewis. Among those who assisted in the preparation of this book are several practicing politicians, journalists, newspaper editors, state and local government personnel, librarians, and professors in Texas universities and community colleges—especially colleagues in our own departments. The following reviewers read all or part of the manuscript and provided many useful comments and suggestions for which we are grateful:

Jack Barbour, Angelo State University; Jill Clark, University of Texas, Arlington; Michael J. Flavin, Midwestern State University; and Timothy Howard, North Harris College.

Finally, we dedicate *Practicing Texas Politics: A Brief Survey*, Sixth Edition, to Texas college and university students and instructors who, we hope, will be the chief beneficiaries of our work.

Lyle C. Brown
Joe E. Ericson
Robert S. Trotter, Jr.
Joyce A. Langenegger
Ted Lewis

Chapter 1

★

THE ENVIRONMENT OF TEXAS POLITICS

"KICK RUMP OPRAH!"

Copley News Service.

*D*istributed nationwide by the Copley News Service, the preceding cartoon illustrates how Texas government and politics sometimes attract national attention. After agricultural interests pressured the Texas Legislature to pass the state's False Disparagement of Perishable Food Products act in 1995, persons became liable for knowingly spreading false information stating or implying that a perishable food product is unsafe for human consumption. By 1998, a total of 13 states had similar "veggie libel" laws; and millions of Americans knew that the nation's most famous TV talk-show hostess had been sued in the Lone Star State.

Texas Beef Group v. *Oprah Winfrey*

Under Texas's false disparagement law and related civil statutes, Paul Engler and other Panhandle feedlot operators sued Oprah Winfrey, vegetarian activist Howard Lyman, and Harpo Productions, Inc. The plaintiffs sought more than $10 million in actual damages, plus unspecified punitive damages, for statements made on Winfrey's "Dangerous Foods" show aired nationwide on April 16, 1996. In the course of this program, Lyman declared that the since-banned practice of feeding protein-enhanced meal containing ground-up dead livestock could spread the "mad cow disease." Although there was no evidence of this disease in the United States, it had hit Great Britain's cattle industry and, according to the British government, most likely caused the deaths of some people who ate contaminated beef. Winfrey responded, "It has just stopped me cold from eating another burger." Subsequently, Chicago Mercantile Exchange prices for future delivery of live cattle dropped sharply.

For six weeks in January and February 1998, the Chicago-based *Oprah Winfrey Show* attracted national attention to Amarillo. There, Winfrey taped her show nightly in the city's Little Theater and spent weekdays in court in the A. Marvin Jones Federal Building. Although state law was involved, the case was tried in a U.S. district court because Winfrey was a resident of Illinois and damages of more than $75,000 were sought by Engler and each of the other plaintiffs. On February 17, U.S. District Judge Mary Lou Robinson ruled that there was no proof that the defendants had made knowingly false statements or that live cattle are a perishable food. Nevertheless, she continued the trial under the state's general business-defamation law. This meant that Engler's group would have to prove damaging statements had been made "of and concerning" them, with reckless disregard for the truth or malicious intent. Finally, on February 26, an all-white, twelve-member jury (4 men and 8 women) found that Winfrey, her production company, and Lyman were not liable. Subsequently, Engler and others announced that they would appeal to the Fifth U.S. Circuit Court of Appeals in New Orleans.

Later, in a separate lawsuit, Winfrey, Lyman, and Harpo Productions were sued by seven feedlot companies (including Engler's Cactus Feeders, Inc.) on behalf of more than 100 ranchers and businessmen residing in Texas, 17 other states, Canada, and Mexico. All had fed or owned cattle in Engler's Texas feedlots at the time of Winfrey's "Dangerous Foods" show, and each claimed damages up to $75,000. Because no plaintiff claimed damages in excess of $75,000, this second veggie libel suit was filed in Judge Ron Enns' state district court in the Panhandle town of Dumas (population 13,400) located 50 miles north of Amarillo. Winfrey's lawyer expressed outrage at the renewed attack on her freedom of speech; the court's crowded docket indicated a lengthy delay before any trial could be held; and Winfrey's fans faced the possibility of future shows taped in the cowtown that is celebrated in song as the home of the Ding Dong Daddy who likes to strut his stuff. Also of importance is the fact that Dumas is the county seat of Moore County, where beef is the second most important industry and Engler is a major employer.[1]

Legislative actions and court proceedings, as well as popular elections and lobbying activities, are parts of the political struggle that determine, in the words of political scientist Harold Lasswell, "who gets what, when, and how."[2] **Politics** involves conflict between political parties and other groups that seek to elect government officials or to influence those officials when they make public policy, such as enacting and interpreting the Texas veggie libel law.

Political Behavior Patterns

This book focuses on politics as it is practiced within the Lone Star State. Our analysis of the politics of Texas's state and local governments today aims to help readers understand political action and prepare them for participation in the political affairs of this state and of its counties, cities, and special districts. In addition, we will introduce readers to some important **political actors,** most of them high-ranking party activists or government officials who have been elected or appointed to public office. In politics, as in athletics, people need to be able to identify the players to understand the game.

Government, Politics, and Public Policy

Government may be defined as a public institution with the authority to allocate values in a society. In practice, values are allocated when a state or local government formulates, adopts, and implements a **public policy,** such as raising taxes to pay for more police protection or better streets and highways. At the state level, each public policy is a product of political activity that may involve both conflict and cooperation among legislators, between legislators and the governor, within the courts, and among various governmental agencies, lobby groups, and citizens.

Policymaking involves political action intended to meet particular needs or achieve specific objectives. For example, a state policy to promote public health by reducing or eliminating the use of certain pesticides alleged to cause cancer might be proposed to a legislator by the governor or another government official, by a nongovernmental organization such as the environmentalist Sierra Club, or by any interested person. Next, the proposal would be incorporated into a bill and submitted to the Texas Legislature by a state senator or representative favoring a new policy. Then, in committee hearings and on the floor of the Senate and the House of Representatives, the bill would be discussed and debated in the presence of lobbyists representing interest groups, journalists reporting the news, and concerned citizens. When the bill is passed by the legislature and signed by the governor, the pesticide proposal becomes law. Next, the new public policy must be implemented, or put into operation. That responsibility might be assigned by law to the Texas Department of Agriculture or to some other governmental agency. But the policy measure could be challenged in court. Judges might uphold all or part of the legislation or nullify it entirely if it violates some provision of the Texas Constitution or the U.S. Constitution. In sum, politics is the moving force that produces public policy, which in turn determines the ultimate course pursued by government.

Political Culture

Politics is influenced by **political culture,** which consists of attitudes, habits, and general behavior patterns that develop over time. Political culture is the result of both remote and recent political experiences. The foundations of Texas's political culture were laid and developed under the flags of six national governments: Spain, France, Mexico, the Republic of Texas, the Confederate States of America, and the United States. Unlike most of the other 49 states, Texas was not a U.S. territory prior to statehood. As an independent republic (1836–1845), Texas was given diplomatic recognition by the governments of the United States, England, France, Holland, and Belgium. With a popularly elected president and congress, the republic maintained its own army and navy, operated a postal system, printed paper money, administered justice through its courts, and provided other governmental services.

Individualism and Conservatism According to Professor Daniel Elazar, "culture patterns give each state its particular character and help determine the tone of its fundamental relationship, as a state, to the nation."[3] Elazar asserts that the political culture of Texas is strongly individualistic in that government is supposed to maintain a stable society but intervene as little as possible in the lives of the people. Elazar identifies the state's politics with economic and social conservatism, strong support of personal politics, distrust of political parties, and minimization of parties' importance. He states that a majority of Texans are descendants of immigrants from traditionalistic southern states, where conservatism, elitism (upper-class rule), and one-party politics were long entrenched.

Although urbanization and industrialization, together with an influx of people from other states and countries, are changing the cultural patterns of Texas's population, Elazar insists that the traditionalistic **influence of the Old South** still lingers. He notes that many Texans have inherited southern racist attitudes, which for decades were reflected in state laws that discriminated against African Americans and other minority groups in party membership, voter registration, and voting.

The traditionalistic **influence of Mexico** is discernible among some Mexican-American Texans who are affected by a political culture featuring the elitist *patrón* (protecting political boss) system that still dominates certain areas of South Texas. For more than 20 years, however, the old political order of that region has been challenged—and, in many instances, defeated—by a new generation of Mexican Americans.

With regard to Elazar's appraisal of Texas's conservative political culture, important questions arise: How long will particular sociocultural influences last? Are not cultural influences of the past being ever replaced by new ones? Will Texas's cultural identities, inherited largely from the nineteenth century, survive indefinitely in the face of widespread urbanization, industrialization, and population change?

The Frontier Experience Another source of Texas's conservatism is the nineteenth-century **frontier experience**. This concept has been enlarged over time by historians and fiction writers emphasizing the violent aspects of Texans' struggle for independence from Mexico and their clashes with Native Americans who unsuccessfully resisted the westward movement of Anglo settlers. Thousands of natives and settlers—men, women, and children—were slain on the Texas frontier from the 1820s to the mid-1870s. This period of frontier warfare lasted longer in Texas than in other states.

After the Texas frontier was secured, there remained the task of bringing law and order to the land. In some areas, range wars, cattle rustling, and other forms of violence continued to menace law-abiding citizens into the twentieth century. As a result of these experiences, many Texans grew accustomed to the use of force in settling disputes and struggling for survival. In 1995, when the legislature legalized the carrying of concealed handguns by licensed owners, some people interpreted the action as another influence of frontier days, when many Texans carried concealed weapons or bore pistols openly in holsters. Today, shootings and other violence may be as common in Texas's inner cities and elsewhere as they were on the state's frontier in the nineteenth century.

Professor Mody C. Boatright and others have questioned the traditional emphasis on violence as an important aspect of life on the Texas frontier. They have pictured an environment in which settlers developed a spirit of community cooperation as they built schools and churches, harvested crops, participated in house-raisings and logrollings, and rounded up cattle.[4] Regardless of differing views concerning the frontier influence, the Lone Star State's political culture will continue to be shaped by immigration, urbanization, communication, and education, along with other national and even international developments.

The Land

Like people everywhere, Texans are influenced by their geography as well as by their history. Thus, Texas's mountains, plains, seacoasts, climate, mineral deposits, and other geographic features affect the state's economy, its political culture, and the part the Lone Star State plays in national and international affairs. By the end of the twentieth century, Texans had cleared the land to establish and operate thousands of farms and ranches, built hundreds of towns and cities, organized many banks and businesses, and produced much of the nation's oil and natural gas, cotton and mohair, fish and meat, wheat and sorghum, fruits and vegetables, and computers and computer chips.

The Politics of Geography

From the start, Texas politics and public policy have been molded in part by the state's size. Its very large area and diverse physical geography create strong regional interests. Regardless of where they live, however, most citizens of the Lone Star State strongly identify with their state and are proud to be called Texans.

Size With about 267,000 square miles of territory, Texas is second only to Alaska in area. The Lone Star State is as large as the combined areas of New York, Pennsylvania, Ohio, Illinois, and the six New England states.

Moving south in a straight line from the northwestern corner of the Texas Panhandle to the state's southern tip on the Rio Grande near Brownsville, one must travel 800 miles. Almost equally long is the distance from Newton County's Louisiana border (south of the Sabine River's Toledo Bend Reservoir) to the New Mexican border near El Paso. Believe it or not, Texarkana is closer to Chicago than to El Paso, and Brownsville is closer to Mexico City than to the Panhandle town of Texline. Such great size has necessitated the building of about 274,000 miles of roadways in the state, including more than 71,000 miles of major highways constructed and maintained under the supervision of the Texas Department of Transportation. No other state has so many miles of roadways.

Due to their state's vast size and **geographic diversity,** Texans developed a concept of five areas—North, South, East, West, and Central Texas—as five potentially separate states. In fact, the congressional resolution by which Texas was admitted to the Union in 1845 specifies that up to four states "in addition to said state of Texas" may be formed out of its territory and that each "shall be entitled to admission to the Union." Various plans for carving Texas into five states have been proposed to the Texas Legislature, none of which has been taken seriously by most Texans.

FIGURE 1.1 Texas Geographic Regions

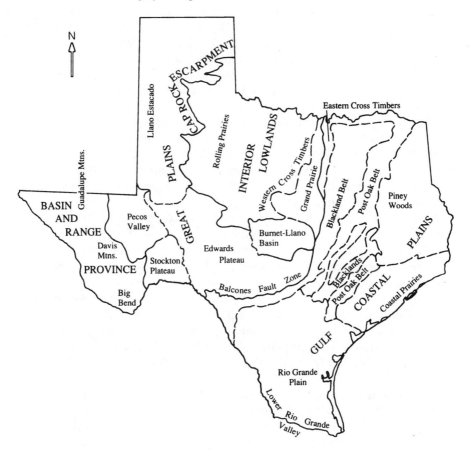

Source: *1990–91Texas Almanac and State Industrial Guide* (Dallas: A. H. Belo Corporation, 1989), p. 70. Reprinted with permission from the *Texas Almanac*. Further reproduction, without specific permission, not licensed.

Regions Geographically, Texas is at the confluence of several major physiographic regions of North America. The four principal **physical regions** of the state are the Gulf Coastal Plains, the Interior Lowlands, the Great Plains, and the Basin and Range Province. (For a map showing these regions, see Figure 1.1.)

The Gulf Coastal Plains region in East Texas is an extension of the Gulf Coastal Plains of the United States, a region that stretches westward from the Atlantic coast and then southward into Mexico. The internal boundary of the Gulf Coastal Plains follows the Balcones Fault, so named by Spanish explorers because the westward-rising hills resemble a line of balconies. Immediately east of the fault line is the Blackland Belt. From 15 to 70 miles in width, this strip of black soil stretches southward from the Red River, which marks the eastern half of the Oklahoma border, to the Mexican border. The international boundary follows the Rio Grande in its southeastern course from

El Paso to Brownsville and the Gulf of Mexico. (Mexicans call this international stream the Rio Bravo, which means "brave river" or "fierce river.")

Bordering the Gulf of Mexico, between the Piney Woods of East Texas and the Rio Grande Plain of South Texas, is the Coastal Prairies area. This flat region has been the scene of Texas's greatest industrial growth since World War II, particularly in the section between Beaumont and Houston. Here are the state's chief petrochemical industries, which are based on petroleum and natural gas.

The Interior Lowlands region encompasses the North Central Plains of Texas. That territory is bounded by the Blackland Belt on the east, the Cap Rock Escarpment on the west, the Red River on the north, and the Colorado River on the south. Farming and ranching are important activities within this largely prairie domain. Major cities in the region are Abilene, Dallas, Fort Worth, and Wichita Falls.

Immediately west of the Interior Lowlands and rising to higher altitudes, the Texas Great Plains area is a southern extension of the Great High Plains of the United States. From Oklahoma at the northern boundary of the Panhandle, this area extends southward to the Rio Grande. The Panhandle and South Plains portion of the region is known principally for its large-scale production of cotton and grain sorghum. These irrigated crops draw their water from the Ogallala Aquifer, formed thousands of years ago by runoff from the Rocky Mountains. This underground, water-bearing rock formation extends northward from Texas to North Dakota and underlies parts of eight states. Chief cities of the Panhandle–South Plains are Lubbock and Amarillo.

Centered in Nevada, the Basin and Range region of the United States enters western Texas from southern New Mexico. The only part of the Lone Star State classified as mountainous, this rugged triangle provides Texans and non-Texans with a popular vacation area that includes the Davis Mountains and Big Bend National Park. The state's highest mountains, Guadalupe Peak (8,749 feet) and El Capitan (8,085 feet) are located here.

Economic Geography

Although geographic factors do not directly determine political differences, geography greatly influences the economic pursuits of a region's inhabitants, which in turn shape political interests and attitudes. Geography has encouraged rapid population growth, urbanization, and industrialization in East Texas; in arid West Texas, it has produced a sparsely populated rural and agricultural environment. In the course of its economic and political development, the Lone Star State has been influenced greatly by three land-based industries: cattle, cotton, and oil.

Cattle The origin of Texas's **cattle ranching** may be traced to Gregorio de Villalobos, who transported Spanish-Moorish cattle from Spain to Mexico in the early years of the conquest. Subsequently, Francisco Vásquez de

Coronado and other Spanish explorers and settlers brought livestock into Texas. Later, cattle from Mexico were crossbred with cattle brought by Anglo settlers to produce the hardy Texas longhorn that thrived on the open range.

Plentiful land and the relative absence of government interference encouraged the establishment of huge cattle empires by determined entrepreneurs such as Richard King and Mifflin Kenedy. Today the famous King Ranch is composed of four separate units that total more than 825,000 acres in Kleberg County (with the county seat at Kingsville, near the ranch headquarters) and five other South Texas counties.[5] Ownership of the Kenedy Ranch's 370,000 acres has been contested by the descendants of José Manuel Ballí. They claim that Kenedy acquired this land illegally.

After the Civil War (1861–1865), an estimated 5 million cattle ranged over Texas's nearly 168 million acres of land. During the 25 years following that war, about 10 million longhorns were driven from Texas to Abilene (Kansas) and other northern railheads. In time, the beef business as a political and economic force leveled off in the wake of newly emerging industries. Yet today, Texas still has more cattle than any other state: about 15 million, including 400,000 dairy cows.

Cotton Before Spaniards brought cattle into Texas, cotton was already growing wild in the region. Spanish missionaries were the first to cultivate the plant. In the 1820s, the first hybrid or improved cotton was introduced

Cowboy Manuel Silva and cutting horse Corral separate a cow from a herd of King Ranch cattle. (Courtesy of King Ranch Archives, King Ranch, Inc.)

into Texas by Colonel Jared Groce, known as the founder of the Texas cotton industry. Groce and other Anglo Texans first cultivated cotton in East and Central Texas, where crop conditions most closely resembled those in the Old South. Prior to the Civil War, while slaves were available to perform much of the field labor, cotton production spread. During that war, revenue from the sale of Texas cotton to European buyers aided the Confederacy. As more frontier land was settled, **cotton production** moved westward and increased in volume.

Currently, the High Plains region of West Texas accounts for about 60 percent of the state's annual cotton yield. With more than 5.6 million acres of Texas farmland devoted to cotton production (about 40 percent of the country's cotton acreage), the annual harvest usually exceeds 5 million bales of lint and 2 million tons of cottonseed. The annual value of this crop has ranged from $1.0 billion to $1.7 billion in recent years. Much of Texas cotton is exported.

Oil Before the twentieth century, Texas petroleum was an unknown quantity and had very limited commercial value. Not until 1901, when the **Spindletop Field** was developed near Beaumont, did petroleum usher in the industry that dominated the state's economy for nearly a century. After the Spindletop boom, other wells were drilled across Texas. In 1919, the legislature gave the Texas Railroad Commission limited regulatory jurisdiction over the state's oil and natural gas industry.

At its peak in the early 1980s, the Texas petroleum industry employed half a million workers earning more than $11 billion annually. By that time, the state's oil business had expanded into gasoline refineries, petrochemical plants, and factories for manufacturing a wide range of tools and equipment used in drilling, transporting, and refining operations. Meanwhile an increasing number of banks willingly financed these costly enterprises. In 1982, an oil price slump began that produced a near panic in the industry, and the number of operating drilling rigs plunged from more than 1,000 to near zero by 1986. At that time, the price of oil dropped to less than $10 per barrel, its lowest level in more than a decade. As a result, many oil operators, businesspeople in related industries, and real estate developers were unable to meet their loan obligations. Thus, hundreds of banks and savings and loan associations became insolvent and were closed or merged with healthier financial institutions that were often controlled by out-of-state interests.[6] At the same time, tens of thousands of laborers, technicians, engineers, managers, and others lost their jobs and joined the ranks of the unemployed or left Texas to find jobs elsewhere.

By 1998, the oil and gas industry accounted for less than 10 percent of the state's economy and provided employment for only about 160,000 Texans. Nevertheless, most oil and gas jobs (including those in refineries and other petrochemical plants) pay relatively high wages and salaries. Meanwhile, there is a growing awareness that oil-based fuels burned in automobiles, trucks, buses, and airplanes are the world's principal source of atmospheric pollution. In addition, immeasurable harm to the world's oceans has resulted from oil spills in the Gulf of Mexico and other waters around the globe.

In the century-long development of the Texas oil industry, its political impact has been inevitable. Because of the large amounts of oil money contributed to candidates for public office and collected as revenue from taxes and lease holdings by state and local governments, Texas politics could hardly escape the industry's influence. In recent years, however, reduced petroleum production and relatively low oil prices (except for the brief period of the Gulf War sparked by Iraq's invasion and occupation of Kuwait) have been accompanied by declining political contributions from the industry.

The People

Texas has a large, ethnically diverse population. In every decade since 1850, it has grown more rapidly than the overall population of the United States. Like the population of the nation, Texas's population is aging as the post–World War II baby-boom generation reaches middle age. More than one-third of all Texans are either African Americans or Hispanics; the remainder are predominantly Anglos (non-Hispanic whites), with a small but rapidly growing number of Asians and fewer than 70,000 Native Americans.

Demographic Features

According to the federal census of 1990, Texas's population totaled 16,986,510. After the release of this census figure, Sunbelt states called for a revision, claiming the region had 1.8 million uncounted people, including 482,000 in Texas. The majority of unreported Texans were Hispanics living in South Texas, the most undercounted area in the United States. In the decade before the 1990 census, the number of Texans increased by 2.8 million. This amounts to a decennial growth rate of 19.4 percent; the national growth rate for that period was only 9.8 percent. Of the state's total 1990 population, 10.9 million (64.7 percent) had been born in Texas.

Population Distribution Just as Texas's physical geography makes the state a land of great contrasts, so does the distribution of its inhabitants. Densely populated, humid eastern areas contrast with sparsely populated, arid regions in the west. At one extreme is Harris County (containing Houston and most of its suburbs). Located in the southeastern part of the state, that county has more than 2.8 million inhabitants. At the other extreme is Loving County, on the New Mexican border, where the 1990 census counted only 107 people. Texas's four most populous counties (Harris, Dallas, Bexar, and Tarrant) have a combined population of more than 7 million, about

42 percent of all Texans. These four urban counties (along with Travis County) are located within the Texas Triangle, which is roughly outlined by segments of interstate highways 35, 45, and 10. (See Figure 1.2.)

During the 1980s, **population shifts** within Texas matched the national pattern: movement from rural to urban areas and from large cities to suburbs. Regions where the economy depended largely on oil and agriculture either decreased in total population or grew more slowly than the state as a whole. With an average growth rate of slightly more than 50 percent, suburban counties experienced the most rapid population increases in the 1980s. Some grew by nearly 90 percent. In sharp contrast, urban and rural counties grew by only 10 percent and 6 percent, respectively.

Population Changes Between 1970 and 1990, nearly 3 million people migrated to Texas from other states. Migrants entering Texas from other

FIGURE 1.2 The Texas Triangle

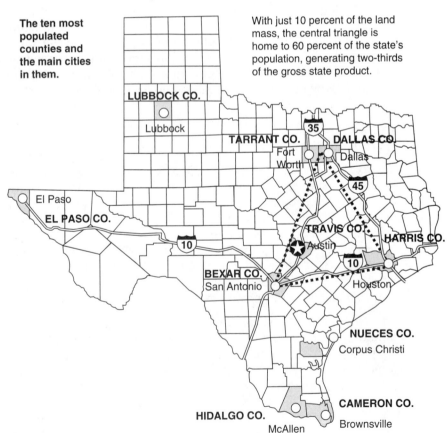

Source: "Demographic Graphics," *The Dallas Morning News,* May 8, 1994. Reprinted with permission of *The Dallas Morning News.*

states are adding significantly to the Lone Star State's population increase, but both legal and illegal immigration from Mexico and other countries also contribute to this growth.

The U.S. Census Bureau estimated that the population of Texas grew by 2.14 million from 1990 to 1996, an increase slightly higher than the estimated 2.12 million growth in California during those years. Although 55 percent of Texas's population rise was due to more births than deaths within the state, 23 percent consisted of immigrants from Mexico and other countries and 22 percent of immigrants from other parts of the United States.[7]

To provide today's public policymakers and businesspeople with demographic information that will allow them to plan for the future, Dr. Steven H. Murdock and his associates in the Population Estimates and Projections Program of the Department of Rural Sociology at Texas A&M University—College Station prepared alternative scenarios of population growth. According to Murdock, if the number of people migrating to Texas each year between 1990 to 2030 were offset by an equal number leaving, the state's population would still increase to nearly 21.8 million by 2030. If the rates of net migration from other countries and other states decreased to one-half of those for 1980–1990, Texas would have nearly 26.7 million people by 2030. If the rates of net migration remained the same as those for 1980–1990, the figure for the year 2030 would be more than 33.8 million. Finally, if net migration rates rose by 25 percent over those for 1980–1990, the population of Texas would grow to nearly 38 million.[8]

Urbanization   Migration of people from rural regions to cities results in **urbanization**. Urban areas are composed of one or more large cities and surrounding suburban communities. A suburb is a relatively small town or city, usually outside the boundary limits of a central city. For a century after statehood, Texas remained primarily rural. Then came urbanization, which progressed at an accelerated rate. Whereas Texas was 80 percent rural at the beginning of the twentieth century, by 1970 it was 80 percent urban. In the late 1990s, Texans living in metropolitan areas constitute more than 80 percent of the state's population. Suburbs adjoining or near central cities spread into rural areas and surrounding counties. This is especially true of Houston's suburbs, which have a combined population nearly as large as that of Houston.

Metropolitanization   Suburbanization on a large scale creates a metropolitan area, a core city surrounded by a sprawl of smaller cities and towns. Like most states, Texas is experiencing suburbanization on a very large scale. **Metropolitanization** concentrates large numbers of people in urban centers, which become linked in a single geographic entity. Though socially and economically integrated, a metropolitan area is composed of separate units of local government, which include counties, cities, and special districts.

Since 1910, federal agencies have defined metropolitan areas for census purposes. In 1950, a set of standard metropolitan statistical areas (SMSAs), composed of groups of urbanized counties, was developed. Later these areas were redefined. The word *standard* was dropped, and three new area classifications based on population were adopted:

■ **Metropolitan statistical area (MSA):** the basic unit, comprising a freestanding urbanized area with a total population of at least 50,000
■ **Primary metropolitan statistical area (PMSA):** composed of two or more MSAs with a total population of 100,000 or more
■ **Consolidated metropolitan statistical area (CMSA):** a megalopolitan area consisting of two or more PMSAs and a total population of 1 million or more

The United States (including Puerto Rico) contains 258 MSAs (22 in Texas), 76 PMSAs (5 in Texas), and 19 CMSAs (2 in Texas). Each of the Dallas and Fort Worth urbanized areas is designated a PMSA; combined they form a CMSA. The only other CMSA in Texas is composed of the Houston PMSA, the Galveston–Texas City PMSA, and the Brazoria PMSA.

With a population of about 4 million in 1990, the Dallas–Fort Worth Metroplex became the eighth most populous metropolitan area in the nation. Between 1980 and 1990, its population grew nearly 30 percent, for a gain of more than 950,000 people, as it became the most populous area in Texas. During the same period, the Houston-Galveston-Brazoria metropolitan area (population 3,750,000 in 1990) grew by 20 percent to become second in population. In the 1990s, rapid population growth continued in both CMSAs.

Cities are eager to obtain the highest possible statistical designation because many congressional appropriations are made accordingly. For example, to qualify for mass transit funds, an area must be an MSA. The business community also uses data on population concentrations for market analysis and advertising.

Texas's rate of population growth is consistently greater in the MSAs than throughout the state as a whole. Most of these population concentrations are in the eastern part of the state. Texas's MSAs contain 82 percent of the state's population but include only 48 of the 254 counties. It is politically significant that these 48 counties potentially account for four out of every five votes cast in statewide elections. Thus, governmental decision-makers are answerable primarily to people living in one-fifth of the state's counties. The remaining four-fifths, constituting the bulk of the state's area, have only 18 percent of the people. Urban voters, however, are rarely of one mind at the polls; they do not tend to overwhelm rural voters by taking opposing positions on all policy issues.

Racial/Ethnic Groups

Today, three major groups comprise 98 percent of the Texas population: Anglos, Hispanics (mostly Mexican Americans but including other persons of Spanish origin), and African Americans. The remaining 2 percent is composed largely of Asian Americans and Native Americans.

The size of its combined African American and Hispanic (or Latino) groups distinguishes Texas from the country as a whole. In 1980, one Texan in three was non-Anglo, that is, a member of a racial or an ethnic minority. The national ratio in that year was one in five. By 1990, African American and Hispanic minorities together constituted more than 37 percent of Texas's population, compared to only 24 percent for the nation.

Professor Steven Murdock projects the following population percentages for the year 2010 if the rate of net migration to Texas that occurred from 1980 to 1990 remains the same: Anglo, 48.6; Hispanic, 36.1; African American, 10.9; and other (Asian and Native American), 4.4. In this scenario, Anglos would no longer constitute a majority; they would be outnumbered by the combined total of other groups. In a similar scenario, Murdock's projections for the year 2030 are as follows: Anglo, 36.7; Hispanic, 45.9; African American, 9.5; and other, 7.9. At this point there would still be no majority, but Hispanics would outnumber Anglos.[9]

Native Americans   In the 1990s, **Native Americans** constitute fewer than 1 percent of Texas's residents, but their number was never large. Estimates of the number of Native Americans in the area when the first Spaniards arrived range from 30,000 to 150,000. Traveling in Texas in 1856, after three decades of Anglo-Indian warfare, one observer estimated the state's Native American population at about 12,000.[10] As of 1990, the Native American population of Texas was nearly 66,000. Most Native Americans reside in towns and cities, where they work in a variety of jobs and professions.

Only three small tribal groups live on reservations in Texas. About 550 Native Americans, the remnants of the Alabama and Coushatta tribes, are found on a 4,351-acre reservation in Polk County in the Big Thicket region of East Texas. Far across the state, near Eagle Pass on the United States–Mexico border, live a few hundred members of another Indian group, the Kickapoo tribe. The governments of Mexico and the United States allow them to move back and forth between Texas and the Mexican state of Coahuila. The state's third Native American group, the 1,400-member Tigua tribe, inhabits a 100-acre reservation near El Paso. Because of widespread intermarriage with non-Tiguas, only five Tiguas of unmixed ancestry remained in 1997, and these were women over 50 years of age.[11]

African Americans   The first **African Americans** entered Texas as slaves of Spanish explorers in the sixteenth century. Three hundred years later, about the time slavery was abolished in Mexico, Anglo settlers brought larger numbers of black slaves from the United States to Texas. In addition, a few free African Americans came from northern states before the Civil War. By 1847, African Americans accounted for one-fourth of the state's population; in 1880, they numbered about 400,000. By 1990, Texas had 2 million African Americans, about 12 percent of the state's population. Today Texas has the third-largest number of African Americans in the nation after New York and California. Most are located in southeast, north-central, and northeast

Texas, where they are concentrated in large cities. In recent years, a significant number of Africans have emigrated to the United States and settled in Texas; for example, more than 30,000 African immigrants live in the Dallas area.

Like other Texans, African Americans have largely abandoned farms and villages for the state's urban areas. Their search for employment and their desire for a higher standard of living have prompted this migration. Today half of the state's African Americans reside in and around Houston, Dallas, Fort Worth, San Antonio, and Beaumont. More than 20 percent live in Harris County.

Hispanics   Until 1836, Texas history was part of the history of Spain and Mexico. After the Texas Revolution of that year, immigration from Mexico all but ceased; it resumed after 1900, especially during the decade of the Mexican Revolution, which began in 1910. In the second half of the twentieth century, Texas's Hispanic population has been enlarged by a relatively high birth rate and a surge of illegal immigration from Mexico and other countries in the Western Hemisphere.

In the 1980s, Texas's Hispanic population became more diverse in terms of country of origin. This resulted from an increase in immigrants from Central America, South America, and the islands of the Caribbean. By 1990, Texas **Hispanics** numbered about 4.3 million, or nearly 26 percent of the state's population. Today, the populations of no fewer than 13 Texas counties are more than 80 percent Hispanic, and in 36 counties minority residents (chiefly Hispanics) are in the majority. This gives Texas the most minority-dominated counties in the nation.

More than 90 percent of Texas Hispanics are of Mexican origin. Texas ranks second in the nation in the number of Spanish-surnamed residents; only California, with about 7.7 million in 1990, has more.

San Antonio and El Paso are the largest cities in the United States with Hispanic majorities. In both Houston and Corpus Christi, African Americans and Hispanics together constitute more than 50 percent of the population. Both the economic strength and the political influence of Texas's Spanish-surnamed citizens are on the increase. Hispanics have larger families and are younger than the Anglo population. Immigration from Mexico and other Spanish-speaking countries is expected to continue throughout the remainder of the twentieth century and beyond. (See the reading on pages 28–31 for a description of relations between people in El Paso and Ciudad Juarez, twin cities on the border.)

Asian Americans   Few members of Texas's three largest ethnic populations (Anglo, Hispanic, and African American) are aware that the Lone Star State is home to one of the largest **Asian American** populations in the nation. Most of Texas's Asian-American families have immigrated to the United States from Southeast Asia (Cambodia, Laos, and Vietnam in particular). Only a small percentage are American born. Compared to Hispanics and African Americans, Asian Americans are newcomers to Texas. By the mid-

1990s, however, 4 percent of all Asian Americans in the United States were living in the Lone Star State.

Most Asian Americans settle in the state's largest urban centers, Houston and the Dallas–Fort Worth Metroplex. Many are unskilled laborers, but about half of Texas's first generation Asian Americans entered this country with college degrees or completed degrees later. The intensity with which the state's young Asian Americans focus on education is revealed by enrollment data for the University of Texas at Austin. Although Asian Americans account for about 2 percent of the total population of the state, they comprised more than 17 percent of the total freshman class enrollment in the University of Texas at Austin in the fall semester of 1998.

Anglos As commonly used in Texas, the term **Anglo** is not restricted to persons of Anglo-Saxon lineage. Traditionally, the term applies to all whites except Hispanics. The 1990 census indicates that more than 60 percent of Texas's population is composed of "non-Hispanic whites." Although the first non-Spanish-speaking immigrants to Texas were largely of English ancestry, some were of Scottish, Irish, and Welsh ancestry. A significant number of German immigrants established settlements in the Hill Country west and north of San Antonio before the Civil War. Additional European immigrant groups include French, Scandinavian, and Eastern European peoples, together with a scattering of Italians, Greeks, and others.

Some Social and Economic Policy Issues

Social and economic influences on government, politics, and policymaking have been recognized since the days of ancient Greece. In recent years, Texas has experienced a wave of uncontrolled immigration and rapid economic change. Both of these developments pose problems for policymakers.

Immigration: Federal and State Problems

Since Texas became part of the Union, meandering the 1200-mile Rio Grande boundary with Mexico has been the source of many controversies.[12] Controlling the flow of aliens across the river, deciding how long they can remain within U.S. territory, determining what labor (if any) they may perform, and other immigration policy matters are issues that affect state, national, and international politics. Persons entering the United States in violation of federal immigration laws are called **undocumented aliens**. Although they supply Texas employers with cheap labor, some compete with U.S. citizens for jobs and require costly social services for themselves or for their children who come into this country or are born here. As with immigration issues involving other racial and ethnic groups today and in earlier periods of American history, passions and prejudices produce explosive politics.

In response to heavy political pressure and 14 years of debate and political maneuvering, the U.S. Congress enacted into law the Immigration Reform and Control Act of 1986. This federal statute was designed to restrain the flow of illegal immigrants into the United States by penalizing employers who knowingly hire undocumented aliens and appropriating funds to provide more enforcement personnel for the U.S. Immigration and Naturalization Service (INS), especially border patrol officers, whom Hispanics refer to as *la migra*.

In fact, hundreds of thousands of undocumented aliens have continued to enter Texas each year since 1986. Many are arrested, detained, and subsequently expelled from the country. Others voluntarily return to Mexico and other countries after earning money to support their families. But many thousands of undocumented aliens remain in Texas and often are able to arrange for family members to join them. Some undocumented aliens are shamelessly exploited by employers, merchants, and landlords. Others receive fair wages and humane treatment. All, however, live and work in fear of arrest and deportation.

In the 1990s, an anti-immigration groundswell developed throughout most parts of the United States. Central to the controversy is the issue of costs and benefits resulting from both legal and illegal immigration. In 1994, Texas joined other states in suing the federal government to recover various costs (for example, health, welfare, education, and law enforcement) incurred from illegal immigration. That same year, President Bill Clinton appointed former U.S. representative Barbara Jordan to chair the Commission on Immigration Reform, and U.S. border patrol personnel intensified their efforts to halt the influx of undocumented aliens. Meanwhile, immigration issues continued to attract the attention of social scientists, special-interest groups, politicians, the general public, and policymaking officials at all levels of government in Texas and throughout the country. In 1995, official estimates placed the total number of undocumented aliens in the United States at more than 3.5 million, with 300,000 to 427,000 located in Texas.

With the approach of congressional and presidential elections in 1996, the matter of undocumented aliens became a "hot-button" issue that some politicians exploited. Before the November election, the U.S. Congress enacted the Immigration Control and Financial Responsibility Act of 1996. It was co-sponsored by Representative Lamar Smith, a Republican from San Antonio. In addition to doubling the number of border patrol officers, the new ban increases penalties for immigrant smuggling and speeds up the deportation of illegal immigrants who use false documents or commit other crimes while in the United States.

Meanwhile, low wages and high levels of unemployment in Mexico motivate masses of Mexican workers to cross the border in search of jobs. At the same time, many businesspeople, farmers, and ranchers in Texas and elsewhere are willing to violate U.S. law (and run the risk of incurring fines) by hiring undocumented aliens. They do so because other labor is unavailable or because illegal immigrants will work harder for lower wages.

Searching for New Economic Directions

Once identified in the popular mind with cattle barons, cotton kings, and oil millionaires, the image of the Lone Star State is changing. Today, Texas is part of middle-class America, with its share of professionals and businesspeople employed by varied enterprises: law firms; universities; federal, state, and local government bureaucracies; real estate and insurance companies; wholesale and retail sales firms; and manufacturing, communication, and transportation industries.

Industry For more than half a century, petroleum production and related enterprises led Texas's industrial development. Then, devastated by plunging oil prices in the mid-1980s, the entire Texas petroleum industry declined sharply. Nevertheless, other businesses have spread across the state and now play an important role in the national economy. In *Fortune*'s 1998 listing of the 500 largest private corporations in the United States, 36 were headquartered in Texas. Only three states had a larger proportion of the 500 than Texas: New York, 61; California, 52; and Illinois, 41. Among the 15 cities having 6 or more of the Fortune 500, there were 2 in Texas: Houston was third with 15, while Dallas was sixth with 9.[13]

Traditionally, the state's government performs poorly in financing public education and providing basic social services. In attempting to attract new industries, leaders of Texas government and business emphasize that the state does not levy a personal income tax. When deciding whether to locate or relocate to Texas, however, corporate executives are more concerned about the quality of the state's human resources and public services. They are apt to be adversely impressed by a system of public education that is inadequately and inequitably financed. In the area of social services, they will note that Texas compares unfavorably with most other states in almost every category. Nevertheless, Texas's economy has outperformed the national economy in the 1990s. New enterprises involving high technology and biotechnology are part of the Lone Star State's drive toward industrial growth and diversification.

High Technology The term **high technology** applies to research, development, manufacturing, and marketing of a seemingly endless line of electronic products. Among these are computers, calculators, digital watches, microwave ovens, telecommunications devices, automatic bank tellers, aerospace guidance systems, medical instruments, and assembly-line robots. Although high-technology businesses employ less than 6 percent of Texas's labor force, these enterprises contribute about 10 percent of all wages paid to private-sector employees. Most "high-tech" jobs are in manufacturing. Approximately 85 percent of all high-tech employment is centered in Austin, Dallas, El Paso, Fort Worth, Houston, and San Antonio. Major high-tech manufacturers include Motorola, Dell Computer, Compaq Computer, Texas Instruments, and Applied Materials (which produces machinery for manufacturing semiconductors).

The occupational structure of many high-tech companies differs from those of most other industrial firms. High-tech enterprises employ larger percentages of professional, technical, and managerial personnel. More than one-third of all high-tech jobs are in these categories, and wages and salaries are well above average. In January 1997, the American Electronic Association released a 50-state survey revealing that Texas was second only to California in high-tech employment, with more than 300,000 high-tech jobs. This was less than half the number for California, but Texas manufactures more microchips.[14]

Biotechnology Today **biotechnology** ("biotech") is exerting a growing influence on the state's economy. This multibillion-dollar industry produces many new medicines and vaccines, exotic chemicals, and other products that benefit medical science, human health, and agricultural production. Biotech-related jobs have increased substantially since 1983, four times faster than the overall increase in employment in Texas.

Agriculture Endowed with a wide range of climates, hundreds of thousands of acres of arable land, an abundant supply of labor, and adequate transportation and harbor facilities, Texas's farmers and ranchers are well equipped to produce and market huge amounts of food and fiber. Today, the Lone Star State leads the nation in total acreage of agricultural land and numbers of farms and ranches, as well as in production of beef, grain sorghum, cotton, wool, and mohair (from Angora goats).

Gross income from the products of Texas **agriculture** amounts to about $15 billion annually. The estimated value of agricultural assets in the state (such as land, buildings, livestock, and machinery) is more than $100 billion. Texas leads the nation in exported cotton, much of which goes to Korea and Taiwan. Mexico is the largest buyer of Texas's farm and ranch products, and Japan is a major consumer of Texas-grown wheat and corn. Beef is the state's most important meat export, but horsemeat processed for human consumption has a $100-million-a-year foreign market. Half of Texas's exported horsemeat goes to France, Italy, Switzerland, Belgium, and Japan. Nevertheless, only 3 percent of the state's jobs and total income are provided by farming and ranching. Furthermore, most agricultural commodities are shipped abroad or to other parts of the United States without being processed in Texas by Texans. Consequently, industrial development for processing food and fiber is needed if Texas is to derive maximum economic benefit from the products of its farms and ranches.

The number and size of Texas farms and ranches have changed greatly over the past seven decades. These developments are due largely to the availability of labor-saving farm machinery and the use of chemicals to kill weeds, defoliate cotton before harvesting, and protect crops from insects and diseases. In the 1930s there were more than 500,000 farms and ranches in Texas, with an average size of 300 acres. By 1997 the number of farms and ranches was about 205,000, while the average size was approximately 630 acres.[15]

Services One-fourth of all employed Texans work in the **service industry,** and this sector continues to provide new jobs more rapidly than all others. Service businesses include those that provide health care (hospitals and nursing homes), personal services (hotels, restaurants, and recreational enterprises such as bowling alleys and video arcades), and commercial services (printers, advertising agencies, data processing companies, equipment rental companies, and management consultants). Other service providers include investment brokers, insurance and real estate agencies, banks and credit unions, and a large variety of merchandising enterprises.

Most service jobs pay lower wages and salaries than employment in manufacturing firms that produce goods. Thus, Austin journalist Molly Ivins warns, "The dream that we can transform ourselves into a service economy and let all the widget-makers go to hell or Taiwan is bullstuff. The service sector creates jobs all right, but they're the lowest paying jobs in the system. You can't afford a house frying burgers at McDonald's, even if you're a two-fryer family."[16]

Texas in the Course of National Affairs

During more than 150 years of statehood, Texas's influence on national affairs has often matched or even exceeded its physical size. For example, the Lone Star State's exploding population has resulted in increased representation in the U.S. House of Representatives (up from 27 to 30 as a result of reapportionment after the 1990 census). Also important is the fact that Texas has the third-largest number of electoral votes (32 for presidential elections from 1992 through the year 2000). Furthermore, a succession of prominent Texas-based politicians in White House and cabinet positions has added greatly to the state's national importance.[17]

Evidence of Texas's influence at the highest level of government was apparent during the 12-year Reagan-Bush era. After serving as vice president of the United States from January 1981 to January 1989, adopted-Texan George Bush was president of the United States from January 1989 to January 1993. Serving in the Bush cabinet were three Texans: James Baker III, secretary of state; Robert Mosbacher, Sr., secretary of commerce; and Lauro Cavazos, secretary of education. According to *The Dallas Morning News,* no fewer than 450 other Texans were serving in various positions in the Bush administration at the beginning of 1990. Perhaps one reason for the large number of prominent Texan officeholders was that the state's donors contributed $2 million to the Bush election campaign in 1988.

In 1992, Republicans held their presidential convention in Houston, Bush's adopted hometown. Texas voters responded by giving Bush a plurality of the popular vote in the November election. Nevertheless, for the first time since Texas joined the Union, a Democratic party candidate won the presidential election without the electoral votes of the Lone Star State. As a result, many

Texans feared that President Bill Clinton would all but ignore Texas during his administration beginning in 1993. Some of this anxiety was dispelled when Clinton selected U.S. senator Lloyd Bentsen, Jr., a Texan, as secretary of the Department of the Treasury and appointed Henry Cisneros, former mayor of San Antonio, secretary of the Department of Housing and Urban Development. Norma Cantu, a native of Brownsville, was named to head the Office of Civil Rights within the Department of Education.

After Bentsen's move to Clinton's cabinet, where he served for two years before retiring from public life, a Texan no longer chaired the powerful Senate Finance Committee. On the positive side, however, Texans would continue to chair three important committees in the U.S. House of Representatives: Kika de la Garza of McAllen (Agriculture), Jack Brooks of Beaumont (Judiciary), and Henry B. Gonzalez of San Antonio (Banking, Finance, and Urban Affairs). In 1993, Texas's congressional delegation ranked third in influence according to *Roll Call,* a Capitol Hill newspaper.

In the election of November 1994, Representative Brooks lost the House seat he had held for 40 years. Representatives de la Garza and Gonzalez were re-elected, but they lost their committee chairs as Republican majorities dominated both houses of the 104th Congress, which convened in January 1995. Included among Texas Republicans with seniority and influence in the 104th Congress were Senator Phil Gramm, the first Republican to announce he would seek his party's nomination as its presidential candidate in 1996; Representative Dick Armey, the House majority leader; Representative Tom DeLay, the House majority whip; and Representative Bill Archer, chair of the House Ways and Means Committee, which considers proposals for new federal tax laws. All four of these Texas Republicans continued in office after being re-elected in 1996 to the Republican-dominated 105th Congress. But with the resignation of Henry Cisneros as secretary of the Department of Housing and Urban Development at the end of President Clinton's first term, Texas lost its only cabinet member.

Meeting New Challenges

As we move into the twenty-first century, Texans will be greatly affected by public policy decisions concerning their state's economy and its entire social order. The most important of these decisions will relate to protection of the ecological system, job-creating economic development, technological changes in communications and industry, and restructuring and financing of public and higher education in the state.

Environmental Protection

In the 1990s, Texas's environment deteriorated as pollution by the state's petrochemical industries, deforestation, toxic waste generation without adequate disposal facilities, acid rain, and air and water pollution continued to pose hazards for all living creatures. Many human health problems are caused by the low quality of the air we breathe and the impurity of the water we drink. Some effects of environmental pollution are revealed in observations concerning fish and wildlife populations. For example, Texas (along with California, Hawaii, and Florida) leads all other states in the number of endangered fish and wildlife species.

Bordered by Florida, Alabama, Mississippi, Louisiana, and Texas, the Gulf of Mexico covers nearly 700,000 square miles, or seven times as much area as the Great Lakes. Industries in each of these states and Mexico release toxic chemicals directly into the gulf or into rivers that flow into it, especially the Rio Grande, which divides Texas and Mexico. Also contributing greatly to **environmental problems** in the gulf is the continuing flow of nitrate-laden rivers that draw their water from the chemically fertilized farms of rural areas and the lawns and gardens of cities large and small. With declining catches of fish, shrimp, and oysters from Gulf waters, Texans must do with less seafood or import it from abroad at rapidly rising prices. Of course, another solution to the problem would be environmental protection measures designed to clean up the Gulf of Mexico and restore its productivity.[18]

Education for Economic Development

Along with a poor record of environmental protection, Texas gets low marks in other critical areas that affect its residents' quality of life and economic welfare. In a 1990 report by the Corporation for Economic Development, experts at this national "think tank" faulted Texas for a dismal performance in education and its failure to develop a skilled work force, eliminate an imbalance between rich and poor areas, and overhaul an antiquated and counterproductive tax system. In the late 1990s, these shortcomings were still evident.

Success in dealing with educational needs will be especially important in determining Texas's ability to compete nationally and internationally in business as well as in science and technology. The urgency of this matter is suggested in studies that rank Texas near the bottom among the states in **literacy** of its residents. Of special concern to employers is the fact that one out of every three Texans cannot read and write well enough to fill out a simple job application. Moreover, the Texas Department of Economic Development estimates that the state loses many billions of dollars annually because most illiterate Texans are doomed to unemployment or low-paying jobs and thus generate little or no tax revenue.

Poverty and Social Problems

Although many of America's public figures stress the importance of family values, serious social and economic problems affect homes throughout the country. Since the 1980s, there have been alarming numbers of children living in **poverty,** births to unwed teenagers, juvenile arrests, violent acts committed by teenagers, pre-adolescents, and children in single-parent homes. Today nearly one of every four Texas children lives in poverty, and many children at all levels of society suffer from abuse and neglect. In 1997, the state's homeless population was estimated at between 85,000 and 225,000 according to a report by the Texas Department of Mental Health and Mental Retardation. The Texas Office for the Education of Homeless Children predicted that more than 123,000 of the state's children would be homeless sometime during that same year.

Texas's limited response to the social and economic needs of its people continues to be the subject of much debate. Some Texans argue that any public assistance for the poor is too much. They believe government hand-outs encourage dependence on government and discourage self-reliance, personal initiative, and desire to work. Other Texans advocate greatly increased government spending to help people who are unable to care for themselves and their families because of mental or physical health problems, lack of job opportunities, or age. Between these extremes are Texans who support a limited role for government in meeting human needs but call for churches and other nongovernmental organizations to play a more active role in dealing with social problems.[19] Texas voters, however, tend to support candidates for public office who promise lower taxes, tighter government budgets, fewer public employees, and reduction or elimination of social services. As a result, the Lone Star State ranks near the bottom of the 50 states in governmental responses to poverty and social problems.

Restructuring the Economy

Because the petroleum industry is not expected to regain its former leading role in Texas business, the restructuring of the state's economy has been vigorously pursued for more than a decade. In so doing, leaders in business and government have been forced to launch new industrial programs within the context of rapidly changing national and international circumstances.

A continuing struggle to provide jobs and market goods and services calls for effective public policies, a productive labor force, an adequate supply of capital, and sound managment practices. Of special importance to Texas is the fact that trade with Mexico has expanded greatly in recent years. In 1993, the U.S. Congress approved the **North American Free Trade Agreement (NAFTA),** to which the United States, Canada, and Mexico are parties. By reducing and then eliminating tariffs over a 15-year period, the agreement has stimulated U.S. trade with both Canada and Mexico.

Because 60 percent of U.S. exports to Mexico are produced in Texas or transported through the Lone Star State from other states, an expanding foreign trade should produce more jobs for Texans, more profits for the state's businesses, and more revenue for state and local governments. At the same time, however, a growing volume of trucking on highways between Mexico and Canada is producing serious traffic problems that endanger the lives of all motor vehicle drivers and passengers while slowing the transportation of goods.[20]

Since 1995, a succession of political and economic crises in Mexico have raised serious questions concerning the future of NAFTA. In fact, the survival of Mexico's political system has been jeopardized by assassinations of public figures, kidnappings of wealthy businesspeople, drug-related corruption of government officials, attacks on tourists, widespread unemployment and hunger in both urban and rural areas, and acts of armed rebellion (especially in the southern states of Chiapas, Oaxaca, and Guerrero). Today, Mexico has a population of more than 95 million; thus, another nationwide civil war such as the Mexican Revolution of 1910–1917 may drive millions of refugees northward across the border and into the United States.[21] Such a development would have a tremendous impact on the four U.S. border states of Texas, New Mexico, Arizona, and California.

Looking Ahead

As the process of economic development and diversification goes forward in Texas, some of the state's cherished values are being sorely tried. Many jobs are lost while others are being created, and old industries decline or die as new ones are established. Meanwhile, the lives of all Texans are affected—some for better and others for worse. Critical environmental problems—including air, water, and soil pollution—must be resolved at the same time the state's water supply is declining.[22]

Natural disasters such as hurricanes, tornadoes, floods, and droughts will continue to present problems for individuals, businesses, and governments at all levels. Further, as indicated by federal census statistics, together with economic and social data from other sources, Texas policymakers must deal with an expanding aging population and a high incidence of poverty. Above all, both ordinary citizens and public officials must realize that their ability to cope with public problems now and in the years ahead depends largely on how well our homes and schools prepare young Texans to meet the crises and demands of an ever-changing state, nation, and world.[23]

In the next chapter, we will examine the position of the states within the federal Union and look at the constitutional development of the Lone Star State, especially its much-amended Constitution of 1876.

Notes

1. For more details on the Winfrey affair, see Skip Hollandsworth and Pamela Colloff, "How the West Was Won Over," *Texas Monthly,* March 1998, pp. 100–103, 118–120; Karen Olsson, "Mad Cows and Cattlemen," *Texas Observer,* February 13, 1998, pp. 8–11; and John W. Gonzalez, "New Beef with Oprah: Irate Cattlemen Across Amercia Are Suing Talk-Show Host Over Disparaging Comments," *Houston Chronicle,* April 26, 1998, pp. 1A, 14A.

2. Harold Lasswell, *Politics: Who Gets What, When, How* (New York: McGraw-Hill, 1936).

3. Daniel Elazar, *American Federalism: A View from the States,* 3rd ed. (New York: Harper & Row, 1984), p. 134.

4. Mody C. Boatright, "The Myth of Frontier Individualism," *Southwestern Social Science Quarterly* 22 (June 1941), pp. 14–32. See also Chandler Davidson, *Race and Class in Texas Politics* (Princeton, N.J.: Princeton University Press, 1990), pp. 35–36.

5. See Jane Clements Monday and Betty Bailey Colley, *Voices from the Wild Horse Desert: The Vaquero Families of the King and Kenedy Ranches* (Austin: University of Texas Press, 1997); Armando C. Alonzo, *Tejano Legacy: Rancheros and Settlers in South Texas, 1734–1900* (Albuquerque: University of New Mexico Press, 1998).

6. For details concerning Texas's economy in the 1980s, see M. Ray Perryman, *Survive and Conquer, Texas in the 80s: Power-Money-Tragedy . . . Hope!* (Dallas: Taylor Publishing, 1990).

7. Tom Bowers, "Texas Approaches 20 Million to Lead U.S. in Population Growth," *San Antonio Express News,* January 1, 1997.

8. See Steven H. Murdock et al., *The Texas Challenge: Population Change and the Future of Texas* (College Station: Texas A&M University Press, 1997), pp. 11–14.

9. Ibid., p. 21.

10. Frederick Law Olmsted, *A Journey through Texas* (New York: Dix, Edwards, 1857; reprint, Burt Franklin, 1969), p. 296. For more information on Texas Indian tribes, see Richard L. Schott, "Contemporary Indian Reservations in Texas: Tribal Paths to the Present," *Public Affairs Comment* (Lyndon B. Johnson School of Public Affairs, University of Texas at Austin), 39:3 (1993).

11. Laura Smitherman, "Tejas Work to Save Tribe," *El Paso Times,* February 15, 1997.

12. For a collection of readable and informative essays that focus on life along the Mexican border, see Bobby Byrd and Susannah Mississippi Byrd, eds., *The Late Great Mexican Border* (El Paso: Cinco Puntos Press, 1996). See also Timothy J. Dunn, *The Militarization of the U.S.-Mexican Border, 1978–1992: Low Intensity Conflict Doctrine Comes Home* (Austin: CMAS Books, Center for Mexican American Studies, University of Texas at Austin, 1996).

13. *Fortune,* April 27, 1998, p. F-32.

14. Kirk Ladendorf, "Study Says Texas No. 2 in High-Tech," *Austin American-Statesman,* January 30, 1997, p. C-1.

15. These statistics were provided by the Texas Agricultural Statistics Service, Texas Department of Agriculture.

16. Molly Ivins, "Top to Bottom Reform of Financial Structures Essential," *Dallas Times Herald,* June 3, 1990.

17. See Kenneth E. Hendrickson, Jr., and Michael L. Collins, eds., *Profiles in Power: Twentieth Century Texans in Washington* (Arlington Heights, Ill.: Harlan Davidson, 1993).

18. For information on all aspects of Texas's environmental problems, see *Texas Environmental Almanac* (Austin: Texas Center for Policy Studies, 1995).
19. See Governor's Advisory Task Force on Faith-Based Community Service Groups, *Faith in Action: A New Vision for Church-State Cooperation in Texas,* Full Report (Austin, December 1996).
20. Roger Croteau, "Supporters Say Dangerous I-35 Needs Bypass," *San Antonio Express News,* March 9, 1997.
21. See Denise Dresser, "Mexico: Uneasy, Uncertain, Unpredictable," *Current History* 96 (February 1997) pp. 51–54.
22. For an excellent overview of the state's water problems, see Ann Walther, *Texas at a Watershed: Planning Now for Future Needs,* House Research Organization Report No. 75-13 (Austin: Texas House of Representatives, April 15, 1997).
23. To provide guidance for Texas government, business, communities, and individuals to the year 2015, Comptroller John Sharp and his staff produced an impressive two-volume study that is of special value to Texans seeking more information on ways to meet new challenges. See *Forces of Change: Shaping The Future of Texas* (Austin: Research Division, Office of the Comptroller of Public Accounts, 1994).

Key Terms and Concepts

politics	primary metropolitan statistical area (PMSA)
political actor	
government	consolidated metropolitan statistical area (CMSA)
public policy	
policymaking	Native American
political culture	African American
influence of the Old South	Hispanic
influence of Mexico	Asian American
frontier experience	Anglo
geographic diversity	undocumented alien
physical region	high technology
cattle ranching	biotechnology
cotton production	agriculture
Spindletop Field	service industry
population shift	environmental problems
urbanization	literacy
metropolitanization	poverty
metropolitan statistical area (MSA)	North American Free Trade Agreement (NAFTA)

SELECTED READING

*El Paso–Juarez: In the Foothills of the Future**

Research Division, Office of the Comptroller of Public Accounts

The Texas-Mexico border's largest twin cities are viewed as a single entity by the more than two million people who live there. Every day they exchange their cultures and economies, their difficulties and vitalities. Each has a past entwined with the others'. Sometimes they don't admit it, but they share the future, too.

People here already live in the future of Texas. Some of them have blond hair and blue eyes. Many speak English without musical inflections or soft vowels. Most hustle off each morning to jobs in car dealerships, factories, and banks. They send their kids to school dressed in the trendiest duds their wallets can afford. They make business deals over lunch and attend high school football games on Friday nights. They fret about taxes, traffic, and other trappings of modern life in the United States. But there are few real gringos here.

Bilingual by Necessity

In some ways, of course, the Texas future will be different from the glimpse of it you see here today. There will be no ethnic majority in Texas a generation from now, but 70 percent of El Paso's 600,000 residents today are Hispanic—and their numbers are growing. Across the bridge, Ciudad Juarez boasts an unofficial population of nearly 1.5 million. In other ways, though, tomorrow arrived here long ago. Most people on either side are bilingual, at least to the degree necessary to carry on commerce and cultural exchange, even as overall state trade increasingly ties itself to Mexico and other nations throughout the hemisphere. Between the slopes of the Sierra Juarez to the south and the foothills of the Franklin Mountains to the north, El Paso–Juarez constitute the world's largest international city, with a combined population of more than 2 million. One-fifth of all U.S. trade with Mexico flows through the area. Still, 72 percent of the region's retail business is internal. And together, residents of these twin cities work out local solutions to local problems they believe are mainly imposed by remote governments with little sense of the texture of the border and a way of life whose history and landscape predate Columbus.

*From *Forces of Change: Shaping the Future of Texas,* Vol. 1 (Austin: Comptroller of Public Accounts, 1994), pp. 260–264. Reprinted by permission; headings have been added.

Finding the Real Border

"Folks in El Paso understand folks in Mexico, both culturally and socially," says Henry King, director of the Census Data Affiliate for West Texas. "We have the technology to increase the value of the human and natural resources across the border." That border is rarely what it appears to be. Even where it begins and ends—except as a meandering abstract line in some cartographer's imagination—is largely a matter of opinion. Some say it stretches into parts of Houston, San Antonio, Chicago and Miami, or that it can be found in North Denver, East L.A., Oakland, and San Francisco's Mission District—approximately the same outpost boundaries that marked the height of the Spanish expansion north from Mexico during the seventeenth and eighteenth centuries.

Wherever the real border is, in EPJAZ, as planners call El Paso–Juarez, it increasingly resembles a fault line between two tectonic plates accumulating the economic tensions that originate far from the epicenter. The two cities have different histories, too, although they are unambiguously a single metropolis today. El Paso del Rio del Norte, the name given to the river valley by conquistador Don Juan de Oñate more than 400 years ago, has long since settled into a unique juxtaposition of the modern world's advances and the old ways. It was once a city, until the Mexican-American War connected the portion north of the Rio Grande to the United States.

Cities that Have Seen It All

El Paso became the county seat in 1883, wrestling the honor away from the once-larger Ysleta, where Texas' oldest mission, built by Franciscan missionaries and Tiguas in 1768, still stands. That's when Anglo merchants and financiers, a distinct minority, began to dominate local political and business circles. And if their status isn't as entrenched as in the past, many Hispanics in the El Paso–Juarez area might still be forgiven for believing that lighter colors continue to rise to the top—along with most of the money. First the northeast, then the northwest arms of El Paso's sprawl encircle the Franklin Mountains, effectively segregating the community and its schools. Real estate values to the south of the Interstate 10 dividing line are about half those to the north. And El Paso's Hispanics, outnumbering their Anglo friends nearly three to one, are crowded into the smaller south side of town.

As for Juarez, it has felt the alternating jolts of economic prosperity and depression in unique ways. Never feeling much of a link to distant Mexico City, its fortunes have nevertheless been dependent on decisions made there. In the 1880s, with new railroads along the Santa Fe–Chihuahua Trail, the capital granted Juarez unrestricted trade zone status, and the area bloomed. But other regions of Mexico protested the flow of foreign goods into the interior, and what Mexico City had granted, it soon took away. The next boom came with Prohibition in the United States. Maybe more than anything in the first half of this century, booze built the border. But it was the *maquiladora* program that put the finishing touches on the Juarez economy, with more than 200 twin plants eventually bringing tens of thousands of jobs and a tenuous sense of financial independence.

So from the pioneer expansion to the coming of the railroads, from outlaws and gunslingers to Pancho Villa and the Texas Rangers, from prospectors looking for the Lost Padre Mine to undocumented workers in search of any prospects period—the isolated region has seen it all. The nearest metropolitan neighbor in any direction—Tucson, Albuquerque, Chihuahua or Lubbock—is 300 miles away. The area has survived this sweep of history the way families weather tragedy by clinging to each other.

Bound by a Reckless Symbiosis

If you ask someone on an El Paso street for directions to the nearest hardware store, he's likely to direct you a few blocks down and a couple over—landing you in the middle of Juarez. Despite El Paso's distinction of having the lowest per capita income of any large U.S. city, stop a Juarez woman to inquire where she works, and chances are the answer will be across the way—in El Paso. After 150 years, the cities' economies have grown together in ways that each would sometimes prefer to ignore or deny. Not that life on one side of the border is identical to the other. The contrast is particularly stark toward the west, where students and professors in the modern buildings of the University of Texas at El Paso can peer a thousand yards through the early morning desert light at whole families living in improvised shanties of cardboard and scrap iron. It's a reckless symbiosis that binds these twins together.

"How can life on the border be other than reckless?" Graham Greene asked in his 1940 novel, *The Power and the Glory.* "You are pulled by different ties of love and hate." Forty-five years later, Carlos Fuentes, Mexico's leading man of letters, suggested an answer. "On both sides of this frontier, we gaze at one another, and we can do two things," Fuentes said. "We can be shocked by our differences and deny the other, or we can try to understand our differences and see ourselves through the eyes of the other. This is the constant challenge of that frontier—not to destroy the other because he's different."

Today, the metropolis is being meshed even closer together by the challenges of the future. El Paso, a strategic center of air defense and space programs that are under Congress' budget-cutting knife, is now fighting to consolidate its natural advantage as one of the most important gateways to Latin American commerce. Meanwhile, Juarez, an energetic, cacophonous city in constant motion, is also positioning itself for the onslaught of free trade while trying to cope with the pressures of being Mexico's fastest-growing city.

Challenges and Opportunities

There are many challenges. "We're trying to redefine our regional identity," says Bert Diamondstein of the Industrial Development Council at the El Paso Chamber of Commerce. "We hope to lead the way in addressing the environmental, health, and infrastructure requirements of the border. We'd even like to boost our business from Pacific Rim exporters to the North American market."

There are many opportunities, too. Public schools on both sides of the border have made bilingualism the order of the day in a region with more children per capita than any other in either nation. In Rivera Elementary, on El Paso's west side, and in Rusk Elementary, in the city's central core, a first-of-its-kind pilot program is designed to meet the needs of students with limited English skills while providing Spanish instruction to non-Spanish speakers. The programs are taught by one bilingual teacher and one monolingual teacher, and this team-teaching approach is winning high marks for helping students gain proficiency in two languages while mastering their academics.

In Juarez, public schools take a different approach. There, they try not just to immerse students in English as a second language classes from the earliest grades, but to counter the substitute for culture that students find at the conjunction of entertainment and advertising—from modern movies to Madonna. The children read inexpensive editions of classic literature and learn to do logarithms in the language of the north.

The emotional issues of nationalism voiced by bilingual opponents who worry that the schools' programs set out to destroy every vestige of the old culture, and the arguments of bilingual proponents who cite the program as a path to cultural enrichment, have given way to a relatively simple business proposition: People who know two languages have a better chance of getting ahead. As the hemisphere veers toward a *de facto* free trade zone status, the practical value of both English and Spanish will increase.

As they look ahead then, the two partners see a future as inseparable as their common past.

Chapter 2

★

FEDERALISM AND THE TEXAS CONSTITUTION

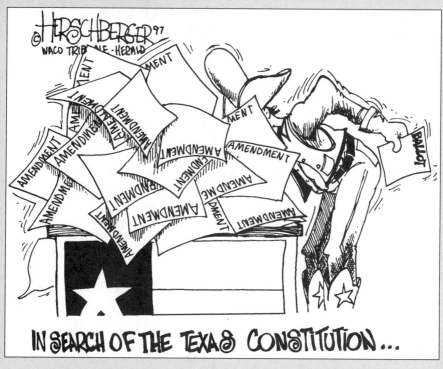

IN SEARCH OF THE TEXAS CONSTITUTION...

Waco/Tribune-Herald/Herschberger.

*T*he Texas Constitution, adopted in 1876, serves as the Lone Star State's fundamental law. It has been amended frequently over the past 12 decades (as illustrated by Vern Herschberger's cartoon at the beginning of this chapter). But on three occasions, Texans have expressed strong opposition to proposals for wholesale constitutional revision. Nevertheless, the document's length and lack of organization are frequently criticized by newspaper editors, lawyers, political scientists, government officials, and others who, consult it. The Texas Constitution is, however, one source of the government's policymaking power; the other major source is membership in the federal Union.

The American Federal Structure

A federal structure of government is characterized by the division of powers between a national government and associated regional governments. The heart of the federal system in the United States lies in the division of powers between the national government (with its seat in Washington, D.C.) and the governments of the 50 states. Since 1789, the U.S. Constitution has prescribed a federal system of government for the nation, and since 1846 the State of Texas has been a part of that system.

Described by North Carolina's former governor Terry Sanford as "a system of states within a state," American federalism has survived two centuries of stresses and strains. Among the most serious threats were the Civil War, which almost destroyed the Union from 1861 to 1865, and a number of economic crises such as the Great Depression that followed the stock market crash of 1929.

The Distribution of Powers

Division of powers and functions between the national government and state governments was originally accomplished by spelling out in the U.S. Constitution the powers of the national government and by adding the **Tenth Amendment**. The latter asserts: "The powers not delegated to the United States by the Constitution, nor prohibited by it to the States, are reserved to the States, respectively, or to the People." Although the Tenth Amendment may seem to endow the states with powers comparable to those delegated to the national government, Article VI of the Constitution contains the following clarification: "This Constitution, and the laws of the United States which shall be made in pursuance thereof; and all treaties made, or which shall be made, under the authority of the United States, shall be the supreme law of the land; and the judges in every State shall be bound thereby, anything in the Constitution or laws of any State to the contrary notwithstanding." This **national supremacy clause** emphasizes that the U.S. Constitution and the laws and treaties made under it by the national government must prevail over the constitutions and laws of the states.

Delegated and Implied Powers   Article I, Section 8, of the U.S. Constitution lists powers granted specifically to the national government. Included are powers to regulate interstate and foreign commerce, borrow and coin money, establish post offices and post roads, declare war, raise and support armies, provide and maintain a navy, levy and collect taxes, and establish uniform rules of naturalization. To these specifically **delegated powers** was added a clause that gives the national government the power "to make all laws which shall be necessary and proper for carrying into execution the foregoing powers, and all other powers vested by this Constitution in the government of the United States, or in any department or officer thereof." Since 1789, Congress and the federal courts have used this grant of **implied powers** to expand the authority of the national government.

Limitations on the States   As members of the federal Union, Texas and the other states are constrained by limitations imposed by Article I, Section 10, of the U.S. Constitution. They may not enter into treaties, alliances, or confederations or, without the consent of Congress, participate in interstate or foreign compacts. Furthermore, they are forbidden to levy import duties on another state's products and must accept the Constitution, laws, and treaties of the United States as the supreme law of the land. From the Civil War and the U.S. Supreme Court's landmark ruling in ***Texas* v. *White*** (1869), Texans learned that states cannot secede from the Union. In the *White* case, the court ruled that the national Constitution "looks to an indestructible union, composed of indestructible states."

Neither Texas nor any other state may constitutionally deny anyone the right to vote because of race, gender, failure to pay a poll tax, or age (if the person is 18 years of age or older). No state is permitted to deny anyone the equal protection of the laws or the privileges and immunities of citizens of the United States. Furthermore, no state may deprive persons of life, liberty, or property without due process of law.

Guarantees to the States   The U.S. Constitution provides all states with an imposing list of **constitutional guarantees**. For example, Texas may be neither divided nor combined with another state without the consent of the legislatures concerned and Congress. At the same time, each state is entitled to protection against invasion and domestic violence and is guaranteed a republican form of government (that is, representative government). In addition, Texas may have its own militia (National Guard units) and is assured that trials by federal courts for crimes committed in Texas will be conducted in Texas. Each state is guaranteed that it will have equal representation with the other states in the U.S. Senate and will have at least one member in the U.S. House of Representatives. In fact, each state has two senators in Washington and, after the 1990 census, Texas was apportioned 30 representatives in the House. Finally, Texas and the other states participate equally in approving or rejecting proposed amendments to the U.S. Constitution.

Interstate Relations

Article IV provides: "Citizens of each state shall be entitled to all **privileges and immunities** of citizens in the several states." Thus, residents of Texas who are visiting in another state are entitled to all the privileges and immunities of citizens of that state. It does not mean, however, that Texas residents who visit another state are entitled to all the privileges and immunities to which they are entitled in their home state. In 1823, the U.S. Supreme Court defined privileges and immunities broadly as follows: protection by government, enjoyment of life and liberty, right to acquire and possess property, right to egress and ingress (to leave and enter), and right to the use of courts. Although corporations are legal persons, they are not included under the privileges and immunities clause.

Article IV of the Constitution also states that "full faith and credit shall be given in each State to the public acts, records, and judicial proceedings of every other State." The **full faith and credit clause** means that any legislative enactment, state constitution, deed, will, marriage, divorce, or civil court judgment of one state must be officially recognized and honored in every other state. This clause does not apply to criminal cases. A person convicted in Texas for a crime committed in Texas is not punished in another state to which he or she has fled. Such cases are handled through **extradition,** whereby the fugitive would be returned to the Lone Star State at the request of the governor of Texas. The U.S. Supreme Court ruled in ***Puerto Rico* v. *Brandstadt*** (1987) that a governor must comply with an extradition request. Furthermore, for some felonies, the U.S. Congress has made it a federal offense to flee from one state to another for the purpose of avoiding arrest.

State Powers

Nowhere in the U.S. Constitution is there a list of state powers. Instead, according to the Tenth Amendment, all powers not specifically delegated to the national government are reserved to the states or to the people. The **reserved powers** of the states are therefore undefined. We will not attempt here to define or list the states' reserved powers; however, political scientists usually group these powers into four categories:

- Police power (protection of the health, morals, and convenience of citizens)
- Taxing power (raising revenue to pay salaries of state employees and meet other costs of government)
- Proprietary power (public ownership of property such as airports, energy-producing utilities, and parks)
- Power of eminent domain (taking private property for highway construction or other public use at a fair price)

Needless to say, states today have imposing powers, responsibilities, and duties. They are, for example, responsible for all of the nation's public elections—national, state, and local. There are no nationally operated election facilities. State courts conduct most trials (both criminal and civil), operate the public and higher education systems, and maintain most of the nation's prisons. One must be cautious in attempting to identify state powers or mark the boundary line between state and national powers. The reason is that since the establishment of the American federal system, the states have operated within a constitutional context that has been modified to meet changing conditions.

An Evolving Process

In creating a federal republic, the framers of the U.S. Constitution sought to provide a workable balance of powers between national and state governments that would sustain the Union indefinitely. The fact that the American federal system has endured more than 200 years of stresses and strains attests to their wisdom and foresight. The supreme test of endurance came with the Civil War, which pitted North against South in a struggle to settle the issue of states' rights versus national supremacy. The nationalist victory in 1865 did not end federalism, however. Policymaking authority of the national government after the war was no broader than before the war. Each state's position within the Union was left much as before, but southern states could no longer mandate slavery.

Between 1865 and 1930, Congress acted vigorously to regulate railroads and interstate commerce and, through grants of money to the states, it influenced state policymaking. With the onset of the Great Depression of the 1930s, the number and size of **federal grants-in-aid** grew apace as Congress sought to assist the states financially. As these federally initiated programs multiplied, the national influence on policymaking widened accordingly, with loss of state control over many areas. Since the 1980s, however, state and local governments have been given more freedom to spend federal funds, although in some areas they have been granted less money to spend. Consequently, Texas and other states are forced to assume more responsibility in formulating and funding their own programs in education, highways, mental health, welfare, and other areas.

This latest development in federal-state relations has been named the "Devolution Revolution." The concept underlying **devolution** is to bring about a reduction in the size and influence of American national government by reducing federal taxes and expenditures and shifting many federal responsibilities to the states. Since one feature of this "revolution" involves sharp reductions in federal aid, states will be compelled to assume important new responsibilities with substantially less revenue to finance them.

Another important feature is an increasing utilization of block grants by Congress when distributing money to state and local governments. Block grants are fixed sums of money awarded to state and local governments on an automatic formula-allocation basis. This means allocations are made on the basis of a formula already determined by Congress. Thus, receiving governments have greater flexibility in spending within broad functions of government. (See Chapter 3, page 71, for a discussion of federal grants.)

The Texas Constitution: Politics of Policymaking

"Humbly invoking the blessings of Almighty God, the people of the state of Texas do ordain and establish this Constitution." These are the words of the **preamble** to the 28,600-word document that became Texas's seventh supreme law in 1876. By the beginning of 1999, it had been changed by no fewer than 377 amendments and had grown to more than 80,000 words, making it the second-longest state constitution in the nation. (Table 2.1 provides information concerning the length and number of amendments of the longest and shortest state constitutions.) Although nearly 90 years younger than the U.S. Constitution, the Texas Constitution is 10 times as long and has about 14 times as many amendments as the federal document. If the past rate of amendment continues to the year 2000, the Texas Constitution will by then have accumulated approximately 400 amendments.

Legal scholars and others who examine fundamental laws generally believe constitution makers should not attempt to solve specific policy problems; rather, they should state clearly who is to solve them, both in the present and in the future. If this rule is followed, later generations will have

TABLE 2.1 Comparative Data for Selected State Constitutions, (1996)

State	Number of Words	Year Adopted	Number of Amendments	Average Number of Amendments per Year
Alabama	220,000*	1956	582*	14.6
Texas	80,806	1876	364	3.0
Oklahoma	68,800	1907	151	1.7
California	54,645	1879	491	4.2
Louisiana	54,112	1974	72	3.3
North Carolina	11,000	1970	27	1.0
Utah	11,000	1895	84	0.8
Indiana	10,230	1857	38	0.3
Connecticut	9,564	1965	28	0.9
New Hampshire	9,200	1784	143	0.7
Vermont	6,880	1793	52	0.3

*Includes numerous local amendments that apply to only one county. Approximately 70 percent of all amendments are local.

Source: *The Book of the States, 1996–1997* (Lexington, Ky.: The Council of State Governments, 1996), pp. 3–4.

no need to adopt numerous amendments. In the case of a state, it is the legislature's job to enact specific laws authorized by its constitution. For example, a constitution may provide for the election of government officials, but the legislature enacts the laws that schedule and regulate the elections.

The major faults of the present Texas Constitution are unwieldy length and a lack of coherent organization of provisions. The Texas Constitution has grown by amendment chiefly because the framers spelled out policymaking powers and limitations in minute detail. This, in turn, made frequent amendments inevitable, as constitutional provisions had to be altered to fit changing times and conditions. For more than a century, the document has continued to grow through an accumulation of amendments, most of which are essentially statutory (resembling a law made by a legislature) in nature. The result is a constitution that more closely resembles a code of laws than a fundamental instrument of government.

Within the federal structure of government in the United States, the Texas Constitution is the fundamental law of the Lone Star State. This document establishes the government, defines governing powers, and imposes limitations thereon. It is subject only to the U.S. Constitution and federal statutes and treaties, which together constitute "the supreme law of the land."

Historical Developments

The Texas Constitution provides the legal basis on which the state functions as an integral part of the federal Union. But it is more than this. The Texas Constitution is a product of history and an expression of the dominant political philosophy of its citizens. It is a reflection of the moral and social principles of the people who adopted it and later generations who have amended it.

Despite the idealistic sentiment commonly attached to constitutions in the United States, the arts of drafting and amending a constitution are essentially political in nature. Although many people may see political aspects of constitution making as shady operations carried out through secret, under-the-table deals, more knowledgeable and realistic observers view constitution drafters as pragmatic men and women.

The **constitutional history of Texas** began nearly two centuries ago, when Texas was a part of Mexico. Each of its seven constitutions has reflected the political situation that existed when the document was drafted.[1] In this chapter, we see the political process at work as we examine the origins of these constitutions and note efforts to revise and amend the current Texas Constitution.

The First Six Constitutions In 1824, three years after Mexico gained independence from Spain, Mexican liberals established a republic with a federal constitution. Within that federal system, the former Spanish provinces of Tejas and Coahuila became a single Mexican state that adopted its own constitution. Thus, the Constitution of Coahuila y Tejas, which was promulgated in 1827, marked Texas's first experience with a state constitution. Political unrest among Texans, who wanted more representation than the two seats they held in the 12-member Texas-Coahuila legislature, arose almost immediately. On March 2, 1836, at Washington-on-the-Brazos, a delegate convention of 59 Texans issued a declaration of independence from Mexico. Then the delegates drafted the Constitution of the Republic of Texas, modeled largely on the U.S. Constitution.

Sam Houston's Texans defeated the Mexican forces under General Antonio López de Santa Anna, in the Battle of San Jacinto, on April 21, 1836. The young republic petitioned the U.S. government for admission into the Union. In 1845, annexation was authorized by a joint resolution of Congress after repeated attempts to bring it about through a treaty of annexation.

Texas president Anson Jones called a constitutional convention, whose delegates drew up a new state constitution and agreed to accept the invitation to join the Union. In February 1846, after Texas voters ratified both actions of the constitutional convention, Texas became the 28th state of the United States. The Constitution of 1846 lasted until the outbreak of the Civil War.

When the Secession Constitution was adopted in 1861, the aim of the convention that drafted it was to make as few changes as possible in the structure and powers of the government. Only those changes necessary to equip the government for separation from the United States were included. The Reconstruction Constitution of 1866, however, confronted a different set of conditions. Initially it had to restore Texas to the Union with the fewest possible changes in existing social, economic, and political institutions. Thus, the Constitution of 1866 was based on the Constitution of 1846, but it recognized the right of former slaves to sue in the state's courts, to enter into contracts, to obtain and transfer property, and to testify in court actions involving blacks (but not whites). Although the Constitution of 1866 protected the personal property of African-American Texans, it did not permit them to vote, hold public office, or serve as jurors.

The relatively uncomplicated reinstatement of the Lone Star State into the Union ended abruptly when the Radical Republicans gained control of the U.S. Congress following the election of November 1866. Refusing to seat Texas's two senators and three representatives, Congress set aside the state's reconstructed government, enfranchised former slaves and other African Americans, disenfranchised prominent whites, and imposed military rule across the state. Military officers replaced civil authorities. In 1868, a constitutional convention drafted yet another state constitution, which guaranteed a full range of rights for former slaves. It was ratified a year later. With elections supervised by the military and African Americans voting and running for office, Radical Republicans gained control of the Texas Legislature and elected E. J. Davis, a former Union army general, governor of Texas.

Governor Davis imposed martial law in some places and used police methods to enforce his decrees. Historians have alleged his administration to be one of the most corrupt in Texas history, characterized by extravagant public spending, property tax increases to the point of confiscation, gifts of public funds to private interests, intimidation of newspaper editors, and control of voter registration by the military. Although the Constitution of 1869 is associated with the Reconstruction era and the unpopular administration of Governor Davis, the machinery of government it created was quite modern. This fundamental law called for annual sessions of the legislature, a four-year term for the governor and other executive officers, and gubernatorial appointment (rather than popular election) of judges. It abolished county courts and raised the salaries of government officials. These changes centralized more governmental power in Austin and weakened government at the grassroots level.

The Davis regime survived from 1870 to 1874. In perhaps the most fraudulent election ever conducted in Texas, Davis (with 42,633 votes) was badly defeated in December 1873 by Democrat Richard Coke (with 85,549 votes). Democrats had gained control of the legislature in 1872; two years later, they were able to wrest control of the state courts from the Republicans. The next step was to rewrite the Texas Constitution.

Drafting the Constitution of 1876 In the summer of 1875, Texans elected 75 Democrats and 15 Republicans (6 of whom were African Americans) as delegates to a constitutional convention; however, only 83 attended the gathering in Austin. Half were members of the Texas Grange (the Patrons of Husbandry), a farmers' organization committed to the cause of economy and limited government. Its slogan of "retrenchment and reform" became the major goal of the convention. So strong was the spirit of economy among delegates that they refused to hire a stenographer or to allow publication of the convention proceedings. As a result, no official record was ever made of the convention that gave Texas its most enduring constitution.[2] Delegates, as a body, represented the unreconstructed element of the state rather than those who had been sympathetic to the Davis regime.

In their zeal to undo Reconstruction policies, the delegates overreacted on occasion. Striking at Reconstruction measures that had given Governor Davis control over voter registration, the overwrought delegates inserted a statement providing that "no law shall ever be enacted requiring a registration of voters of this state." Within two decades, however, the statement had been amended to permit voter registration laws.

As they continued to dismantle the Davis administration machinery, the determined delegates inserted numerous pages of specific policy provisions, resulting in a document that read more like a legal code than a basic fundamental law. They reduced the governor's salary, powers, and term (from four to two years); made all executive offices (except that of secretary of state) elective for two-year terms; and tied the hands of legislators with biennial (once every two years) sessions, low salaries, and restricted legislative powers. All judges became popularly elected for relatively short terms of office. Public services were trimmed to the bone. As further concessions to taxpayers, the delegates lowered salaries of public officials, reinstated racially segregated public education, and repealed the school attendance law. They limited the public debt and severely curbed the taxing and spending powers of the legislature. Local government was stimulated by the establishment of justice of the peace courts, county courts, and district courts. In addition to prohibiting voter registration, the convention restored precinct elections and allowed only taxpayers to vote on many local bond issues.

Texas's most enduring constitution was put to a vote in 1876 and was approved by more than a two-to-one majority. Although Texans in the state's largest cities—Houston, Dallas, San Antonio, and Galveston—voted against it, the much larger rural population voted for approval.

Today: After More than a Century of Usage

With all its shortcomings, the **Constitution of 1876** has endured for more than 120 years. The disadvantage of its excessive length is compounded by its structural disarray and confusion. The wordy document contains misnumbered sections, misspelled words, and articles left blank. One sentence contains 756 words. Some sections devoted to the same subject are scattered throughout the body of the Constitution rather than grouped in a single article. Chiefly because of its length, complete printed copies of the Texas Constitution are not readily available to the public. However, each edition of the *Texas Almanac,* published every other year by *The Dallas Morning News,* includes the complete text. A copy of the constitution is also located on the World Wide Web <http//www.capitol.state.tx.us/>.

Distrust of Government Sharing in the prevailing distrust of government, the framers of the Constitution of 1876 sought with a vengeance to limit and thus control policymaking by placing many restrictions in the state's fundamental law. Prevailing opinion of the day held that a state government could exercise only those powers that were listed in the state constitution. Therefore, instead of being permitted to exercise powers not denied by the national or state constitutions, for over a century Texas lawmakers have been limited to those powers that are spelled out in the state's basic law. The inevitable result is a lengthy constitution that has grown longer with time. Amendments have been added in response to new policy demands resulting from changing circumstances. For example, in 1875 delegates saw fit to include pages of details on state regulation of Texas railroads, which are now regulated exclusively by the federal government. Today legislative efforts must be devoted to building highways and regulating motor vehicle traffic. The same is true of the changing policy needs of education, public health, crime control, and a wide variety of social services unforeseen in 1875.[3]

Need for Amendments It was inevitable that filling the Texas Constitution with statutory detail in 1875 would soon lead to constitutional amendments to move the state into and through the twentieth century. As a consequence, virtually any substantive change in Texas government requires an amendment. For example, an amendment is needed to change the way the state pays bills, to abolish an unneeded state or county office, or to authorize a bond issue pledging the revenues of the state. Urbanization, industrialization, the communication revolution, the population explosion, growing demands in education, and countless needs for social services have all produced pressures for constitutional change.

Most amendments that have been adopted, however, apply to policy issues that should have been resolved by statute alone. Instead, an often uninformed and usually apathetic electorate has decided the fate of each policy issue.

A sample of the utter absurdity of **policymaking by constitutional amendment** is provided by one of the 13 proposed amendments on the ballot in 1991. Proposition 9 authorized the land commissioner to grant clear title to a certain type of land "held under color of the law for at least fifty years." Approved by almost two-thirds of the voters, this amendment was needed to clear a cloud on the title to only 62 acres of rural land claimed by a Hays County rancher. Another amendment to clear title to approximately 4,428 acres claimed by 146 families in Fort Bend and Austin Counties was included among the 14 proposed amendments that voters approved in November 1993.

An additional 15 amendments were voted on in 1997, one on August 9 and the remaining 14 on November 4. The August amendment increased homestead exemptions from property taxation to $15,000. The November proposals ranged from two concerning local officials to equity borrowing on homes, water development and conservation, and funds for crime victims. Voters approved the August proposal and another 12 in November, bringing the total number of amendments to 377.

Constitutional Revision and Amendments

Attempts to revise the Constitution of 1876 began soon after its adoption. A legislative resolution calling for a constitutional revision convention was introduced in 1887 and was followed by many more, but none was implemented until 1972. However, some gains were realized in 1969, when an amendment removed 56 obsolete provisions.

Major Reform Efforts

The most comprehensive movement to achieve constitutional revision began in 1971, but, like earlier attempts, it failed to produce a revised basic law for Texas. The 62nd Legislature began the process with a joint resolution that proposed an amendment authorizing the appointment of a study commission and naming the members of the 63rd Legislature as delegates to a constitutional convention. Except for the Bill of Rights, any part of the Constitution of 1876 could be changed or deleted. Submitted to the voters in 1972 as a proposed constitutional amendment, the resolution was approved by a comfortable majority (1,549,982 affirmative and only 985,282 negative votes).

Constitutional Revision Commission A six-member committee (composed of the governor, the lieutenant governor, the speaker of the House, the attorney general, the chief justice of the Texas Supreme Court, and the presiding judge of the Court of Criminal Appeals) selected 37 persons to serve as members of a **Constitutional Revision Commission**. The commission prepared a draft constitution based on opinion and information gathered at public hearings conducted throughout the state and from various authorities on constitutional revision. One-fourth the length of the present constitution, the completed draft was submitted to the legislature on November 1, 1973.

Legislative Constitutional Convention On January 8, 1974, members of both houses of the Texas Legislature met in Austin as a constitutional convention. Previous Texas constitutions had been drafted by convention delegates popularly elected for that purpose. When the finished document was put to a vote, the result was 118 for and 62 against. Thus, the two-thirds majority of the total membership needed for final approval was missed by only three votes. (A total of at least 121 votes for approval was necessary.) Attempts to reach compromises on controversial issues proved futile.[4]

Perhaps there has been no better demonstration in Texas of constitution making as a political process than the **1974 constitutional convention**. First, the convention was hampered by a lack of positive political leadership. Governor Dolph Briscoe maintained a hands-off policy throughout the convention; Lieutenant Governor Bill Hobby similarly failed to provide needed political leadership; and the retiring speaker of the House, Price Daniel, Jr., pursued a nonintervention course. Other members of the legislature were distracted by their need to campaign for reelection.

A primary reason the convention failed by a razor-thin margin to agree on a proposed constitution was the phantom "nonissue" of a right-to-work provision. With a statutory ban on union shop labor contracts in effect since 1947, adding this prohibition to the constitution would not have strengthened the legal hand of employers to any significant degree. Nevertheless, conservative, anti-labor forces insisted on it, and a pro-labor minority vigorously opposed it. The controversy aroused much emotion and at times produced loud and bitter name calling among delegates on the floor and spectators in the galleries.[5]

A Legislative Proposal Stung by widespread public criticism of the 1974 convention's failure to produce a proposed constitution for public approval or rejection, the 64th Legislature resolved to submit a proposal to Texas voters. In 1975, both houses of the legislature agreed on a constitutional revision resolution comprising ten articles in eight sections to be submitted to the Texas electorate in November. The content of the articles was essentially the same as that of the final resolution of the 1974 convention. If all eight propositions had been approved by voters, only the Bill of Rights of the Constitution of 1876 would have been retained in the new constitution.

The People Decide   The revision proposed in 1975 represented years of work by men and women well informed on the subject of constitution making. Recognized constitutional authorities evaluated the concise and orderly document as one of the best-drafted state constitutions ever submitted to American voters.[6] Although new and innovative in many respects, the proposal did not discard all of the old provisions. In addition to retaining the Bill of Rights, the proposed constitution incorporated such basic principles as limited government, separation of powers, and bicameralism (a two-house legislature).

Nevertheless, Texas voters demonstrated a strong preference for their old constitution by rejecting each proposition; voters in 250 of the state's 254 counties rejected all eight. Only 23 percent of the estimated 5.9 million registered voters cast ballots, meaning that only about 10 percent of the state's voting-age population participated in this important referendum. When asked to explain the resounding defeat of the eight propositions, Bill Hobby, then lieutenant governor, responded, "There's not enough of the body left for an autopsy."

In 1995, Senator John Montford (D–Lubbock) drafted a streamlined constitution that incorporated many of the concepts contained in the failed 1975 proposal. Montford's plan also called for a voter referendum every 30 years (without legislative approval) on the question of calling a constitutional revision convention. With Montford's resignation from the Senate to become Chancellor of the Texas Tech University system in 1996 and with such issues as tax reform, welfare reform, and educational finance pressing for attention, the 1997 Legislature did not seriously consider constitutional revision.[7]

In 1998 Senator Bill Ratcliff (R-Mount Pleasant) and Representative Rob Junell (D-San Angelo) with assistance from San Angelo State University students, prepared a complete rewrite of the 1876 document.

Piecemeal Revision   After defeat of the proposed constitution, in 1997 Texas legislators sought to achieve some measure of revision by other means, including legislative enactments and piecemeal constitutional amendments. In 1977, for example, the 65th Legislature enacted into law two parts of the 1975 propositions defeated at the polls. One established a procedure for reviewing state administrative agencies (the sunset process described on pages 218–219); the other created a planning agency within the governor's office. In 1979, the 66th Legislature proposed six amendments designed to implement parts of the constitutional revision package rejected in 1975. Three were adopted by the voters and added to the Texas Constitution:

- Establishing a single property tax appraisal district in each county (see pages 66–67)
- Giving criminal appellate jurisdiction to 14 courts of appeals that formerly had exercised civil jurisdiction only (see page 239)
- Allowing the governor restricted removal power over appointed statewide officials (see page 197)

Other amendments constituting piecemeal revision continue to be added,[8] including 11 that were adopted in 1995, and another 13 that were adopted in 1997.

Fewer than 8 percent of Texas's registered voters participated in the November 1995 constitutional amendment election. This low voter turnout fueled efforts to give Texans the powers of initiative and referendum. If adopted, the initiative process would allow individuals or groups to gather signatures required for submitting proposed constitutional amendments and statutes (ordinary laws) to direct popular vote, bypassing the legislature. The referendum process would allow voters to gather signatures to challenge and potentially overturn statutes passed by state lawmakers.

Proponents believe adoption of the two processes will put Texans back in control of their government by:

- Making government more responsive by holding legislators accountable and making representative democracy work better
- Allowing citizens to put issues that matter to them on the ballot
- Allowing citizens to participate directly in the legislative process

Those opposed argue that the initiative and referendum are bad, even dangerous, public policy. They point out that the procedures

- Can become tools of special interests, allowing big money to dominate the processes
- Circumvent representative democracy
- May be used to impose discriminatory measures
- Allow majorities to trample the rights of minorities

If initiative and referendum procedures should be adopted, Texans would join voters in 24 other states in being able to propose and adopt their own laws.

As the 75th legislative session drew to a close in May 1997, legislation had been proposed to submit an amendment; but members of the legislature awaited an outpouring of favorable public opinion before taking the necessary action. Since that was not forthcoming by session's end, Texas voters did not have an initiative and referendum option when they voted on other proposed amendements in 1997.

The Amendment Process

Each of the 50 American state constitutions contains means for changing the powers and functions of government. Without a provision for amendment, most constitutions could not survive for long. Revisions may produce a totally new constitution to replace an old one. Courts may alter constitutions by interpreting the wording of these documents in new and different ways. Finally, constitutions may be changed by **formal amendment,** the chief method by which the Texas Constitution has been altered.

Because the Lone Star State's registered voters have an opportunity to vote on one or more proposed amendments nearly every year—and sometimes twice in a single year—an understanding of the steps in the amending process is important. Article XVII, Section 1, provides a relatively simple procedure for amending the Texas Constitution. The basic steps in that process are as follows:

- A joint resolution proposing an amendment is introduced in the House or in the Senate.
- A joint resolution is adopted by 100 or more votes of the House membership and 21 or more votes of the Senate membership (two-thirds of each house).
- The secretary of state prepares an explanatory statement describing the proposed amendment.
- The attorney general approves the explanatory statement.
- The explanatory statement is published twice in Texas newspapers that print official state notices.
- A copy of the proposed amendment is posted in each county courthouse at least 30 days before the election.
- The voters approve the proposed amendment by a simple majority vote in a regular or special election.
- The governor, who has no veto power in the process, proclaims the amendment.

In a regular session of the legislature (held at the beginning of odd-numbered years), any member of the House or Senate may introduce a joint resolution proposing a constitutional amendment. Also, if requested by the governor, an amendment may be proposed during a special session. To be valid, a proposed amendment must be approved by a recorded vote of two-thirds of the entire membership of each house. The legislature also decides whether a proposed amendment will be submitted to the voters in the November general election of an even-numbered year or in a special election scheduled for an earlier date. In 1997, for example, the regular session of the 75th Legislature produced 15 proposed amendments that were submitted to Texas voters that same year.

The Texas Constitution: A Summary

Although this textbook does not include the entire Texas Constitution, each chapter looks to Texas' basic law for its content. However, to introduce readers to some details of the document's 17 articles, the pages that follow present a brief summary.[9]

The Bill of Rights

Eleven of the 30 sections of Article I, the Texas Constitution's **Bill of Rights,** provide protections for people and property against arbitrary governmental actions. Guarantees such as freedom of speech, press, religion, assembly, and petition are included. The right to keep and bear arms, prohibitions against taking of property by government action without just compensation, and forbidding impairment of the obligation of contract are also incorporated. An additional group of rights was added by constitutional amendment in 1989 that aimed to guarantee the "rights of crime victims." Most of the rights spelled out in the Texas Constitution are also protected by the U.S. Constitution. Thus, with their basic rights guaranteed in both national and state constitutions, Texans have a double safeguard against arbitrary governmental actions.

With regard to some rights, the Texas Constitution is even more protective than the U.S. Constitution. For example, attempts nationwide to add the proposed **Equal Rights Amendment (ERA)** to the U.S. Constitution failed between 1972 and 1982 (even though it was approved by the Texas Legislature). Nevertheless, in 1972, Texas voters approved the following amendment to Section 3 of their state Constitution: "Equality under the law shall not be denied or abridged because of sex, race, color, creed or national origin." Prohibitions against imprisonment for debt, outlawry (the process of putting a convicted person outside of the protection of the law), transportation (punishing a convicted citizen by banishment from the state), and monopolies are included within the Texas Bill of Rights but not in the U.S. Constitution.

Thirteen sections relate to rights of persons accused of crimes and to rights of individuals who have been convicted of crimes. For example, one section concerns the right to release on bail; another prohibits unreasonable searches and seizures; and a third declares that "the right to trial by jury shall remain inviolate." These provisions are closely related to similar language in the national Bill of Rights.

Three sections contain philosophical observations that have no direct force of law. Still smarting from what they saw as the "bondage" years of Reconstruction, the angry delegates to the constitutional convention of 1875 began their work by inserting this statement: "Texas is a free and independent state, subject only to the Constitution of the United States." They also asserted that all political power resides in the people and is legitimately exercised only in their behalf and that those people may at any time "alter, reform, or abolish their government." To guard against the possibility that any of the rights guaranteed in the other 29 sections would be eliminated or altered by the government, section 29 proclaims that "everything in this 'Bill of Rights' is excepted out of the general powers of government, and shall forever remain inviolate."

The Powers of Government

Holding fast to the principle of limited government, the framers of the Constitution of 1876 firmly embedded in the state's fundamental law the familiar doctrine of **separation of powers**. In Article II, they assigned the lawmaking, law-enforcing, and law-adjudicating powers of government to three separate branches identified as the legislative, executive, and judicial departments, respectively.

Legislative powers are vested in the bicameral legislature, composed of a House of Representatives with 150 members and a Senate with 31 members. Article III is titled the Legislative Department. A patchwork of 65 sections, this article provides vivid testimony to more than 120 years of amendment. For example, in November 1936, an amendment added a section granting the Texas Legislature the authority to levy taxes to fund a retirement system for public school, college, and university teachers. Almost 40 years later, in April 1975, this amendment was repealed and a new retirement system was instituted for those state employees.

Article IV, the Executive Department, states unequivocally that the governor "shall be the Chief Executive Officer of the State" but then provides for the sharing of executive power with four other popularly elected officers who are independent of the governor: the lieutenant governor, attorney general, comptroller of public accounts, and commissioner of the general land office. The office of state treasurer was originally included in this list, but a constitutional amendment adopted in 1995 abolished the office. With this and other forms of division of executive power in the Constitution, the Texas governor is little more than first among equals in the Executive Department.

Through Article V, the Judicial Department, Texas joins Oklahoma as the only states in the Union with two courts of final appeal: one for civil cases (the Supreme Court of Texas) and one for criminal cases (the Court of Criminal Appeals). Below these two supreme appellate courts are the courts authorized by the Constitution and created by the legislature: the intermediate appellate courts (14 courts of appeals) and many courts of original jurisdiction (district courts, county courts, and justice of the peace courts). In a constitution with separation of powers, the ideal judicial article need only create a court system, name at least one court, and specify the mode of selection and tenure of judges. In contrast, Article V of the Texas Constitution is full of legalistic wording addressed principally to lawyers and judges.

Suffrage

The right to vote is called **suffrage**. Article VI, entitled Suffrage, is one of the shortest articles in the Texas Constitution. Prior to 1870, states had definitive power to conduct elections. Since that time, amendments to the U.S. Constitution, acts of Congress, and rulings by the U.S. Supreme Court have vastly diminished this power. Within the scope of current federal regulations, the Texas Constitution establishes qualifications for voters, provides for registration of citizens for voting, and governs the conduct of elections. In response to decisions of the U.S. Supreme Court, this article was amended to abolish the payment of a poll (head) tax or any other form of property qualification for voting in the state's elections.

Local Governments

The most disorganized part of the Texas Constitution concerns units of **local government**: counties, municipalities (cities), school districts, and other special districts. Although Article IX is titled Counties, the subject of county government is scattered through four other articles. To find all that is contained on the subject, one must also read Article XI, Municipal Corporations; Article V, Judiciary; Article VIII, Taxation and Revenue; and Article XVI, General Provisions. Moreover, the basic structure of county government is defined not in Article IX on counties but in Article V on the judiciary. Article XI on municipalities is equally disorganized and inadequate. Only four of the sections of this article relate exclusively to municipal government. Other sections concern county government, taxation, public indebtedness, and forced sale of public property.

Along with counties and municipalities, the original Constitution of 1876 referred to school districts but not other types of special-district government. Authorization for special districts, however, crept into the Constitution with a 1904 amendment that authorizes the borrowing of money for water development and road construction by a county "or any defined district." Thereafter, special districts have been created to provide myriad services, such as drainage, conservation, urban renewal, public housing, hospitals, and airports.

Other Articles

The nine remaining articles also reflect a strong devotion to constitutional minutiae. Titles are as follows: Education, Taxation and Revenue, Railroads, Private Corporations, Spanish and Mexican Land Titles, Public Lands and Land Office, Impeachment, General Provisions, and Mode of Amendment. The shortest is Article XIII, Spanish and Mexican Land Titles; its entire text was deleted by amendment in 1969, because its provisions were deemed obsolete. The longest article is Article XVI, General Provisions. This article, for example, provides for county poorhouses for the indigent, prohibits the charging of usurious (excessively high) interest rates, regulates the manufacture and sale of intoxicants, permits the use of convict labor to build public roads, and provides for pensions for retired Texas Rangers (law enforcement officers, not the baseball team).

Looking Ahead

Later chapters will demonstrate how the Texas Constitution affects the structure, functions, and procedures of the three branches of the state's government, the operation of political parties and interest groups within the state, and the financial arrangements for state and local units of government in Texas. However, a clarification is desirable at this point. Local governments in the American federal system derive their powers and responsibilities from the state governments that create them. Texas's local governments may derive their organizational arrangements from constitutional provisions or from legislative requirements. Chapter 3 directs our attention to local governments.

Notes

1. For a more detailed account of early Texas constitutions, see John Cornyn, "The Roots of the Texas Constitution: Settlement to Statehood," *Texas Tech Law Review* 26:4 (1995): 1089–1218.
2. Our best source on the proceedings is Seth Shepard McKay, ed., *Debates in the Texas Constitutional Convention of 1875* (Austin: University of Texas Press, 1930). McKay drew heavily on contemporary newspapers for debate material.
3. For criticism of the Texas Constitution, see W. Frank Newton, "Why Texas Needs a New Constitution, Now," *Texas Lawyer,* February 12, 1990, pp. 26–27.
4. A detailed account of the convention appears in Janice C. May, *The Texas Constitutional Revision Experience of the 70s* (Austin: Sterling Swift, 1975).
5. The 1947 act of Congress known as the Taft-Hartley Act prohibits closed-shop labor contracts, which bar the hiring of nonunion workers. As amended, it also permits states to adopt statutory or constitutional right-to-work provisions banning the union shop (that is, prohibiting any employer-employee labor contract requiring union membership to obtain or keep a job). Texas has a right-to-work law that was enacted in 1947 by the 50th Legislature.
6. See Janice C. May, "The Proposed 1976 Revision of the Texas Constitution," *Public Affairs Comment* 21 (August 1975), pp. 1–8.
7. Montford, along with Jerry Hall, his former chief of staff and veteran journalist, are preparing a book focusing on the need to overhaul the Texas Constitution.
8. For an analysis of amendments proposed between 1976 and 1989, see James G. Dickson, "Erratic Continuity: Some Patterns of Constitutional Change in Texas Since 1975," *Texas Journal of Political Studies* 14 (Fall–Winter 1991–92), pp. 41–56.

9. For a more detailed analysis of the contents of the Texas Constitution, see Janice C. May, *The Texas State Constitution: A Reference Guide* (Greenwood, Conn.: Greenwood Press, 1996), and George D. Braden, *Citizen's Guide to the Texas Constitution* (Austin: Texas Advisory Commission on Intergovernmental Relations, 1972).

Key Terms and Concepts

Tenth Amendment	constitutional history of Texas
national supremacy clause	Constitution of 1876
delegated power	policymaking by constitutional
implied power	amendment
Texas v. *White*	Constitutional Revision
constitutional guarantee	Commission
privileges and immunities	1974 constitutional convention
full faith and credit clause	formal amendment
extradition	Bill of Rights
Puerto Rico v. *Brandstadt*	Equal Rights Amendment (ERA)
reserved power	separation of powers
federal grant-in-aid	suffrage
devolution	local government
preamble	

SELECTED READING

The Texas Constitution: A Patchwork Quilt?

Joe E. Ericson

In this original article, the author analyzes reasons for frequent amendments to the Texas Constitution and highlights some of the consequences.

In 1961, the League of Women Voters of Texas described the Texas Constitution as a "patchwork quilt," a document held together by an ever-growing series of amendments. Composed originally of less than 30,000 words, by 1998 it had grown to more than 80,000 words as a result of 377 amendments.

Today, Texas has a fundamental law that has been described by critics as "a cluttered, overly detailed, inflexible instrument"[1] that is "obsolete, cumbersome and inefficient"[2] and has "little relevance for the 21st Century."[3] Defended by some individuals, including former Secretary of State Tony Garza, as a "living document,"[4] the Constitution has been criticized frequently by other individuals, including some of the state's leading attorneys, jurists, academics, and editorial writers. In fact, a movement for revision was launched barely fifty years after it was adopted in 1876, and efforts have flared anew every ten to twenty years since. None, however, has been entirely successful. Instead, Texans have opted for "batches of amendments," for revision by piecemeal changes (patches and sometimes patches on patches).

Frequency of Amendment

From 1964 to 1997, a total of 296 proposed amendments, an average of slightly more than nine per year, were submitted to Texas voters for approval; 206 were adopted, an average of more than six per year. During those 34 years, 18 or more amendments were presented to voters in five different elections—28 in 1987 (an "all-time" record), 27 in 1965, 20 in 1966, 19 in 1983, and 18 in 1971. Because most amendments appear on November election ballots, voting on proposed amendments has become a "familiar rite of fall" that has been repeated 21 times in

---

*This article was written especially for *Practicing Texas Politics*. Joe E. Ericson is a professor of political science, Stephen F. Austin State University.

32 November elections; amendment elections also have been scheduled periodically in other months.

Individuals participating in amendment elections are frequently confronted with complex questions that may or may not be of interest or pertain to them. For example, in 1997, one proposition asked electors to approve the elimination of duplicate numbering of constitutional provisions; another sought voter consent to limit the amount of state debt payable from the general revenue fund. Voter turnout is normally low, in part because citizens have been asked too many times to patch up the outmoded and overly restrictive content of the Lone Star State's fundamental law. Texans have also failed to vote in large numbers on constitutional issues because of confusing and ambiguous ballot language that makes understanding proposed amendments almost impossible. Thus, in 1995 only 8 percent and in 1997 only 10 percent of registered voters cast ballots on constitutional issues. Only when highly controversial questions are presented do voters cast ballots in greater numbers. In 1987, for example, adoption of a state lottery attracted 31 percent and parimutuel gambling on horse and dog races interested 26 percent.

Consequence of Frequent Amendment

This process of revision by piecemeal amendment has caused Texans to create a constitution characterized by a number of distinct features. Four of the most prominent are excessive verbiage, needless detail, rigorous restraints, and widespread disorganization.

Excessive verbiage   The League of Women's Voters' 1961 study concluded that approximately 21,000 of the Constitution's words could be eliminated by careful editing (for example, rewriting and simplifying many sections) without altering the essential meaning or changing the intent of any provision. Obsolete or outdated material could be removed, such as a section in Article IV that authorizes the governor to call out the state militia to "protect the frontier from hostile incursions by Indians or other predatory bands," or another in Article XVI stating that "any person who conscientiously scruples to bear arms shall not be compelled to do so, but shall pay an equivalent for personal service."

Vacant sections or articles could also be erased. Article XIII now contains no sections, all having been repealed by a 1969 amendment. Articles X and XIV have only one section each, while Article III contains eight and Article XVI 20 has vacant sections. Duplicate numbering of sections could likewise be corrected. Article VII has two duplications, and Article III has four repetitions.

Needless detail   The Constitution is also cluttered with details not needed, such as a provision for appointment of notaries public; another authorizing the legislature to enact parole, fencing, and livestock laws; and still others concerning bonded debt that are now merely a matter of historical record. The 1961 study conducted by the League of Women's Voters identified one sentence containing 756 words.

Rigorous restraints The 1876 document imposed tight restraints on all phases of government operation within the state. These restraints were designed to keep the state's government out of the hands of Radical Republicans, carpetbaggers, and newly freed slaves in the years immediately following Reconstruction; to reduce the authority of the state government, especially that of the governor; to curtail sharply taxation and spending by all governments; and to give average Texans a greater voice in making government policy. So tight are these controls that citizens statewide are often called on to decide matters that pertain to only one or at most a few counties, cities, or special districts. In the November 1997 special amendment election, the ballot covered such weighty questions as the qualifications of constables, the tax rate limit for fire prevention districts in Harris County, and the jurisdiction of elected municipal (city) court judges.

At other times, voters have been asked to allow Mills, Reagan, and Roberts Counties to abolish the office of constable. Additional proposed amendments concerned the issue of Dallas County road bonds, the authority of the legislature to regulate cattle brands, and the term of office for Fort Bend County's district attorney. The consequence of such restraints and excessive detail is page after page of trivia, contradictions, and obscurity.

Rigid limitations also force repeated amendment of the same section or portion of a section. Article III, Section 49 so limited the purpose for which state debts could be created that by 1997 this section alone had been amended eight times. Moreover, many other sections have also been amended more than one time.

Widespread disorganization In the original document, before any amendments were added, each article of the Texas Constitution covered almost exclusively the subject matter specified in its heading. Today, after hundreds of changes, the document has lost much of its organizational cohesiveness and consistency. In the late 1990's, almost two-thirds of Article III, Legislative Department, dealt with such subjects as state appropriations, state debt, financial assistance or compensation by either the state or its political subdivisions, and local government finance. All of these matters would be more logically located in Article VIII, the finance article.

Provisions relating to local government are located in Article IX, Counties; Article XI, Municipal Corporations; Article V, Judicial Department; Article VIII, Taxation and Revenue; and Article XVI, General Provisions. Concerned individuals seeking information about the structures and powers of county governments will need to consult Article V, Judicial Department. A state ad valorem (property) tax is now prohibited, but seven sections in Articles VII and VIII still contain material relating to that tax. One section authorizing a special appropriation for John Tarleton Agricultural College (now Tarleton State University) was adopted in 1946 without either article or section number. So confusing had the constitution's organization become that in 1997 voters approved the elimination of duplicate numbered provisions in Articles III and VII.

The End Result

One fundamental fact clearly emerges from this and other analyses of the Texas Constitution. Rewriting the document piecemeal at an accelerating rate through random amendments has not served to create a basic law that citizens can read and understand. They need one that is consistent in its requirements and serves the needs of today's Texans.

Despite the necessity for a new constitution for Texas, in 1998, an Austin editorial writer warned "that recasting a constitution" was not a "chore for the squeamish." It is, he concluded, "a job the Legislature is going to have to undertake and the sooner they get started the better."[5]

1. "Amendment Fatigue," *Austin American Statesman*, November 6, 1997.
2. "Obsolete Constitution Needs to Be Replaced," *Amarillo Daily News*, November 2, 1997.
3. Gary Scharrer, "State Constitution Has No Relevance in 21st Century," *El Paso Times*, November 9, 1997.
4. Tony Garza, "Texas Constitution Is a Living Document," *Dallas Morning News*, October 24, 1995.
5. Arnold Garcia, "Rewriting a Constitution Isn't for the Weak," *Austin-American Statesman*, June 8, 1998.

Chapter 3

LOCAL GOVERNMENTS

Thadeus & Weez   **by Charles Pugsley Fincher**

Copyright 1998 by Charles Pugsley Fincher.

*A*s we approach the year 2000, practicing Texas politics primarily features urban-based political groups jockeying for power. At the same time, inner-city residents attempt to cope with escalating crime, mounting traffic woes, aging populations, declining property values, and rising neighborhood concerns (racial, ethnic, environmental, and educational). Many local government issues stem from increasing property taxes. (See the cartoon at the beginning of this chapter.)

Overview of Grassroots Problems

Who are the policymakers for **grassroots governments,** and what differences do their decisions make in our daily lives? Answering these fundamental questions requires an understanding of American federalism, discussed in Chapter 2. Texas local governments, like those of other states, are at the bottom rung of the governmental ladder. Cities, counties, and special-district governments are creatures of the State of Texas, which is subordinate to federal authority as specified by Article VI of the U.S. Constitution.

For much of the Lone Star State's population, the fast-paced metropolitan scene is the center of attention. Because more than 80 percent of all Texans reside in these heavily populated urban and suburban areas, their most immediate concerns include violent crimes, drug trafficking, the AIDS epidemic, decaying infrastructures (roads and bridges), and dysfunctional schools. Frustrated by their inability to obtain adequate public services, many African-American and Hispanic citizens seek access to local power structures long dominated by Anglos. "Suburban sprawl," "inner-city decay," and "white flight" are not mere jargon in social science literature. Determining how Texas's local governments should deal with these problems is a challenge that drives most policy debates at the grassroots level.

Opportunities for individuals to participate in local politics begin with registering and voting. (See pages 86–87 for voter qualifications and registration requirements under Texas law.) Some citizens may even seek election to a city council, county commissioners court, school board, or other policymaking body. Short of winning public office, however, an individual may become politically active through homeowners' or renters' associations, voter registration drives, and election campaigns of others seeking local offices. Nevertheless, it is not uncommon to find fewer than 10 percent of a community's qualified voters participating in a local election. Voter apathy disappears when citizens understand that grassroots problems in Texas can be solved only through political participation. By gaining influence in city halls, county courthouses, and special-district offices, citizens may address grassroots problems through the democratic process.

Municipal Governments

Perhaps no level of government influences the daily lives of its citizens more than municipal (city) government. Whether taxing residents, arresting criminals, collecting garbage, circulating library books, or repairing streets, municipalities determine how millions of Texans live in more than 1,100 incorporated communities. Knowing how and why public policies are made within this multiplicity of governments requires an understanding of the organizational and legal framework within which they function.

Legal Status of Municipalities

Powers of city governments are outlined and restricted by municipal charters, state and national constitutions, and statutes. There are two legal classifications of cities in Texas: general-law cities and home-rule cities. An area with a population of 201 or more may become a **general-law city** through a charter prescribed by a general law enacted by the Texas Legislature.[1] A city of more than 5,000 people may be incorporated as a **home-rule city,** with a locally drafted charter that is adopted, amended, or repealed by majority vote in a citywide election. Once chartered, a general-law city does not automatically become a home-rule city just because its population rises above 5,000, nor does home-rule status change when a population declines to less than 5,000. Local voters must decide the legal designation of their city, but the Texas Legislature reserves the right to change a home-rule city's government.

As of late 1998, there were 301 home-rule cities and 892 general-law cities in Texas. The principal advantage of home-rule cities is greater flexibility in determining their structures and forms of municipal government. Citizens draft and adopt city charters that spell out procedures for passing ordinances and establishing powers, salaries, and terms of offices for city council members and mayors. Some cities, such as Austin, provide a process for removing elected officials through a popular vote. This process is referred to as **recall**. Along with initiative and referendum, recall is restricted to home-rule cities in Texas government. An **initiative** is a citizen-drafted measure proposed by a certain number or percentage of qualified voters. If approved by popular vote in a **referendum** election, it repeals an **ordinance** (local law) without city council approval.

Forms of Municipal Government

Four principal forms of municipal government, with many variations, operate in the United States and Texas: strong mayor-council, weak mayor-council, commission, and council-manager. The council-manager form prevails in more than 80 percent of Texas's home-rule cities, and some variation of the mayor-council system operates in many general-law cities.

A typical question from citizens is "How do you explain the structure of municipal government in my town? None of the four models accurately depicts our government." The answer lies in **home-rule flexibility**. Various combinations of the forms discussed in the following sections are permissible under a home-rule charter, depending on voter preference, provided they do not conflict with state law.

Strong Mayor-Council Among larger American cities, the **strong mayor-council form** continues as the predominant governmental structure. Of the nation's ten largest cities, only Dallas and San Antonio operate with a structure (council-manager) other than some variation of the strong mayor-council system. In New York, Chicago, Philadelphia, Detroit, Boston, and St. Louis, the mayor is the administrative as well as political head of the city. Houston and El Paso also have the strong mayor-council form of government, but the balance of Texas's larger, home-rule cities have rejected this form of government. Perhaps this is due to a dislike for so-called machine or ward-heeling politics, a style that once characterized the strong mayor-council form in some northern cities and frequently resulted in corrupt municipal administrations. In Texas, cities operating with the strong mayor-council form have the following characteristics:

- A council composed of members elected from single-member districts
- A mayor elected at large, with power to appoint and remove department heads
- Budgetary power (for example, preparation and execution of a plan for raising and spending city money) given to the mayor, subject to council approval before the budget may be implemented
- Veto power over council actions given to the mayor

Houston has a variation of the strong mayor-council form that features a powerful mayor aided by a citizens' assistance office and an elected controller who is responsible for the budget. (See Figure 3.1.) Such an arrangement allows the mayor to delegate much administrative work to the chief of staff, whom the mayor appoints and may remove. Duties of the chief of staff include coordinating the activities of city departments, the mayor's office, and council members' offices. Houston elected its first African-American, Lee Brown, as mayor in 1997.

Weak Mayor-Council As the term **weak mayor-council form** implies, this model of local government gives limited administrative powers to the mayor, who is popularly elected along with members of the city council, some department heads, and other municipal officials. A city council has power to override the mayor's veto. The mayor's position is weak because the office shares appointive and removal powers over municipal government personnel with the city council.

Instead of being a chief executive, the mayor is merely one of several elected officials who are responsible to the electorate. Significantly, none

FIGURE 3.1   Strong Mayor-Council Form: City of Houston

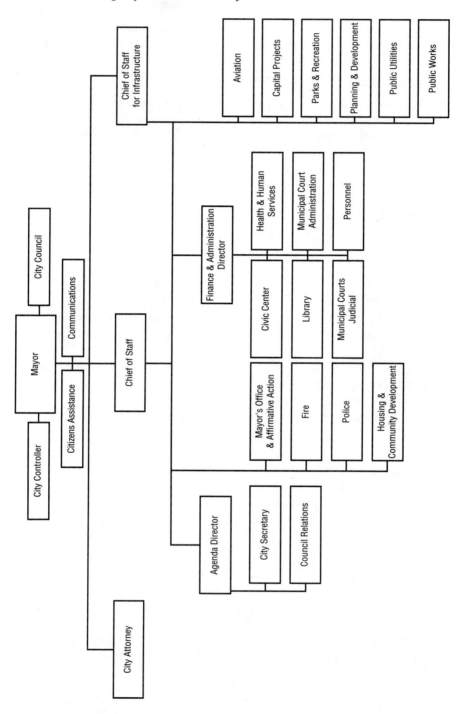

Source: Office of the Mayor, City of Houston.

Houston Mayor Lee Brown, left, chats with Karen Pernell before convening his first town-hall-type meeting. (Betty Tichich/Chronicle)

of the ten largest cities in Texas now operates under the weak mayor-council form of municipal government because of problems in trying to administer large bureaucracies without a chief executive. Although some small general-law and home-rule cities in Texas and other parts of the country operate on the weak major-council plan, the trend is away from this form.

Commission None of Texas's home-rule cities has chosen to operate under a pure **commission form** of municipal government, in which each commissioner administers a department. This form does not provide a single executive but relies instead on elected commissioners constituting a policymaking board. Individually, each commissioner administers a department (for example, public safety, finance, public works, welfare, or legal). Most students of municipal government are critical of this form because it lacks a chief executive and has a dispersed administrative structure. Texas municipalities that have a variation of the commission form of government designate city secretaries or other officials to coordinate departmental work. By state law, some general-law cities, such as Gorman (in Eastland County), must have a commission form of government.

Council-Manager Utilized by most home-rule cities in Texas is the **council-manager form** (sometimes termed the **commission-manager form**). This structure has the following characteristics:

▪ City council or commission members elected at large or in single-member districts
▪ A city manager who can be appointed and removed by the council and is responsible for budget coordination
▪ A mayor, elected at large, who is the presiding member of the council (See Figure 3.2.)

The city council makes decisions after deliberation and debate on policy issues such as taxation, police protection, and zoning ordinances. Once a policy is made, the city manager's office directs an appropriate department to implement it.

When Amarillo and Terrell adopted the council-manager form in 1913, a new era in municipal administration began. Aside from Houston and El Paso, Texas's largest cities are governed with a council-manager system. Typically, city councils require professionally trained managers. Successful applicants usually possess graduate degrees in public administration. City councils, in turn, look to their managers for preparations of annual budgets and policy recommendations. Final decisions are made by the council.

In theory, council-manager systems attempt to separate policymaking from administration. Councils are not supposed to "micro-manage" departments. Practice demonstrates, however, that elected leaders experience difficulties in determining where to draw the line between administrative oversight and meddling in departmental affairs. Nevertheless, about 250 Texas home-rule cities are governed under this form.

Municipal Politics

Elected city councils or commissions are focal points of policymaking. No longer controlled by wealthy elites, council members increasingly reflect Texas's cultural diversity. All that remains constant for municipal politics are state-mandated **nonpartisan elections,** in which candidates are not listed on the ballot by party label; rather, aspirants to a city council or mayoral position are endorsed and supported by community groups. This system paves a relatively easy path to political influence by concerned citizens.

Municipal politics is influenced by two significant developments: emergence of single-member districts for city councils and rising expectations of African Americans and Hispanics. When a city adopts **single-member districts** for electing council members, each voter casts a ballot for a candidate who resides within that voter's district. In an **at-large system,** all council members are elected on a citywide basis. By 1997, more than 40 Texas cities were using **cumulative voting,** rather than single-member districts, to increase African-American and Hispanic representation on city councils. Where multiple vacancies occur in an at-large council system, voters

FIGURE 3.2 Council-Manager Form: City of Dallas Organization Chart

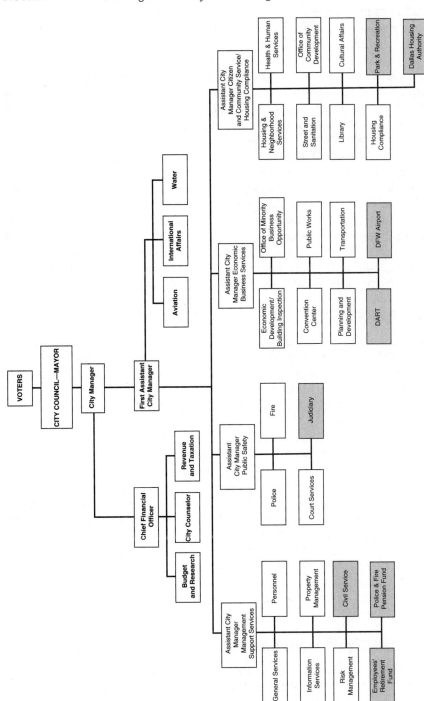

Source: Office of City Secretary, City of Dallas.

may cast one or more of the specified number of votes for one or more candidates in any combination. Only whole votes may be cast and counted in a city where cumulative voting is used.

Prompted by lawsuits and minority group pressures, four of the largest Texas cities operate with single-member district plans. Each council member in Dallas (14), San Antonio (10), El Paso (6), and Fort Worth (8) is elected from a single-member district. Houston, however, continues to function with five council members elected at large (citywide), while nine are from single-member districts. In some cities, the mayor is chosen by (and is a member of) the council.

Mayors of Austin, Dallas, El Paso, Fort Worth, Houston, and San Antonio are elected at large and preside over weekly council meetings. Charters for all of those cities except El Paso allow the mayor to vote on any matter before the council. El Paso's mayor has only a tie-breaking vote.

Some cities, such as Austin, use a **place system** to elect council members. Under this structure, city council candidates file for a numerically designated place, and those candidates who file for the same place run against one another. Council members are then elected on an at-large basis, with all voters in the city voting in each place contest. Austin's mayor is elected citywide.

Municipal Services

Use of single-member districts has altered the power structures in the largest cities of Texas and changed municipal service agendas. Increasing numbers of African Americans and Mexican Americans have migrated from small towns and rural areas to the inner cities of Austin, Dallas, El Paso, Fort Worth, Houston, and San Antonio. This, coupled with more single-member districts, forced the white, male, business-oriented network of power brokers to "cut the pie" to make municipal government more responsive to the demographic and economic realities of the central city.

Cities operating with home-rule charters possess ordinance-making powers. Zoning restrictions, consumer affairs, traffic safety, pollution control, planning, building safety, and other municipal affairs are ordinance regulated. City councils pass, repeal, or amend ordinances. Most cities establish appointed boards and commissions that function in an advisory capacity with municipal departments in implementing municipal ordinances. Interestingly, Houston remains the only city among Texas's ten largest municipalities without zoning powers. Examples of zoning controversies erupting into often heated debate occur when city councils change residential areas into commercial zones.

Municipal Government Revenue

What people want most from their local governments are public services paid for with low taxes. Although city hall is a favorite target of angry taxpayers, the Texas Legislature receives its share of pressure because of strict statutory and constitutional limitations on cities.

Taxes Texas municipalities are constitutionally empowered to levy general property taxes and miscellaneous occupation taxes. Also, by 1998, more than 1,000 cities were collecting nearly $2 billion in sales taxes each year as authorized by state law. In addition, the legislature may authorize new revenues from nontax sources.

Fees Texas municipalities may levy fees for issuing beer and liquor licenses as well as for granting building and plumbing permits. Authorized to maintain municipal courts, cities also obtain revenue from court costs, fines, and forfeitures. This revenue may be substantial, especially if traffic regulations are enforced vigorously.

Texas cities may charge a **franchise fee** based on the gross receipts of public utilities (for example, telephone and cable TV companies) operating within their jurisdictions. Texas courts hold that this is fundamentally a "street rental" or "alley rental" charge. Trailing only property and sales tax revenues, franchise fees are steadily growing as a significant revenue source for the Lone Star State's major cities.

Texas municipalities are authorized to own and operate water, electric, and gas utility systems. If a city decides to offer these services, it may collect revenues large enough to permit profits, which are transferred to general funds. Charges also are levied for services such as sewage disposal, garbage and trash collection, hospital care, and use of city recreation facilities. A **user fee** may mean that a service requires only a small subsidy from a city's general revenue fund, or perhaps no subsidy.

Bonds Taxes and fees normally produce enough revenue to allow Texas cities to cover day-to-day operating expenses, but money for capital improvements (such as construction of city buildings) and for emergencies often must be obtained through the sale of municipal bonds. The Texas Constitution allows cities to issue bonds in any amount, provided they annually assess and collect sufficient revenue to pay the interest and retire the principal without exceeding legal tax limits. Cities are authorized to issue general obligation bonds and revenue bonds. **General obligation bonds** are redeemed out of a city's general revenue fund. **Revenue bonds** are backed by and redeemed out of the revenue from the property or activities (such as convention centers) financed by the sale of the bonds.

Recent Developments

Appropriations from state and federal lawmakers are shrinking as sources of municipal revenue. Although construction of expressways by the Texas Department of Transportation assists cities with traffic movement, pressing human needs receive no direct state financial aid. Foremost among inner-city problems is dilapidated housing, which blights neighborhoods and contributes to other social problems, including crime and strained racial relations.

Tax Reinvestment Zones Following a national trend, some Texas cities are opting for an innovative revenue-raising plan. The legislature authorizes municipalities to create **tax reinvestment zones (TRZs),** through temporary tax abatements (eliminating property taxes) or **tax increment financing (TIF)**. The TIF process involves cities that dedicate zones for redevelopment through tax incentives for businesses to locate in blighted inner-city areas. Once established, TRZs "freeze" commercial and residential property tax rates and valuations within their boundaries, thereby giving tax breaks to property owners. Any increment (increase) in property taxes within the zone is used for property improvements and retirement of bonds. Legal restrictions prevent a city from placing more than 15 percent of its taxable real property and more than 10 percent of its residential property in a TRZ. For example, when Dallas voters authorized a new sports arena, a new TRZ was created in the West End of downtown.

Given the pressures to refrain from raising property tax rates, Texas cities are forced to cut budgets and look for new revenue sources. Compounding the problem are difficulties in passing bond issues.

Often confronted with budget shortfalls, city councils are forced to opt for one or more of the following actions, none of which is an inducement to economic growth:

- Create new fees or raise current fees on services such as garbage collection
- Raise property taxes
- Impose hiring and wage freezes for municipal employees
- Cut services (such as emergency medical services) that are especially important for inner-city populations.

Unlike many big cities outside the Sunbelt, Texas cities can levy neither personal nor corporate income taxes.

Property Tax Issue   Heavy reliance on an ad valorem tax on home and business property brings many Texas communities to the brink of a taxpayers' revolt. Not only do municipal governments rely on the property tax as their major revenue source, but so do counties and most special districts, including public school systems. A 1997 amendment to the Texas Constitution grants a maximum 20 percent homestead exemption for school property taxes.

All business and residential property within each Texas county is assessed for tax purposes by the **countywide tax appraisal district**. Each of these 254 tax districts is responsible for appraising all real estate and commercial property within its county. Prior to 1982, counties, cities, and special districts appraised property irregularly and with different valuation systems. Today city councils, county commissioners courts, and school boards in each county appoint appraisal district board members in addition to setting tax rates for their respective governments.

To offset somewhat the burden of higher taxes resulting from reappraisals of property values, local governments (including cities) may grant homeowners a 20 percent **homestead exemption** on the assessed value of their homes. After reappraisal, taxing units (cities, counties, and special districts) are not allowed to raise tax rates more than 3 percent annually without public hearings allowing citizens to ask questions and state their opinions. Voters may force local governments to roll back a tax rate if it represents more than an 8 percent increase above the previous year's rate. A rollback election must be conducted if 10 percent of the people who voted in the last general election sign a petition. For a school district, the referendum is automatic, unless the tax increase is due to larger enrollment or loss of state aid.

Recently the Texas Legislature has attempted to force cities and other local governments to compensate property owners for regulations that result in "taking" their property or reducing their property values. Zoning ordinances that convert residential areas into commercial tracts are exempt from this restriction.

Counties

Article IX of the Texas Constitution is titled Counties, although it says little about county government. The **county** is an administrative arm of the state, created to serve its needs and purposes. State supervision of county operations, however, is minimal. As an agent of the state, each of the 254 Texas counties (more than any other state) issues state automobile licenses, enforces state laws, registers voters, conducts elections, collects some state taxes, and helps administer justice. In conjunction with state and federal governments, the county conducts health and welfare programs, maintains records of vital statistics (such as births and deaths), issues various licenses, collects fees, and provides a host of other public services.

Texans tend to regard the county's governmental functions as local rather than statewide in nature. Most people cannot distinguish between functions performed for the county and those conducted for the state. For example, the county sheriff and county judge enforce and administer state law. These officials are therefore state functionaries, yet they are elected by the voters of the county and are paid from the county treasury.

Structure and Operation

Operation of county government in Texas is influenced by the Jacksonian principle of popular election of public officials. Texas counties have the same basic governmental structure, as mandated by the state constitution, despite extreme demographic and economic discrepancies between rural and urban counties.

Although many people question the desirability of this arrangement, any change would require amendment of the Texas Constitution. That document requires the election of county commissioners, a county attorney and four district attorneys, a county sheriff, a county clerk, a district clerk, a county tax assessor-collector, and a county treasurer, as well as judicial officers, including justices of the peace and a county judge. All elected county officials serve four-year terms.

Commissioners Court Policymaking is performed by many county officials, but mainly by a body called the **commissioners court.** Its members are the county judge, who presides, and four elected commissioners. The latter serve staggered terms so that two commissioners are elected every two years. Each commissioner is elected by voters residing in a commissioner precinct. Boundary lines for a county's four commissioner precincts are set by its commissioners court. Precincts must be of substantially equal population as mandated by the "one-man, one-vote" ruling of the U.S. Supreme Court in *Avery* v. *Midland County* (1968).

Commissioners court is actually a misnomer, because its functions are administrative rather than judicial. The court's major functions include adopting the county budget and setting tax rates. In performing these duties, commissioners must observe state constitutional limitations on types of taxes and maximum tax rates. State law mandates that counties provide jails, build and maintain county roads and bridges, operate a courthouse, and administer county health and welfare programs. Beyond this, a county is free to decide whether to enter other programs authorized, but not required, by the state. Within these limits, the commissioners may establish and operate county hospitals, libraries, parks, airports, museums, and other public facilities. Increasing citizen demands for services rendered by these agencies impose on most counties an ever-expanding need for money.

Another major function of the commissioners court is the conduct of elections. The state leaves the administration (and expense) of virtually all general and special elections—national, state, and local—to the county. Exceptions are elections for municipal and special-district offices, which are financed by the city or special district conducting the election. Each county is divided into voting precincts by its commissioners court, which also canvasses, or checks, county election returns.

In addition to their collective responsibilities, commissioners court members have individual duties. Each commissioner serves as road and bridge administrator in a precinct, except in the more than 50 counties where a unit road system is established under the direction of a county engineer. Frequently, money allotted for county roads and bridges is divided among the four precincts regardless of need. Waste of money, lack of coordination, and faulty administration are the inevitable results.

County Judge Major responsibility for administrative operations of the commissioners court is vested in a **county judge**. Acting in an administrative capacity, the county judge presides over meetings of the commissioners court. In a judicial capacity, the judge in most counties hears cases in county court but is not required to be a lawyer. (See pages 235–237 for information on county judges, justices of the peace, and constables.) The judge also fills vacancies within the commissioners court, is authorized to perform marriages, and serves as a **notary public** (an individual who certifies documents, takes sworn statements, and administers oaths).

County Attorney and County Sheriff The **county attorney** represents the state in civil and criminal cases. Some counties, such as Harris, elect both a county attorney and a district attorney, with the latter representing the state in only criminal cases. Nearly 50 counties do not elect a county attorney because the functions of that office are performed by a resident district attorney. Other counties elect a county attorney but share the services of a district attorney with two or more neighboring counties.

The **county sheriff,** as chief law enforcement officer, is charged with keeping the peace in the county. In this capacity, the sheriff appoints deputies and is in charge of the county jail and its prisoners. A Texas sheriff must be at least 21 years old, become a state-licensed peace officer within two years after taking office, and have no record of felony conviction. In a county with a population of less than 10,000, the sheriff also serves as tax assessor-collector, unless that county's electorate votes to separate the two offices.

Rarely do write-in candidates for public office (including sheriff) succeed in electoral politics. Only four county sheriffs in Texas history have been elected as write-ins. For example, in 1996, San Augustine County's write-in votes elected a sheriff by a margin of 66 votes.[2]

County Clerk and County Tax Assessor-Collector A **county clerk** keeps records and handles a variety of paperwork chores for both the county court and the commissioners court. In addition, the county clerk files legal documents (such as deeds, mortgages, and contracts) in the county's public records and maintains the county's vital statistics, including birth, death, and marriage records. Responsibility for administration of elections also extends to the county clerk, who certifies each candidate for a place on the general election ballot and prepares the ballot (unless the commissioners court appoints an administrator of elections).

Another county office receiving considerable statewide attention is that of the **county tax assessor-collector,** which, partially at least, is a misnomer. The Texas Constitution stipulates that a county with a population of at least 10,000 must have a tax assessor-collector. Following adoption of a state constitutional amendment in 1982, however, the boards of county tax appraisal districts (defined on page 66) have assessed property values in each county. Therefore, county tax assessor-collectors no longer perform tax assessment (appraisal) duties. Issuing certificates of title and collecting license fees for motor vehicles are additional functions of the office. Unless a county creates an election administrator, the county tax assessor-collector serves as voting registrar.

County Treasurer and County Auditor The **county treasurer** receives and pays out all county funds authorized by the commissioners court. Voter approval of constitutional amendments abolished several county treasurer offices in the 1980s and 1990s, including those of Tarrant County (Fort Worth) and Bell County (Temple). Since elimination of these offices, county commissioners have assigned treasurer duties to the county auditor.

A county of 10,000 or more people must have a **county auditor,** who is appointed by the district court judge or judges having jurisdiction in the county. The auditing function involves checking the account books and records of all officials who handle county funds. Any county having a population of more than 225,000 may have a budget officer, who is appointed by the commissioners court.

County Surveyor The **county surveyor** is a constitutionally prescribed elected officer who draws no salary but is paid to conduct specific surveys of land within the county. Most counties use the services of private surveyors and do not fill the office. When the office is occupied, surveyors enjoy rent-free space in the county courthouse or annex locations as a means of publicizing their business. Texas counties may abolish the office of surveyor on a local option basis.

Appointed Officials Depending on the population of a county and with commissioners court approval, several appointed officers exist in counties across the state. Whenever a county engages in activities authorized but not required by the Texas Constitution or state statutes, the commissioners court must appoint an administrative head to oversee the program. For example, a county may have an administrator as head of a health department. Federal grants-in-aid also involve the counties in programs requiring administrators for welfare, agricultural extension, and other services.

County Finance

Just as the structure of county governments is frozen in the Texas Constitution, so is the county's power to tax and, to a lesser extent, its power to spend.

Taxation The Texas Constitution authorizes county governments to collect taxes on property. Although occupations may also be taxed, no county implements that provision.

Money collected from the basic property tax is distributed among general revenue, permanent improvement, road and bridge, and jury funds in each county treasury. Additional property taxes may be imposed by a commissioners court, but only after statutory authorization by the Texas Legislature and approval by a majority of the county's qualified voters.

Counties and other local taxing units may exempt from taxation temporarily based property such as commercial aircraft. To qualify for the exemption, the items may not be in the state for more than 175 days. In 1993, this so-called **freeport amendment** to the Texas Constitution was lobbied through the legislature by special interests representing businesses heavily engaged in interstate commerce, such as airlines. Since 1993, pollution control equipment installed by businesses is exempt from county and other local property taxation.

Although state constitutional restrictions limit categories of taxable property, counties now operate with a broader definition of valuation. Since 1978, valuation of farmland and ranch land is taxed on productivity rather than market value. If wildlife (such as deer) are fed or hunted on a farm, the property may qualify for an agricultural exemption. All other **real property** (such as buildings, mines, and quarries) continues to be assessed at market value or at least some percentage of market value. Also subject to ad valorem taxation is **tangible personal property** (goods located in the state). Exempted from taxation are government-owned property; household goods and personal effects not used in the production of income (boats, aircraft, and recreational vehicles); holdings of certain designated private, charitable, educational, and religious institutions; farm products in the hands of producers; and supplies for farm and home use. Any motorized vehicle may be exempted on a local option basis. A commissioners court also may grant tax abatements (reductions or suspensions) and reimbursements to attract or retain commercial businesses.

Revenues from Nontax Sources Special laws allow counties to issue bonds, subject to voter approval. Revenue from the sale of bonds is used for capital outlays such as payment for a new county courthouse or county jail. County indebtedness is limited by the Texas Constitution to 35 percent of a county's total assessed property value.

As additional sources of income, counties may impose fees for permitting the sale of liquor, wine, and beer. They also receive a percentage of the state gross receipts tax on liquor. Texas statutes allow each county to share in revenues obtained from state motor vehicle registration and license fees (50 percent after the first $250,000 collected in the county), motor fuel taxes (25 percent), motor vehicle sales taxes (5 percent), fees for issuing certificates of title for motor vehicles (50 percent), and traffic (speeding) fines issued in unincorporated areas (outside city limits).

Federal grants-in-aid are another source of county revenue, but this source has continued to shrink with block grant funding. Typically the U.S. Congress makes counties eligible to receive any and all aid extended to cities and towns, including grants for construction of hospitals, airports, and public housing. For counties that have military installations, grants of federal money increase.

Despite various revenue sources, Texas counties, like other units of local government, are pressured to raise property taxes. Demands for county services and administrative costs continue to increase, but sources of county revenue are not expanding.

Expenditures Although county expenditures are restricted by legal requirements and state administrative directives, patterns of spending vary considerably from county to county. (See Reading 3.1 on the politics of Harris County spending.) The county judge, auditor, or budget officer prepares the budget, but the commissioners court is responsible for final adoption of an annual spending plan. Maintenance of county roads and bridges continues to require the largest expenditures in rural counties throughout Texas.

Counties do not have complete control over their spending because state statutes and administrative directives require that certain county services be furnished and regulatory activities be conducted. Thus, counties are required to raise and spend funds for some purposes dictated by state authorities, not by county commissioners. Examples of such expenditures include welfare and mental health programs.

County Government Reform

Two basic problems underlie any organizational or power changes in county government: (1) the government structure established in the Texas Constitution and (2) voter apathy toward local governments in general and county government in particular. Media coverage can do much to overcome the latter problem. Whenever investigative reporting uncovers abuses of power and wrongdoing in county government, activities of county officials may be held up to closer public scrutiny. (See reading, pp. 79–82.) Only a home-rule amendment to the Texas Constitution can overcome most structural defects. Merging counties into some regional or "supercounty" arrangement would also require a constitutional amendment.

Ordinance-Making Power   County officials generally agree that their governments need ordinance-making power to regulate unincorporated areas outside city limits. Only when counties successsfully lobby the Texas legislature for local laws (ordinances) can they regulate problems such as where to locate landfill sites.[3] Moreover, the Lone Star State is among 12 of the 47 states having county governments that do not grant home-rule status to counties.

County Chief Executive   Another change, as advocated by many students of county government, would entail establishing a single chief executive for each county. Such a reform would go far toward eliminating lengthy ballots and centering administrative responsibility in a single chief executive elected directly by the people or appointed by the commissioners court.

County Road System   Under continual scrutiny is the county road system, which in many counties is inefficient and uncoordinated. Wherever budgeted money for roads and bridges is divided four ways among precinct commissioners, the result is often a four-way struggle for power that sees commissioners concerned primarily with padding their individual road and bridge budgets to benefit political cronies. When each commissioner is free to carry out a road and bridge program on an individual basis, there is no guarantee that plans and operations of the four commissioners will be coordinated and public funds will be spent most effectively.

Special Districts

Among local governmental units, the least known and least understood are **special-district governments**. They fall into two basic categories: school districts and nonschool districts. Created by an act of the legislature or, in some cases, by local ordinance (for example, a public housing authority), a special district usually has one function and serves a specific group of people in a particular geographic area. Special districts must be classified as units of government because they have the following characteristics:

- An organized existence
- A governnmental character (for example, many exercise taxing power)
- Substantial independence from other units of government

Public School Districts

Citizen concerns over public education cause local school systems to occupy center stage among special-district governments. More than 1,000 Texas **independent school districts (ISDs),** created by the legislature, are governed by popularly elected, nonsalaried boards of trustees. Either three- or four-year terms of office are determined by each board for its members, who may serve more than one term.

Given the nonsalaried status of the office, why would citizens seek membership on a school board? The answer lies in the many duties conferred on these boards by the Texas Legislature. Included among the more important powers are the following:

- Setting personnel policy
- Determining salary schedules
- Providing for construction and maintenance of school buildings
- Selecting textbooks
- Setting the property tax rate for the district

Beginning in 1995, school boards have been given increased local autonomy following legislative changes supported by Governor George W. Bush. State policy directives, however, are administered by the Texas Education Agency (see pages 207–208), including control of school districts that fail to meet state standards.[4]

Junior or Community College Districts

Another example of a special district is the **junior college** or **community college district,** which offers two-year academic programs beyond high school and provides various technical and vocational programs. Operated by 50 districts (some with two or more campuses), Texas's 68 public junior or community colleges enroll more than 400,000 students and constitute the state's fastest-growing level of postsecondary education. (See Table 3.1 for the ten largest district enrollments.)

Unlike fully supported state universities and technical colleges, all public two-year colleges are financed in part by local taxes. Approximately 30 percent of their financial support comes from local or district tax revenues, while students pay 20 percent in tuition and fees. About 50 percent comes from state appropriations, which for fiscal years 1998 and 1999 reached a combined total of more than $1.3 billion. The remainder of their support comes from federal aid and miscellaneous sources, such as local scholarships. Beginning in 1998, the Texas Legislature requires counties outside community college districts and with more than 1,000 students enrolled to pay local taxes to the college district serving these students. Financial responsibilities of a two-year college board member include setting property tax rates, issuing bonds (subject to voter approval), and adopting the annual budget.

Nonschool Districts

As if 1,193 municipalities, 1,043 school districts, 50 community/junior college districts, and 254 counties were not enough local governments for Texas taxpayers to bear, hundreds of others have been created. Each carries out a special function. Heading the list in numerical order are more than 1,000 water or utility districts, followed by more than 300 housing authorities, 200 soil and water conservation districts, 80 hospital districts, and 40 hospital authorities. Mass transit authorities provide public transportation for cities in seven metropolitan areas: Austin, Corpus Christi, Dallas, El Paso, Fort Worth, Houston, and San Antonio. Local voters determine whether a city joins a mass transit authority.

Counties may also establish special districts for emergency medical services, jails, rural rail systems, fire prevention, mosquito control, health programs, airports, noxious weed control, wind erosion conservation, waste disposal, and ground water subsidence.

Special districts often overcome restrictions placed on municipalities and counties by the Texas Constitution. For example, many public hospitals are

TABLE 3.1 Texas Public Community (Junior) College Districts: Ten Top Enrollments and State Funding

College District (Major City)	Enrollment Fall 1997	% of Total Enrollment	State Funding Fiscal Year 1998	% of Total State Funding
Alamo (San Antonio)	38,332	9.40%	$50,522,758	7.66%
Austin (Austin)	25,796	6.32%	34,338,313	5.21%
Collin County (Plano)	11,047	2.71%	15,077,454	2.29%
Dallas County (Dallas)	45,153	11.06%	70,732,978	10.72%
Del Mar (Corpus Christi)	10,399	2.55%	18,875,074	2.86%
El Paso County (El Paso)	19,371	4.75%	29,698,424	4.50%
Houston (Houston)	31,926	7.83%	57,819,554	8.74%
North Harris (Houston)	22,185	5.44%	28,348,039	4.30%
San Jacinto (Houston)	18,283	4.48%	28,386,437	4.30%
Tarrant County (Fort Worth)	26,692	6.54%	32,502,984	4.93%
All Others (40)	158,839	38.93%	293,418,859	44.49%
Grand Total	407,985	100.00%	$659,518,870	100.00%

Source: Texas Higher Education Coordinating Board.

built by hospital districts because they operate on a multicounty basis, reaching beyond city limits and county lines. In 1997, the Texas Legislature also authorized construction of sports facilities, governed by appointed special-district boards from multiple cities and counties, following voter approval.

The Politics of Special Districts

Underlying creation of special districts are political maneuverings of extreme variety and complexity. Private financial gain lies in cozy relationships among many land developers, bankers, and legislators. Out of this axis of power spring hundreds of municipal utility districts (MUDs) and other water districts around Texas's central cities. In the Houston area alone, more than 400 MUDs operate in Harris and surrounding counties.

Special-district governments may raise revenue with property or sales taxes and various fees, depending on statutory directives. Mass transit authorities, such as Houston's Metro and Dallas's DART, rely on a l percent sales tax as their principal funding source. Fort Worth's Crime Control and Prevention District levies a one-half-cent sales tax for its anti-crime operations. These examples are symptomatic of a relentless trend in local governance nationwide, namely, trying to solve problems by creating more governments.

Metropolitan Areas

Eighty percent of Texas's more than 19 million people live in 22 metropolitan areas. Ringing these and other Texas cities are rapidly growing suburban communities with municipal and special-district governments that further fragment local governance. An ever-tightening squeeze brought on by escalating property taxes underlies metropolitan problems. Many scholars question urban policies that attack regional issues related to transportation, education, pollution, crime, and housing through special-district governments. Hundreds of water districts are glaring examples of how fragmentation of services impede regional planning.

How will metropolitan areas be governed in the future? Given legal and political impediments to any comprehensive overhaul of existing governmental structures, quick and easy answers to that question are unrealistic. Entrenched officeholders, particularly county politicians, resist efforts to merge their duties with those of municipal officials. Long-range solutions must begin with an understanding of how and why urban problems transcend existing governmental boundaries.

Councils of Governments

Looking beyond city limits, county lines, and special-district boundaries requires expertise from planners who think regionally. In 1966, the legislature created the first of 24 regional planning bodies known as **councils of**

governments (COGs) or, in some areas, planning/development commissions/councils.

Governmental membership in a COG is voluntary. Furthermore, COGs do not attempt to usurp local autonomy of any governmental unit. They perform regional planning activities and provide services requested by member governments or as directed by federal and state programs. Stringent guidelines for federal grants to local governments require COG expertise. Through review-and-comment procedures, local officials join with COGS to draft and implement state- and federally funded programs. The term **review-and-comment** refers to a COG's evaluation of grant proposals submitted by member governments. Assume, for example, that a city wants to construct a new water treatment facility with federal or state funds. Before approving the project, a COG determines how that facility would affect other governments in the COG.

Some critics of COGs argue that these regional forums are the first step toward metro government, which currently exists in Toronto, Ontario (Canada); Miami, Florida; Nashville-Davidson County, Tennessee; and, on a smaller scale, Portland, Oregon. **Metro government** results in consolidation of existing local governments in an urban area under one umbrella authority.

Stopgap Approaches

Aside from COG services, other means of coping with metropolitan problems tend to be cosmetic solutions for serious illnesses. Three approaches are possible under state laws.

Municipal Annexation In an attempt to provide statewide guidelines for home-rule cities grappling with suburban sprawl, the Texas Legislature enacted a municipal annexation law in 1963. This statute allows home-rule cities to annex territory beyond their corporate limits, with the following restrictions:

- Generally, territories annexed during a calendar year may not exceed 10 percent of a city's area as of January 1 and, depending on the city's population, must be within one-half mile to five miles of the city limits
- When the unincorporated area is annexed, the city must provide services (for example, water and sewer) for the area, or the annexed area's residents can petition a state district court for deannexation
- A suburban municipality adjoining the central city may be annexed by the central city, but only after voter approval in both the central and suburban communities

Controversies occur when city councils adopt ordinances annexing unincorporated areas, thus depriving residents in subdivisions of opportunities to determine whether they will be annexed. (Exceptions are general-law cities that must provide unincorporated areas with water and sewer services before annexation occurs.)

Intergovernmental Contracting Another trend in metropolitan areas is for local governments to contract for services when one government lacks funds to do the job alone. Community college districts contracting with their county tax assessor-collectors to collect college property taxes are one example. Such contractual arrangements facilitate intergovernmental cooperation but are not long-range solutions to governing metropolitan areas.

New Districts Without state supervision of special districts, interest groups flex their political muscle with their legislators, who respond with favorable laws creating dozens of new governments each legislative session. Political expediency, therefore, says, "Pass my special-district bill, and don't bother me with how my metropolitan area is affected." That common attitude represents a formidable challenge to Texas's local government reformers.

Looking Ahead

Practice of local politics in Texas is as disjointed as the organizational structures of grassroots governments attempting to deliver services. City hall politics, county politics, school board politics, and transit board politics present a bewildering array of officeholders to frustrated taxpayers who are already skeptical and often cynical about politicians in general. To whom, then, do grassroots residents turn for answers? How can a sense of community and cooperation be developed within Texas's complex urban areas? Answers to these and related questions must begin with more citizen involvement.

Grassroots enfranchisement gives rise to hope that Texas's local governments can become more regionally oriented. Increased voter registration, particularly in central cities, may provide the key for unlocking doors that block political and economic progress. Aided by single-member districts, newly empowered African Americans and Hispanics are changing political agendas.

What remains is for citizens to take advantage of opportunities to participate in politics at every level of government—local, state, and national. That first step toward building individual political efficacy (self-empowerment) is essential for democracy to flourish. The following chapter describes how citizens can vote and work through political parties to affect primaries and general elections.

Notes

1. See "Local Government Code," Sections 1.001–140, Chapters 6–8, *Vernon's Texas Codes Annotated* (St. Paul, Minn.: West, 1988).
2. Emily Manis, "San Augustine Overlooked Box Opened by Clerk," *The Daily Sentinel* (Nacogdoches), November 11, 1996, p.1.

3. Cindy Horswell, "Chambers Officials Vow to Reduce Size of Future Landfills," *Houston Chronicle*, February 19, 1998, p. 21A. See also Patrick Barta, "Counties Are Taking Steps to Curb Rural Growth," *Wall Street Journal*, March 26, 1998, pp. T1, T4.
4. For a list that rates 3,172 of Texas's elementary schools from "four-star" to "no-star," evaluated according to the Winich-Toenjes method, see "Our Best Schools," *Texas Monthly*, November 1996, pp. 112–119, 155, 157, 159, 160.

Key Terms and Concepts

grassroots government	homestead exemption
general-law city	county
home-rule city	commissioners court
recall	*Avery* v. *Midland County*
initiative	county judge
referendum	notary public
ordinance	county attorney
home-rule flexibility	county sheriff
strong mayor-council form	county clerk
weak mayor-council form	county tax assessor-collector
commission form	county treasurer
council-manager form	county auditor
commission-manager form	county surveyor
nonpartisan election	freeport amendment
single-member district	real property
at-large system	tangible personal property
cumulative voting	special-district government
place system	independent school district
franchise fee	(ISD)
user fee	junior college or community
general obligation bond	college district
revenue bond	council of governments (COGs)
tax reinvestment zone (TRZ)	review-and-comment
tax increment financing (TIF)	metro government
countywide tax appraisal district	

SELECTED READING

---★---

Contractual Friendships*

Bob Sablatura

 Why lucrative no-bid contracts are awarded to politically connected contractors and law firms by Harris County officials is the subject of this look at how Texas's most populated county is governed. What follows is another example of investigative journalism exposing the realities of money-driven politics.

Harris County Judge Robert Eckels had breakfast one morning last month (February 1998) with a few of his closest friends. Before his meal was properly digested, he had socked away more than an estimated $250,000 for his upcoming election campaign. The event was the annual Friends of Eckels appreciation breakfast put on every year by a who's who of the city's engineers, architects, attorneys, construction contractors, and financial advisors. Although a seemingly diverse group from the outside, most of these people have one thing in common: they get high-dollar, lucrative no-bid contracts from the county. They also donate generously to the campaigns of the five elected officials who dole out the tens of millions of dollars in such contracts each year. Since 1994, the county judge and four commissioners accepted more than $5 million in campaign donations, most from individuals and companies doing business with Harris County. (See Table 1.)

Legalized Bribery?

Eckels said it is no secret that most contributions come from people who receive county contracts, but he believes they support him—and others on the Commissioners Court—because he has shown a desire to focus on basic infrastructure within the county. "I don't think individually they expect more contracts because they contribute to me," Eckels said.

County Commissioner Steve Radack said it may sometimes appear that the amount of campaign contributions is the motivating factor in contract awards, but most contractors are selected because of existing working relationships. "All things being equal, you give the business to your friends," Radack said. "It is human nature to want to work with people you know and trust."

---

*From the *Houston Chronicle*, March 29, 1998. This article is the last in a series of three articles on Harris County politics. Bob Sablatura is a staff writer for the *Chronicle*. Reprinted by permission.

TABLE 1 Greasing the Political Machine

Company	Contributions	Contracts
James Edmonds (lobbyist for NYLCare)	$79,500	$5,004,996*
Turner, Collie & Braden	72,500	12,473,469
Hermes & Read Partnership	70,505	1,850,114
Mayor, Day, Caldwell & Keeton	69,500	1,373,395
Vinson & Elkins	69,000	3,029,373
Fulbright & Jaworski	68,500	558,935
Pepe Engineering	65,106	572,055
Costello Inc.	63,000	1,114,911
Geotest Engineering	59,000	2,074,412
Klotz Associates, Inc.	55,750	1,423,589
JNS Consulting Engineers	54,500	819,397
Carter & Burgess	54,500	1,497,089
Dannenbaum Engineering	53,000	4,498,463
Landtech Consultants	51,000	824,734
Pierce, Goodwin, Alexander & Linville	50,000	8,863,628

*Represents annual fee to administer the county's health insurance plan. NYLCare receives $417,083 per month. Edmonds also represented other clients receiving contracts from Harris County during this period.

Source: Contributions are from candidates' official campaign contribution reports and contract amounts are from the Harris County Treasurer's office.

Richard Bean, an economist with the University of Houston, said the private sector would never allow its decision-makers to accept such favors from contract recipients. Bean said he has an aquaintance who has the responsibility of selecting engineering contractors to work for his employer, a local oil company. "He can't take a lunch or even a calendar from one of these companies," Bean said. "If he does, he's fired, and his $150,000-a-year job is gone with him." The bottom line, Bean said, is that companies donate money to candidates in order to influence decisions on contract awards. Regardless of how elected officials portray it, he said, the practice is nothing more than legalized bribery. "You can call it anything you want, but it is a bribe," Bean said.

Contracting for Professional Services

Harris County regularly contracts for services provided by professionals, such as engineers, accountants, surveyors, architects, and attorneys. According to state law, these contracts cannot be competitively bid. The cost of the contract is determined through negotiation with the firm providing the services. Most professional services are provided in connection with road construction projects. In contrast, contracts for actual construction of the roads are awarded after a competitive bid process, pitting competing firms against one another as they attempt to offer the lowest price for the job.

The largest contributors to county campaigns are people associated with the firms that get contracts without a bidding process. Of the top 15 contributors since 1994, only one firm does not receive no-bid contracts. That firm, whose lobbyist was the largest contributor to county campaigns, is NYLCare, the county's insurance provider. NYLCare must submit a cost proposal to county officials.

In Harris County, the recipients of professional services are selected by the individual commissioners and the county judge. Commissioners usually choose the firms when a project is to be built in their precincts, and the county judge chooses firms associated with the issuance of bonds.

Radack said that while he recommends the county engineer negotiate with a certain firm on a job, he doesn't dictate that the contract be awarded regardless of cost. "If the county engineer comes back to me and says the company wants a ridiculous amount of money for the job, I tell them to find someone else," Radack said.

Radack said there are many firms clamoring to do business with the county, and he works hard to select a wide range of qualified companies for the work, without regard to whether they contribute to his campaign. "I wish there was enough work to give everybody all the contracts they want, but there isn't," Radack said.

Eckels said the county hires a pretty broad group of contractors. "You see the same names come up over and over again on campaign reports, but there are a lot of them," Eckels said. "We try to support our local economy and our local businesses as much as we can. We are lucky to have enough local talent to do that."

Bond Issues

One example of that is the three local law firms that act as bond counsel on county bond issues. Mayor, Day, Caldwell & Keeton; Fulbright & Jaworski; and Vinson & Elkins get the vast majority of such work. All three are among the 10 largest givers to county campaigns. For years, the county only used two firms for such work, but former County Attorney Mike Driscoll pushed the Commissioners Court a decade ago to start awarding business to Mayor, Day, Caldwell & Keeton.

Assistant County Attorney Rosalinda Garcia said there is no reason county bond work could not be performed by other law firms. There are a lot of local, state, and national firms that are qualified to do the job, but do not get the opportunity in part because of the financial support given to county officials by the three local firms. Garcia said she also believes that the county could save money by forcing the law firms to submit formal proposals for the work.

While the county cannot ask the firms to bid against one another, she said, there is no reason the county cannot seek proposals that spell out what rates the firms would charge for legal services or types of bonds. "We would not be asking them for a baseline amount they could not exceed, but we could get enough information so we would be able to compare apples to apples," Garcia said.

Quid Pro Quo?

Texas law makes it illegal for public officials to accept contributions or anything else of value in return for a contract. But experts on ethics laws agree that it is almost impossible to prove a "quid pro quo" or that a contract was awarded as the direct result of a campaign contribution.

Professional organizations often have codes of ethics that apply to their membership. And while many of the ethics guidelines sound like they would prohibit campaign contributions of the sort given by professional firms to county officials, they often do not apply. The National Society of Professional Engineers, for example, has ethics guidelines geared specifically toward campaign contributions.

The ethics code prohibits its members from making political contributions "intended to influence the award and administration of contracts involving a public authority, or which may have the appearance of influencing the award and administration of contracts involving a public authority." The ethics code, however, goes on to allow contributions of any type as long as they are reported.

Arthur Swartz, a spokesman for the association, said engineers should not be penalized for taking an interest in local politics. "Everyone has the right to participate in the political process," Swartz said. "As long as our members comply with the campaign reporting laws, they are not violating our policies."

Chapter 4

★

The Politics of Elections and Parties

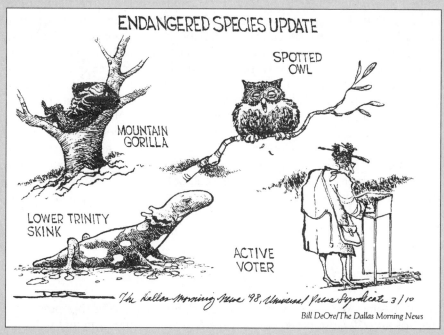

Bill DeOre/*The Dallas Morning News*

Texas voters have indeed become as rare as any of the endangered species shown in Bill DeOre's opening cartoon. In 1998, the Republican and Democratic primaries attracted only 11.3 percent of registered voters to the polls. This turnout resulted in the lowest number of voters casting ballots since 1970 when only one-third as many Texans were registered to vote. Participation in primary run-off elections was even more dismal, with only 3.8 percent of registered voters casting a ballot.[1]

Low voter turnout is one of four trends that were highlighted in the 1998 elections. While voter participation declined, voter registration increased. Approximately 80 percent of voting-age Texans (those 18 and older) were registered to vote in 1998, the highest percentage in history. The Democratic party continued to weaken as the Republican party demonstrated greater strength than in previous elections. Republican judgeships, in particular, increased because many judicial Republican candidates had no Democratic opponents. Governor George W. Bush, a Republican, received endorsements for re-election from several Democratic elected officials, including Lieutenant Governor Bob Bullock. Finally, competition for the increasing number of Hispanic voters intensified between the Democratric and Republican parties.

Candidates for Texas's public offices, except persons seeking municipal or special-district offices or running in a special election, are nominated by major parties in their primaries. In general election contests, Texans may vote for nominees of either the Democratic or the Republican party; candidates of minor parties, such as the Libertarian party; or independent candidates. In special elections, voters choose from among all of the people who have decided to run for a particular office.

The Politics of Elections

The U.S. Supreme Court has declared the right to vote to be the "preservative" of all other rights. For most Texans voting is the principal political activity, and for many it is their only exercise in practicing Texas politics. Casting a ballot brings individuals and their government together for a moment and reminds people anew that they are part of a political system. We begin our study of the electoral process in the Lone Star State by focusing on voters and voting.

Voters

The right to vote has not always been as widespread in the United States as it is today. **Universal suffrage** did not become a reality in Texas until the mid-1960s.

Democratization of the Ballot In America, obstacles to voting or suffrage have been removed by successive waves of democratization. Adopted after the Civil War, the Fourteenth and Fifteenth Amendments to the U.S. Constitution were intended to prevent denial of the right to vote because of race. But for the next 100 years, African-American citizens in Texas and other states of the former Confederacy, as well as many Mexican-American voters, were prevented from voting by one barrier after another, legal and otherwise. For example, the white-robed Ku Klux Klan and other lawless groups used terrorist tactics to keep African Americans from voting.

The so-called **white primary,** a product of political and legal maneuvering within the southern states, was designed to deny African-American and some Mexican-American citizens access to the Democratic primary.[2] That primary was the real election in predominantly one-party southern states, where white Democrats nominated white candidates who almost invariably won the general elections. This practice lasted from 1923 to 1944, when it was declared unconstitutional by the U.S. Supreme Court in *Smith* v. *Allwright*.[3]

Beginning in 1902, Texas required that citizens pay a special tax, called a **poll tax,** to become eligible to vote. The cost was $1.75 ($1.50 plus $.25, which was optional with each county). For the next 62 years, many Texans—especially low-income persons, including disproportionately large numbers of African Americans and Mexican Americans—frequently failed to pay their poll tax during the designated four-month period from October 1 to January 31. This, in turn, disqualified them from voting during the following 12 months in party primaries and in any general or special election. With ratification of the Twenty-fourth Amendment to the U.S. Constitution in January 1964, the poll tax was abolished as a prerequisite for voting in national elections. Then, in *Harper* v. *Virginia State Board of Elections* (1966), the U.S. Supreme Court invalidated all state laws that made payment of a poll tax a prerequisite for voting in state elections.

To democratize the ballot even more, Congress passed the Voting Rights Act of 1965. As amended in later years, this law (together with federal court rulings) abolished the use of literacy tests in voter registrations, prohibited residency requirements of more than 30 days for voting in presidential elections, and required all states to provide some form of absentee or early voting.

In 1993, Congress passed the National Voter Registration Act, or **motor voter law,** which simplified voter registration by permitting registration by mail; at welfare, disability assistance, and motor vehicle licensing agencies; and at military recruitment centers. In addition, in cases where citizens believe their voting rights have been violated in any way, federal administrative and judicial agencies are now more directly available. This imposing body of congressional legislation, together with federal court orders, has removed almost every obstacle to exercising the right to vote. In practice, these new safeguards are particularly applicable to situations involving racial minority groups.

Amendments to the U.S. Constitution also expanded the American electorate. The Fifteenth Amendment prohibits the denial of voting rights because of race; the Nineteenth Amendment precludes denial of suffrage on the basis of gender; the Twenty-fourth Amendment prohibits states from requiring payment of a poll tax or any other tax as a condition for voting;

and the Twenty-sixth Amendment forbids setting the minimum voting age above 18 years.

In Texas, as in other states, determining voting procedures is essentially a state responsibility. All election laws currently in effect in the Lone Star State are compiled into one body of law, the **Texas Election Code**.[4] In administering this legal code, state and party officials must protect the voting rights guaranteed by federal law.

Qualifications for Voting To qualify to vote in Texas, an individual must be

- A native-born or naturalized citizen of the United States
- At least 18 years of age on election day
- A resident of the state and county for at least 30 days immediately preceding election day and a resident of the area covered by the election on election day
- A registered voter for at least 30 days immediately preceding election day

Most adults who live in Texas meet the first three qualifications for voting, but registration is required before a person can vote.

Voter registration is intended to determine in advance whether prospective voters meet all the qualifications prescribed by law. Most states, including Texas, use a permanent registration system. Under this plan, voters register once and remain registered unless they change their mailing address and fail to notify the voting registrar within three years or otherwise lose their eligibility to register. Since the requirement of voter registration may deter voting, the Texas Election Code provides a number of voter registration centers in addition to those sites authorized by Congress under the motor voter law. Texans may also register at local marriage license offices, in public high schools, with any volunteer deputy registrar, or in person at the office of the county voting registrar. This official is the tax assessor-collector unless the county commissioners court designates the county clerk to perform the function or appoints another individual to serve as **elections administrator.**

Between November 1 and November 15 of each odd-numbered year, the registrar mails a registration certificate effective for the succeeding two voting years to every registered voter in the county. A certificate mailed to the address indicated on the voter's application form may not be forwarded by postal authorities if the applicant has moved to another address; instead, it must be returned to the registrar. This enables the county voting registrar to maintain an accurate list of names and mailing addresses of persons to whom voting certificates have been issued. Registration files are open for public inspection in the voting registrar's office, and a statewide registration file is available in Austin.

The color of certificate cards mailed to eligible voters in November of odd-numbered years differs from the color of the cards sent two years earlier. For example, blue cards were mailed to voters in 1997, and yellow is the color designated for cards mailed in 1999.

Anyone serving a jail sentence as a result of a misdemeanor conviction or not finally convicted of a felony is not disqualified from voting. The Texas Constitution, however, bars from voting anyone who is incarcerated, on parole, or on probation as a result of a felony conviction and anyone who is "mentally incompetent as determined by a court." A convicted felon may vote immediately after completing a sentence or following a full pardon. (See Table 8.1, page 230, for examples of misdemeanors and felonies.)

Two Trends in the Suffrage From our overview of suffrage in Texas, two trends emerge. First, there has been a steady expansion of voting rights to include virtually all persons of both sexes who are 18 years of age or older. Second, there has been a movement toward uniformity of voting policies among the 50 states. In fact, however, democratization of the ballot has been pressed upon the states largely by the U.S. Congress, by federal judges, and by presidents who have enforced laws and judicial orders.

Voters and Nonvoters Now that nearly all legal barriers to the ballot have been swept away, the road to the voting booth seems clear for rich and poor alike, for minority groups as well as for the majority, and for individuals of all races, colors, and creeds. But universal suffrage has not resulted in a corresponding increase in **voter turnout,** either nationally or in Texas.

Voter turnout in Texas is well below that of the nation as a whole, with Texas ranking 48 out of 50 in the 1996 presidential election. Few citizens believe their vote will determine an election outcome, but some races have actually been won by only a single vote. In 1998, two nominations in the Democratic primaries (one in Kleberg and another in Chambers Counties) were determined by a coin toss because of a tie vote.

In local elections at the city or school district level, a turnout of 25 percent is relatively high. Low citizen participation in elections has been attributed to the influence of pollsters and media consultants, voter fatigue resulting from too many elections, negative campaigning by candidates, lack of information about candidates and issues, and feelings of isolation from government.

Decisions by people to vote or not vote are made in the same way other decisions are made: on the basis of anticipated consequences. A strong impulse to vote may stem from peer pressure, a perception of one's own self-interest, or a sense of duty toward one's country, state, local community, political party, or interest group. Decisions about whether to vote are also made on the basis of cost measured in time, money, experience, information, job, and other resources.

Of all the socioeconomic influences on voting, education is by far the strongest. Statistics clearly indicate that as educational level rises, people are more likely to vote, assuming all other socioeconomic factors remain constant. The effect of education on voting is greatest for those with the least education. More schooling tends to reduce the cost of voting. For example, educated people usually have more income and leisure time for voting; moreover, education enhances one's ability to learn about political parties, candidates, and issues. Educated persons can more easily comply with voting regulations, learn how and when to register, understand instructions for completing forms, and follow and interpret coverage of political campaigns by television, newspapers, and other media.

Though far less important than education, gender and age also relate to voting behavior. Nationally, women are slightly more likely to vote than men. Young people (ages 18–25) have the lowest voter turnout of any age group. The highest voter turnout is among middle-aged Americans (ages 40–64).

Race and ethnicity also influence voting behavior. The turnout rate for African Americans is still substantially below that for Anglos. African Americans tend to be younger, less educated, and poorer than Anglos. Though Hispanic voter turnout rates are slightly below the state average in primaries and general elections, findings by scholars indicate that the gap is narrowing.

Voting Early: In Person and by Mail Opportunities to vote early in Texas are limited to in-person **early voting**, voting by mail, and voting by facsimile machine by military personnel and their dependents in combat zones or hostile areas. Electronic voting on election day is now available to astronauts on space flights.

Texas law allows voters to vote "early," that is, for almost three weeks preceding a scheduled election or first primary and for ten days preceding a run-off primary. Early voting ends, however, four days prior to any election or primary.

In less populated rural counties, early voting is done at the courthouse; in more populous urban areas, the county clerk's office accommodates voters by maintaining branch offices for early voting. Polling places are generally open for early voting on weekdays during the regular business hours of the official responsible for conducting the election. If requested by 15 registered voters, polling places must also be opened on Saturday or Sunday.

Registered voters who qualify may vote by mail during an early voting period. Anyone can vote by mail-in ballot who

- Will not be in his or her county of residence during the entire early voting period and on election day
- Is at least 65
- Is or will be physically disabled on election day, including those who expect to be confined for childbirth on election day
- Is in jail during the early voting period and on election day
- Is in the military or a dependent of military personnel and has resided in Texas

When early voting was used for the first time in the primary and general elections of 1988, about 20 percent of Texas's registered voters cast ballots during the early voting periods. In 1996, the percentage of early voters was approximately 17 percent in the general election. Although they make voting easier, these changes have not increased the percentage of total voter turnout in elections across Texas.

Primaries

Among the states, party primaries are held every two years. Presidential primaries occur every four years and provide a means for Democrats and Republicans to select delegates to their parties' national conventions, where candidates for president and vice president are nominated. Other primaries occur every two years when party members go to the polls to choose candidates for the U.S. Congress and for many state, district, and county offices.

Development of Direct Primaries A unique product of American political ingenuity, the **direct primary** was designed to provide a nominating method that would avoid domination by party bosses and allow wider participation by party members. This form of nomination permits party members to choose their candidates directly at the polls. For each office (except president and vice president of the United States and some local officials), party members select by popular vote the person they wish to represent their party in the **general election,** in which candidates of all parties compete. An absolute majority of the vote (more than 50 percent) is required for nomination. When the first primary fails to produce such a majority, a **run-off primary** is held to allow party members to choose a candidate from the first primary's top two vote getters.

Three basic forms of the direct primary have evolved in America. A few states use an **open primary,** which requires no party identification of the voter. In **blanket primaries,** all eligible voters receive the same ballot, on which are printed the names of all candidates and their respective party labels. Thus, regardless of party affiliation, the voter may vote for anyone seeking nomination. Most states use some form of **closed primary,** which requires the voter to show party identification, either when registering or when voting in a party primary.

Texas Primaries The Texas Election Code requires voters to identify their party affiliation at the time of voting, making Texas a combination of a closed primary state and an open primary state. Voter registration certificates are stamped with the party label when voters participate in a primary. Qualified voters may vote in the primary of any party, so long as they have not already voted in another party's primary or convention in the same year. All voters are notified of the restriction on voting on the primary ballot. It contains the following statement: "I am a Democrat (Republican) and understand that I am ineligible to vote or participate in another political party's primary election or convention during this voting year." Violation of a party pledge is a misdemeanor offense punishable by a fine of $500.

Bonds of party loyalty in Texas loosen at general election time. Beginning in the early 1950s, it became common practice in Texas for persons to participate in the primaries of the Democratic party and then legally cross over to vote for Republican candidates in the general election. Crossover voting is evidence of a long-term trend toward voter independence of traditional party ties. Although historically Texas Republicans were more likely to engage in crossover voting (perhaps because the Republican primary ballot carried the names of fewer candidates for various offices), a turning point occurred in 1996. For the first time in Texas history, Republican primaries were conducted in all 254 Texas counties. Of even greater political significance, more Texans voted in Republican primaries than in Democratic primaries, another first in the Lone Star state's history. This trend reversed in 1998, when Democrats had a higher turnout in their primaries than Republicans. There were, however, more contested statewide races on the Republican ballot.

This increased competion for Republican party nominations was the continuation of a trend that began much earlier. The increase in Republican voting strength was demonstrated by electing Republican governors Bill Clements (1978 and 1986) and George W. Bush (1994 and 1998), winning the state for the national Republican ticket in eight of the twelve presidential elections from 1952 to 1996, and allowing the Republican party to capture control of the Texas Senate in 1996. For the first time since Reconstruction, Republican candidates were elected in every statewide election contest in 1998.

Throughout the 1980s and 1990s, the state GOP (Grand Old Party) increased its representation in the Texas Legislature while also growing stronger at the county and precinct levels of government. When more office seekers sought nomination as Republican candidates and when more offices were won by Republicans, GOP voters became less tempted to vote in Democratic primaries and were more attracted to the primaries of their own party.

Administering Primaries   In most states, primaries are administered by the political parties sponsoring them. The Texas Election Code allocates the responsibility for conducting Texas primaries to each political party's county executive committee. Primary elections (including voting on election day and during the early voting periods described on pages 88–89) are actually conducted by the county clerk or the county elections administrator. Political parties whose gubernatorial candidate received 20 percent or more of the vote in the preceding general election must nominate all of their candidates in direct primaries. Scheduled in even-numbered years, the first primary and a run-off primary (if a run-off is needed) are held on the second Tuesdays in March and April, respectively.

Individuals who want to run in a direct primary for their party's nomination for statewide office must file the necessary papers with their party's state chair, who in turn certifies the names of these persons to each county chair in counties in which the election is administered. Prospective candidates desiring to have their names placed on the primary ballot for a county or precinct office must file with the county chair of their party. County primary committees for each political party supervise the printing of primary ballots. If the parties conduct a joint primary, the county clerk administers the election. If each party conducts its own primaries, county chairs arrange for voting equipment and polling places in the precincts. With the approval of the county executive committee, the county chair obtains supplies and appoints a presiding judge of elections in each precinct. Together with the state executive committee, the county executive committee determines the order of names of candidates on the ballot and **canvasses** (that is, confirms and certifies) the vote tally for each candidate.

Financing Primaries   Major expenses for administering party primaries include renting facilities for polls (the places where voting is conducted), printing ballots and other election materials, and paying election judges and clerks. In recent years, approximately 20 percent of the cost of holding Texas primaries has been covered by the collection of filing fees paid by candidates. For example, candidates for the office of U.S. senator pay $4,000, and candidates for governor and all other statewide offices pay $3,000. Candidates for the Texas Senate and the Texas House of Representatives pay $1,000 and $600, respectively.

In lieu of paying a fee, a candidate may file a nominating petition containing a specified number of signatures of people eligible to vote for the office for which that candidate is running. A candidate for statewide office must obtain 5,000 signatures. Candidates for district, county, or precinct office and for offices of other political subdivisions must obtain either 500 signatures or the equivalent of 2 percent of the area's votes for all candidates for governor in the last general election, whichever is less. The difference between the amount collected in filing fees and the total cost of conducting first run-off primaries is paid by the state. The cost of each Democratic first primary from 1992 to 1998 ranged from slightly more than $5.5 million to $7.1 million, whereas the cost of Republican first primaries for that period ranged from nearly $3.8 million to more than $5.2 million.

General Elections

A clear distinction must be made between general elections and party primaries. General elections determine which candidates will fill government offices. These electoral contests are public in nature and are conducted, financed, and administered by state and county governments. Primaries are party functions that allow party members to select nominees to run against the candidates of opposing parties in general elections. This distinction is valid even though the U.S. Supreme Court has ruled that primaries are so necessary in the selection of general election candidates as to be subject to government regulation. Thus, even though the state regulates and largely finances primaries, they serve only as a means for political parties to nominate candidates.

Election Schedules   Throughout the United States, the date prescribed by law for congressional elections is the first Tuesday following the first Monday in November of even-numbered years. Presidential elections take place on the same day in November every four years (for example, 1996, 2000, and 2004). In Texas, general elections for state, district, and county officials are held every even-numbered year (for example, 1998, 2000, and 2002).

Many cities and special districts hold annual elections; others schedule elections in odd-numbered years only.

In Texas's general elections involving candidates for state, district, and county offices, the candidate who polls a plurality in a contest is the winner. Thus, even if a majority is not obtained because of votes received by third-party or independent candidates, a run-off election is not held. Elections for governor and other statewide officers serving terms of four years are scheduled in the off-year. These **off-year elections** are held in November of the even-numbered years between presidential elections (for example, 1998 and 2002). Along with most other states, Texas follows this schedule to minimize the influence of presidential campaigns on the election of state and local officials. Elections to fill offices for two-year or six-year terms must be conducted in both off-years and presidential years.

Voting Systems In general elections, Texas uses three voting systems: the paper ballot, manually operated voting machines, and electronic voting machines. In every county, the county commissioners court determines the system that will be used. Each system has advantages and disadvantages with regard to such matters as ballot and equipment costs, ease of use by voters, accuracy of counting, labor cost, and time required to count the votes. For example, paper ballots are relatively cheap and easy to use, but counting them is a slow, laborious, and error-prone process.

For paper ballots, the Texas Election Code provides that the party obtaining the highest number of votes in the previous gubernatorial election will be assigned the first party column on the left, next to the office column. Strategically this is the best position, because uninformed voters are apt to vote for candidates whose names are listed in the first party column on the left. Political parties whose candidates for governor finished second or lower in number of votes received in the preceding gubernatorial general election are ranked in succeeding columns from left to right on paper ballot forms. Parties that are not organized in Texas but have national candidates are listed next, followed by columns of independent candidates.

On machine and punch-card ballot forms, the order of the columns is essentially the same as that for paper ballots, except that they begin at the top of the ballot rather than on the left. First is a list of parties for straight-party-ticket voting, followed by lists of candidates for national, state, district, and local offices in that order. (Figure 4.1 shows a sample machine ballot used in presidential election year 1996.) Punch-card ballots have space for names of write-in candidates on a detachable portion of the ballot card. A list of all write-in candidates who have filed an appropriate declaration is posted in each precinct polling place on the day of election.

Special Elections

Texas voters participate in **special elections** to fill vacancies in U.S. congressional and state legislative offices, act on proposed state constitutional

FIGURE 4.1 Sample Ballot, General Election, November 5, 1996

OFFICIAL BALLOT
(BOLETA OFICIAL)

GENERAL ELECTION
(ELECCION GENERAL)

(Condado de)
McLENNAN COUNTY, TEXAS

NOVEMBER 5, 1996

(5 de noviembre de 1996)

INSTRUCTION NOTE:
Vote for the candidate of your choice in each race by darkening in the oval provided to the left of the name of that candidate.
You may cast a straight-party vote (that is, cast a vote for all the nominees of one party) by darkening in the oval provided to the left of the name of that party. If you cast a straight-party vote for all the nominees of one party and also cast a vote for an opponent of one of that party's nominees, your vote for the opponent will be counted as well as your vote for all the other nominees of the party for which the straight-party vote was cast. You may vote for a write-in candidate by writing in the name of the candidate on the line provided and darkening in the oval provided to the left of the line.
Use only the marker provided.
(NOTA DE INSTRUCCION:
Vote por el candidato de su preferencia en cada carrera llenando completamente el espacio ovalado a la izquierda del nombre de ese candidato.
Usted podrá votar por todos los candidatos de un solo partido político (es decir, votar por todos los candidatos nombrados del mismo partido político) llenando completamente el espacio ovalado a la izquierda del nombre de dicho partido político. Si usted vota por un solo partido político ("straight-ticket") y también vota por el contrincante de uno de los candidatos de dicho partido político, se computará su voto por el contrincante tanto como su voto por todos los demás candidatos del partido político de su preferencia. Usted podrá votar por inserción escrita escribiendo el nombre del candidato en la línea provista y llenando completamente el espacio ovalado a la izquierda de la línea. Solamente use el marcador provisto.)

Straight Party
(Partido Completo)

○ Republican
(Republicano) (REP)

○ Democratic
(Democrático) (DEM)

○ Libertarian
(Libertariano) (LIB)

○ Natural Law
(Ley Natural) (NLP)

○ U.S. Taxpayers
(Pagadores de Impuestos) (UST)

President and Vice President
(Presidente y Vice Presidente)

○ Bob Dole /
Jack Kemp (REP)

○ Bill Clinton /
Al Gore (DEM)

○ Harry Browne /
Jo Jorgensen (LIB)

○ John Hagelin /
Mike Tompkins (NLP)

○ Howard Phillips /
Herbert W. Titus (UST)

○ Ross Perot /
James Campbell (IND)

○ _____
Write-in *(Voto Escrito)*

United States Senator
(Senador de los Estados Unidos)

○ Phil Gramm (REP)

○ Victor M. Morales (DEM)

○ Michael Bird (LIB)

○ John Huff (NLP)

**United States Representative,
District 11**
(Representante de los Estados Unidos, Distrito Núm. 11)

○ Jay Mathis (REP)

○ Chet Edwards (DEM)

○ Ken Hardin (NLP)

Railroad Commissioner
(Comisionado de Ferrocarriles)

○ Carole Keeton Rylander (REP)

○ Hector Uribe (DEM)

○ Rick Draheim (LIB)

○ Paul Pigue (NLP)

Chief Justice, Supreme Court
(Juez Presidente, Corte Suprema)

○ Tom Phillips (REP)

○ Andrew Jackson Kupper (DEM)

○ David Parker (LIB)

Justice, Supreme Court, Place 1
(Juez, Corte Suprema, Lugar Núm. 1)

○ John Cornyn (REP)

○ Patrice Barron (DEM)

○ Thomas Stults (LIB)

Justice, Supreme Court, Place 2
(Juez, Corte Suprema, Lugar Núm. 2)

○ James A. Baker (REP)

○ Gene Kelly (DEM)

○ Eileen Flume (LIB)

**Justice, Supreme Court, Place 3,
Unexpired Term**
(Juez, Corte Suprema, Lugar Núm. 3, Duración Restante del Cargo)

○ Greg Abbott (REP)

○ John B. Hawley (LIB)

**Judge, Court of Criminal
Appeals, Place 1**
(Juez, Corte de Apelaciones Criminales, Lugar Núm. 1)

○ Sue Holland (REP)

○ Bob Perkins (DEM)

**Judge, Court of Criminal
Appeals, Place 2**
(Juez, Corte de Apelaciones Criminales, Lugar Núm. 2)

○ Paul Womack (REP)

○ Charles Holcomb (DEM)

**Judge, Court of Criminal
Appeals, Place 3**
(Juez, Corte de Apelaciones Criminales, Lugar Núm. 3)

○ Tom Price (REP)

○ Frank Maloney (DEM)

**Member, State Board of
Education, District 5**
(Miembro de la Junta Estatal de Instrucción Pública, Distrito Núm. 5)

○ Bob Offutt (REP)

○ Nettie Ruth Bratton (DEM)

State Representative, District 57
(Representante Estatal, Distrito Núm. 57)

○ Barbara Rusling (REP)

○ Jim Dunnam (DEM)

**Chief Justice, 10th Court of
Appeals District, Unexpired Term**
(Juez Presidente, Corte de Apelaciones, Distrito Núm. 10, Duración Restante del Cargo)

○ Rex Davis (REP)

○ Joe Cannon (DEM)

**Justice, 10th Court of
Appeals District**
*Juez, Corte de
Apelaciones, Distrito Núm. 10)*

○ Bill Vance (DEM)

District Judge, 19th Judicial District
(Juez del Distrito, Distrito Judicial Núm. 19)

○ Bill Logue (DEM)

District Judge, 74th Judicial District
(Juez del Distrito, Distrito Judicial Núm. 74)

○ Alan Mayfield (DEM)

Sheriff
(Sherife)

○ Danny Volcik (REP)

○ Jack Harwell (DEM)

County Tax Assessor-Collector
(Asesor-Colector de Impuestos del Condado)

○ Tom McPeak (REP)

○ A.F. "Buddy" Skeen (DEM)

○ _____
Write-in *(Voto Escrito)*

Constable, Precinct No. 7
(Condestable, Precinto Núm. 7)

○ Jesse Kelly (DEM)

0007F

013

amendments, vote on local bond issues, and, occasionally, elect members of city councils and school boards. If no candidate obtains a majority in a special election, a run-off contest between the top two contenders must be conducted to obtain a winner. Vacancies in state judicial and executive offices are filled by gubernatorial appointment until the next general election and do not require special elections.

Administering Elections

The Texas Constitution authorizes the legislature to provide for the administration of elections. State lawmakers, in turn, have made the secretary of state the chief election officer for Texas but have left most details of administering elections to county officials.

Voting Precincts The basic geographic area for conducting national, state, district, and county elections is the **voting precinct**. Texas has almost 9,000 voting precincts, drawn by the county commissioners courts (county judge and four commissioners) after each decennial census. Citizens vote at polling places within their voting precincts or, if voting precincts have been combined for an election, at a polling place convenient to each of the combined voting precincts. Municipal precincts must follow the boundary lines of county-designed voting precincts adjusted to city boundaries. Subject to this restriction, municipal and special-district voting precincts are designated by the governing body of each city and special district, respectively.

Election Officials Various county and political party officials participate in the administration of elections. The county clerk or elections administrator prepares general and special election ballots based on the certification of candidates by the appropriate authority (the secretary of state for state and district candidates and the county clerk or elections administrator for local candidates). The county election board consists of the county judge, county clerk or elections administrator, sheriff, and chairs of the two major political parties. Board responsibilities include selecting polling places, printing ballots, and providing supplies and voting equipment.

County commissioners courts appoint one **election judge** and one alternate judge, each from different political parties, to administer elections in each precinct for a maximum term of two years. Furthermore, each county's commissioners court canvasses election results. Each election judge selects as many clerks as will be needed to assist in conducting general and special elections in a precinct. Clerks must be selected from different political parties. In city elections, judges are appointed by the city secretary.

Vote Counting and Recounting Some precincts in sparsely populated areas continue to use paper ballots, which must be counted by hand. Voting machines automatically count each vote as the ballot is cast. If a punch-card device is used, ballots can be electronically counted as soon as the polls close. Purchase and storage of mechanical and electronic voting equipment are expensive, but the use of such equipment can reduce the cost of conducting elections when many voters are involved.

In some instances, candidates for nomination or election to an office may request a recount of ballots if they believe vote tabulations are inaccurate. The Texas Election Code also provides detailed procedures for settling disputed elections. Since the 1960s, several changes in voting procedures have been made to encourage full, informed participation in elections.

Additional Requirements All registration and election materials used in all counties must be printed in both English and Spanish. Also, Texas voters can now take voting guides, newspaper endorsements, and other printed material into the voting booth. Civil rights groups have filed lawsuits in an attempt to force counties to make polling places and voting booths accessible to physically disabled voters.

Party Structure

Although neither the U.S. Constitution nor the Texas Constitution mentions political parties, these organizations are an integral part of the American governmental process. A **political party** can be defined as a combination of people and interests whose primary purpose is to gain control of government by winning elections. In Texas, as throughout the United States, the Democratic and Republican parties are the two leading political parties. State election laws have contributed to the continuity of the two-party system. These laws specify that a general election is won by the candidate who receives the largest number of votes (a plurality) without a run-off. Thus, third-party candidates have little chance of winning an election by defeating the two major-party nominees.

American political parties exist on four levels: national, state, county, and precinct. In part, this is in response to the federal organization of government in the United States. Each major party is loosely organized so that state and local party organizations are free to decide their positions on party issues. State- and local-level organizations of the two major parties are encouraged to support national party policies, but this effort is not always successful.

Temporary Organization

As mandated by the Texas Election Code, Texas's two major parties are alike in structure. Each has permanent and temporary organizational structures. (See Figure 4.2.) The **temporary party organization** consists of primaries and conventions in which party members of the major political parties select their candidates for public office. State-level party officers are elected at conventions. Primary election voting periods may also include run-off voting. Conventions are scheduled at the precinct level, the county and state senatorial district level, and the state level. Each lasts for only a

FIGURE 4.2 Texas Political Party Organization

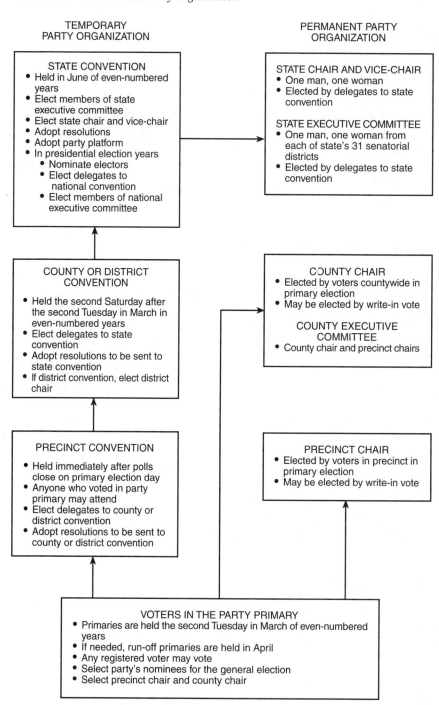

TEMPORARY PARTY ORGANIZATION

PERMANENT PARTY ORGANIZATION

STATE CONVENTION
- Held in June of even-numbered years
- Elect members of state executive committee
- Elect state chair and vice-chair
- Adopt resolutions
- Adopt party platform
- In presidential election years
  - Nominate electors
  - Elect delegates to national convention
  - Elect members of national executive committee

STATE CHAIR AND VICE-CHAIR
- One man, one woman
- Elected by delegates to state convention

STATE EXECUTIVE COMMITTEE
- One man, one woman from each of state's 31 senatorial districts
- Elected by delegates to state convention

COUNTY OR DISTRICT CONVENTION
- Held the second Saturday after the second Tuesday in March in even-numbered years
- Elect delegates to state convention
- Adopt resolutions to be sent to state convention
- If district convention, elect district chair

COUNTY CHAIR
- Elected by voters countywide in primary election
- May be elected by write-in vote

COUNTY EXECUTIVE COMMITTEE
- County chair and precinct chairs

PRECINCT CONVENTION
- Held immediately after polls close on primary election day
- Anyone who voted in party primary may attend
- Elect delegates to county or district convention
- Adopt resolutions to be sent to county or district convention

PRECINCT CHAIR
- Elected by voters in precinct in primary election
- May be elected by write-in vote

VOTERS IN THE PARTY PRIMARY
- Primaries are held the second Tuesday in March of even-numbered years
- If needed, run-off primaries are held in April
- Any registered voter may vote
- Select party's nominees for the general election
- Select precinct chair and county chair

limited amount of time: from less than an hour to a few days. These events are temporary because they are not ongoing party activities.

Conventions are used at the state level to select party leaders who are chosen by delegates elected at the local level. Rules of the state Democratic and Republican parties mandate that party policy be determined at their conventions. This is done by passing resolutions, which occurs at both local and state conventions, and adopting a platform at the state conventions. A party's **platform** is a document that sets forth the party's position on current issues. In presidential election years, conventions on all levels are used to select delegates who attend a party's national convention. Here candidates are chosen for president and vice president of the United States. All Texas political conventions must be open to the media according to state law.

Precinct Conventions   In Texas, **precinct conventions** are conducted every even-numbered year on the second Tuesday in March, which is the first primary day. At the lowest level of temporary party organization, these conventions (both Democratic and Republican) assemble in almost all of the state's voting precincts. Usually precinct conventions are sparsely attended. By state law, only individuals who voted in the party primary are permitted to participate. The main business of the precinct convention is to elect delegates to the county or district convention. Under the rules of both the Democratic and Republican parties, precinct conventions may elect one delegate to the county (or district) convention for every 25 votes cast in the precinct for the party's gubernatorial nominee in the last general election. Resolutions express the positions of precinct convention participants on any number of issues from immigration to abortion to the national debt. Likewise, resolutions may be submitted to a county or district convention.

County and District Conventions   State law requires that **county** and **district conventions** occur 11 days after the precinct conventions. These conventions are always held on a Saturday. District conventions, rather than a single county convention, are held in heavily populated counties (such as Harris, Dallas, and Bexar) that have more than one state senatorial district.

The main business of county and district conventions is to elect delegates to the state convention. Under party rules for both the Democratic and Republican parties, county and district conventions may select one delegate to the state convention for every 300 votes cast in the county or district for the party's gubernatorial nominee in the last general election. Rules of the Democratic party allow state delegates to be selected by precinct delegations. If all delegate positions are not filled in this manner, the remaining state delegates are proposed by the county or district convention's nominations committee. Under Republican party rules, all delegate candidates are submitted by the county or district convention's committee on nominations for approval by the county or district convention participants. Both parties' rules also allow the adoption of resolutions to be submitted to the state convention.

State Conventions In June of even-numbered years, each Texas political party must hold a biennial **state convention** to conduct party business, which includes the following four tasks:

- Certifying to the secretary of state the names of party members nominated in the March and April primaries for Texas elective offices
- Drafting and adopting a party platform
- Adopting resolutions regarding issues that are too specific to be included in the party platform
- Selecting members of the party's state executive committee

In presidential election years, the June convention also performs the following three functions:

- Elects delegates to the national presidential nominating convention (The total number for Texas is calculated under national party rules)
- Elects members from Texas to serve on the party's national committee
- Elects a slate of potential presidential electors to cast Texas's electoral votes if the party's ticket wins a plurality of the state's popular presidential vote

Beginning with the 1992 presidential election and continuing through the presidential election of 2000, Texas is allowed 32 electoral votes. A state's electoral college vote is equal to the number of its members in the U.S. Congress (for Texas, 30 representatives and 2 senators).

Selection of National Convention Delegates

Delegates to a national party convention are selected based on their support for particular candidates for the party's presidential nomination. In a presidential preference primary, rank-and-file party members are permitted to vote directly for the presidential candidates of their choice. In states where primaries are used, voting is by precinct. Based on the results of the primary vote, delegates to the party's national convention are chosen. At the respective national conventions, the parties' candidates for president and vice president are nominated.

The caucus-conference is another plan used in many states to select delegates to a national convention. Party members assemble in caucuses at the respective precinct, county, and state levels. Here they choose national convention delegates who either are pledged to support a particular presidential candidate or are uncommitted.

Democratic Selection Texas Democrats combine the two plans and therefore have a primary-caucus plan. At each of the conventions in presidential years, participants must indicate their presidential preferences. Individuals may indicate they are uncommitted and do not want to pledge their support to any candidate. Presidential candidates are awarded delegates to local and state conventions in proportion to the number of their supporters in attendance. In 1996, Bill Clinton won the support of all Texas delegates to the national Democratic convention. His delegates included 159 who were selected in the senatorial district caucuses, 42 who were selected on an at-large basis from among all of the convention delegates, 25 political leaders who had pledged their support to Clinton, and three superdelegates who were unpledged party and elected officials.

Republican Selection The Republican party selects national delegates based on the results of the presidential preference primary. At the 1996 state convention, 90 delegates were selected by congressional district caucuses and 33 were chosen on an at-large basis by the entire convention. Any presidential candidate who wins 50 percent or more of the popular vote in the primary in a particular congressional district or statewide is entitled to all of the district or at-large delegates, respectively. Nominating committees at the congressional-district level and the state level recommend national delegates. State convention delegates, however, make the final decision.

Permanent Organization

Each major political party in the United States consists of thousands of virtually autonomous executive party committees at local, state, and national levels. For both Democrats and Republicans, these executive committees nationwide are linked only nominally. At the highest level, each party has a national committee. In Texas, the precinct chairs, together with the county, district, and state executive committees, comprise the **permanent party organization** of the state parties.

Precinct Chair The basic party official in both the temporary and permanent party structures in Texas is the **precinct chair,** who is elected by precinct voters in the party primaries for a term of two years. If both parties are evenly matched in strength at the polls, the precinct chairs become more vital in getting people out to vote. A precinct chair, who is an unpaid party official, arranges for the precinct convention and serves on the county executive committee. (For a discussion of the role of the precinct chair, see the reading on pages 119–123.)

County and District Executive Committees Each party organization at the county level is headed by a **county executive committee,** composed of all the precinct chairs, and the county chair, who is elected on a countywide basis by party members in the primaries. The Texas Election Code also provides for a **district executive committee,** composed of the county chairs from each county in a given district (senatorial, representative, or judicial). County executive committees conduct primaries and arrange for county conventions. At the local level, the county chair is the key party official.

State Executive Committee For each major political party, the highest permanent party organization of the state is the **state executive committee**. As mandated by state law, an executive committee is composed of one man and one woman from each of the 31 state senatorial districts, plus a chair and a vice chair, one of whom must be a woman. In 1998, both the Democratic and Republican parties selected women to their respective state chairs—Molly Beth Malcom and Susan Weddington. For both the Democratic and Republican parties, the state executive committee of 64 members is elected at the party's state convention. On that occasion, delegates from each of the 31 senatorial districts choose two members from their district and place these names before the convention for its approval. At the same time, the chair and vice chair are chosen at large by convention delegates.

The state executive committee of each party must canvass statewide primary returns and certify the nomination of party candidates. In addition, it conducts the state convention, seeks to promote party unity and strength, maintains relations with the party's national committee, and raises some campaign money for party candidates (although most campaign funds are raised by the candidates themselves).

Political Democracy

Today's politics in the Lone Star State reflects Texas's political history. Traditions based on centuries of political experience influence current attitudes toward parties, candidates, and issues. Nevertheless, Texans' changing demands and expectations have forced revisions in party platforms and affected the campaigns of candidates for public office. Political parties cannot remain static and survive, nor can politicians win elections unless they are in step with the opinions of the voting majority. Increasing competition between Texas's Democratic and Republican parties has brought more women, Hispanics, and African Americans into the state's political system. As a result of this new competitiveness, party politics has become more democratic and more nationalized. Compared to the politics of earlier years, Texas politics today is more partisan (party centered). But internal feuding among competing groups exists within both the Democratic and Republican parties.

Ideology

Since the 1930s, the terms *liberal* and *conservative* have meant more to many Texas voters than the names of political parties. In view of long-standing ideological differences between liberals and conservatives, this terminology must be explained. These ideological labels almost defy definition, however, because meanings change with time and circumstances and because each label has varying shades of meaning for different people. In Texas, both Democrats and Republicans tend to be conservative; but the Republican party is dominated by right-wing conservatives, whereas the Democratic party is influenced (but not dominated by) left-wing liberals. Despite the use of *right-left* terminology throughout the United States, the Texas Legislature does not use partisan or ideological criteria for assigning floor seats to members.

Conservativism In its purest form, modern conservative doctrine envisions ideal social and economic orders that would be largely untouched by government. According to this philosophy, if all individuals were left alone (the doctrine of laissez-faire) to pursue their self-interests, both social and economic systems would benefit and the cost of government would be low. **Conservatives,** therefore, are generally opposed to government-managed or government-subsidized programs such as assistance to poor families with dependent children, unemployment insurance, and federal price support programs for the benefit of farmers producing commodities such as cotton and wheat. Today's fiscal conservatives give the highest priority to reduced taxing and spending; on the other hand, social conservatives (such as those associated with the Christian Coalition) stress the importance of their family values, especially opposition to abortion.

Liberalism **Liberals** favor government regulation of the economy to achieve a more equitable distribution of wealth. Only government, liberals insist, is capable of guarding against pollution of air, water, and soil by corporations and individuals. Liberals claim that government is obligated to aid the unemployed, alleviate poverty (especially for the benefit of children), and guarantee equal rights for minorities and women. As is the case with their conservative opponents, many Texas liberals are ideologically inconsistent. For example, a liberal who advocates government regulation to protect the environment might oppose an anti-pollution measure requiring installation of a costly emission control device on his or her automobile.

Major Political Parties

From the Reconstruction era following the Civil War until the 1950s, Texas and other former Confederate states had a one-party identity that featured a strong Democratic party and a weak Republican party. Contests between the liberal and conservative factions within the Democratic party were more meaningful than those between the two major parties. After the middle of the twentieth century, however, Texas moved toward a two-party system similar to that of most other states. By 1998, although Democrats filled over two-thirds of all partisan-elected offices in Texas, Republicans held over 70 percent of statewide offices.[5]

Some political scientists interpret recent polling and election results as evidence that there has been a **dealignment** of Texas voters. These scholars explain that the large percentage of Texans who claim to be independent (as high as 44 percent of all Texans by 1998) have abandoned allegiance to any political party (especially the Democratic party) but tend to vote for Republican candidates. Other political scientists assert that the rising tide of Republican electoral victories (especially from 1992 to 1998) demonstrates that many Texans have switched their political affiliation and loyalty to the Republican party in a **realignment** of voters.

Republican Party Evidence of the growing strength of the Texas GOP was sharply revealed in 1961 with the election to the U.S. Senate of Texas

Republican John Tower. Originally elected to fill the vacancy created when Lyndon Johnson left the Senate to become vice president, Tower won successive elections until his retirement in 1984. He was replaced by another Republican, Phil Gramm, a former Democrat and former member of the U.S. House of Representatives.

In 1978, Texas Democrats were stunned by the election of Republican Bill Clements as governor, the first Republican chief executive since Reconstruction. Four years later, Clements was unseated by Democrat Mark White. In 1986, however, many conservative Democrats, former Democrats who had turned Republican, and independents helped Texas Republicans elect Clements to a second term.

Republican gubernatorial candidate Clayton Williams lost the 1990 election to liberal Democrat Ann Richards, but in 1994 she was defeated by Republican George W. Bush, who benefited greatly from voter mobilization by the Christian Coalition. A hallmark of Governor Bush's 1998 re-election campaign was the level of support he received from some of Texas's most influential Democrats, including then-Lieutenant Governor Bob Bullock and state Representative Rob Junnell, chair of the 75th Legislatures House Appropriations Committee. Other Democratic candidates, such as John Sharp (who was the Democratic nominee for lieutenant governor) refused to endorse any gubernatorial candidate, including the Democratic nominee, Garry Mauro. Of special importance is the fact that the Republican party carried Texas in eight of the twelve presidential elections between 1952 and 1996, including the last five elections in that period (1980, 1984, 1988, 1992, and 1996).

Texas GOP strongholds are in West Texas, the Panhandle–South Plains, some small towns and rural areas in East Texas, the Dallas–Fort Worth Metroplex, and the suburbs of Houston, San Antonio, and Austin. With the exception of Democratic El Paso, West Texas Republicanism extends from the Permian Basin (Midland-Odessa) through the Davis Mountains and the German Hill Country. This West Texas region, like the Panhandle–South Plains area to the north, is populated primarily by conservative farmers and ranchers, along with people connected with the oil and gas industry in Midland, Odessa, and other parts of the Permian Basin area.

Democratic Party Democratic voting strength is concentrated in El Paso, South Texas, parts of East Texas, the Golden Triangle (Beaumont, Port Arthur, and Orange), portions of the diverse Central Texas region, and the lower-income neighborhoods of Dallas, Houston, and San Antonio. Straight-ticket voting for all Democratic candidates on the general election ballot has declined, however, as fewer Texans (especially those in rural East Texas) choose to remain "yellow dog Democrats." This term has been applied to people whose party loyalty is said to be so strong that they would vote for a yellow dog if it were a Democratic candidate for public office.

Republican expansion has strengthened partisan competition throughout the state and has diminished the intensity of factional politics within the

Democratic party. Nevertheless, Democrats are divided by many interests and issues. Before the opening of recent Democratic state conventions, for example, delegates have split into several caucuses to draft platform planks and resolutions reflecting the preferences of ethnic and racial minorities, women, gays and lesbians, teachers, farmers, labor union members, motorcyclists, and other groups.

Third Parties

Americans commonly apply the term *third party* (or *minor party*) to any political party other than the Democratic or Republican party.

Libertarian Party Since 1980, the Libertarian party has provided Texas voters with alternatives to Democratic and Republican candidates. Never a serious threat to either of the two major parties, the Libertarian party finds its strongest support in urban areas. Libertarians advocate minimizing the performance of government at all levels while maximizing individual freedom and rights. For example, Libertarian platforms have consistently opposed foreign aid spending, public health programs, and agricultural subsidies for farmers and ranchers. Both the U.S. Department of Energy and the U.S. Department of Education are subject to frequent Libertarian criticisms. At the same time, Libertarians oppose laws regulating sale and use of drugs and restricting the right of abortion.

Reform Party Dallas billionaire Ross Perot exploded onto the American political scene in 1992 with a media-centered petition drive that placed him on the presidential ballot as an independent candidate in Texas and all other states. Though not the winner of that election, the computer tycoon continued to spend huge amounts of his personal fortune to publicize proposals for revolutionizing the political process and revitalizing America. In response, millions of mainstream Americans joined Perot's new political organization, United We Stand America (UWSA).

While Perot insisted that the role of UWSA was to serve as a "watchdog" to monitor the Clinton administration, early in 1995 a decision was made to hold a conference in Dallas to consider the organization of a political party. When the meeting was held in mid-August, no decision was made on either a new party or a presidential bid by Perot in 1996. On September 25, however, Perot appeared on CNN's *Larry King Live* to announce that he would launch a new party for independent voters. Named the Reform party, Perot's organization was placed on the ballots of most states but did not meet ballot requirements in his home state. Nevertheless, Perot campaigned in Texas as an independent presidential candidate, and his name was printed on the Texas ballot. He received 378,537 votes, which amounted to about 7 percent of the total popular vote for the state.[6] In 1998, Reform party volunteers failed to obtain the necessary signatures to secure a place on the general election ballot. Attorney Mark Brown campaigned for attorney general as a Reform party write-in candidate.

Recent Electoral Contests

Republicans are apt to view their recent victories as signs of a new era in which the GOP will dominate the state's political scene at all levels of government. In the 1998 elections, many Republican candidates had no Democratic challengers. Only three of thirteen statewide races had more than one candidate in the Democratic primary, while Republicans fielded multiple challengers in numerous local and statewide races. Democrats insisted, however, that continued decline of their political power was not inevitable and that the political tide would change in their favor.

For political scientists, practicing politicians, and concerned citizens of the Lone Star State, the U.S. senatorial special election of 1993 and the primaries and general elections of 1994, 1996, and 1998 stand out as important milestones in Texas's political development. The following sections on the electoral politics of the 1993–1998 period provide an essential background for understanding and practicing Texas politics from the late 1990s through the beginning of the twenty-first century.

1993: A Special Election to Fill a U.S. Senatorial Seat

For Texas Republicans, the outcome of a special election in 1993 raised expectations of future electoral victories. In January of that year, Democrat Lloyd Bentsen resigned his seat in the U.S. Senate to become secretary of the treasury in President Bill Clinton's cabinet. Pending the result of a special election scheduled for May 1, Governor Ann Richards appointed Railroad Commission member Bob Krueger to fill the vacancy. A total of 24 candidates entered the special election contest: 5 Democrats (including Krueger), 10 Republicans (including Texas Treasurer Kay Bailey Hutchison), 6 independents, 1 Libertarian, 1 member of the Socialist Workers party, and 1 member of the People's party.

After the votes were counted, Hutchison and Krueger finished first and second, respectively. Because no candidate received an absolute majority (more than 50 percent), a run-off election was conducted. The result was a landslide victory for Hutchison. Elected to serve through 1994, Republican Hutchison joined Republican Phil Gramm in Washington to give the GOP control of both Texas seats in the U.S. Senate.

1994: A Gubernatorial Election Year

Shortly after Hutchison's run-off triumph in 1993, veteran Texas Democratic leader Robert Strauss spoke to the National Press Club in Washington. He predicted that the Texas Democratic party would have difficulty winning statewide elections in nonpresidential election years. Observing that "the core Democratic vote is getting smaller," Strauss commented, "we don't get out a minority vote very well for ordinary races."[7] For Governor Ann Richards and other Democratic candidates who were defeated in 1994, this comment by Strauss was prophetic.

The 1994 Primaries Slightly more than 1 million voters participated in the Democratic party's first primary, conducted on March 8, 1994; about 555,000 Texans voted in the Republican party's first primary on that same day. Total turnout for the two primaries amounted to fewer than 18 percent of the state's registered voters. In part, this low turnout resulted from lack of competition for the gubernatorial nomination within both parties. Republican George W. Bush, son of former president George Bush, easily won the Republican party's gubernatorial nomination with 93 percent of the votes. Governor Ann Richards won 78 percent of the votes in the Democratic primary.

The 1994 General Election By November 1994, more than 8.6 million Texans were registered to vote, but only 51 percent voted that year. In the contest involving U.S. senatorial candidates, whose names appeared at the top of the ballot, Republican Kay Bailey Hutchison led with 2.6 million votes (61 percent). Democrat Richard Fisher came in second with 1.6 million votes (38 percent). Among the 30 U.S. representatives elected, 19 were Democrats and 11 were Republicans.

For several weeks before election day, pollsters reported that Democrat Ann Richards and Republican George W. Bush were running neck and neck in the gubernatorial race. Bush, however, scored a stunning victory with 2.35 million votes (53 percent). Richards came in second with 2 million votes (46 percent).

Although unofficial exit polls indicate that Bush received about 60 percent of the Anglo vote and 70 percent of the Asian vote, Richards attracted about 76 percent of the Hispanic vote and more than 90 percent of the African-American vote. Carrying fewer than one-third of Texas's 254 counties, Richards received her strongest support in South Texas, Central Texas, and scattered counties in East Texas and West Texas. Bush ran strongly in most suburban precincts, to which many "new Texans" from other states have in-migrated.

The five Democratic incumbents immediately below the governor on the ballot (Lieutenant Governor Bob Bullock, Attorney General Dan Morales, Comptroller John Sharp, Treasurer Martha Whitehead, and Land Commissioner Garry Mauro) defeated Republican challengers by smaller margins, but Republican incumbent Agriculture Commissioner Rick Perry was re-elected. All six Republican candidates below Perry on the ballot also were elected, giving the GOP two Railroad Commission members, two Supreme Court justices, and two Court of Criminal Appeals judges. On lower judicial levels, the wave of GOP voting in 1994 spelled defeat for many Democratic judges. At the same time, GOP gains in the Texas Legislature were minimal. The number of Republican senators increased from 13 to 14, and the number of Republican representatives rose from 60 to 61. Backed by the Christian Coalition, Republicans won 3 of the 6 contested seats on the State Board of Education and thus obtained a majority of 8 on the 15-member board.

1996: A Presidential Election Year

Late in 1995, as both parties prepared for the 1996 presidential campaign, there was speculation that Democrats would write off Texas while concentrating on California and other closely contested states where President Bill Clinton's prospects for gathering electoral votes were brighter. Adoption of this strategy would mean that Democrats running for Texas's congressional, state, and local offices could not expect Clinton's campaign and the Democratic National Committee to finance a strong, statewide get-out-the-vote drive that also would help them. The logic of this strategy was supported by the fact that Clinton had won the White House in 1992 without the electoral votes of the Lone Star State.[8]

The 1996 Primaries On March 12, 1996, about 1,900,000 Texans voted in the first primaries of the two major parties. For the first time since the primary system was established in 1906, more voters participated in the Republican primary (1,019,803) than in the Democratic primary (921,256). Nevertheless, the total number of participants was about 535,000 less than in 1992, the previous presidential election year. On each first-primary ballot were the names of persons seeking nomination as a candidate for the office of U.S. senator.

Following many months of intensive campaigning for nomination as the Republican party's presidential candidate, U.S. senator Phil Gramm had recently dropped out of that contest after disappointing performances in the Iowa caucus and the Louisiana primary. His popularity among Texas Republicans remained high, however, and he received 85 percent of their votes in his primary bid for re-nomination for a third term in the U.S. Senate.

On the Democratic ballot were the names of four men who sought nomination as their party's candidate to oppose Gramm. Two were members of the U.S. House of Representatives: liberal John Bryant, from Dallas, and conservative Jim Chapman, from Sulphur Springs in East Texas. The third, John Odam from Houston, was a moderate Democrat who had campaigned unsuccessfully for nomination as a candidate for attorney general in 1990. Victor Morales, an unknown government teacher from Mesquite, was the fourth candidate. Morales's political experience was limited to serving as a city council member. Most observers believed that either Bryant or Chapman would lead with less than an absolute majority in the first primary and would then face each other in a run-off. But when the votes were counted, Morales finished first and Bryant was second.

Using a few thousand dollars from his savings, Morales had driven throughout the state in his white Nissan pickup, talking to prospective voters wherever he could find them. His message was simple: Morales was a common citizen without plans for solving the nation's problems, but he would draw on his own experience to represent them better than any of his Democratic opponents or Phil Gramm. Helped by free media coverage of his unique campaign, Morales drew support from Hispanics, from some confused voters who thought he was Attorney General Dan Morales, and from many thousands of Texans who were tired of professional politicians but could identify with an "everyman" candidate. After his first-primary triumph, Morales continued to campaign throughout the state in his Nissan pickup.

Victor Morales drives his white pickup truck in San Marcos, Texas, in the Cinco de Mayo parade in 1996. He drove the same truck while campaigning successfully for the Democratic nomination for the U.S. House of Representatives in 1998. (Copyright ©1996 Alan Pogue)

Then, in the run-off primary, Morales scored another upset victory by narrowly defeating Bryant.

The 1996 General Election   Only 53 percent of the state's 10.5 million registered voters went to the polls in the general election in 1996. Although Clinton paid more attention to Texas in 1996 than in 1992, the amount of money spent to mobilize Democratic voters within the Lone Star State was nowhere near as much as the amount collected in Texas and spent elsewhere. In the presidential race, Republican Bob Dole carried Texas with 49 percent of the popular vote, Democrat Bill Clinton received 44 percent, and independent candidate Ross Perot finished third with 7 percent. At the same time, Gramm defeated Morales in the U.S. senatorial race, 55 percent to 45 percent. Likewise, Republican candidates won all other statewide contests. This involved defeats for Democratic candidates in four Supreme Court races, three Court of Criminal Appeals races, and one Railroad Commission race.

As a result of this November election and subsequent special elections in December and January, Republicans gained two seats in the Texas delegation to the U.S. House of Representatives, four seats in the Texas House of Representatives, and three seats in the Texas Senate. The state senatorial victories produced a Republican majority in that legislative chamber for the first time since the Reconstruction era.

1998: Another Republican Gubernatorial Election Year

The 1998 elections focused on changes in the political makeup of Texas. Even Democrats seemed to recognize the ability of Republicans to attract independent voters in general elections, as no Democratic candidates filed for many judgeships. Most statewide offices attracted only one Democrat seeking nomination in the primaries.

Governor George W. Bush began his campaign for the Republican nomination for governor with over $13 million in funds and an approval rating of over 60 percent from all Texas voters. These advantages ensured his renomination and seemed to guarantee that he would make Texas history by being the first governor elected to consecutive four-year terms. His bipartisan popularity only enhanced his chances for the Republican presidential nomination in 2000, a goal he actively pursued with out-of-state appearances during his gubernatorial campaign. When polled in 1997, over 60 percent of Texans said they would support the governor's presidential bid. Democratic gubernatorial nominee Garry Mauro attempted to make a campaign issue of the governor's presidential aspirations by claiming that the Lone Star State did not need a "part-time governor."[9]

Although Republican candidates continued to seek the support of the Christian Coalition and other social conservative groups in 1998, the impact of these groups on statewide elections weakened. When less than 6 percent of registered voters participated in the first Republican primary in March, it was assumed that well-organized social conservatives would have a disproportionate influence on the results. Yet two candidates who were actively supported by the Christian Coalition (Tom Pauken who ran for attorney general and Steve Stockman who ran for a seat on the Railroad Commission) were defeated. Social conservatives' second choice for attorney general, Barry Williamson, lost the primary run-off election in April. This election attracted only 2.1 percent of registered voters. Although voters elected Republicans to all statewide offices in 1998, this level of support did not extend to social conservative candidates. Appealing to moderate voters, Governor Bush insisted he would unite, not divide, Texans.

Women in Politics

The role of women in Texas politics has increased throughout the twentieth century. As noted above, by 1998 the two major political parties were led by female state chairs. Numerous women were successful candidates for office in the 1998 elections. Texas female voters outnumbered male voters and Ann Richards was elected governor. Nevertheless, Texas women did not begin to vote and hold public office for three-quarters of a century after Texas joined the federal Union in 1846.

Through 1982, only two women had won statewide elective office in Texas. In 1918, Dr. Annie Webb Blanton, a highly respected educator, was elected state superintendent of public instruction. Subsequently, Miriam Amanda "Ma" Ferguson was twice elected governor of Texas. Ferguson's election in 1924 and 1932, however, resulted from the influence of her husband, former governor James E. "Pa" Ferguson. (Her campaign slogan was "Two governors for the price of one.") As expected, Jim Ferguson functioned as the state's unofficial chief executive during his wife's terms. Since 1982, several women have won statewide offices, including Ann Richards (state treasurer and governor), Kay Bailey Hutchison (state treasurer and U.S. Senator), and Rose Spector (justice of the Supreme Court of Texas). In 1998, Justice Spector was defeated by Republican Harriet O'Neill in an all-female race for a position on the Texas Supreme Court. A candidate's gender appears to be declining in importance to Texas voters.

In the early 1990s, Texas women served as mayors in about 150 of the state's towns and cities, including the first four in population (Houston, Dallas, San Antonio, and El Paso). As mayor of Dallas (1988–1991), Annette Strauss was fond of greeting out-of-state visitors with this message: "Welcome to Texas where men are men and women are mayors."[10] Convinced that gender was no longer a factor in election or appointment to public office in the Lone Star State, Mayor Strauss could point out that Dallas's city manager, city attorney, and school board president were women.

Despite their electoral victories in Texas and elsewhere across the nation, fewer women than men seek elective public office. There are several reasons for this situation, chief of which is the difficulty in raising money to pay campaign expenses. Some potential donors are reluctant to give money to women candidates, perhaps because they think women cannot win.

Under ordinary circumstances, women candidates cannot expect large contributions from their female supporters, because most Texas women donors do not control as much money as male contributors do. There is also a tendency for women contributors to donate less money than equally affluent men to political campaigns. Thus, many women are discouraged from seeking elective office. There are, however, other reasons fewer women than men seek public office. While women are enjoying increasing freedom, they still shoulder more responsibilities for family and home than men do (even in two-career families). Some mothers feel obligated to care for children in the home until the children finish high school. Such parental obligations, together with age-old prejudices, deny women their rightful place in government. Yet customs, habits, and attitudes do not remain static; new opportunities for women in public service are expanding accordingly.

Racial/Ethnic Politics

More than 37 percent of Texas's total population is composed of Hispanics (chiefly Mexican Americans) and African Americans. Politically, the state's principal ethnic and racial minorities wield enough voting strength to decide any statewide election and determine the outcomes of local contests in areas where their numbers are concentrated. Most of Texas's African-American and Hispanic voters participate in Democratic primaries and vote for Democratic candidates in general elections. Nevertheless, the Texas Poll conducted in August 1997 showed that 16 percent of African Americans and 27 percent of Hispanics did not identify with either the Republican or the Democratic party. Instead, they claimed to be politically independent.

African Americans

In April 1990, the Texas State Democratic Executive Committee filled a candidate vacancy by nominating Potter County Court-at-Law Judge Morris Overstreet, an African-American Democrat, for a seat on the Texas Court of Criminal Appeals. This historic action guaranteed that the state's voters would select the first African American elected to a statewide office since the Reconstruction era. In the subsequent general election, Judge Overstreet faced Judge Louis Sturns, an African-American lawyer from Fort Worth. Sturns had been appointed in 1990 by Governor Clements to a seat on the Court of Criminal Appeals, thereby becoming the first African American to hold a statewide office. Overstreet won the general election of 1990 and was re-elected in 1992. He sought the Democratic nomination for attorney general in 1998. He lost, however, to former attorney general Jim Mattox in the Democratic primary. Many African Americans criticized the Democratic leadership for encouraging Mattox to run against Overstreet. In a conciliatory move, Overstreet was selected to co-chair the 1998 Democratic Convention. He had a prominent role as he shared the job of presiding over the convention with then-party Chair Bill White. There were no African-American Democratic candidates for statewide office on the 1998 general election ballot.

For more than half a century, African-American Texans have tended to identify with the Democratic party. With a voting-age population in excess of 1 million, they constitute about 10 percent of the state's potential voters. Most of Texas's African-American citizens say they are Democrats, and only 5 percent are declared Republicans. The remainder are independents. More than 90 percent of the state's African Americans of voting age support Democratic candidates and tend to remain with the Democratic party regardless of income. Since 1970, African Americans have substantially increased their membership in the Texas Legislature. At the time, four African-American Democrats have represented a Houston district in the U.S. House of Representatives: Barbara Jordan, Mickey Leland, Craig Washington, and Sheila Jackson Lee. Eddie Bernice Johnson, also an African-American Democrat, has represented a Dallas district in the U.S. House of Representatives since 1993. During the 1970s, a total of 174 African-American Texans were elected to public offices; even more were chosen in the 1980s; and in the late 1990s, more than 500 were serving in elected offices at state and local levels.

Hispanics

The term *Hispanic* is a broad one that includes people with Spanish surnames and others who identify with this ethnic group. Most Hispanic Texans or their ancestors came to Texas from Mexico and other Spanish-speaking countries in the Western Hemisphere. More than 90 percent of all Texas Hispanics are of Mexican lineage and are U.S. citizens, with the right to vote and hold public office.[11] It is essential, therefore, that this distinction be made clear: the term *Mexican American* applies to the large majority of Hispanic Texans who are of Mexican ancestry. One Texas political organization has chosen the title Mexican-American Democrats (MAD). This organization was greatly weakened when the Tejano Democrats were formed in 1995 and became "an official arm of the Texas Democratic Party."[12] Tejano Democrats claim to represent the entire Hispanic community. Another organization, the Mexican-American Legal Defense and Education Fund (MALDEF), provides legal services to Hispanics who are litigants in civil rights cases. Nearly all Hispanics who participate directly or indirectly in Texas politics are Mexican Americans. Texas has the second-largest Hispanic population in the nation; California ranks first. With more than 2,000 Hispanics holding elective public offices in 1998, Texas led the nation in the number of elected Hispanics.

Although Mexican Americans have played an important role in South Texas politics throughout the twentieth century, not until the 1960s and early 1970s did they begin to have a major political impact at the state level. Founded in 1969 by José Ángel Gutiérrez of Crystal City and others, the Raza Unida party mobilized many Mexican Americans who had been politically inactive and attracted others who had formerly identified with the Democratic party. By the end of the 1970s, however, Raza Unida had disintegrated. According to Ruben Bonilla, former president of the League of United Latin American Citizens (LULAC), the main reason Raza Unida did not survive as a meaningful voice for Texas's Mexican-American population was "the maturity of the Democratic party to accept Hispanics."

In the 1980s, Mexican-American election strategy became more sophisticated as a new generation of college-educated Hispanics sought public office and assumed leadership roles in political organizations. Among them were Hector Uribe of Brownsville, who won a seat in the Texas Senate, and Henry Cisneros (educated at Texas A&M, Harvard, and George Washington universities), who served four terms as mayor of San Antonio before serving from 1993 to 1997 in President Clinton's cabinet as secretary of the Department of Housing and Urban Development. In 1986, Raul Gonzalez was elected to the Texas Supreme Court, after first having been appointed to that office by Governor Bill Clements. Five years later, Fortunato "Pete" Benavides became the first Texas Hispanic to serve on the Texas Court of Criminal Appeals. In 1992, Benavides was defeated in his bid for re-election to the court. Early in 1994, however, President Clinton appointed him to the U.S. Fifth Circuit Court of

Appeals. This 13-judge court is based in New Orleans and hears appeals from federal district courts in Texas, Louisiana, and Mississippi.

On issues related to religion and abortion, Mexican Americans are more conservative than Anglos, but on most civil rights issues, they are much more liberal. Mexican-American voters are strongly motivated by economic issues, especially the problem of unemployment. These interests continue to draw a large majority of Mexican Americans to the Democratic party. Republican candidates, however, are making some progress in getting the vote of upwardly mobile, urban Mexican Americans who have achieved middle-class or higher economic status. In the 1998 general election, the best known Hispanic candidate for statewide office was Republican Tony Garza, a former Texas secretary of state, who was elected to a position on the Texas Railroad Commission.

In 1990, Democratic gubernatorial candidate Ann Richards was supported by more than 250,000 of the 330,000 Hispanics who voted. Also benefiting from the large Hispanic turnout in 1990 was Democratic Representative Dan Morales of San Antonio, who was elected attorney general of the Lone Star State. In defeating his Republican opponent, Senator J. E. "Buster" Brown of Lake Jackson, Morales became the first Mexican American elected to a non-judicial statewide office and the second to win any statewide office in Texas. Morales was re-elected for another four- year term in 1994 with 88 percent of the Hispanic vote. His decision not to seek re-election in 1998 shocked Texas Democrats. The only Hispanic Democratic candidate for statewide office in 1998 was Representative Richard Raymond who ran unsuccessfully for land commissioner. However, almost one-half of Hispanic voters supported Governor Bush, and Republican Tony Garza won the Railroad Commission race.

Recognizing the increasing importance of the Hispanic vote in Texas, Governor Bush appointed two Hispanics to the position of Texas's secretary of state—first selecting Tony Garza and later replacing him with Houston attorney Al Gonzales. Both the state Democratic and Republican parties actively sought the support of Hispanic voters in 1998.[13]

Political Campaigns

Elections in Texas are conducted to fill national, state, county, city, and special-district offices. With so many electoral contests, citizens are frequently besieged by candidates seeking votes and asking for money to finance their election campaigns. It is through the democratic election process, however, that Texans have an opportunity to influence public policymaking by expressing preferences for candidates and issues when they vote.

Conducting Campaigns in the 1990s

Campaigns are no longer limited to speeches by candidates on a courthouse lawn or from the rear platform of a campaign train. Today prospective voters are more likely to be harried by a barrage of campaign publicity involving television and radio broadcasting, newspapers, billboards, yard signs, and bumper stickers. Moreover, they probably will encounter door-to-door canvassers, receive political questionnaires and propaganda leaflets in the mail, be asked to answer telephone inquiries from professional pollsters or locally hired telephone bank callers, and be solicited for donations to pay for campaign expenses.

Nonissue Campaigns Only a minority of Texans, and indeed other Americans, are actively concerned with politics. But even among those interested in political affairs, there is a growing impatience with current styles of campaigning. Upon retirement in 1986 from long service in the U.S. Senate, Thomas Eagleton of Missouri observed, "The whole nature of the political campaign has degenerated into a war of meaningless little TV spots and meaningless little newspaper articles about the periphery of the campaign, but never the substance."[14]

Importance of the Media With more than 11 million potential voters to be reached in 254 counties, Texas is by necessity a media state for political campaigning. To visit every county personally during a primary campaign, a candidate would need to go into four counties per day, five days a week, from the filing deadline in January to the March primary date. Such extensive travel would leave little time for speechmaking, money raising, and other campaign activities. Therefore, Texas campaigners must rely more heavily on television and radio exposure than candidates in other states.

Across Texas, there are no fewer than 60 television stations and 350 radio stations, along with about 100 daily and more than 400 weekly newspapers. Of the television outlets, those in Houston and the Dallas–Fort Worth Metroplex reach the largest number of prospective voters but are the most expensive. For candidates seeking statewide offices, exposure via stations serving the largest and most heavily populated viewer areas is essential. For one major television outlet, a one-minute ad cost $25,000, a 30-second ad $12,500 and a 10-second "sound bite" $6,250.

Candidates in 1998 also relied on computers to communicate with prospective voters. Most campaigns had web sites. Some candidates experimented with the use of e-mail, weighing its low cost against computer-users' resistance to "spam" (electronic junk mail).

Mudslide Campaigns Following Ann Richards's victory over Jim Mattox in the Democratic run-off primary of April 1990, one journalist reported that Richards had "won by a mudslide." This expression suggests the reaction of many citizens, who were disappointed, if not infuriated, by the candidates' generally low ethical level of campaigning and their avoidance of critical public issues.

Concern over the shortcomings of American election campaigns has given rise to organized efforts toward improvement. One group, the Markle Commission on the Media and the Electorate, concluded after two years of study that candidates, media people, consultants, and the electorate are all blameworthy. Candidates and consultants, wishing to win at any cost, employ negative advertising and make exaggerated claims. The media emphasize poll results and the "horserace" appearance of a contest rather than basic issues and candidate personalities that relate to leadership potential. The Markle Commission found that television news devotes less attention to issues than do newspapers. The electorate too must share the blame for the low ethical level of political campaigning. Only when voters become a corrective force will reform be achieved. Of necessity, the improvement will take place over time, if it happens at all. Because the bottom line of campaign reform involves educating citizens, little can be achieved overnight.[15]

Financing Campaigns

On more than one occasion, President Lyndon Johnson bluntly summarized the relationship between politics and finance with the statement "Money makes the mare go." Although most political scientists would state this fact differently, it is obvious that money is needed to pay necessary expenses of election campaigns. Certainly a candidate for statewide office in Texas cannot win without first communicating with a large percentage of the state's voting population. But the postage alone for mailing a postcard to every Texan 18 years of age or older would cost more than $2 million. Many Texans are qualified to hold public office, but relatively few can afford to pay their own campaign expenses or are willing to undertake fund-raising drives designed to attract significant campaign contributions by others.

Most routine work involved in Texas election campaigns is still performed largely by volunteer workers: people who do door-to-door canvassing, distribute campaign literature, and put up yard signs. But huge sums of money must be raised to pay for media advertising and hire professionals who know how to plan, organize, and direct a campaign. Candidates for statewide office, for example, can no longer rely entirely on volunteers to operate phone banks. For greater assurance of victory, hundreds of paid telephone callers are needed. Because of the professionalization of political campaigning, it is unlikely that candidates for most statewide offices and many district offices in Texas, especially those for governor and U.S. senator, could win without the aid of highly paid specialists in political campaigning and public opinion polling.

Polls are essential but expensive. They help candidates determine where to focus media efforts, which issues to emphasize, which strengths to exploit, and how to remedy weaknesses. A single statewide poll may cost a Texas candidate $5,000 to $35,000, depending on the size of the sample and the number of questions asked. But because favorable polling results may attract contributors who are looking for a winner, polls can help a candidate raise campaign funds. Newspapers and billboards constitute other media forms essential to election campaigning. A billboard on the freeway of a major Texas city will cost about $3,000 per month, while a full-page ad in one of the state's major newspapers will cost up to $60,000 per weekday (and more for Sunday).

Contributions by PACs A **political action committee (PAC)** is a legal device used by corporations, labor unions, and other organizations to raise large sums of money to be channeled into political campaigns. Federal law permits a PAC to give a candidate up to $5,000 for each primary, run-off, and general election. An individual may contribute only $1,000 in each instance. At the state level, there is no limit to the amount of money a PAC may contribute. Ordinarily, PACs strongly favor incumbents over challengers for an obvious reason: persons already in office are more likely to be elected than their opponents.

Regulation of Campaign Financing

Both federal and Texas state laws have been enacted to regulate various aspects of campaign financing. Texas laws on the subject are relatively weak and tend to emphasize reporting of contributions. Federal laws are more restrictive, featuring both reporting requirements and limits on contributions by individuals and PACs.

Federal Regulation The Federal Election Campaign Act of 1972, as amended, permits a taxpayer to designate $3 of an annual U.S. income tax payment, or $6 on a joint return, to be placed in the presidential campaign fund as a contribution to the public funding of presidential campaigns. This was the first step taken toward public funding of elections. But an even broader step was taken in the Federal Election Campaign Act of 1974 and subsequent amendments.

The Federal Election Campaign Act of 1974 applies only to election campaigns for president, vice president, and members of Congress. Contributions by individuals are limited as follows: $1,000 per campaign, $5,000 per year to any PAC, $20,000 per year to a national party organization, and $25,000 per year to all federal candidates. PAC contributions are limited to $5,000 per election campaign, and candidates are required to make periodic reports on contributions and expenditures. A bipartisan Federal Elections Commission administers the law. The 1996 elections demonstrated that federal campaign finance laws failed to limit the amount of money contributed to campaigns. Bipartisan attempts at reform by Congress in 1998 did not succeed, however.

State Regulation Texas's state ethics law is designed to "control and reduce the cost of elections" and to disclose information related to election expenditures and contributions. The **Texas Ethics Commission** administers the rules governing ethical behavior in government.

Texas's Campaign Reporting and Disclosure Law (1973) and its Ethics Law (1991) prescribe requirements for campaign reporting and disclosure for office seekers in the Lone Star State. Every candidate for nomination and election to any state, district, county, or municipal office (along with every political committee involved in such elections) must designate a campaign treasurer before accepting contributions or making expenditures. Contributions to candidates by labor unions and corporations are prohibited. Candidates and political committees may not accept more than $100 in cash from a contributor, but there is no limit on the amount received by check. Neither candidates nor political committees may knowingly accept political contributions of more than $500 from any out-of-state political committee unless they report the names of contributors of $100 or more. Contributions may not be converted to personal use. Wealthy candidates running for statewide office may spend unlimited amounts of their own money on their campaigns. Limits are set, however, on amounts that may be recouped (repaid to a candidate) from contributions by others. These limits are $500,000 for a gubernatorial candidate and $250,000 for a candidate seeking any other statewide office.

Candidates and treasurers of campaign committees are required to file periodically with the State Ethics Commission. Sworn statements list all contributions received and expenditures made during designated reporting intervals, plus the name and address of each donor of amounts in excess of $50. Any candidate or campaign treasurer who fails to file these reports is liable to each opposing candidate for double the amount of the unreported contributions or expenditures and to the state for triple that amount. These reports reveal the names and the amounts given by donors of more than $50, but there is no limit on the amount that may be contributed. In practice, both federal and state campaign finance laws have largely failed to cope with the problem of influence buying through transfers of money in the form of campaign contributions. It may well be that as long as campaigns are funded by private sources, they will remain inadequately regulated.

Nevertheless, the legislature took a significant step when it enacted the Judicial Campaign Fairness Act. This statute limits both the contributions to judicial candidates and the time during which donations can be made. Voluntary campaign spending limits range from $2 million for judicial candidates for statewide office to $100,000 for persons running for a judicial office in a district with a population of fewer than 250,000. Noncomplying candidates must note this fact on their campaign materials; their complying opponents will be exempt from spending and contribution limits.

Looking Ahead

Under the freedom of speech clause of the U.S. Constitution, Americans have a right to give money to the candidates of their choice. The U.S. Supreme Court has ruled that campaign contributions may be limited, but independent expenditures in support of a specific candidate may not. Furthermore, in *Buckley* v. *Valeo* (1976), the U.S. Supreme Court held that candidates may not be prohibited from spending their own money on their campaigns. In the face of these guaranteed rights, political parties are weakened in turn. When PACs can collectively contribute millions of dollars to a candidate for a statewide office, the candidate no longer needs to remain obligated to a party. **Public funding of elections** by state governments could, however, either strengthen or weaken political parties. If state funds were to go directly to candidates, parties would hardly benefit. But if public money were given to parties, they in turn could parcel it out to candidates and thereby strengthen party loyalty.

It is interesting to speculate on how candidates and voters would respond to or be affected by public funding of Texas elections. First, challengers would be placed on a more equal financial footing with incumbents. Private financing favors incumbents in raising campaign money. Texas legislators are well aware of this, and they will surrender their advantage only in the face of strong public pressure. Second, public funding would run counter to Texas tradition. The Lone Star State has never tried it, and many citizens are undisturbed by big-money domination of politics. Moreover, some Texans believe public financing of elections would violate their freedom of the ballot. Public funding would open the way, they believe, for an individual's tax money to be used to finance a candidate the taxpayer opposes. Others object to public funding on the grounds that adoption of the plan would be a dangerous departure from the private enterprise system.

These and other objections to public funding of elections indicate that for the foreseeable future, Texas will continue to allow wealthy individuals and powerful interest groups to buy political favors from government under the guise of making campaign contributions. The following chapter provides extensive coverage of interest groups.

Notes

1. "Too Many Elections?" *Houston Chronicle*, April 16, 1998, p. 32A.
2. David Montejano, *Anglos and Mexicans in the Making of Texas, 1836–1986* (Austin: University of Texas Press, 1987), p. 143.
3. Other U.S. Supreme Court cases involving the Texas white primary are *Nixon* v. *Herndon* (1927), *Nixon* v. *Condon* (1932), and *Grovey* v. *Townsend* (1936).
4. The Texas Election Code is a compilation of state laws that govern voter qualifications, procedures for nominating and electing party officials and government officials, and other matters related to suffrage and elections.
5. Sam Attlesey, "Dwindling Dominance," *The Dallas Morning News*, January 13, 1998.
6. For detailed but readable accounts of Ross Perot's political crusade, see Carolyn Barta, *Perot and His People: Disrupting the Balance of Political Power* (Fort Worth: The Summit Group, 1993), and Gerald Posner, *Citizen Perot: His Life and Times* (New York: Random House, 1996).
7. Kathy Kiely, "Strauss Says Texas Is Losing Its Clout," *Houston Post,* June 25, 1993, p. 31A.
8. See Sam Attlesey, "Parties Jockeying for Positions in State Races," *The Dallas Morning News,* November 19, 1995, p. 46A.

9. Clay Robison, "Bush Can Handle 'Part-time' Governor Tag," *Houston Chronicle*, April 26, 1998, p. 2C.

10. *The Dallas Morning News,* September 18, 1990, p. 12A.

11. Peggy Fikac, "First Hispanic Joins High Criminal Court," *San Angelo Standard-Times,* April 27, 1991, p. 1A. Two studies of Mexican Americans in Texas and nationwide are Arnoldo De León, *Mexican Americans in Texas: A Brief History* (Arlington Heights, Ill.: Harlan Davidson, 1993), and Peter Skerry, *Mexican Americans: The Ambivalent Minority* (New York: The Free Press, 1993).

12. *Tejano Democrats*, "Main Page," <http//www.tejanodemocrats.org>.

13. See Bill Clements, "Attracting Hispanics Is Crucial to the Texas GOP's Future," *Corpus Christi Caller Times*, January 8, 1998; and Jorge A. Ramirez, "Texas Hispanics: Ties to Democratic Party Remain Strong," *The Dallas Morning News*, January 25, 1998.

14. *San Angelo Standard-Times,* November 3, 1986.

15. Dave McNeely, "Election Reform Starts with the Awakening of the Electorate," *Austin American-Statesman,* June 3, 1990.

Key Terms and Concepts

universal suffrage	political party
white primary	temporary party organization
poll tax	platform
motor voter law	precinct convention
Texas Election Code	county convention
voter registration	district convention
elections administrator	state convention
voter turnout	permanent party organization
early voting	precinct chair
direct primary	county executive committee
general election	district executive committee
run-off primary	state executive committee
open primary	conservative
blanket primary	liberal
closed primary	dealignment
canvass	realignment
off-year election	political action committee (PAC)
special election	Texas Ethics Commission
voting precinct	public funding of elections
election judge	

SELECTED READING

A Fly on the Wall at Polling Place #315*

Kelli Montgomery

On March 12, 1996, Super Tuesday, County *magazine sent staff writer Kelli Montgomery to Precinct #315 in Hays County where both the Democratic and Republican primaries were being held. Turnout was slow and steady all day, but it's what went on behind the scenes that's the real story.*

This is a story about the precinct workers who manned the polls from dawn to dusk; it's about who they are and what they do. What goes on when they're not pushing ballots? It's also a look at the people who trailed in and out of precinct #315 that day. Why did they come out to vote, and how much do they know about the local races? What happened outside the polls?

For those who have ever run or plan to run for office some day, understanding the dynamics behind the neighborhood polling place may prove insightful.

Super Tuesday began in a fog. My directions to the polling site were somewhat sketchy, but the larger-than-life campaign signs dotting the roadway led me straight to my observation post: the Dorie Miller Junior High Cafeteria, the new and improved polling site for Precinct #315.

For years the Hays County precinct held its elections in the local veterinary clinic. Aside from the less-than-pleasant odors ingested, voters occasionally would get a glimpse of an operation or two being performed after a hospital door had mistakenly been left open. Before that, a tent was erected for elections; bathrooms were down the street at the filling station. The one consensus that crossed party lines all day was that the air-conditioned cafeteria beat the previous sites by far.

Other things besides the location had changed too. Precinct #315, for example, used to be strongly Democrat. Voters would stream in the door obtrusively marked "Democratic Primary," while volunteer workers on the other side sat idle. In recent years, however, support in the county for the GOP has climbed. The ratio of Republicans to Democrats at the precinct this time was roughly double, presumably the result of a more contested ballot.

Something else, too. Not unlike precincts everywhere, early voting had curtailed much of the election day momentum. Super Tuesday this year was like watching the Super Bowl without any pre-game hype. One voter told *County* magazine there used to be a line "clear out the door and around the building" at Precinct #315.

*From *County,* May/June 1996, pp. 31–35. *County* magazine is published by the Texas Association of Counties. Printed with permission.

Early Bird on a 12-Hour Shift

"Boy, this is going to be a long day," I thought, walking into the cafeteria about 7 A.M. Students were off on spring break. Few voters had arrived. Not much action happening outside the poll, either. Several campaign signs decorated the front of the schoolyard. Most were knocked down later in the day by the wind. Inside, the lunchroom was divided—Democrats on one side, Republicans on the other. Three stretch tables stacked with chairs provided a subtle physical boundary. Even separate doors marked separate primaries.

I perched mid-way between the two parties and observed, feeling at times more like a judge in a tennis match than a writer. *Point, right side, Point, left side, Point right side,* I noted as voters trickled in. One man in sunglasses entered through the GOP-marked door, grabbed a ballot and mistakenly headed over to the opposing party's side. "Hey, what are you doing?" the Democratic precinct workers motioned. "Ya'll look like a hostile bunch," he joked, seeing their empty booths.

Another man came in. "I'll vote for candidate ABC—Anybody But Clinton," he bantered. Everyone laughed. The atmosphere was friendly and relaxed. About 10 A.M., an older couple wanted to know "where all the Democrats were?" after seeing a voter tally sheet posted on the primary door. "It's never been this slow."

By late afternoon, the pace picked up. "The headaches start about 5:15 P.M.," one precinct worker said. Sure enough, that's when the vehicles started streaming in. Booths filled up on both sides. Turnout was highest ten minutes before the polls closed. In the end, the final voter tally was Republicans, 267, Democrats, 141, a low turnout by most accounts. By comparison, a few years ago, turnout in both Super Tuesday primaries reached closer to 1,900 at the precinct.

Getting to Know the Volunteer Precinct Workers

On each side of the room, three workers sat ready for action behind long cafeteria tables stacked with papers. Each party's setup looked almost identical, barring different colored ballots and signs. Along the walls were four space-aged looking voting booths that transformed into briefcases once the polls closed. A punch card system was set up inside. On a chair nearby sat a gray, plastic file box sealed by a lock. A sign taped to the top indicated it was a third degree felony for anyone but the election judge to open the box; punishable by two to ten years in prison.

I introduced myself to the Democratic precinct workers first. Turns out precinct judge Carol Kutscher, Becky Cultra, and Sterling Rogers had worked elections together for years. Real pros, you could tell. When they weren't pushing ballots, they reminisced about their kids, past elections, the rising costs of buying houses and so on like old chums.

Rogers, an artist, filled me in on some election-day folklore, like the time Precinct #315 ran out of ballots right before the polls closed. "There wasn't time to re-stock. People were lined up. We had to use scratch paper and write in the list of candidates," he recalled. It was a perfectly acceptable improvisation. Another time, election officials saw someone accidentally drop two ballots that were stuck together into the box. "We were able to report it as invalid," Rogers said. Lucky thing, too. It could have meant workers staying late into the night trying to figure out why the number of ballots didn't match the voter tally. On the Republican side, precinct judge Stan Livingston, his wife, Mildred, and Glen McEntire were seasoned veterans, too. Their stories were similar.

All day, the volunteers taught me about the ins and outs of precinct protocol; like "don't wear political memorabilia," it's prohibited inside the polls. (Albeit, one guy in a Ross Perot t-shirt made it through okay, but his vote in a party primary made him ineligible to sign any Perot petitions.) Also, to prevent "electioneering," campaigning within 100 feet of a primary entry is illegal. Two distance markers mounted to trees prohibited political influencing. "No electioneering or loitering beyond this point," the signs read. "It's a manifestation from the early days when political bosses would usher voters into the polls and literally show them who to vote for," Rogers explained. These days, campaigners are relegated to the parking lots.

The Elections Process, A Calculated Science

On each precinct table, there was a 30-page reference handbook distributed by the Texas Secretary of State's Office about what to do in virtually any situation that may arise. Precinct #315's workers, fortunately, already knew the rules. If someone forgets his registration card, for example, the voter must sign an affidavit saying he is who he says he is and that he "misplaced it, forgot it, or lost it." If a person shows up at the wrong precinct, he may only vote in those races not precinct related.

The way the process works is each primary is given duplicate lists of all the voters in the precinct. Volunteers check the registration card of the voter against the master list. If the person voted early, his name will appear checked off on the list. Registration cards are also stamped Democrat or Republican if a person votes in either primary to prevent double voting. Each primary also gets identical supply boxes, provided by the county's election administrator, that contain all the necessary forms, tally sheets, highlighters, maps, precinct packets, and so on.

When the polls close, five envelopes addressed to the presiding officer of the local canvassing authority, the custodian of election records, the presiding judge, the voter registrar, and the county chair will be filled with everything from the day's events. For instance, *Envelope No. 1* must contain a certificate verifying the machines were properly secured, a tally list, the original copy of election returns, and so on. *No. 2* includes, among other things, the poll list, signature roster, early voting list, affidavits of voters without certificates. Other envelopes contain similar items. "It's a lot of work to have precinct elections. After the polls close, the work really begins," explained Mildred Livingston. "That's when you've got to get all the paperwork together and get the ballots over to the central headquarters to be counted."

"Why Work?" I Asked the Volunteers

After a while, I began to wonder what makes these volunteer workers tick. It's a 12- to 15-hour shift with few, if any, breaks at polling sites that are rarely comfortable or accommodating. The pay is meager. Occasionally, you get the disgruntled voters, too. About 4 P.M., for instance, I watched on one primary's side for more than ten minutes. "Why was the precinct's location changed? Why weren't there more contested races on the ballot?" she wanted to know. "It took me forever to get here. It's not even worth it!"

Livingston, who has manned the polls for 13 years, said it's not really a question of wanting to do it, "it's more an understanding that someone must do it." Kutscher, a 14-year volunteer poll worker, shared a similar view. "I guess I felt like it was sort of a civic duty. A neighbor called and asked me to do it years ago. I've been doing it ever since."

For the most part, the volunteers say they enjoy the work. "It gives us a chance to visit with our neighbors. It's fun," Cultra said. In truth, few people line up to work the precinct elections at all. *County* asked Hays County Election Administrator Joyce Cowan how she gets people to watch the booths each time. "We beg them," she said lightheartedly.

Why Vote?

I polled random people who had just cast their ballots. The phrase "civic duty" kept popping up again and again like a rehearsed theatrical line. Rick Johnson, an engineering draftsman, said he didn't really know why he voted. He just felt like it was something he needed to do, he said. Accompanying him was his school-aged daughter who helped him pick the questionable candidates. She said she based most of her decisions on the names she liked.

Some people said they voted to align themselves with a particular platform. "I think it makes a difference, even if my candidate doesn't win," said accountant Barney Howard. "It helps me identify with the party's stand at least." Others said they came out to the polling site to show support for friends or acquaintances who were running for office.

One couple, who spoke Spanish during the interview, said they vote regularly because it's a privilege. "In other countries, you don't have the opportunity to express your opinion like you do here. You may even be risking your life just to stand in line and cast a vote," said Raul Ovalles, before greeting his daughter and son-in-law who arrived during our interview to cast their ballots too.

Overall, the majority of voters said they came out mainly for the state and national races. Most told *County* they didn't know much about the local candidates aside from what they read in the newspapers. They'd like to know more, though. "One guy who was running for local office called me himself," said Ken Jenkins, a wallpaper employee who was drinking coffee outside the polling place. "I know everyone can't do that, but I was impressed. I voted for him."

Electioneering, a Softer Sell Today

In the parking lot, "Remember to vote for Flores," a young woman repeated quietly to voters on their way in. "My dad's running for JP." "I'm hoping people will remember his name if I stand out here. I think it helps candidates who aren't really known in the county yet," Flores said. She said her four other sisters were stationed at precincts around town.

Few campaigners were out that day. At high-turnout times like around 8 A.M. and 5:30 P.M., a few vehicles decorated with signs or streamers drove through the parking lot. Two off-duty law enforcement officers held up signs supporting their friend who was running for a sheriff's spot. They moved from precinct to precinct throughout the day.

Several voters told *County* if supporters for a candidate are out campaigning, they are more likely to vote for that person; if nothing else, just because they remember the name. One voter suggested, if a political candidate has campaign signs, put the party affiliation on it.

The Countdown and the Counting

Ten minutes before the polls closed, voters began to line up. Some came later to attend the precinct conventions being held at 7:15 P.M. That's where the delegates [to the Democratic and Republican county conventions] are elected. Others, I think, just liked the excitement of closing down the polls.

One 18-year-old man spent several minutes reading through the ballot, selecting his candidates very carefully. His father waited nearby in anticipation, grinning as the 18-year old dropped the ballot in the box. Turns out, it was the young man's first time to vote.

At 7 P.M., the polls closed. Precinct judges quickly began filling the five envelopes. Volunteer workers folded up the booths and helped load supplies. I followed as the judges took the lock boxes to a central headquarters, the Hays County Judicial Center. In the parking lot, police with flashlights and flares motioned precinct officials to a spot where they could unload their cars at the headquarters.

It wasn't until I drove off that I realized what an interesting day it had been. I understood a lot more about the dynamics of election day. Precinct volunteers were there because the job needed to be done. Voters voted at the precinct because they were part of the process and the community. Neighbors greeted neighbors. People brought their kids.

On the way home, I wondered what candidates would win, if there would be a run-off, and what the six dedicated workers would talk about next time at Precinct #315.

Chapter 5

THE POLITICS OF INTEREST GROUPS

IT'S MY SMALL ROLE IN THE SYSTEM: GREASING THE POLITICAL PALMS THAT GREASE THE POLITICAL WHEELS.

CAMPAIGN FINANCE HIGH-ROLLERS

©1996, Houston Chronicle Publishing Company.
Reprinted with permission. All rights reserved.

Money and politics have become almost synonymous. Texas politicians need funding to finance their campaigns or discourage others from running against them. Special interest groups want favorable laws and policies from elected decision makers. As the cartoon that opens this chapter illustrates, special interest groups and individual "highrollers" are eager to provide funding to gain access to elected officials. This relationship is highlighted in a publication released in 1998 entitled *Mortgaged House*. The report notes that over $14.6 million was contributed to the 1996 election campaigns of the 150 members of the Texas House of Representatives. Most of this money was donated by special interests.[1]

Politics focuses on the nomination and election of persons to public office; however, it includes much more. Politics is perhaps best understood as the process of influencing public policy decisions to protect and preserve a group, achieve group goals, and distribute benefits to group members. Organized citizens may demand policies that promote their group's financial security, health and welfare, education, and protection.

Governments make and enforce public policy decisions. Therefore, people constantly try to influence those who make and apply society's rules or policies to their benefit. One important approach is through group action. This involves the interaction of individuals organized to achieve common goals. Experience demonstrates that individuals who form groups for political action are usually more effective in achieving their goals than persons acting alone.

Interest Groups in the Political Process

When attempting to influence political decisions or the selection of the men and women who will make them, people usually turn either to political parties (examined in Chapter 4) or to interest groups (the subject of this chapter).

What Is an Interest Group?

A political **interest group** (sometimes referred to as a **pressure group**) is an organization whose members share common views and objectives and actively support programs designed to influence government officials and their policies. Some examples of interest groups in action include the Texas Students Association, a statewide coalition of public university students, lobbying the legislature to increase appropriations for their universities; Texans for Lawsuit Reform and Citizens Against Lawsuit Abuse proposing new legislation reducing opportunities for litigation aimed at businesses and limiting damage awards to those who sue businesses; and the Gay and

Lesbian Task Force gearing up to campaign against candidates for office who might further restrict homosexual conduct.

Political Parties and Interest Groups

Although both political parties and interest groups attempt to influence policy decisions by government officials, they differ in their methods. Political parties try to gain control of government by

- Electing candidates to public office
- Recruiting leaders to fill party offices
- Formulating policies to resolve public problems
- Serving as intermediaries between citizens—especially voting citizens— and officers of government

The principal purpose of party activity is to gain control of government and its powers in order to achieve party goals.

In contrast, an interest group seeks to influence government officials to decide issues to the advantage of the group. Interest groups try to influence policy decisions by

- Using persuasion to mobilize their own members and supporters
- Attempting to sway public opinion
- Building coalitions with other groups whose interests are identical or closely related
- Obtaining access to key decision makers

Generally, an interest group wants government policies implemented in ways preferred by the group without seeking to place its members in office.

Economic groups (for example, the Texas Bankers Association) and social groups (such as the Texas Congress of Parents and Teachers) serve as vehicles by which policy preferences of special interests are made known to government officials. Because they speak for citizens who share a common interest but who may reside throughout the state, interest groups supplement the formal system of territorial (geographic) representation used for electing most officeholders. They provide an internal system of **functional representation**. Thus, interest groups offer a form of representation and protection for such functional groups as businesspeople, laborers, farmers, Roman Catholics, African Americans, Mexican Americans, teachers, and college students. These groups are composed of people who have similar interests but may not constitute a majority in any city, county, legislative district, or state.

Interest Groups in American Politics

The growth and diversity of interest groups in the United States continue unabated. Although many citizens are not affiliated with any group, others are members of several. Over one in every four Americans is affiliated with three or more interest groups.[2]

In *NAACP* v. *Alabama* (1958), the U.S. Supreme Court recognized the **right of association** through the right of assembly granted by the first amendment of the U.S. Constitution. This decision greatly facilitated the development of interest groups. As a result, the right of individuals to organize into groups for political, economic, religious, and social purposes is ensured. Traditionally, the nation's political and legal culture has encouraged individuals to organize themselves into a bewildering array of associations—religious, fraternal, professional, and recreational, among others. Americans have responded by creating literally thousands of such groups. Three other factors have also fostered group formation and participation in American politics:

- A decentralized structure of government
- Absence of a unified and responsible party system
- The low ideological content of American politics

Decentralization of National and State Governments   Nowhere in the American system is governing power highly centralized or concentrated. **Decentralized government** is achieved in two principal ways. First, the federal system divides power between the national government and the 50 state governments. In turn, each state shares its power with a wide variety of local governments, including counties, cities, and special districts. Second, within each level of government, power is separated into three branches or departments: legislative, executive, and judicial. This separation of powers is especially apparent at the national and state levels.

A decentralized structure increases the ability of interest groups to influence governmental activities. This structure permits groups to fight their battles at different levels of government and within different branches at each level. Public utilities (such as Texas Utilities, which provides electric power to local communities in East Texas) are often able to charge consumers higher rates and obtain other concessions by appealing to federal courts, state regulatory agencies, and municipal governing bodies.

Dispersal of power within branches or departments of government further enhances an interest group's chance of success. Divided power makes public officials more vulnerable to interest group influence.

Texas officials are especially susceptible to interest group pressure because of the public's long tradition of withholding power from the government. Few state constitutions equal that of Texas in devotion to the principle of restricting the power of public officials. For example, largely as the result of pressure exerted by the Grange and other farm organizations, the Texas Constitution requires a two-thirds vote of the Texas Legislature to tax any farm products owned by the producing farmer.

Decentralized Party System   Another result of decentralized government is a **decentralized political party system**. Absence of a unified and responsible party system further magnifies opportunities for effective interest group action. Policymakers (state and local) are particularly affected by the lack of strong, organized political parties. A cohesive party can provide policymakers with the strength to resist pressure from well-organized interest groups. Cohesiveness enables a relatively large number of state legislators, for example, to stand united in the face of determined pressure from interest group lobbyists. Texas legislators are likely to be impressed by any reasonably convincing demonstration of an organized demand, although lawmakers may lack knowledge of the weight or influence of the interest group.

De-emphasized Ideologies The Texas Democratic party has liberal and moderate factions, and the Texas Republican party has fiscal conservative and social conservative factions. Nevertheless, **ideologies**—well-developed systems of political, social, and economic beliefs—are not strong factors in Texas politics. Texas voters do not act in accordance with their commitment to ideological programs, although the advent and growth of the faith-based social conservatives may be in the process of changing this situation. Thus, the appeals of interest groups fall on more receptive ears than would be the case if citizens and their political leaders were dedicated to ideological objectives.

Organization of Interest Groups

As mentioned earlier, an interest group is an organization of individuals who seek to influence governmental decisions, usually without trying to place the group's own members in public office. The organization provides members with information, rallies them in meetings, and otherwise tries to "educate" them. Such a description implies that American interest groups are organized. Moreover, it suggests that any organization becomes an interest group when it decides to influence government decisions.

Organizational Patterns

Because of group diversity, there are almost as many **organizational patterns** as there are interest groups. This variety arises from the fact that, in addition to lobbying, most interest groups carry on nonpolitical functions of paramount importance to their members. A religious organization, for example, may on occasion undertake political activity, while most of the time it emphasizes charitable and spiritual activities.

Some interest groups are highly **centralized organizations** (in which a group takes the form of a single body without affiliated local or regional units). An example of such a centralized group currently operating in Texas is the National Rifle Association. Other groups are **decentralized,** consisting of loose alliances of local and regional subgroups. Their activities may be directed at either the local or the central level. Many trade associations (such as the Texas Association of Business and Chambers of Commerce) and labor unions (such as those affiliated with the AFL-CIO) are examples of decentralized organizations active in Texas politics.

Membership in Interest Groups

Interest groups are composed chiefly of individuals from professional and managerial occupations. Members tend to be homeowners with high levels of income and formal education, and they are likely to enjoy a high standard of living. For example, a lawyer or an accountant is much more likely to be active in an interest group than a janitor or a grocery clerk.

Leadership in Interest Groups

An organized group of any size is almost invariably composed of an active minority and a passive majority. As a result, decisions are regularly made by the minority, which may range from a small elite of elected officers to a larger group composed of delegates representing the entire membership. Organizations tend to leave decision making and other leadership activities to a few people. Widespread apathy among rank-and-file members and the difficulty of dislodging entrenched leaders probably account for limited participation in most group decisions.

Other factors influence **group leadership**. These include the financial structure of the group (members who contribute most heavily usually have greater weight in making decisions), the time-consuming nature of leadership duties (only a few people can afford to devote the time without compensation), and the personality traits of leaders (some individuals have greater leadership ability and motivation than others).

Classification of Interest Groups

The great variety of American interest groups at the national, state, and local levels of government permits them to be classified in several ways. We have just seen how they may differ in degree of centralization. They may also be categorized according to the level or branch of government to which they direct their attention. Some groups exert their influence at all levels of government and on legislative, executive (including administrative), and judicial officials. Others may try to spread their views among the general public and may be best classified according to the subject matter they represent.

Some groups do not fit readily into any category, whereas others fit into more than one. Thus, the classifications that follow are necessarily arbitrary and certainly not exhaustive. They do illustrate that interest groups are involved in most decisions at all levels of Texas government.

Economic Groups

Many interest groups exist primarily to promote the economic self-interest of their members. These organizations are known as **economic groups**. Traditionally, people contribute significant amounts of their money and time to obtain economic benefits. Thus, some organizations exist to further the economic interests of a broad group, such as small businesses. Others are created to protect the interests of a single type of business, such as bowling centers. The Texas Association of Business and Chambers of Commerce is an example of this broader type of interest group known as an **umbrella organization**. Often, individual corporations, such as Southwestern Bell, use the political process to promote the company's economic interests.

Business American businesspeople understand they have common interests that may be promoted by collective action. They were among the first to organize and press for adoption of favorable public policies by national, state, and local governments. Business organizations advocate lower taxes, a lessening or elimination of price and quality controls, and minimal concessions to labor unions. At the state level, business organizations most often take the form of **trade associations** (groups that act on behalf of an industry). Some of the many Texas trade associations are the Texas Association of Builders, the Texas Good Roads and Transportation Association, and the Texas Wine and Grape Growers Association.

More than 60 associations own their headquarters buildings in the city of Austin because they need to be near the legislature and other state agencies. Others lease or rent buildings or office suites. This proximity to the capitol provides regular contact with state officials and gives the associations a path to influence in government.[3]

Although Texas businesses and their representatives were most successful in having their agendas enacted into law during the 1995 session of the Texas Legislature, they were not so influential in the 1997 session. Issues such as juvenile justice, funding for education at all levels, and property tax reform pitted businesses against one another and shattered their united front.

Labor Unions representing Texas workers are almost as active, but not as powerful, as business-related groups. **Organized labor groups** seek, among other goals, government intervention to increase wages, reduce hours, and provide adequate unemployment insurance and other benefits for workers.

Texans are traditionally sensitive to the potential political power of organized labor. Only two industrial labor organizations are generally regarded as significant in Texas government: the Texas affiliates of the AFL-CIO (comprising approximately 60 percent of all Texas union members) and the Texas Oil and Chemical Workers Union. It is doubtful that organized labor's influence really lives up to public perceptions, because union membership is relatively small (but more than 200,000 members) and very few elected or appointed officeholders in Texas come from union ranks.

Professional Groups

Closely related to the economic interest groups are groups dedicated to furthering the interests of a profession or an occupation. **Professional groups** are especially concerned with matters such as standards of admission to a profession or an occupation and licensing of practitioners. Examples of Texas professional and occupational associations are the Association of Engineering Geologists, the Texas Health Care Association, and the Texas Society of Certified Accountants.

Racial and Ethnic Groups

Leaders of **racial and ethnic groups** recognize that only through effective organizations can they hope to achieve their cherished goals (for example, elimination of racial discrimination in employment and representation in state legislatures, city councils, school boards, and other policymaking bodies of government). Racial and ethnic organizations, however, have not exhibited great stability. Most of them have failed to attract and maintain enough members, resources, and member dedication to survive. With some notable results in school integration and local government redistricting, the National Association for the Advancement of Colored People (NAACP) persists as a successful example. The Coalition of Black Democrats has organized within the Democratic Party to support candidates and party positions with which they agree.

In Texas, Hispanic organizations are more numerous than African-American groups, but competition among them has sometimes weakened their impact. The oldest Hispanic group, the League of United Latin American Citizens (LULAC) was founded in 1929. It has worked to acheive equal educational opportunities for Hispanics, as well as full citizenship rights. The Mexican-American Legal Defense and Education Fund (MALDEF) has often used the courts in its efforts to obtain political eqality for Hispanic citizens. Within the Texas Democratic Party, both the Tejano Democrats and the Mexican American Democrats (MAD) attempt to influence party positions and elected officials for the benefit of Hispanics, and especially Mexican Americans. In 1995, a majority of the MAD organization decided to form the Tejano Democrats to be more inclusive in its membership and to represent all Hispanic Democrats, not just Mexican Americans.

Public Interest Groups

A growing number of interest groups claim to represent the public interest rather than narrower private interests. Environmental, consumer, political participation, civil rights, peace, and church groups are often identified as **public interest groups**.

Public interest organizations pursue diverse goals. Common Cause of Texas, for example, focuses primarily on governmental and institutional reform, including support for open-meeting laws, public financing of political campaigns, registration of lobbyists, and financial disclosure laws. Texans for Public Justice also direct their efforts to campaign finance reform. They seek limitations on campaign contributions and electronic filing of contribution information. The Women's Political Caucus promotes equal rights for women and greater participation by women in political activities. The Texas Wildlife Association promotes environmental protection and preservation of the state's wild animals, birds, and fish. The Christian Life Commission (a Baptist agency) deals with many social concerns, such as child care and aging, but has gained more public attention for its opposition to all types of gambling.

In an effort to limit the effectiveness of highly vocal public interest groups, Texans for Lawsuit Reform launched a campaign in 1996 aimed at portraying these groups as big-monied, special-interest organizations. The reform organization intends to limit or eliminate consumers' ability to file lawsuits against businesses in injury cases and to lessen the effects of public interest groups in promoting such lawsuits. Especially targeted have been Citizen Action, the Consumers Union, and Public Citizen, as well as environmental groups such as the Sierra Club, Greenpeace, and the Audubon Society.

Public Officer and Employee Groups

Officers and employees of state and local governments organize to obtain better working conditions, higher wages, more fringe benefits, and better retirement systems. Through their organizational activities, **public officer and employee groups** are able to resist efforts to change the size of state and local governmental bureaucracies. County judge and justice of the peace associations, for example, have been instrumental in blocking reform of justice of the peace courts and county courts in Texas.

At the state level, the largest group is the Texas Public Employees Association (TPEA). Teachers organized on the local level include the Texas State Teachers Association (TSTA), Texas Association of College Teachers (TACT), and Texas Community College Teachers Association (TCCTA). City government groups include the Texas Municipal League, City Management Association, and City Attorneys Association.

Texas Power Groups

Texas legislators readily identify the types of interest groups they consider most powerful: business-oriented trade associations (oil and gas, railroads, and chemicals), professional associations (physicians, lawyers, and teachers), and organized labor groups. Specifically, they often identify the following as wielding above-average influence: lawyers, teachers, brewers, truckers, oil and gas producers, physicians, automobile dealers, bankers, and realtors. Each of these groups maintains a strong linkage with legislators (whose policy decisions control group interests) and with bureaucrats (whose regulatory activities vitally affect group operations).

Business Among the most influential business power groups operating in Texas are the Alliance for Responsible Energy Policy, representing the Texas Railroad Association, the Texas Mining and Reclamation Assocation, and the Association of Electric Companies of Texas; ConnecTexas, which lobbies for the Texas Telephone Association, Southwestern Bell, and GTE

Southwest; and the Texas Conference for Homeowners Rights, including the Texas Bankers Association, Independent Bankers Association of Texas, and Texas Credit Union League. The aim of each group is to produce a show of grassroots support for what are essentially business disputes.

Christian Coalition   With a majority of Texans identifying themselves as conservative Christians,[4] the **Christian Coalition** has emerged as one of Texas's most influential political forces. It is a social interest group that engages in political action primarily within the Republican party. Composed largely of conservative Christians who believe modern society has turned away from basic moral principles, the Christian Coalition advocates a return to strong family values. Issues that have precipitated the Christian Coalition's entrance on the political scene are abortion, homosexuality, limits on prayer in public schools, and the decline of the traditional nuclear family. Mobilizing many pastors and other church leaders, this group aids candidates who voice support for their policy positions. Figure 5.1 presents an example of the campaign literature the group distributed in 1996.

According to Dick Weinhold, the Lone Star State's Christian Coalition chair, during the years 1991 through 1996 a new chapter was formed in Texas almost every week. As a result, by 1996 Texas had the largest Coalition membership of any state. Beginning in 1991, the Coalition had 10,000 members in 38 chapters in Texas; by 1993, its membership had grown to 50,000 in 96 chapters; and in 1996, the membership had increased to 120,000 in 145 chapters.[5] Moreover, Weinhold has been identified as one of "a few people" to whom Governor George W. Bush routinely turns for political advice. Texas, according to Weinhold, is fertile ground for the Coalition's message. He has identified the state's long history of conservative theology and the migration of conservatives to suburban cities as major factors in the growth of the group's membership.

Responding to the Coalition's maneuvering, in 1995 Cecile Richards, daughter of former governor Ann Richards, organized the Texas Freedom Network. Other individuals organized the Texas Freedom Alliance. Both organizations watch the activities of the "radical right," muster mainstream Texas voters, and provide an alternative voice on current political issues.[6] In 1996, two additional groups were formed to combat Coalition activities: the Texas Mainstream Voters Project, which published an alternative "Voters Guide" for the 1996 election, and the Texas Faith Network, which called on religious leaders statewide to resist the Coalition's tactics.

Organizer Weinhold, in assessing the reasons for the Coalition's growth and success, has stressed that "grassroots organization is the key" and that the Coalition's members must be adept at using such political tools as phone banks, high-speed fax networks, and satellite broadcasts.[7] Money for those operations and for newsletters and voter guides, he reported, was obtained from the sale of videos, books, and audiotapes as well as from donations.

Although the Christian Coalition and its allies were not notably successful in influencing the nomination of candidates for top-of-the-ballot positions

FIGURE 5.1 Page 1 of the Christian Coalition's Pro-Family Voter's Guide, distributed widely throughout Texas just prior to the primary elections in March 1996.

PRO-FAMILY
Voter's ★ Guide

PRESIDENTIAL CANDIDATES	Lamar Alexander	Pat Buchanan	Bob Dole	Steve Forbes	Alan Keyes	Dick Lugar
Flat-Rate Federal Income Tax	OPPOSES	SUPPORTS	SUPPORTS	SUPPORTS	OPPOSES	OPPOSES
Religious Freedom Amendment	SUPPORTS	SUPPORTS	SUPPORTS	SUPPORTS	SUPPORTS	UNDECIDED
Prohibit Abortion (Exception: Danger to Mother's Life)	OPPOSES	SUPPORTS	OPPOSES	OPPOSES	SUPPORTS	UNCLEAR
Prohibit Abortion (Exception: Rape, Incest, Mother's Life)	SUPPORTS	OPPOSES	SUPPORTS	OPPOSES	OPPOSES	SUPPORTS
Stop Federal Funding of Planned Parenthood	SUPPORTS	SUPPORTS	SUPPORTS	NO RESPONSE	SUPPORTS	OPPOSES
Prohibit Pornography on the Internet	OPPOSES	SUPPORTS	SUPPORTS	SUPPORTS	OPPOSES	SUPPORTS
Reverse "Don't Ask, Don't Tell" Gay Policy	SUPPORTS	SUPPORTS	SUPPORTS	UNCLEAR	SUPPORTS	OPPOSES
Abolish Congressional Pension System	SUPPORTS	SUPPORTS	UNDECIDED	SUPPORTS	SUPPORTS	OPPOSES

U.S REPRESENTATIVE, DISTRICT 2 (R) CANDIDATE ISSUES	Bruce Babin	Ben Bius	Bob Currie	Jim Hughes	Donna Peterson
Prohibit Abortion (Excluding Mother's Life)	SUPPORTS	UNDECIDED	SUPPORTS	SUPPORTS	SUPPORTS
American Flag Protection Amendment	SUPPORTS	UNDECIDED	SUPPORTS	SUPPORTS	SUPPORTS
Taxpayer Funding of Congressional Campaigns	OPPOSES	OPPOSES	SUPPORTS	OPPOSES	OPPOSES
National Study Commission on Gambling	SUPPORTS	SUPPORTS	OPPOSES	UNDECIDED	SUPPORTS
Prohibit Military Women in Combat	SUPPORTS	SUPPORTS	SUPPORTS	SUPPORTS	UNDECIDED
Restrict Lobbying of Federally-Funded Groups	SUPPORTS	SUPPORTS	SUPPORTS	SUPPORTS	UNDECIDED

U.S REPRESENTATIVE, DISTRICT 3 (R) CANDIDATE ISSUES	Kevin Brady	Gene Fontenot	Don Henderson	Daniel New	Betty Reinbeck	Fred Thornberry
Human Life Amendment	NO RESPONSE	SUPPORTS	UNDECIDED	SUPPORTS	NO RESPONSE	SUPPORTS
Physician-Assisted "Right to Die"	NO RESPONSE	OPPOSES	UNDECIDED	OPPOSES	NO RESPONSE	SUPPORTS
Prohibit Fetal-Tissue Research Funding	NO RESPONSE	SUPPORTS	UNDECIDED	SUPPORTS	NO RESPONSE	OPPOSES
Abolish Congressional Pension System	NO RESPONSE	SUPPORTS	OPPOSES	SUPPORTS	NO RESPONSE	UNDECIDED
Prohibit Military Women in Combat	NO RESPONSE	SUPPORTS	UNDECIDED	SUPPORTS	NO RESPONSE	UNDECIDED
Presidential Line-Item Veto	NO RESPONSE	SUPPORTS	SUPPORTS	OPPOSES	NO RESPONSE	SUPPORTS
Parental Choice in Education (Vouchers)	NO RESPONSE	SUPPORTS	SUPPORTS	OPPOSES	NO RESPONSE	OPPOSES
Stop Federal Funding of Planned Parenthood	NO RESPONSE	SUPPORTS	SUPPORTS	SUPPORTS	NO RESPONSE	UNDECIDED
Reverse "Don't Ask, Don't Tell" Gay Policy	NO RESPONSE	SUPPORTS	SUPPORTS	SUPPORTS	NO RESPONSE	UNDECIDED

This 1996 Primary Voter's Guide is a project of Texas Christian Coalition, American Family Association of Texas, Concerned Women For America, Texas Eagle Forum, Texas Home School Coalition and Texans United For Life. This voter guide is provided for educational purposes only and is not to be construed as an endorsement of any candidate or political party. Each candidate running in a contested primary was sent a 1996 Issues Survey by certified mail. When possible, positions of candidates on issues were verified or determined using voting records and/or public statements. For additional copies, call (817) 545-4044 or (915) 367-1700.

in 1998 (for example, attorney general), they were able to claim victory in a number of down-ballot races (congressional and state legislative) in the Republican primaries. Political commentators have noted that the Christian Coalition is more successful in influencing the outcome of low-profile races in which little is known about any candidate.[8]

Interest Group Activities and Techniques

Interest groups are involved in all types and areas of political activity, many of which overlap the activities of political parties. Group leaders and lobbyists participate in recruiting candidates for government office, defining conflict and shaping consensus (agreement), and building support within and for a political system.

A government sometimes delegates the power to make public policy decisions regarding a profession to an interest group. For example, the State Bar of Texas is an administrative agency of the judicial branch. To practice law in Texas, a licensed attorney must pay dues to the bar and conform to its rules. In effect, the state government has delegated to the state bar the authority to regulate the legal profession. This professional group also attempts to get court reform measures adopted, procedural rules for court actions modified, and methods of selecting state judges reformed.

Group Activities

When interest groups urge their members and others to become involved in activities designed to influence agents of government, they are recruiting people into the political system. Local property taxpayers' associations frequently put forward candidates for both public school and municipal offices in an effort to keep property taxes at a minimum. Organizations of real estate salespeople gain a distinct advantage when their members are appointed to local planning and zoning commissions.

When interest groups serve as an outlet for the discussion of questions of public interest, they help to develop conflict or consensus. Conflict is the more usual outcome because each group is bent on pursuing its own limited ends; this, in turn, leads to clashes with other groups seeking their own ends. In a local school district, for example, an organization of parents and teachers seeking higher pay for teachers and a better physical plan for the school system often is opposed by a local taxpayers' association demanding lower taxes for property owners.

Finally, because governments need support for their policies, interest groups seek to build that support—mostly, of course, for those policies that are in harmony with a particular group's goals. For example, in 1997 the Texas State Teachers Association (TSTA) supported legislative efforts to increase the number of offenses for which disruptive students can be expelled from public school.

Techniques of Interest Groups

Observers soon learn that **interest group techniques** are as varied as their leaders' imaginations. For convenience, these techniques may be classified as lobbying, electioneering, campaign financing by political action committees, and bribery and related illegal practices.

Lobbying   Perhaps the oldest and certainly the best-known interest group tactic is **lobbying.** It is carried on today by **lobbyists**, individuals who attempt to influence government decision makers on behalf of others.[9] Lobbying is most often associated with legislatures and the lawmaking process.

The first task of the lobbyist is to gain access to legislators and other government decision makers. Once the lobbyist has obtained access and captured the desired attention, he or she may use a variety of techniques to make the government official responsive to the group's demands, preferences, and expectations.

One of the principal **lobbying techniques** is personal communication with legislators and other public policymakers. The immediate goal of lobbyists, who are often former members of the Texas Legislature, is to inform the legislators of their group's position on an issue. For maximum effectiveness in using this technique, a lobbyist must select the proper target (for example, a key legislative committee chair, regulatory agency administrator, county commissioner, or city zoning board member).

During the 1997 session of the legislature, registered lobbyists outnumbered legislators by a margin of about nine to one. The 31 senators and 150 House members faced more than 1,600 registered lobbyists, among them many former legislators such as former House Speakers Gib Lewis (who represented 37 clients ranging from Correctional Services Corporation to the University of Mary Hardin Baylor in Belton) and Billy Clayton (who represented almost 30 clients, including R.J. Reynolds Tobacco and the Texas Wine and Grape Growers Association).

The lobbyist chooses the best time and place to speak with an official and determines how best to phrase arguments so they will have a positive impact. Successful lobbyists tend to rely heavily on computers, calculators, radios, pagers, cellular telephones, Internet communications, and other high-tech devices to store and communicate information. They also use such political campaign techniques as direct mailings, television and newspaper advertisements, and grassroots committee action. The purpose of these communication methods is to generate information favorable to an interest group's cause and spread it widely among legislators, other policymakers, and the general public.

A former Texas legislator compared lobbyists to pharmaceutical salespeople who explain new medicines to doctors too busy to keep up with the latest developments. To do their jobs well, successful lobbyists should clearly indicate whom they represent, define their interests, make clear what they want to do and why, answer questions readily, and provide enough information for politicians to make judgments. (For a discussion of effective

In March of 1997, school children, shown here with their sponsor and Senator Mike Moncrief (D-Fort Worth) testified before the Senate Health and Human Services Committee. They were protesting the operation and location of cigarette vending machines. (Courtesy of Texas Senate Media Services.)

lobbying techniques recommended by the TSTA, see the reading on pages 145–148.) Successful lobbyists also befriend as many legislators as possible, especially influential legislative leaders, and get to know their interests and needs. An important study of interest group politics in Texas has concluded that lobbying in Texas has shifted from an emphasis on personal argument to information-based communications.[10]

Yet another influential technique is the creation of an image of broad public support for a group's goals, support the group can readily mobilize when the situation demands. Thus, professional lobbyists rarely ask outright for a favorable vote. Instead, they rely heavily on a grassroots network. The TSTA and the National Rifle Association (NRA) are extremely effective at rallying grassroots support.

A third important technique involves providing favors for legislators and other government decision makers. Some common favors include daily or weekly luncheon and dinner gatherings; free liquor, wine, or beer; tickets for entertainment events, air transportation, and athletic contests; and miscellaneous gifts.

Prompted by media reports of big spending by lobbyists and a grand jury investigation into influence peddling, the 72nd Legislature created the eight-member **Texas Ethics Commission** to enforce new legal standards for lobbyists and public officials. This 1991 legislation enhanced the power of public prosecutors to use evidence that contributions to lawmakers by lobbyists and other individuals are more than mere campaign donations. It expanded disclosure requirements for lobbyists and legislators, put a $500 annual cap on lobbyist-provided food and drink for a lawmaker, and banned honoraria (gratuitous payments in recognition of professional services for which there is no legally enforceable obligation to pay) and lobby-paid pleasure trips (unless a legislator makes a speech or participates in a panel discussion). There is no indication, however, that campaign contributions have been reduced significantly.

Detailed records of political contributions and how they are spent must be filed between two and seven times each year with the Texas Ethics Commission. Those records are open to the public. Politicians may file their reports electronically either by modem or on a computer disk. These reports are posted almost instantly on the commission's electronic bulletin board. Anyone can dial into the system with a personal computer modem and call up electronically filed reports. The commission's web site lists the names of lobbyists and their clients as well as a range of payments received by each lobbyist. In addition the Ethics Commission includes opinions on campaign finance and other matters at this site. The Texas Ethics Commission's site on the World Wide Web can be found at <http://www.ethics.state.tx.us>.

Disclosures required by the ethics law of 1991 reveal that some legislators and lobbyists are business partners. Examples of such arrangements include joint ownership with lobbyists of a West Texas vineyard by House Speaker Pete Laney and a South Texas radio station by Senator Rodney Ellis.

The Texas Ethics Commission is authorized to hear ethics complaints against state officials, candidates for office, and state employees. Its budget allows about 60 reviews each year.

An analysis of registered lobbyists during the 74th Legislature bears out the close connection between lobbyists and legislators. At least half of the top-spending lobbyists were former lawmakers, former aides to a House speaker, former state executives, or former high-level bureaucrats. Moreover, a total of some 50 ex-legislators were registered lobbyists.

Spurred by the disclosure provisions of the 1991 ethics legislation, more than 1,600 special-interest lobbyists registered in 1997. Most of them pushed the agendas of insurance companies, banks, energy producers, and other businesses.Not all lobbyists are full-time professionals. Most work for businesses and occasionally go to Austin to speak to lawmakers about their concerns. There are also lobbyists who represent consumers rather than businesses.

When elected speaker in 1993, James E. ("Pete") Laney pledged that he would not immediately seek employment as a lobbyist after leaving the speaker's office. He also placed a similar restriction on his top staff members. Laney's action was prompted by the growing number of staff members who had resigned to become more highly paid lobbyists.

Electioneering Participating in the process of nominating and electing persons to public office, commonly called **electioneering,** is widespread among interest groups. If a candidate who favors a group's goals can be elected, the group has a realistic expectation that its interests will be recognized and protected once the candidate takes office. Because of the danger of antagonizing party factions, however, most interest groups participate in the nominating process in a less public manner.

Interest group participation in the election process takes a variety of forms. Publishing or otherwise publicizing the political records of incumbent candidates is one of the simplest and most common **forms of interest group participation**. Providing favored candidates with group membership information and mailing lists is a valuable contribution that helps candidates solicit money and votes. Groups also may allow candidates to speak at their meetings, thus giving them opportunities for direct contact with voters and possible media coverage.

A third type of group participation in electioneering involves getting out the vote—the favorable vote. Typically this entails mailing campaign propaganda publicly endorsing specific candidates, making telephone calls to members, transporting voters to the polls, and door-to-door canvassing (soliciting votes).

Campaign Financing by Political Action Committees Because political campaigns are becoming more expensive with each election, contributions from interest group members constitute an important form of participation. Although individual group members continue to supply money, goods, and services, there is a growing tendency for financial assistance to come from **political action committees (PACs)**. Texas statutes prohibit political contributions by corporations and labor unions to individual candidates but not to political parties. These and other groups, however, may form PACs composed of their members and then delegate to the PACs the task of raising funds or obtaining free goods and services for office seekers.

A PAC may also provide support in political campaigns involving issues affecting the group's vital interests. For example, in the 1996 legislative campaigns, Texans for Lawsuit Reform (a group trying to limit damage awards against businesses) contributed over $600,000 to selected candidates for the Texas House of Representatives.

In the 1996 campaigns, the top ten political contributors from January 1995 through June 1996 were all PACs. This was made possible, in large measure, because in Texas there are no effective limits on what PACs can raise and dispense. During the 1995–1996 period, PACs contributed more than $27 million to candidates for positions in the Texas Legislature. Another $17 million went to candidates for other elective offices.

PAC activity continues to increase, with more than 1,000 PACs reported in Texas in 1998. Although PACs bring together people who are able to make campaign contributions, their influence does not end there. Individual PACs also cooperate to form coalitions or alliances, thus linking their activities in electoral politics to other areas of the political process. Two examples of this latter type of activity, called **power linkage,** are registering and turning out voters and lobbying the Texas Legislature.

Perhaps the purest form of linkage between PACs and state and local governments is the connection between PACs' election campaign contributions and the lobbying activities of their related organizations. It is therefore a joining of influence in one part of the political process (the campaign) to influence another part (the legislative process). In this way, interest groups are able to exercise far greater influence over the output of the Texas Legislature than their number would indicate.

Bribery and Unethical Practices Bribery and blackmail, although not common practices in Texas, nevertheless have taken place in state and local government. There were, for example, some well-publicized scandals in the 1950s involving Texas legislators. In the 1970s, the Sharpstown Bank scandal involved Speaker of the House Gus Mutscher and others. Each scandal has rocked the state with charges of **bribery and related practices**.

In February 1980, on the basis of an FBI investigation, House Speaker Billy Clayton accepted (but did not spend) $5,000 to influence the awarding of a state employee insurance contract. Because he had not cashed the checks, a federal district court found Clayton innocent of all bribery charges. In January 1981, he was elected to a fourth term as Speaker of the House.

In 1991, five-time Speaker Gib Lewis was indicted on two misdemeanor ethics charges by a Travis County grand jury. Rather than face a trial subjecting him to a stiffer penalty, Lewis agreed to a plea bargain, was fined $2,000, and announced his decision not to seek re-election to the House of Representatives in 1992. As noted on page 165, he is now a very successful lobbyist.

Gross and flagrant illegalities occur infrequently because of the risk involved and the effectiveness of laws governing the conduct of public officials. Ethics legislation enacted by the 72nd Legislature in 1991 defines any campaign contribution accepted with an agreement to act in the contributor's interest as a felony. The ethics law prohibits a candidate or official from receiving a contribution in the capitol building itself.

Interest Group Power and Public Policy

The **political influence of interest groups** is determined by several factors. It is argued by some that a group with a sizable membership, above-average financial resources, knowledgeable and dedicated leadership, and a high degree of unity (agreement on and commitment to goals among the membership) will be able to exert virtually irresistible pressure on government decision makers. Critics of this position insist that other factors external to the group are also highly relevant. Research indicates that a strong relationship exists between the larger socioeconomic conditions in a state and the power of interest groups. These findings have led some observers to conclude that states with high levels of population, industrialization, per capita wealth, and formal education are likely to produce strong political parties and relatively weak interest groups.

Others point out that the extent to which the aims of an interest group are consistent with broad-based community beliefs greatly increases the probability that the group will be successful and wield considerable power. They also observe that if interest groups are well represented in the structure of the government itself, their power will be enhanced materially; weak governments ordinarily will mean strong interest groups.

Interest Groups and Public Policy in Texas

Given the preceding analysis of the influence of interest groups, let us consider the **role of interest groups in making public policy** in Texas. As Chapter 1 shows, Texas is among the most heavily industrialized and urbanized states; thus, it possesses many of the characteristics that tend to produce strong political parties and relatively weak interest groups. The analysis of Texas political parties in Chapter 4, however, fails to confirm this tendency.

Texas is included among those states with very strong interest groups and relatively weak political parties. Three circumstances explain why industrial, urban, wealthy Texas does not fit the expected pattern. First, many Texas interest groups identify with free enterprise, self-reliance, and other elements of the state's culture; thus, they are readily accepted. Texans are predisposed by temperament to distrust government and its agents but trust interest groups and their lobbyists.

Second, until recently, the century-long one-party tradition in Texas rendered interparty competition negligible. The absence of strong parties and meaningful competition among them has made Texas government vulnerable to the pressures of strong interest groups and their lobbyists.

Finally, the Texas Constitution of 1876 and its many amendments have created state and local governments beset by weak and uncoordinated institutions. Faced with a government lacking sufficient strength to offer any real opposition, interest groups often obtain decisions favorable to their causes.

Texas government is well known as one that is controlled by interest groups, but the Lone Star State interest groups' actual control over government probably falls short of their reputation for complete domination. In many cases, however, a network linking lobbyists, regulatory agency officials (bureaucrats), and friendly legislators zealously guards and protects group interests.

Interest Group Power Linkage

As Figure 5.2 illustrates, a triangular relationship frequently links an interest group, the bureaucracy, and the Texas Legislature. Together they function as a team to gain special treatment for each member of the trio. Some specific examples may help illustrate the ways in which the linkage works to the advantage of team members.

The interest group assists bureaucrats by providing testimony favorable to their proposals in legislative committee hearings and by lobbying before committees and influential legislators to obtain additional funds for agency operations. In return, the interest group gains assistance from the bureaucrats in shaping agency programs and regulations, recruits staff personnel for agency advisory committees and noncareer positions, and casts informal vetoes over agency decisions.

Interest groups support the legislative committees by providing campaign contributions to committee members, transportation to gather data, and advice from group lobbyists, who are often experts on the subject under consideration. From committees, interest groups expect to receive formal and informal access to bureaucrats and to funds for programs that benefit the group.

Finally, bureaucrats reward committee members with favorable treatment of the "folks back home," special consideration for the interest group allied with the committee, and advice concerning the distribution of goods, patronage, and government contracts at the disposal of the committee. In return, the committee often develops and acts favorably on legislation giving the bureaucracy more discretion, authority, and money. The committee also is frequently able to help the bureaucracy acquire better physical facilities and more personnel.

Pinpointing Political Power

Assessing the distribution of political power and influence in American government is difficult, and their distribution in Texas is especially complex. There is no simple top-down or bottom-up arrangement; rather, political decisions (especially policy decisions) are made by a wide variety of individuals and groups. Some of these decision makers participate in local ad hoc

FIGURE 5.2 Interest Group Power Linkages

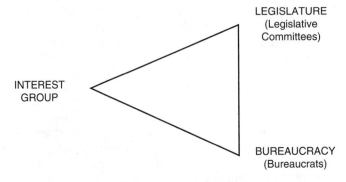

Source: Adapted from Kenneth J. Meier, *Politics and the Bureaucracy* (North Scituate, Mass.: Duxbury, 1979), p. 180.

(specific purpose) organizations; others wield influence through statewide groups. Determining which individuals or groups have the greatest influence often depends on the issue or issues involved.

The political influence of any interest group cannot be fairly calculated by looking at the distribution of only one political asset, whether it is money, status, knowledge, organization, or sheer numbers. Nevertheless, we may safely conclude that organized interest groups in Texas often put the unorganized citizenry at a great disadvantage when public issues are at stake.

Looking Ahead

How and where Texas interest groups exert their influence over public policy decisions are interwoven within the analyses of local governments, the Texas Legislature, executive departments, and the state's bureaucracy. Students should be alert to evidence of interest group participation in Texas government at all levels and in all branches. No better illustration of the power of interest groups in Texas politics can be found than that practiced in the legislative process, the subject of the next chapter.

Notes

1. Lynn Tran and Andrew Wheat, *Mortgaged House: Campaign Contributions to Texas Representatives, 1995–1996* (Austin: Sponsored by Public Citizen's Texas Office, Texans for Public Justice, and U.S. PIRG Education Fund, January, 1998).
2. Steffen W. Schmidt, Mack C. Shelley II, and Barbara A. Bardes, *American Government and Politics Today* (Belmont, Ca.: Wadsworth, 1997), p. 249.
3. H. C. Pittman, *Inside the Third House: A Veteran Lobbyist Takes a 50-Year Frolic Through Texas Politics* (Austin: Eakin Press, 1992), p. 219.
4. Michael Pearson, "Poll: Religious Right Label Irrelevant," *Corpus Christi Caller-Times,* September 4, 1994.
5. Mary Ann Roser, "Might Makes Right," *Austin American-Statesman,* February 25, 1996.
6. Peggy Fikac, "Alliance Formed to Monitor Radical Right," *Houston Chronicle,* October 1, 1995.
7. Roser, "Might Makes Right."
8. Alan Bernstein, "Results Show the Hotze Factor Still Strong but Not Invincible," *Houston Chronicle*, April 16, 1998, p.29A.
9. Ethics legislation enacted in 1991 defines a lobbyist as any person who is paid at least $200 per quarter to influence public officials or who spends at least $200 per quarter to entertain them.
10. Keith E. Hamm and Charles W. Wiggins, "Texas: The Transformation from Personal to Informational Lobbying," in *Interest Group Politics in the Southern States,* ed. Ronald J. Hrebenar and Olive S. Thomas (Tuscaloosa, Ala.: University of Alabama Press, 1992), p. 180.

Key Terms and Concepts

politics
interest group
pressure group
functional representation
right of association
decentralized government
decentralized political party
   system
ideology
organizational patterns
centralized organization
decentralized organization
group leadership
economic group
umbrella organization
trade association
organized labor group
professional group
racial and ethnic groups

public interest group
public officer and employee
   groups
Christian Coalition
interest group techniques
lobbying
lobbyist
lobbying techniques
Texas Ethics Commission
electioneering
forms of interest group
   participation
political action committee (PAC)
power linkage
bribery and related practices
political influence of interest
   groups
role of interest groups in
   making public policy

SELECTED READING

*A Guide to Lobbying**

Texas State Teachers Association

There are certain methods used by effective lobbyists. Common-sense techniques include being courteous and well-informed. This article from the Texas State Teacher's Association's website <http://www.tsta.org> highlights such advice, and it points out other techniques that can make one a successful lobbyist.

"Lobbying" is defined by *Webster's Third New Collegiate Dictionary* as:

- Conduct[ing] activities aimed at influencing public officials and especially members of a legislative body on legislation
- Promot[ing] or secur[ing] the passage of legislation by influencing public officials
- Attempt[ing] to influence or sway a public official toward a desired action

There are different types of lobbying, [including]:

- In-person usually at the legislator's office back home in the district or at the Capitol
- By mail, including letter, fax or telegram, or in some cases, e-mail
- By phone

Becoming an Effective Lobbyist

The most effective lobbyist is one who is knowledgeable about the individual legislator and the issues to be addressed. To be knowledgeable about the issues, read *TSTA Advocate*, the weekly *Legislative Contact* and call the TSTA Hotline on a daily basis. If you have questions, call one of the staff in the Government Relations [GR] Division at TSTA Headquarters.

To be knowledgeable about the legislator, compile a data file on the member as soon as possible. A good source is "A Guide to the Texas Legislature," which includes profiles of all legislators. You can call the GR Division and ask for your legislator's individual profile. Include in your file:

*Reprinted by permission of the Texas State Teachers Association. TSTA is an organization of public school teachers.

- Address and phone number
- Interests, hobbies, etc. (this will help in conversations later)
- Committees and appointments
- Attitude toward public education and TSTA
- People who influence the member
- Staff [members] name[s] and address[es], both in the home office and in Austin. If the legislator has an education aide, note the person's name, phone number, and title.
- Always contact the GR staff to receive the most up-to-date information on an issue, or the current organizational strategy, before contacting the legislator.

General Rules for Effective Lobbying

- Contact the GR staff for the latest information on issues, or the current organizational strategy, before contacting the legislator.
- Always introduce yourself as a member of the Association. A simple "May I have a few minutes of your time?" will set the stage if you have not scheduled an appointment.
- Be gracious to the legislator's receptionist and/or aide. A rude tone will affect your relationship with all in the office, including the legislator. Treat all staff with respect.
- Listen carefully to what the member is saying and write notes after the conversation so you do not forget important points.
- Get down to business quickly. Be brief, be direct, be simple, and above all, be accurate. Do not philosophize. Know your topic and be prepared for questions. Remember that your legislator hears many viewpoints. You want him/her to remember yours, so be factual.
- Be friendly, be persuasive, be professional, and be courteous. Do not argue or belabor the point. Your role is to explain, inform, and persuade. Do not threaten or attack.
- Never make up a position for the Association or give an answer to a question that you are not familiar with. The appropriate response is "I'll get back to you with the answer." Remember, the legislator is depending on you to give accurate information, not guess.
- Think of the hard questions beforehand and be prepared.
- Try to get a commitment if you can. If the legislator refuses to give it to you, ask that he/she get back to you before taking a position against you or say that you will check back before a position or vote is taken.
- Keep in mind that the legislator may try to lobby you. This is especially true if the legislator senses that there is not a firm commitment on the part of our members to our issues. This will hurt our lobby effort.
- When finishing the conversation, always thank the legislator for his/her time. If he/she has asked for follow-up information, quickly send it with a note offering further assistance. Include your name and your local association/TSTA.

- Don't give up if you are not successful the first time. In fact, many times success is in just making the initial contact. Communications established through discussion can aid future lobbying efforts.
- Keep in mind that many or most of the legislators have little or no direct knowledge or experience with the public schools, except that they may have attended public school or their children are in, or have gone through, the public school system. A large part of your job is to help them understand what it is really like to be an educator in the classroom of today.
- Though your appointment is with the legislator, due to his/her busy schedule, last minute changes may result in meeting with the legislator's aide. Do not be discouraged but cordially accommodate the change and make your presentation to the aide. Legislator's aides are very knowledgeable about the issues as it is their job to keep the legislator informed. They are very influential with their legislator and can advocate our point of view.
- Report your progress to the Government Relations Division by mailing a reporting form, letter or brief note, or through a phone conversation.

Lobbying at the Legislature

- Prior to coming to Austin, call the legislator's office and make an appointment. Inform staff in the Government Relations Division that you, and others in your group, will be coming to Austin to meet with your legislator. Ask staff to provide a legislative briefing for your group. The briefings usually take place at the TSTA Headquarters.
- Attend a briefing provided by the Government Relations staff. The briefings will include the latest information on TSTA issues and organizational strategies.
- Introduce yourself to the legislator's receptionist and tell him/her you are there for an appointment. Remember, because of the legislator's busy schedule you may meet with the legislative aide instead.
- After pleasantries, get down to business. Talk about the issues, present facts, and answer questions.
- Leave information, with your name and phone number, for the legislator to read.
- As the session progresses, the level of activity picks up. Therefore, it may be necessary to meet your legislator outside of the House or Senate chamber. This is a very effective place to lobby if you are trying to get the legislator to commit to your position and vote a certain way.
- All legislators are assigned to committees. This is another place that is convenient to lobby legislators. It is also a place to watch your legislator in action. If you are attending a committee meeting of your legislator, be polite and listen to the proceedings. If you need to carry on a lengthy conversation with another TSTA member or member of the audience, step outside.
- Take notes on issues of interest to TSTA and what the legislator says during public discussions in committee meetings.

- When the meeting adjourns, if you need to speak again with the legislator, do so quickly.
- If your legislator voted correctly on a TSTA issue, or spoke favorably on an issue, thank the member when the meeting adjourns. Follow up with a note of thanks.
- While at the Legislature, you may wish to watch your legislator during meetings of the House or Senate. You may do so by sitting in the House or Senate gallery. Rules of the gallery demand that you not engage in loud conversations.
- Debrief with the Government Relations staff, if possible, or report necessary information to the Government Relations Division.

Chapter 6

★

THE LEGISLATURE

Courtesy of Jason Knittle.

*T*he Texas Legislature and its members frequently attract the attention of the state's editorial cartoonists. For example, Jason Knittle's cartoon concerning Representative Irma Rangel (D-Kingsville) responds to Rangel's criticism of the Texas Academic Skills Program test (TASP) prepared by the Educational Testing Service in Princeton, New Jersey.[1] She is reported to have stated, "The TASP is a threatening test instead of an encouraging exam and does not show students' basic skills and knowledge," and "Some students do not need math."[2]

Students must take the TASP test, or one of the alternative tests designated by the Texas Higher Education Coordinating Board, before enrolling in any college-level course at one of the state's public colleges or universities. A satisfactory score on the American College Test (ACT), the Scholastic Assessment Test (SAT), or the Texas Assessment of Academic Skills (TAAS) test exempts a student from the TASP test. Because millions of Texas students and parents are affected, it is natural that legislators will be praised or criticized for their statements and legislative actions regarding public schools and institutions of higher education.

All Texas legislators are popularly elected, so voters must accept credit or blame for the performance of their representatives and senators. The work of these policymakers is vital to everyone. They make the laws that affect the life, liberty, and property of all persons residing in the Lone Star State.

A Preliminary View

Lawmaking by an elected representative body with many members is a slow, frustrating, and often disappointing process. Moreover, most citizens are impatient with political tactics and procedural delays, even if their policy objectives are achieved. Usually they are dissatisfied with the inevitable compromises involved in the **legislative process** by which the Texas Legislature creates and enacts legislation.

Looking down at the House or Senate floor from third-floor gallery seats, visitors to the Capitol are likely to be appalled by the shouting, whistling, pushing, prank playing, and even sleeping that all too frequently occur in the chambers of the Texas Legislature. Debate seldom reflects a high level of statesmanship. Legislative conduct is sometimes best described as bizarre, especially during the hours that mark the end of a session.

On one memorable occasion, a stripper performed in the House lobby to celebrate the birthday of a representative. In the course of the 75th Legislature's regular session, some House members howled and barked at Representative Arlene Wohlgemuth (R–Burleson) as she was presented with a box of dog biscuits. This conduct on the House floor was inspired by Wohlgemuth's defense of her bill authorizing judges to order the killing of dogs that cause injury requiring medical treatment or hospitalization.[3]

Legislative Framework

In all of their state constitutions, Texans have entrusted enactment of bills and adoption of resolutions to popularly elected legislators. This is the essence of representative government. As in a majority of states, the lawmaking branch of Texas government is officially termed the **legislature**. Nebraska has a **unicameral** (single-chamber or one-house) legislature. Texas and all 48 other states have **bicameral** (two-chamber or two-house) lawmaking bodies that are similar to the federal government's Congress in Washington, D.C.

Composition

In Texas and 40 other states, the larger legislative chamber is called the **House of Representatives**. Remaining states use the terms *assembly, house of delegates,* or *general assembly*. In the 49 states with bicameral legislatures, the more numerous chamber ranges in size from 40 members in Alaska to 400 members in New Hampshire. Texas has 150 members in its House of Representatives. The less numerous legislative chamber is called the **Senate**. Alaska has the smallest senate, with 20 members; Minnesota has the largest, with 67. The Texas Senate has 31 members.

Election and Terms of Office

Texas legislators are elected by voters residing in representative and senatorial districts. Representatives are elected for two years; senators are elected for four years. Terms of office for members of both houses begin in January of odd-numbered years.

Senatorial redistricting occurs in the first odd-numbered year in a decade (for example, 2001). A new Senate is elected in the general election of the following year (for example, November 2002). In January of the next odd-numbered year (for example, 2003), Senators draw lots, using 31 numbered pieces of paper sealed in envelopes. The 16 who draw odd numbers will serve for four years; the 15 who draw even numbers will serve for only two years. Thereafter, approximately half of the senators (that is, 15 or 16) are elected in even-numbered years for four-year terms.

If a member of the legislature dies, resigns, or is expelled from office, the vacancy is filled by special election. A legislator may be expelled by a two-thirds majority vote of the membership of the legislator's chamber.

Sessions

A Texas statute requires a **regular session** to begin on the second Tuesday in January of each odd-numbered year. In practice, these regular biennial sessions always run for the full 140 days authorized by the Texas Constitution. **Special sessions,** lasting no longer than 30 days each, may be called by the governor at any time. During a special session, the legislature may consider only those matters placed before it by the governor.

Visitors watch Senate Proceedings from the gallery. (Senate Media Services)

Such limits indicate a deep-seated popular distrust of legislators and a fear of change.

Because special sessions were common until 1993, particularly for the purpose of dealing with budgetary problems, some legislators have advocated annual sessions. In 1993, for example, the Senate approved a joint resolution proposing a constitutional amendment that would have authorized a 55-day budget session in each even-numbered year. Although the proposal died in the House, a similar resolution might be adopted by both chambers in a future session and then submitted to Texas voters in a general or special election. Such budget sessions are used in some other states.

Districting

Providing equal representation in a legislative chamber involves dividing a state into districts with approximately the same number of inhabitants. Population distribution changes constantly due to migration of people and to different birth rates and death rates. Therefore, the boundaries of legislative districts must be redrawn periodically to ensure equitable representation. Such **redistricting** can be politically painful to a legislator. It may take away territory that has provided strong voter support for a particular lawmaker; it may add to a legislator's district an area that produces little support and much opposition; or it may include within a new district the residences

Visitors have a gallery view of House Proceedings. (Senate Media Services)

of two or more representatives or senators, only one of whom can be re-elected to represent the district.

Framers of the Texas Constitution of 1876 stipulated that "the legislature shall, at its first session after the publication of each United States decennial census, apportion the State into Senatorial and Representative districts." Nevertheless, in the decades that followed, the legislature sometimes failed to redivide the state's population and map new districts for legislators. Thus, some districts became heavily populated and greatly underrepresented; others experienced population decline or slow growth, resulting in overrepresentation.

In 1948, the inequities of legislative districting in Texas finally led to the adoption of a state constitutional amendment designed to pressure the legislature to remedy this situation. Under the amendment, failure of the legislature to redistrict during the first regular session following a decennial census brings the Legislative Redistricting Board into operation. This board consists of the following five ex officio (that is, "holding other office") members: lieutenant governor, speaker of the House of Representatives, attorney general, comptroller of public accounts, and commissioner of the General Land Office. The board must meet within 90 days after the legislative session and redistrict the state within another 60 days.

Although new legislative districts were drawn after the federal censuses of 1950 and 1960, the Texas Constitution's apportionment formulas for the House and Senate discriminated against heavily populated urban counties.

These formulas were not changed until after the U.S. Supreme Court held in *Reynolds* v. *Sims* (1964) that "the seats in both houses of a bicameral state legislature must be apportioned on a population basis." This "one person, one vote" principle was applied first in Texas by a federal district court in *Kilgarlin* v. *Martin* (1965).

Over the last three decades, every redistricting measure enacted by the Texas Legislature has resulted in complaints about **gerrymandering**. This process involves drawing districts to include or exclude certain groups of voters and thus influences the outcomes of elections. Usually such districts are odd shaped rather than compact, as was the case with districts created under the guidance of Governor Elbridge Gerry for Massachussetts in 1812. Many state and federal court battles have been fought over the constitutionality of Texas's legislative districting arrangements.

Members of the Texas Senate have always represented **single-member districts;** that is, the voters of each district elect one senator. Most of the 31 senatorial districts cover several counties, but a few big-city senatorial districts are formed from the territory of one county or part of a county. Redistricting according to the 1990 census provides for a population of about 548,000 in each senatorial district.

Until 1971, a Texas county with two or more seats in the House used **multimember districts** to elect representatives at large. Thus, a voter in such a county could vote in more than one House race. In 1971, however, single-member districts were established in Harris, Dallas, and Bexar counties. Four years later, the single-member districting system was extended to all other counties electing more than one representative. Today, all representatives are elected on a single-member district basis. Election results demonstrate that single-member districts reduce campaign costs and increase the probability that more African-American and Hispanic candidates will be elected. As a result of the 1990 census, redistricting provided each state representative district with a population of approximately 113,000.

Not only does the Texas Legislature redraw its own district lines, but in the year following each federal census, it must also establish new districts for all U.S. representative seats apportioned to the Lone Star State by the U.S. Congress. Based on the 1990 census, each of these 30 congressional districts has a population of about 566,000.

Compensation

Many states pay legislators ridiculously low salaries (for example, an average of $300 per year in Rhode Island and $100 per year in New Hampshire). In contrast, lawmakers in California receive an annual salary of $75,600. Members of the Texas Legislature receive low pay, reasonable allowances, and a relatively generous retirement pension after a minimum period of service.

Pay and Per Diem Allowance

Originally, Texas legislators' salaries and per diem (daily) personal allowances during a regular or special session were specified by the state Constitution and could be changed only by constitutional amendment. Thus, a 1975 amendment increased annual salaries from $4,800 to $7,200 for senators, representatives (including the speaker of the House), and the president of the Senate (the lieutenant governor). That amendment also increased their per diem allowance from $12 to $30. Since adoption of a 1991 amendment, however, the Texas Ethics Commission sets the per diem allowance and may recommend salary increases for legislators and even higher salaries for the speaker and the lieutenant governor. Such salary changes must be submitted to Texas voters for approval or disapproval at the next general election.

For the 75th Legislature, which convened in January 1997, the per diem allowance was $95 for senators, representatives, and the lieutenant governor. This amounted to a total of $12,700 per official for the 140-day regular session. (The maximum amount permitted as a federal income tax deduction by the Internal Revenue Service was $101 per day.) No salary increases had been recommended and approved, however, so in 1998 all Texas legislators (including the House speaker) and the lieutenant governor were still receiving an annual salary of only $7,200.

In 1995, Public Citizen (a public interest lobby organization) surveyed Texas legislators to determine the number of hours per week they devoted to legislative affairs and the amount of yearly earnings they lost as a result of legislative service. For the 41 representatives who responded, the average legislative workweek was about 62 hours during a session and 33 hours during the interim between sessions. For the five senators who responded, the average workweek was about 51 hours during a session and nearly 27 hours during the interim. Representatives estimated lost earnings of $47,000 per year, and senators estimated lost earnings of $36,000. Despite the limited number of responses (especially from senators), these data do provide a rough picture of three discouraging aspects of legislative service: long hours, low pay, and lost earnings.

Contingency Expense Allowances

Each chamber authorizes contingency expense allowances for its members. From January 1997 to January 1999, for example, every representative's operating account was credited monthly with $8,500. House members in the 75th Legislature could use money in this account to cover the cost of travel, postage, office operations, and staff salaries.

During the regular session of the 75th Legislature and the following three summer months, each senator was restricted to a total of not more than $25,000 per month for secretarial and other office staff salaries and for staff travel within Texas. For the next 16 months prior to the beginning of the 76th regular session in January 1999, the maximum senatorial staff allowance was set at $24,000 per month. (See the reading on pages 183–185 for information concerning the role of hundreds of college students and recent graduates in the legislative process.)

Retirement Pension

Under the terms of the State Employees Retirement Act of 1975, legislators contribute 8 percent of their salaries to a retirement fund. Retirement pay for senators and representatives amounts to 2.5 percent of a district judge's salary for each year served. As a result of an unpublicized amendment slipped into a state employee benefits bill passed in the closing days of the 72nd regular session in May 1991, a legislator with 12 years of service may retire at age 50 or with 8 years of service at age 60. Thus, Carl Parker of Port Arthur, who served in the House and Senate for a total of 32 years before losing an election in 1994, became eligible for a pension of nearly $55,000 per year after he finished his last term of office. Of course, many legislators do not serve long enough to qualify for a pension.

Membership

Members of the Texas Legislature must meet specific state constitutional qualifications concerning citizenship, voter status, state residence, district residence, and age. Despite such restrictions, millions of Texans possess all the prescribed legal qualifications. As is true of the memberships in other state legislatures, however, the biographical characteristics of members of recent Texas legislatures suggest restricted opportunities for election to either of the two chambers.

Qualifications of Members

The Texas Constitution specifies that House and Senate members must be citizens of the United States, qualified Texas voters, and residents of the districts they represent for one year immediately preceding a general election. In matters of state residence and age, however, qualifications differ between the two chambers. (See Table 6.1.)

A House candidate must have resided in Texas for two years before being elected, whereas a Senate candidate must have five years of state residence. To be eligible for House membership, a person must be at least 21 years of age; to serve in the Senate, a person must be at least 26. If there is a question concerning constitutional qualifications or a dispute over election returns, each legislative chamber determines who will be seated.

Characteristics of Members

The typical Texas legislator is an Anglo, Protestant male between 35 and 50 years of age, was born in Texas, is an attorney or a businessperson, and has

TABLE 6.1 Constitutional Qualifications for Membership in the Texas Legislature

Qualification	House	Senate
Citizenship	United States citizen	United States citizen
Voter status	Qualified Texas voter	Qualified Texas voter
Residence in district to be represented	1 year immediately preceding election	1 year immediately preceding election
Texas residence	2 years immediately preceding election	5 years immediately preceding election
Age	21 years	26 years

Source: Constitution of Texas, Art. 3, Secs. 6 and 7.

served one or more previous terms of office. Such characteristics do not guarantee any predetermined reaction to issues and events, but legislators tend to be influenced by their experience and environment, both of which have policy consequences. Any study of the legislature must pay some attention to the biographical characteristics of legislators.

Gender Classification Anglo males continue to dominate the Texas Legislature, but their number has declined in recent years. At the beginning of the 62nd Legislature's regular session in January 1971, only one woman senator was listed on the legislative rolls. Twenty-six years later, when the 75th Legislature convened in January 1997, the number of women had increased to 33 (3 senators and 30 representatives). Nevertheless, because about 51 percent of Texas's inhabitants and 53 percent of its registered voters are women, their representation in the legislature continues to be disproportionately low.

Racial/Ethnic Classification Representation of racial/ethnic minorities increased substantially from the late 1960s through the early 1990s. Barbara Jordan, the first African American to be elected to the Texas Senate in the twentieth century, served from 1967 until she was seated in the U.S. Congress in 1973.

At the beginning of the regular session of the 75th Legislature in 1997, Senate seats were held by two African Americans and seven Mexican Americans. In the House, there were 14 African-American representatives and 28 Mexican-American representatives. Despite the fact that both African Americans and Mexican Americans have been underrepresented in the Texas Legislature, African-American representation increased from 3 legislators in 1971 to 16 in 1997, and the number of Mexican-American legislators grew from 12 to 35 during that period.

Political Party Affiliation In the election of 1960, no Republican won a seat in the 57th Legislature (1961–1962); 36 years later, 17 Republican senators and 68 Republican representatives were elected to serve in the 75th Legislature (1997–1998). Thus, between January 1961 and January 1997, the political division in the House shifted from a total of 150 Democrats and no Republicans to a majority of 82 Democrats and a minority of 68 Republicans. During that same period, the political lineup in the Senate changed from 31 Democrats and no Republicans to a minority of 14 Democrats and a majority of 17 Republicans.

Most African-American and Mexican-American legislators have been Democrats. Like African-American and Mexican-American legislators, Republican legislators tend to reside in metropolitan areas. But whereas African-American and Mexican-American lawmakers are usually elected by central-city residents, Republican senators and representatives receive their strongest support from suburban voters. Because legislative districts in South Texas tend to have large numbers of Mexican Americans in both rural and urban areas, voters in most of those districts elect Democrats who are Mexican Americans.

Age The minimum age qualifications set by the Texas Constitution are 26 years for senators and 21 years for representatives. Although the ages of senators have tended to be slightly higher than those of representatives, in 1997, the average (arithmetic mean) age of House members was 1.4 years higher than that of Senators. Senators and representatives are rarely under 30.

Occupation Traditionally Texas legislators have included a large number of attorneys, many business owners or managers, lesser numbers of real estate and insurance people, and some farmers and ranchers. Teachers, medical personnel, engineers, and accountants have been very few in number, and almost none have been laborers. Although most legislators are identified with only one occupation, others claim two or more, and several are business executives who also serve on boards of directors of various firms. Such a variety of occupational backgrounds provides a broad range of expertise in dealing with diverse public problems, but individuals with modest or low incomes are seldom elected to either chamber of the Texas Legislature.

Lawyer-legislators may receive retainers from corporations and special-interest groups, with the understanding that legal services will be performed if needed. In some cases, these retainer payments are intended to influence legislation rather than guarantee availability of legal counsel. It is also noteworthy that lawyer-legislators exercise a decisive influence in amending and revising the Penal Code and the Code of Criminal Procedure. Some of them receive big fees for representing clients before state agencies.

Education In government, as in business, most positions of leadership call for college credentials. Thus, it is not surprising to find that nearly all members of recent Texas legislatures attended one or more institutions of higher education and most could claim a bachelor's degree. In 1995, members of the 74th Legislature reported the following degrees: bachelor's, 161;

master's, 41; law, 59; doctorate, 4; dental surgery, 2; theology, 1; medicine, 1; veterinary medicine, 1; and chiropractic, 1.

Religious Affiliation Although the Texas Constitution requires the separation of church and state, religion may play a critical role in the formulation of public policy. Therefore, political analysts must take a legislator's denominational ties and church doctrines into consideration. These factors are especially important when considering legislation involving abortion, birth control, gambling, sale of alcoholic beverages, state aid to parochial schools, Sabbath observance, and other matters of vital concern to some religious groups but not others. In 1997, the four most numerous religious affiliations reported by members of the 75th Legislature were as follows: Roman Catholic, 25 percent; Baptist, 22 percent; Methodist, 15 percent; and Episcopalian, 6 percent.

Legislative Experience In a legislative body, experience is measured in terms of turnover (first-termers replacing experienced members) and tenure (years of service in a legislative chamber). Once elected, senators tend to remain in the Senate longer than representatives serve in the House. To some extent, this tendency is influenced by the fact that representatives occasionally pass up opportunities for nomination and re-election to make a bid for a Senate seat or some other office.

Some legislators simply grow weary of political battle and drop out of politics to pursue a quieter life. Others withdraw because of redistricting problems, financial difficulties, family opposition to continued political activity, or employment opportunities that will not permit legislative service (such as becoming a lobbyist). Frequent special sessions and the burden of interim committee work pose major problems. Legislators cannot live on their meager state salaries, so most practice a profession or manage a business that competes for their time.

As a general rule, lawmakers do not become very effective until they spend two or more years working with constituents, bureaucrats, lobbyists, fellow legislators, and other elected officials. Many Americans believe, however, that long legislative tenure should be discouraged if not prohibited. In the 73rd, 74th, and 75th Legislatures, unsuccessful efforts were made to propose term-limits amendments to the Texas Constitution.

Powers and Immunities

Although bound by restrictions not found in many state constitutions, the legislature is the dominant branch of Texas government and the chief agent in making public policy. Through control of government spending, for example, legislators make state agencies and personnel—and, to some extent, units of local government—dependent on them. In addition to their constitutional powers, lawmakers enjoy certain immunities designed to allow them to function freely.

Legislative Powers

Using language reminiscent of George Orwell's *Animal Farm,* we may say that whereas all powers exercised by the Texas Legislature are, in a sense, legislative, some are more legislative than others. The more typical exercise of legislative power involves making public policy by passing bills and adopting resolutions. Each bill and resolution has a distinctive abbreviation, which indicates the chamber of origin, and every legislative proposal is designated by a number indicating the order of introduction during a session.[4]

Simple Resolution   Abbreviated *H.R.* (House Resolution) if introduced in the House and *S.R.* (Senate Resolution) if introduced in the Senate, a **simple resolution** involves action by one house only and is not sent to the governor. Adoption requires a simple majority vote of members present. Matters dealt with by simple resolution include rules of the House and Senate, procedures for House and Senate operation, and invitations extended to nonmembers to address the chambers.

Concurrent Resolution   After adoption by simple majority votes of members present in the House and in the Senate, a **concurrent resolution** (*H.C.R.* or *S.C.R.*) is sent to the governor, who has two options: sign it, or veto it. Typical examples are resolutions requesting action by the U.S. Congress or information from state agencies, establishing joint study committees composed of senators and representatives, or granting permission to sue the state. An exception is the concurrent resolution to adjourn at the end of a legislative session; this measure does not require approval by the governor.

Joint Resolution   Adoption of a **joint resolution** (*H.J.R.* or *S.J.R.*) requires approval by both houses, but the governor's signature is not necessary. Proposed amendments to the Texas Constitution are examples of joint resolutions requiring a two-thirds majority vote of the membership of each house. To date, all proposed amendments to the U.S. Constitution initiated by Congress, with the exception of the Twenty-first Amendment, have been submitted to state legislatures for ratification. The Texas Legislature ratifies a proposed U.S. constitutional amendment with a joint resolution adopted by simple majority votes of members present in both houses.

Bill   Before enactment, a proposed law or statute is known as a **bill** (*H.B.* or *S.B.*). For purposes of classification, bills are divided into three categories: special, general, and local. A **special bill** makes an exception to general laws for the benefit of a specific individual, class, or corporation. Of greater importance are **general bills,** which apply to all people or property in all parts of Texas. To become law, a bill must pass by simple majority votes of members present in both the House and the Senate, but a two-thirds majority vote of the membership in each chamber is required to pass an emergency measure that will take effect as soon as the governor signs it.

A **local bill** creates or affects a single unit of local government (for example, a city, county, or special district). Such bills are usually passed without opposition if sponsored by all legislators from the affected district. Constitutional limitations on subjects of local bills have led to the enactment of **bracket bills,** which are special bills disguised as general bills. However, House rules prohibit the application of a bracket bill to an unnamed city or another unit of government that is the only one in Texas falling within the specified population bracket. For example, a bill referring to "cities with population between 157,000 and 158,000" would cover only the city of Amarillo, according to the 1990 decennial census.

Other Powers

Although the Texas Legislature exercises its principal powers by passing bills and adopting resolutions, the House and Senate have other important powers. Some of these powers relate only indirectly to the lawmaking function.

Constitutional Amendment Power Both legislative chambers are involved in proposing amendments to the Texas Constitution. A proposal is officially made when the joint resolution is approved by a two-thirds majority vote of the total membership of each house. (The constitutional amendment process is covered in detail on pages 45–46.)

Control over Administration Most appointments made by the governor must be submitted to the Senate and approved by at least two-thirds of the senators present. Thus, one chamber of the legislature is in a position to influence the selection of many important officials. Moreover, the unwritten rule of **senatorial courtesy** requires that the Senate "bust" (reject) an appointment if the appointee is declared "personally objectionable" by the senator representing the district in which the appointee resides.

Further legislative control over administrative matters is exercised through enactment of laws establishing and, in some cases, abolishing various state agencies. The legislature also defines the responsibilities of these agencies and imposes restrictions on them through appropriation of money for their operation and through general oversight of their activities.

One form of administrative supervision involves requiring state agencies to make both periodic and special reports to the legislature. The state auditor, who provides information concerning irregular or inefficient use of funds by administrative agencies, is appointed for a two-year term by the Legislative Audit Committee. This six-member body is composed of the speaker of the House of Representatives, chairs of the House Appropriations Committee and Ways and Means Committee, the lieutenant governor, and chairs of the Senate Finance Committee and State Affairs Committee. The Legislative Budget Board, the lawmakers' own budgeting agency, helps the legislature evaluate government operations for purposes of determining how large appropriations should be for each state agency. (See pages 271–273 for more information concerning the Legislative Budget Board.)

Another important instrument of control over state administration is the Legislature's Sunset Advisory Commission. It makes recommendations concerning the continuation of nearly all state agencies. (See pages 218–219 for details concerning the organization and function of this commission.)

Investigative Power To obtain information about problems requiring remedial legislation, the legislature may subpoena witnesses, administer oaths, and compel submission of records and documents. Such action may be taken jointly by the two houses as a body, by one house, or by a committee of either house. Legislative investigations that led to reforms include probes of higher education in South Texas, rural health care delivery, and the insurance industry.

Impeachment Power The House of Representatives has the power to impeach judges of the state's 396 district courts, justices of the 14 state courts of appeals and the Supreme Court of Texas, and judges of the Texas Court of Criminal Appeals. Also, the House may impeach executive officers, such as the governor, attorney general, comptroller of public accounts, and commissioner of the General Land Office. Impeachment power is rarely used, however.

Impeachment involves bringing charges by a simple majority vote of House members present; it resembles the indictment process of a grand jury. Following impeachment, the Senate renders judgment after a proceeding that resembles a court trial. Conviction requires a two-thirds majority vote of the Senate membership. The only punishment that may be imposed is removal from office and disqualification from holding any other public office under the Texas Constitution. If a crime has been committed, the deposed official may also be prosecuted before an appropriate court like any other person.

Immunities

In addition to their constitutional powers, state senators and representatives enjoy **legislative immunities** conferred by the Texas Constitution. First, they may not be sued for slander or otherwise held accountable for any statements made in a speech or debate during the course of a legislative proceeding. Of course, this protection does not extend to remarks made under other circumstances. Second, they may not be arrested while attending a legislative session or while traveling to or from the legislature's meeting place for the purpose of attending, unless charged with "treason, felony, or breach of the peace."

As illustrated by the case of Senator Drew Nixon (R-Carthage), legislators are not immune from prosecution. Early in 1997, during the 75th session, Nixon was arrested in South Austin after being taped and filmed while offering $35 for sex to an undercover policewoman and carrying an unlicensed handgun in his car. In September of that year, he pled guilty to misdemeanor charges and was sentenced to serve six months in jail and to pay fines totaling $6,000. It was his second handgun conviction.

Travis County Court-at-Law Judge David Puryear allowed Nixon to serve his jail term on weekends, thus freeing him from Monday morning to Friday evening for legislative duties and work in his accounting office in Carthage. Had Nixon been convicted of a felony, he would have been disqualified from continuing in office.

Presiding Officers

Merely bringing 181 men and women together in the Capitol does not ensure the making of laws or any other governmental activity. If several people are to transact official business jointly, there must be organized effort. The basic organization of the legislature is prescribed by the Texas Constitution. For example, it designates the lieutenant governor as president of the Senate and provides for the election of a speaker to preside over the House of Representatives.

President of the Senate: The Lieutenant Governor

The most important function of the lieutenant governor of Texas is to serve as **president of the Senate**. Just as the vice president of the United States is empowered to preside over the U.S. Senate but is not a member of that national lawmaking body, so the lieutenant governor of Texas is not a member of the state Senate.

Chosen by the people of Texas in a statewide election for a four-year term, the lieutenant governor is first in line of succession in the event of death, resignation, or removal of the governor. When the governor is absent from the state, the lieutenant governor serves as acting governor and receives the gubernatorial salary, which amounted to nearly $300 per day at the beginning of 1998. Ordinarily, however, the lieutenant governor's salary is the same as those of senators and representatives: $7,200 per year, which amounts to less than $20 per day.

As president of the Texas Senate, the lieutenant governor exercises the following important powers:

- Appoints all Senate committee chairs and vice chairs (but cannot remove them)
- Appoints Senate committee members
- Recognizes senators who wish to speak on the floor or to make a motion (for example, to take up a bill out of order of calendar listing)
- Votes to break a tie vote in the Senate
- Serves on the Legislative Council (a research arm of the legislature)
- Serves on the Legislative Audit Committee
- Chairs the Legislative Budget Board
- Determines the Senate committee to which a bill will be sent after introduction

Given these powers (most of which have been granted by the Senate rather than the Constitution), the lieutenant governor of Texas is perhaps the most powerful officer in the state, especially when the legislature is in session.

At the beginning of each session, the Senate elects a president pro tempore, who presides when the lieutenant governor is absent or disabled. At the end of a session, a new president pro tempore is named for the interim period. Usually, on the basis of seniority, the office is passed around among those senators who have not yet served as president pro tempore. By custom, the governor and lieutenant governor arrange to be absent from the state for one day during the president pro tempore's term, so that official can serve as governor for one day—an event that involves a swearing in ceremony and celebration.

For more than two decades, the office of lieutenant governor was held by two Democrats: first by William P. Hobby, Jr. (1973–1991) and subsequently by Bob Bullock. Though strong leaders, Hobby and Bullock treated both Republican and Democratic senators fairly, almost without exception, when Democrats occupied a majority of the Senate seats. Bullock's power and popularity were apparent in the fall of 1994 when nearly all the Republican senators attended his campaign fund raiser, despite criticism from Tom Pauken, then chair of the Republican party's state executive committee. Again, in 1996, some senators found it expedient to participate in fund-raising events held for the benefit of the lieutenant governor even though he did not face re-election that year.

After Republicans won a majority of the Senate seats in November 1996, Bullock reprimanded a group of Republican senators, both privately and publicly, when they attempted to extract a promise that he would appoint more Republicans to chair Senate committees. At the opening of the 75th regular session in January 1997, Senate Republicans did not attempt to use their three-vote majority to change Senate rules to weaken Bullock's power to appoint committee members and control the flow of legislation. Shortly after the end of the 75th regular session, Bullock exploded a political bomb when he announced that he would not seek re-election in 1998. In that year Republican Rick Perry won the lieutenant governorship, but the GOP lost one Senate seat and fell short of electing a House majority.

Speaker of the House

The presiding officer of the House of Representatives is the **speaker,** a representative who is elected to that office by the House membership for a two-year term. Like the lieutenant governor in the Senate, the speaker controls proceedings in the House. Included among the speaker's more important powers are the following:

- Appoints all House committee chairs and vice chairs (but cannot remove them)
- Appoints all members of House procedural committees
- Appoints House substantive committee members within limitations of the seniority rule

- Recognizes members who wish to speak on the House floor
- Assigns bills and resolutions to House committees
- Serves on the Legislative Council
- Serves as vice chair of the Legislative Budget Board
- Serves on the Legislative Audit Committee

House rules authorize the speaker to name another representative to preside over the chamber temporarily. The speaker may also name a member of the House to serve as permanent speaker pro tempore for as long as the speaker desires. A speaker pro tempore performs all the duties of the speaker when that officer is absent.

Because of the speaker's power, filling this House office involves intense political activity. Lobbyists make every effort to ensure the election of a sympathetic speaker, and potential candidates for the position begin to line up support several months or even years before a speaker's race begins. Long before election of a speaker, anyone aspiring to that office will attempt to induce House members to sign cards pledging their support. House rules adopted in 1997, however, prohibit soliciting written pledges during a regular session. Once elected, a speaker usually finds it easier to obtain similar pledges of support for re-election in future regular sessions.

Having served as speaker for a record-breaking five terms (1983–1993), Gib Lewis (D–Fort Worth) left that $7,200-per-year office after pleading no contest to charges that he had failed to report his financial interest in a Fort Worth investment company. Then he became a lobbyist, reportedly earning almost $600,000 in his first year (which is more than 80 times the annual salary he received as speaker).[5]

After several months of courting fellow representatives and representatives-elect, cotton farmer Pete Laney (D–Hale Center) announced in November 1992 that he had sufficient pledges of support to guarantee his election as speaker at the beginning of the 73rd regular session in January 1993. Following his election, Laney surprised many observers when he led a movement to reform the House rules (including a slight reduction of the speaker's powers). He also took action to improve the image of the House by banning lobbyists from access to the back of that chamber and ending the practice of bringing margarita machines into the Capitol for the convenience of those legislators, staff personnel, and others who customarily celebrate the end of a regular session with heavy drinking.

At the beginning of the 74th regular session in January 1995 and again in 1997, Laney was re-elected without opposition as speaker. At the end of the regular session of the 75th Legislature, he announced that he would seek a fourth term in 1999.

Committee System

Presiding officers determine the committees to which bills will be referred. (See Table 6.2 for committee titles and numbers of members for House and

TABLE 6.2   Committees and Numbers of Members, 75th Legislature (1997–1998)

House Committees	Senate Comittees
Substantive Committees	**Standing Committees**
Agriculture and Livestock (9)	Criminal Justice (7)
Appropriations (27)	Economic Development (11)
Business and Industry (9)	Education (11)
Civil Practices (9)	Finance (13)
Corrections (9)	Health and Human Services (11)
County Affairs (9)	Intergovernmental Relations (11)
Criminal Jurisprudence (9)	International Relations, Trade, and
Economic Development (9)	Technology (9)
Elections (9)	Jurisprudence (7)
Energy Resources (9)	Natural Resources (11)
Environmental Regulation (9)	State Affairs (13)
Financial Institutions (9)	
Higher Education (9)	**Special Committees**
Human Services (9)	Administration (7)
Insurance (9)	General Investigating (5)
Judicial Affairs (9)	Nominations (7)
Juvenile Justice and Family Issues (9)	Veterans Affairs and Military
Land and Resource Management (9)	Installations (5)
Licensing and Administrative Procedures (9)	
Natural Resources (9)	**Select Committee**
Pensions and Investments (9)	Tax Reform and Public School
Public Education (9)	Finance (11)
Public Health (9)	
Public Safety (9)	**Committee of the Whole Senate**
State Affairs (15)	Legislative and Congressional
State, Federal, and International Relations (9)	Redistricting (31)
State Recreational Resources (9)	
Transportation (9)	
Urban Affairs (9)	
Ways and Means (11)	
Procedural Committees	
Calendars (11)	
General Investigating (5)	
House Administration (11)	
Local and Consent Calendars (11)	
Redistricting (11)	
Rules and Resolutions (11)	
Select Committee	
Revenue and Public Education Funding (11)	

Senate committees in the 75th Legislature.) In addition, and of special importance, is their power to appoint committee members as well as designate all committee chairs and vice chairs. Because both House and Senate committees play important roles in the fate or fortune of all bills and resolutions, selection of committee members goes far toward determining the amount and type of legislative output generated during a session. Consequently, lobbyists attempt to influence committee selection.

Permanent staff personnel are available to assist legislators with committee work between sessions, but tasks that standing committees might perform are often given to interim study committees. Members of these specially created committees are appointed by presiding officers and sometimes by the governor.

House Committees

House rules provide for a limited seniority system for **substantive committees**, each of which considers bills and resolutions relating to the subject identified by a commitee's name (for example, elections or transportation). A maximum of half the membership for each substantive committee (exclusive of the chair and vice chair) is based on seniority, that is, years of cumulative service as a member of the House. When a regular session begins, each representative, in order of seniority, designates three committees in order of preference. A representative is entitled to become a member of the committee of highest preference on which there is a vacant seniority position. Other committee members are appointed by the speaker. Seniority does not apply to membership on the **procedural committees**, each of which considers bills and resolutions relating primarily to an internal legislative matter (for example, calendars or House administration). All members are appointed by the speaker.

Although standing and procedural committees are established under House rules adopted in each regular session, the speaker may independently create **select committees**. Such action may be taken at the beginning of a session so that the House can work on emergency legislation before appointments for standing committees have been made.

To ensure that representatives' efforts are not divided among too many committees, membership is limited to no more than two substantive committees. Chairs of the powerful Appropriations Committee (spending of state money), Ways and Means Committee (taxes), and State Affairs Committee (the most important subjects that do not involve spending and taxing) may not serve concurrently on another substantive committee. At the beginning of the 75th Legislature in January 1997, Speaker Laney appointed Republicans to chair 11 substantive committees and two procedural committees: Redistricting and House Administration.

Senate Committees

Senate rules provide for **standing committees** (similar to House substantive committees) and **special committees** (similar to House procedural committees). In addition, the Senate has the Committee of the Whole Senate on Legislative and Congressional Redistricting, composed of all the senators. The chair and vice chair of each committee are appointed by the lieutenant governor, as noted earlier.

The lieutenant governor's power of appointment extends to membership on all Senate standing committees, special committees, and the two five-member standing subcommittees of the Committee on Natural Resources: Agriculture and Water. A senator serves on a maximum of three standing committees and is restricted to holding no more than one standing committee chair. In 1997, at the beginning of the 75th Legislature, Lieutenant Governor Bullock selected Republicans to chair one special committee (the Veterans Affairs and Military Installations Committee) and five standing committees.

Legislative Caucus System

With the House and Senate firmly controlled for several years by Speaker Gib Lewis and Lieutenant Governor Bill Hobby, caucuses of like-minded members exercised limited influence on the Texas Legislature. Each of these presiding officers sought to absorb potential opponents within his team and to discourage legislative organizations based on partisan, philosophical, racial, or ethnic interests. Later, however, caucus organizations increasd in importance under Speaker Pete Laney and Lieutenant Governor Bob Bullock.

Party Caucuses

Students of American national government are aware of the importance of the Democratic and Republican party caucuses in both houses of the U.S. Congress. In state legislatures, one finds strong party caucus organizations whenever a strong two-party system prevails and party competition is keen. The growing importance of party caucuses in the Texas Legislature is one indication that Texas has become a two-party state. The House Democratic Caucus was organized in 1981 with 37 members. In recent years, all Democratic legislators have been reported as belonging to their party's caucus. The House Republican Caucus was organized at the beginning of the 71st regular session in 1989. It takes policy positions on important legislation (for example, workers' compensation and prison reform measures).

Racial/Ethnic Caucuses

In the U.S. Congress and in many state legislatures, racial and ethnic minorities organize and form voting blocs to maximize their power. Because African Americans and Hispanics constitute significant minorities in the Texas Legislature, it is not surprising that they have formed caucuses for this purpose. Composed of African-American senators and representatives, the **Legislative Black Caucus** concentrates on issues affecting African-

American Texans. In the 1980s, the **Mexican-American Legislative Caucus** successfully pushed legislation placing farm workers under state workers' compensation, unemployment compensation, and minimum wage protection. In the 1990s, pressure from the Mexican-American Legislative Caucus produced larger appropriations for state universities in South Texas and the Mexican border area from El Paso to Brownsville and north to Corpus Christi and San Antonio.

Ideological Caucuses

Two House-based ideological caucuses have emerged. A conservative organization attracts Republicans and conservative Democrats, and a liberal group appeals to many Democrats (including several who are also members of the Legislative Black Caucus and the Mexican-American Legislative Caucus). As might be expected, the conservative and liberal caucuses reflect opposing views on taxing and spending as well as on public interest issues such as environmental protection; but a few representatives belong to *both* caucuses.

Organized in 1985, the **Texas Conservative Coalition** is composed of both Republicans and conservative Democrats. This organization owes its creation to an increased number of Republican legislators elected in the early 1980s and to dissatisfaction with education reforms and tax increases enacted during a special session in 1984. Membership in the Conservative Coalition reached 69 in 1993, and climbed to 93 in 1997. Established in November 1993 with 42 charter members, the **Legislative Study Group** represents the liberal Democrats' response to the Texas Conservative Coalition. The Legislative Study Group has called for ethics in government, campaign finance reform, consumer and environmental protection, long-term solutions to problems involving public safety, and changes in Texas's systems of public education, health and human services, and criminal justice. Membership during the 75th regular session in 1997 was 73.

Procedure

Enacting a law is not the only way to get things done in Austin, but passing bills and adopting resolutions are the principal means whereby members of the Texas Legislature participate in making public policy according to detailed rules of procedure.

Rules

To guide legislators in their work, each chamber adopts its own set of rules at the beginning of every regular session, usually with only a few changes in the rules of the preceding session. Learning these official rules is a matter of great importance for members and others who seek to understand the lawmaking process. Whether a bill is passed or defeated depends heavily on skillful use of House and Senate rules by sponsors and opponents.

Questions concerning interpretation of rules are decided by the lieutenant governor and the speaker, who wield the gavel of authority in their respective chambers. Because procedural questions may be complex and decisions must be made quickly, each chamber employs a **parliamentarian** to assist its presiding officer. Seated on the dais immediately to the left of the lieutenant governor or speaker, this Senate or House expert on rules is ever ready to provide answers to procedural questions.

As an example of the use of House rules, on May 25, 1997, Representative Arlene Wohlgemuth (R-Burleson) raised a point of order that precipitated what Representative Dan Kubiak (D-Rockdale) called the "Memorial Day Massacre." This action killed 52 bills (although some were salvaged later as amendements to other bills). Wohlgemuth acted late in the 75th session when it appeared that opponents of a bill concerning parental notification of abortion performed on minors (S.B. 86) would use the same tactic to prevent a floor vote on that bill. She complained that Calendars Committee Chair Mark Stiles (D-Beaumont) had failed to inform the House concerning the meeting place of his committee before the 52 bills were set for floor action. Speaker Pete Laney upheld her point of order.[6]

A Bill Becomes a Law

The Texas Constitution calls for regular sessions to be divided into three periods for distinct purposes. The first 30 days are reserved for the introduction of bills and resolutions, action on emergency appropriations, and the confirmation or rejection of recess appointments made by the governor between sessions. The second 30 days are meant to be devoted to consideration of bills and resolutions by committees. The remainder of the session, which amounts to 80 days because regular sessions always run the full 140 days allowed, is devoted to floor debate and voting on bills and resolutions. Throughout a session, action may be taken at any time on emergency matters submitted by the governor.

Because the Texas Constitution allows each chamber to determine by a four-fifths majority vote its own order of business, the House has customarily permitted unlimited consideration of bills during the first 60 days. The Senate, however, suspends the constitutional rule on a bill-by-bill basis during the 60-day period. The Texas Constitution specifies that all revenue bills must originate in the House; other kinds of legislation may originate in either chamber.

During a regular session and for a month thereafter, information concerning bills and resolutions may be obtained by calling the **Legislative Reference Library's** toll-free number, 800-253-9693. At other times (and at all times for callers within the Austin area), the library's number is 512-463-1252. Located on the second floor of the capitol, this library is open to the public. Its books, periodicals, government documents, and newspaper clippings provide a wealth of information for anyone engaged in research concerning the Texas Legislature and its work. Many of the Legislative Reference Library's resources (including text and history of bills and resolutions) are available through the Internet <http://www.capitol.state.tx.us>. Video and audio tapes of each day's proceedings may be purchased from the House and Senate audio-video departments.

Although the full process of turning a bill into a law is complex, certain basic steps are clearly outlined. The following paragraphs trace these steps from introduction to action by the governor. For our purposes, we will describe the path of a bill that originates in the House.[7] (The step numbers in Figure 6.1 will help you visualize the bill's progress.)

1. *Introduction in the House* Any House member may introduce a bill by filing 12 copies (14 copies of every bill related to conservation and reclamation districts) with the chief clerk. This staff person supervises legislative administration in the House. Prefiling of bills by members and members-elect is allowed as early as the first Monday following the November general election before a regular session begins in January or 30 days before the start of a special session.

2. *First reading (House) and referral to committee* After receiving a bill, the chief clerk assigns it a number in order of submission and turns the bill over to the reading clerk for the **first reading**. The reading clerk reads aloud the caption and announces the committee to which the bill has been assigned by the speaker.

3. *House committee consideration and report* Before any committee action, the committee staff must prepare a bill analysis that summarizes important provisions of the bill. If requested by the committee chair, the bill's author or sponsor provides an analysis. The committee chair decides whether the bill needs a fiscal note (provided by the Legislative Budget Office), which will project the costs of implementing the proposed legislation for five years. It is a responsibility of the committee chair to decide whether the Legislative Budget Office should prepare impact statements for certain types of bills. As a courtesy to sponsoring representatives, most bills receive a committee hearing at which lobbyists and other interested persons have an opportunity to express their views.

At the discretion of the committee chair, a bill may be sent to a subcommittee for a hearing, followed by submission of a written subcommittee report to the committee. If a majority of a committee's members decides that a bill should be passed, usually with proposed amendments, a favorable report is referred to the chief clerk.

Determining the order in which House bills are cleared for floor action is entrusted to two committees, the Calendars Committee and the Local and Consent Calendars Committee. As a result of changes made in House rules in 1993, meetings of these calendar committees are now open to the public, the press, and all representatives. Within 30 days after receiving a bill, a calendars committee should decide by record vote whether to place the bill on a calendar for floor consideration.

Except in the case of a general appropriations measure, a printed copy of a bill must be placed in the newspaper mailbox of each House member 36 hours before it is considered on the floor during a regular session and 24

FIGURE 6.1 Route Followed by a House Bill from Texas Legislature to Governor

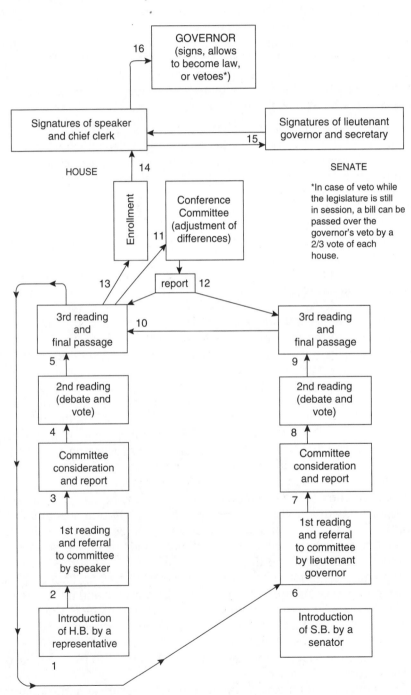

Source: Prepared with the assistance of Dr. Beryl E. Pettus

hours before consideration in a special session. For the general appropriations bill, according to House rules, delivery must be made to "the newspaper mailbox of each member at least 168 hours during a regular session and at least 72 hours during a special session, before such a bill can be considered . . . on a second reading."

4. *Second reading (House)* Usually the **second reading** is limited to caption only. The author of a bill, or the committee member reporting on behalf of the committee, is given the privilege of beginning and ending floor debate with a speech of not more than 20 minutes. Other speakers are limited to not more than 10 minutes each, unless extra time is granted. A computer on the desk of each representative provides easy access to the text of amendments proposed during floor debate. After discussion ends and any amendments are added, a vote is taken on "passage to engrossment" (preparation of an officially inscribed copy). A quorum of two-thirds of the House members must be present.

A record vote usually involves using an electronic system. Votes are recorded and tallied as each representative presses the button on a desktop voting machine that turns on a light by the representative's name on a scoreboard (green, yes; red, no; white, present but not voting). House rules prohibit **ghost voting** (pressing the voting button for an absent representative). In 1991, however, votes by one representative were recorded hours after his death caused by an overdose of crack cocaine. If a member calls for "strict enforcement" of the House rules, the voting clerk locks the voting machine of each member who is absent.

Approval of a bill on second reading requires a simple majority vote. In the event that a bill contains an emergency clause (and, almost without exception, bills contain this clause), a motion may be made to suspend the rules by a four-fifths majority vote of members present and to give the bill an immediate third reading.

5. *Third reading (House)* On the **third reading**, a simple majority vote of members present is required to pass the bill. Amendments may still be added at this stage, but such action requires a two-thirds majority vote. Following the addition of an amendment, a new copy is made, checked over by the engrossing and enrolling clerk, and stamped "Engrossed."

6. *First reading (Senate)* After passing on the third reading in the House, the chief clerk adds a statement certifying passage and transmits the bill to the Senate (where the original House number is retained). In the Senate, the House bill's caption is read aloud by the secretary of the Senate, who also announces the committee to which the bill has been assigned by the lieutenant governor. It is common practice for identical or companion bills to be introduced in both chambers at the same time, thus speeding the legislative process. A senator's sponsorship of a House bill is necessary for the bill to be given serious consideration. (Likewise, a representative's sponsorship of a Senate bill is needed in the House.)

7. *Senate committee consideration and report* Senate procedure differs somewhat from House procedure. If a majority of the committee members want a bill to pass, it is given a favorable report. Then the bill's sponsor in the Senate indicates a desire for floor debate by filing a notice so that the measure will be placed on the Intent Calendar according to the order in which bills are reported favorably.

At the beginning of each session, however, a bill on which floor action is not intended (called a "stopper") is "parked" at the head of the list and left there. Thus, all bills on the Intent Calendar must be taken up outside the regular order of business, an action that requires a two-thirds majority vote of the membership (21 of the senators present).This two-thirds rule enhances the power of the Senate's minority party.

8. *Second reading (Senate)* As with second readings in the House, the Senate at this stage debates the bill, considers proposed amendments, and routinely puts the measure to a voice vote. A computer on the desk of each senator displays the texts of proposed amendments. Votes are registered as the roll is called by the secretary of the Senate, who is employed to supervise legislative administration in that chamber. But unless a senator holds up two fingers to indicate an intention to vote no, the presiding officer usually announces that the chamber unanimously approves the bill after only a few names are called. A quorum of 21 senators must be present when a vote is taken. A simple majority is needed to pass a bill.

Custom permits a senator to speak as long as physical endurance permits, which on one occasion in 1977 amounted to 43 hours. Such **filibustering** is most effective when undertaken during the final hours of a session.

9. *Third reading (Senate)* If passed on the second reading, a bill can have its third reading immediately, assuming the rules have been suspended (as is routinely done in the Senate) by the required four-fifths majority vote of members present. Amending a bill on the third reading requires a two-thirds majority vote of members present.

10. *Return to the House* After passage by the Senate, a House bill is returned to the chief clerk and then sent to the engrossing and enrolling clerk. The latter has the responsibility to supervise preparation of a perfect copy of the bill and deliver it to the speaker. When an amendment has been added in the Senate (as usually happens), the change must be voted on in the House. If the House is not prepared to accept the amended bill, the ordinary procedure is to request a conference. Otherwise, the bill will die unless one of the chambers reverses its position.

11. *Conference committee* When the two houses agree to send the bill to conference, each presiding officer appoints five members to serve on the **conference committee**. Attempts will be made to adjust differences and produce a compromise version acceptable to both chambers. At least three Senate members and three House members must agree before the committee can recommend a course of action in the two houses. The author of the House bill serves as conference committee chair.

12. *Conference committee report* The conference committee's recommended settlement of questions at issue must be fully accepted or rejected by each chamber. Most conference committee reports are accepted. Both houses, however, may agree to return the report to the committee, or, on request of the House, the Senate may accept a proposal for a new conference.

13. *Enrollment* After a conference report has been accepted by both houses, the chief clerk of the House prepares a perfect copy of the bill and stamps it "Enrolled."

14. *Signatures of the chief clerk and speaker* When the enrolled conference committee report is received in the House, the reading clerk of the House reads the bill by caption only. Then it is signed by the chief clerk, who certifies the vote by which it passed, and by the speaker.

15. *Signatures of the secretary of the Senate and the lieutenant governor* Next, the chief clerk of the House takes the bill to the Senate, where it is read by caption only. With certification of the vote by which it passed, the bill is signed by the secretary of the Senate and by the lieutenant governor.

16. *Action by the governor* While the legislature remains in session, the governor has three options: sign the bill; allow it to remain unsigned for ten days, not including Sundays, after which time it becomes law without the chief executive's signature; or, within the ten-day period, veto the measure by returning it to the House unsigned, with a message giving a reason for the veto. A vote of "two-thirds of the membership present" in the first house that considers a vetoed bill (in this case, the House of Representatives) and a vote of "two-thirds of the members" in the second house (in this case, the Senate) are required to override the governor's veto.[8]

After a session ends, the governor has 20 days, counting Sundays, in which to veto pending legislation and file the rejected bills with the secretary of state. A bill not vetoed by the governor automatically becomes law at the end of the 20-day period. The governor's postadjournment veto is of special importance because it cannot be overridden. However, relatively few bills are vetoed.

Ordinarily, an act of the legislature does not take effect until 90 days after adjournment, or even later if specified in the bill. Exceptions to this rule include a general appropriation act (which takes effect when approved) and an emergency measure (which takes effect as specified). The latter must be identified by an emergency statement in the text and must pass each house by a two-thirds majority vote of the total membership (21 votes in the Senate and 100 votes in the House of Representatives).

Influences Within the Legislative Environment

In theory, elected legislators are influenced primarily, if not exclusively, by their constituents. In practice, however, many legislators' actions bear little relationship to the needs or interests of the "folks back home." To be sure, Texas senators and representatives are not completely indifferent to voters, but many of them fall far short of being genuinely representative. One problem is that large numbers of citizens are uninterested in most governmental affairs and have no opinions about how the legislature should act in making public policy. Others may have opinions but are inarticulate or unable to communicate with their legislators. Therefore, lawmakers are likely to yield not only to the influence of the presiding officers in the House and Senate but also to pressure from other powerful political actors seeking to win their voluntary support or force their cooperation.

Governor

We already noted the roles of legislative leaders and the governor's veto power. It is also important to point out that the ever-present threat of executive veto plays an equally important part in legislative behavior. Even though a bill might be popular with many senators and representatives, knowledge that the governor will oppose the measure is often sufficient to discourage its introduction or cause it to be buried in committee, tabled, or defeated on the floor of the House or Senate.

Each chief executive campaigns for office on a platform of promises and then feels compelled to promote certain policies after being elected. Thus, legislators must be influenced to ensure the success of the governor's plans for taxing, spending, building, and educating, among other things. And if there is any doubt as to what the governor wants, gubernatorial policies will be outlined in messages from time to time. Popular support for the chief executive's ideas will make opposition difficult, even though the people in a legislator's district may be adversely affected.

Judges, Attorney General, and Comptroller of Public Accounts

An act that is politically expedient and even popular with constituents may conflict with provisions of the Texas Constitution or the U.S. Constitution. Thus, in their lawmaking, all legislators are influenced by what state and federal judges have done or may do about possible legislative action.

Usually senators and representatives wish neither to spend time nor invest political capital in legislative efforts that will be struck down by judicial decisions or opinions of the attorney general. Therefore, while a bill is being considered, the committee chair may turn to the attorney general for an opinion concerning its constitutionality.

By estimating how much money will be collected under current and projected revenue laws, the state comptroller exercises great influence because the legislature must keep state spending within the limits of anticipated revenue. For example, after an appropriation bill has passed the House and Senate, it is sent to the comptroller. If the comptroller determines that sufficient revenue will not be available, the bill is red-tagged and cannot be enacted unless both houses approve it by a four-fifths majority vote. (See pages 199–200, 202, and 204 for further information concerning the role of this executive official.)

Lobbyists

Lobbying as an interest group tactic is discussed on pages 136–138. Opinions vary concerning the influence of lobbyists on legislative behavior and public policy. In many minds, lobbying carries an image of corruption. Others see lobbyists as performing a useful role by supplying information and serving as links with organized groups of constituents. But it is a nagging fact that special-interest groups spend large amounts of money to induce legislative action (usually to kill a bill) that otherwise would not be taken on a legislator's own initiative or in response to requests by constituents. In fact, many bills are written by lobbyists and "carried" by cooperative legislators.[9]

A Texas statute prohibits campaign contributions to lawmakers during a legislative session. Nevertheless, state senators and representatives are subjected to intensive lobbying activities throughout the year, especially when they convene in Austin for regular and special sessions.

A legislator may not accept loans, cash, or travel and lodging for a vacation trip. But a senator or representative may enjoy a lobby-paid jaunt to attend a trade conference held at a luxury resort by agreeing to make one or two speeches at the meeting. A legislator may accept free meals,entertainment, and gifts from lobbyists, but there is a $500 limit on entertainment and on gifts from a single lobbyist in a year.

Lobbyists are required to register with the Ethics Commission, and lobbying reports mandated by state law are made to that agency. Both lobbyists and political action committees contribute directly to the campaign funds that cover legislators' election expenses and are used to pay for a wide range of political and officeholder activities.[10] In view of this influence, some observers insist that the so-called Third House, composed of well-financed lobbyists, plays a more important role in initiating, strengthening, passing, weakening, or defeating critical bills and resolutions than do the popularly elected senators and representatives who sit in the two houses established by the Texas Constitution.[11]

Legislative Research Organizations

Reliable information is essential to policymakers. Most Texas legislators depend heavily on information provided by their own staffs, administrative agencies, and lobbyists. Three official research bodies have been established to help legislators with their work.

Legislative Council   Authorizing special research projects by its staff is one of the functions of the **Legislative Council,** which is composed of the lieutenant governor (chair), the speaker (vice chair), five senators appointed by the lieutenant governor, and ten representatives appointed by the speaker. Support is offered to legislators, other state officials, and the public in a number of areas. In 1997, the Legislative Council's executive director supervised 353 permanent and 84 sessional employees in providing bill drafting, legislative counseling, legislative research and writing, interim study committee research support, demographic and statistical data compilation and analysis, computer mapping and analysis, publications, and computer services.

House Research Organization A bipartisan steering committee of 15 representatives governs the **House Research Organization (HRO)**. Committee members are independently elected for staggered four-year terms, but their election is subject to approval by the House membership. As an administrative department of the House, the HRO's operating funds are provided by the House Administration Committee. Fourteen staff personnel were employed during the 75th regular session, and approximately half that number work during the interim between sessions. The HRO produces reports on a wide variety of policy issues, and it publishes the *Daily Floor Report* on each day the legislature is in session. The *Daily Floor Report* analyzes important bills to be considered, providing an objective summary of their content and arguments for and against each bill. Within a few months after the close of a regular session, the staff publishes a report on the session's important bills and resolutions, including some that were defeated. (For example, see *Major Issues of the 75th Legislature, Regular Session,* published in 1997.) All representatives receive HRO publications, and senators have access through the capitol computer network. Members of the capitol press corps, law firms, libraries, businesses, political scientists, and others can subscribe to these objectively written and informative publications.

Senate Research Center Organized under the secretary of the Senate, the **Senate Research Center** succeeded the Senate Office of Bill Analysis in 1991. While maintaining the bill analysis function, the center's activities include research in diverse areas. Primarily the center responds to requests for research and information from senators. However, as president of the Senate, the lieutenant governor also utilizes the center's information and expertise. The center's periodic publications range from the semimonthly *Clearinghouse Update,* which presents brief accounts of issues facing Texas and the nation, to the *Summary of Significant Legislation* after each regular session. In addition, the center produces special publications.

Media

It is difficult to measure (or even estimate) the influence of newspapers, magazines, television, and radio on legislative behavior. Legislators are aware that some of their activities will be publicized by newspapers (especially Texas's big-city press), radio and television broadcasts, and magazines such as *Texas Monthly* and the *Texas Observer*, along with newsletters and other publications produced for subscribers or members of special-interest groups. Thus, a legislator may be induced to work for or against a bill to avoid negative publicity or earn favorable publicity. On some policy issues, lawmakers (as well as voters) may be impressed by reasoned opinions expressed in editorials, persuasive analyses from political columnists and commentators, reporters' news stories, and editorial cartoons such as those printed in this edition of *Practicing Texas Politics*.

Most legislators give daily attention to radio and TV news programs, as well as to their hometown newspaper and one or more big-city newspapers or a daily collection of clipping-service articles taken from many Texas publications. Passage of the Ethics Bill in 1991, for example, was in part the result of investigative reporting by *Austin American-Statesman* journalists who focused on lobbying activities and legislative corruption.

Slow Progress Toward Legislative Reform

In its much-publicized comparative study of state legislatures in 1971, the Citizens Conference on State Legislatures ranked the Texas Legislature 38th in the country in terms of legislative capabilities.[12] Later, in a study prepared for the Texas Constitutional Convention of 1974, the Citizens Conference made the following summary assessment (largely valid two decades later) and recommendations:

> Burdened by restrictions from another century, the [Texas] Legislature has been unable fully to rise to the challenges of the present age. Instead of a strong legislature performing its intended tasks of representation, problem resolution, and oversight of state administration, the present Legislature is a weakened body constrained by limited biennial sessions, by its inability to review vetoed bills after adjournment or to call itself into special sessions. These limitations together with constitutionally prescribed salaries, a Senate presided over by an executive branch official, and a multitude of constitutional legislation that restricts the Legislature's power to act effectively should be among the targets for revisions to articles.[13]

Proposition 1 of the proposed constitutional revision package of 1975 was designed to remedy some of the weaknesses listed above, but it was overwhelmingly rejected by the state's voters. In 1989, Texas voters rejected a proposed constitutional amendment linking salaries for the speaker, lieutenant governor, and legislators to the governor's salary. Subsequently, the Texas Ethics Commission was authorized to set per diem allowances and recommend salary increases. More recently, significant reforms have been made in rules governing House organization and procedures. There is no indication, however, that Texans are ready to overhaul the basic structure of their legislature or to increase its powers and effectiveness.

During more than a century of one-party politics and a "no-party" legislature,[14] Texans allowed the Austin lobby, rather than popularly elected legislators, to become the center of the policymaking process. If the Texas Legislature is the "people's branch" of state government, it should be strong and responsive to public opinion at the ballot box. But as long as political action committees and special-interest lobbyists play decisive roles in financing election campaigns and setting the legislative agenda, Texas lawmakers are not likely to respond quickly to the state's critical problems with enlightened and effective public policies. Although most Texas legislators are honest, too many of the Lone Star State's senators and representatives appear to be comfortable with the lobbyists' cynical definition of an honest legislator: one who stays bought.[15]

Looking Ahead

Either Republicans or Democrats could spark legislative reforms Texans need in the twenty-first century. Nevertheless, Texas's political history reveals that significant reform and pressure for ethical conduct in government usually come only after a highly publicized scandal that arouses public indignation.

The following chapter presents more information concerning relations between the legislative and executive branches. In particular, it gives attention to the role of the governor and the state bureaucracy in policymaking and implementation.

Notes

1. *The South Texan*, February 5, 1998, p. 4. *The South Texan* is the campus newspaper of Texas A&M University—Kingsville.
2. Roel Garcia and Roger Hill, "Rangel Lashes Out Against TASP," *The South Texan*, January 29, 1998, pp. 1, 6.
3. Rosanna Ruiz, "Bill Would Allow Dangerous Dogs to Be Destroyed," *Fort Worth Star-Telegram*, April 11, 1997.
4. Each regular session brings forth an avalanche of bills and resolutions. During the regular session of the 75th Legislature (January 14 to June 2, 1997), 3,610 bills were introduced in the House and 1,951 in the Senate. Only 870 of the former and 617 of the latter passed both houses and were sent to Governor George W. Bush. He vetoed 36. See *Major Issues of the 75th Legislature, Regular Session,* House Research Organization Session Focus Report No. 75-11 (Austin: Texas House of Representatives, 1997), p. i.
5. Robert Bryce, "Access Through the Lobby," *Texas Observer,* February 24, 1995, p. 15.
6. For more details concerning the Memorial Day Massacre, see Representative Arlene Wohlgemuth's letter to supporting constituents and the text of personal privilege speeches made on the House floor by Representatives Dan Kubiak, Kent Grusendorf, and Mark Stiles. These documents are printed in Eugene W. Jones and others, *Practic-*

ing Texas Politics, 10th ed. (Boston: Houghton Mifflin, 1998), pp. 417–423.

7. For more detailed descriptions of the lawmaking process, see Thomas M. Spencer, *The Legislative Process, Texas Style* (Pasadena, Tex.: San Jacinto College Press, 1981); and *How a Bill Becomes a Law, 75th Legislature,* House Research Organization, Session Focus Report 75–4 (Austin: House of Representatives, January 20, 1997).

8. As one authority explains, this difference in the two-thirds majorities required by Article IV, Section 14, represents "a mysterious error in the present constitution." See George D. Braden, *Citizens' Guide to the Proposed New Texas Constitution* (Austin: Sterling Swift, 1975), p. 15.

9. For a scholarly yet readable description of lobbying in the Lone Star State, see Keith E. Hamm and Charles W. Wiggins, "Texas: The Transformation from Personal to Information Lobbying," in *Interest Group Politics in the Southern States,* ed. Ronald J. Hrebenar and Clive S. Thomas (Tuscaloosa, Ala.: University of Alabama Press, 1992), pp. 152–180.

10. See Lynn Tran and Andrew Wheat, *Mortgaged House: Campaign Contributions of Texas Representatives, 1995–1996* published in January 1998 and sponsored by Public Citizens' Texas Office (Austin), Texans for Public Justice (Austin), and U.S. PIRG Education Fund (Washington, D.C.).

11. For a personal account of legislative lobbying, see H. C. Pittman, *Inside the Third House: A Veteran Lobbyist Takes a 50-year Frolic Through Texas Politics* (Austin: Eakin Press, 1992).

12. John Burns, *The Sometime Governments: A Critical Study of the American Legislatures* (New York: Bantam Books, 1971), p. 49.

13. *The Impact of the Texas Constitution on the Legislature* (Houston: Institute of Urban Studies, University of Houston, 1973), p. 55.

14. This term is used in an excellent study of the development of the House Democratic Caucus. See Robert Harmel and Keith E. Hamm, "Development of a Party Role in a No-Party Legislature," *Western Political Quarterly* 39 (March 1986), pp. 72–92.

15. For journalist Molly Ivins's criticism—and ridicule—directed at Texas legislators and other politicians she has known, see her three books: *Molly Ivins Can't Say That, Can She?* (New York: Random House, 1991), *Nothin' but Good Times Ahead* (New York: Random House, 1993), and *You Got to Dance with Them What Brung You* (New York: Random House, 1998).

Key Terms and Concepts

legislative process
legislature
unicameral
bicameral
House of Representatives
Senate
regular session
special session
redistricting
gerrymandering
single-member district
multimember district
simple resolution
concurrent resolution
joint resolution
bill
special bill
general bill
local bill
bracket bill
senatorial courtesy
impeachment
legislative immunity
president of the Senate

speaker
substantive committee
procedural committee
select committee
standing committee
special committee
Legislative Black Caucus
Mexican-American Legislative
    Caucus
Texas Conservative Coalition
Legislative Study Group
parliamentarian
Legislative Reference Library
first reading
second reading
ghost voting
third reading
filibustering
conference committee
Legislative Council
House Research Organization
    (HRO)
Senate Research Center

SELECTED READING

*Young Staffers Work in Power's Shadow**

Steve Scheibal

Hundreds of college students and recent graduates work full time or part time in staff jobs and internships in the state capitol. Some police the legislative chambers as assistant sergeants-at-arms, or they assist Senate and House officers in keeping track of bills and resolutions and in producing daily journals. Others are employed by the Legislative Budget Board and by legislative research organizations such as the Legislative Council, House Research Organization, and Senate Research Center. Many find jobs with committees or in the offices of the president of the Senate and the speaker of the House. This reading describes another type of legislative staff employment: service as a legislative assistant in the office of a senator or representative. These staffers are paid from a contingency expense fund authorized for each legislator. As in the case of other legislative staff jobs and internships, some political connection with a legislator is usually an important qualification.

Like many other 20-somethings staffing legislative offices, Raphael Bemporad enjoys access deep inside Texas' halls of power. He insists, though, that access doesn't buy much more than an education. The legislative aide to state Sen. Rodney Ellis, D–Houston, doesn't vote on bills, isn't accountable to voters and virtually never shows up in the newspaper. But Bemporad and his cohorts do a lot more in the 1997 legislative session than answer phones and make coffee. They form the nucleus for the state's next generation of leaders, and as legislation is drafted and debated, their recommendations to members will be felt in every corner of the state. Forget the clichés about disaffected youth and meaningless jobs. These people fill the roles that many of their bosses filled decades ago. Their work in this political grad school has kept the state running for 150 years.

With legislators jamming two years of laws through the five-month session, decision makers such as Ellis depend on staffers such as Bemporad to tell them what they're voting on, the bills' pluses and minuses, and how legislation will affect constituents. "I think our influence is conditioning the frame of the decision," said Bemporad, who is 28. "It doesn't seem like it, but it can make a huge difference."

At the end of last year, nearly a third of the legislative assistants and other full-time staff members were younger than 30. Many are just out of college or between degrees. Few people see these staffers behind the scenes in the Legislature. Yet

*From the *Austin American-Statesman,* February 3, 1997, pp. A1, A5. Steve Scheibal is a staff writer for the *American-Statesman.* Printed with permission.

these people's influence at the Capitol has exploded in recent years as state government has grown and legislators have had to delegate the details to their staffs. "I would say I spend much more time now dealing with staff people than I did, certainly, four or five years ago," said Rusty Kelly, who worked for former House Speaker Billy Clayton and went on to become one of the Capitol's most sought-after lobbyists.

Sink or Swim

Besides being more accessible than their bosses, Kelly said, staff members "help prepare legislation, they talk to other members' staffs, and in many ways, they try to help their members poll to see if they have enough votes. He added that staff jobs "are not unlike what regular lobbyists do for clients."

Legislative staffing jobs have become a way station for political job-seekers or people on their way into or out of graduate school. The stress of activity during sessions creates a sink-or-swim environment in which new staffers learn—quickly—how the process works or they move on to something else. Most aides don't stick around longer than two sessions. The stress can be hard to live with, most say, and the pay seldom makes up for it. According to state payroll records, staffers under 30 earned an average of $25,128 per year—$5,300 less than the 556 staffers older than 30. But high turnover means the swimmers can rise to the top quickly. People with as few as two or three years' tenure can find themselves sifting through job prospects.

One of the ranking young staffers is Eric Wright, 26, director of the budget writing Senate Finance Committee. Wright has worked at the Capitol for fewer than 3½ years, but signed on with Sen. Bill Ratliff, R–Mount Pleasant, who became finance chairman last year. Wright now processes much of the budget information that committee members will use in writing a state budget for 1998–1999. He also epitomizes the ambiguity of a staffer's legislative clout. "We certainly make recommendations to our bosses based on the information we get. Sometimes Senator Ratliff will agree with our recommendations and sometimes he won't," Wright said. "More often than not, we give him a recommendation that a lot of the leadership staff is agreeable to, and I would say that more often than not he is in agreement with our recommendations."

Scent of Power

But while staffers may catch the scent of power as they write up a recommendation for their boss, Wright emphasized that they never get a taste. "I would like to say that I have some influence, but I don't take many steps without my boss's consent," Wright said.

Young staffers, not yet comprehending the almost hourly problems in answering to constituents, appeasing other members, and looking out for the press, usually contemplate their own runs for a seat at the table. "I can't think you can work in this area without entertaining thoughts of running for political office," Wright said. Nevertheless, few staffers will admit to having aspirations for the boss's job, especially when so many receive job offers from lobbying firms, consultants, state agencies and graduate schools, even after just one or two sessions. "The $7,200 per year is not enough to live off of," Wright said of legislators' salaries.

Putting Ideas into Action

Bemporad also eschews the idea of running for office, saying he's learned enough about politics that he doesn't want to get into it any deeper. Besides, he said, staffers have plenty of room to turn ideas into legislation as long as they respect the concerns of their bosses.

Two years ago, when he worked for Rep. Richard Raymond, D–Benavides, and volunteered at the Sustainable Food Center in Austin, Bemporad saw three low-cost ways to help address statewide hunger issues: make electronic food stamps available to farmers' markets, allow open state land to be used for community gardens and create a multiagency anti-hunger task force. After getting Raymond's go-ahead, Bemporad drafted legislation and helped shepherd the three bills through the Legislature, though Gov. George W. Bush eventually vetoed the task force. "I was able to bring something to the table that Richard Raymond believes in," Bemporad said.

In the big scheme, it was a small victory, but it still helps ease the stress, low pay, and long hours that come with the job. "It's a real chance for me to be active on issues that I care about," Bemporad said. "There is a palpable excitement in being part of the process."

Chapter 7

THE EXECUTIVE AND THE STATE BUREAUCRATIC SYSTEM

Copyright 1998 by Charles Pugsley Fincher.

George W. Bush first was inaugurated as governor of Texas on January 17, 1995. Reelected in November 1998, Bush was being touted for a presidential race in the year 2000, after trouncing Garry Mauro, former Texas land commissioner. (See cartoon that begins this chapter.) Although inexperienced in public administration, Bush assumed a high office that many ambitious politicians covet. No other officeholder in the Lone Star State is so widely recognized and gets as much media attention as the governor. Nevertheless, Article IV of the Texas Constitution establishes a multi-headed executive branch within which the governor must share executive power with other elected officials. (See Figure 7.1.) Perhaps *primus inter pares* (first among equals) is a more appropriate description of the Texas governor than the title chief executive, but limited executive power does not discourage gubernatorial candidates who wage multimillion-dollar campaigns in their efforts to win this prestigious office.

Overview of the Governorship

Texas's executive branch functions alongside an alignment of legislators and interest groups (especially the business lobby) that manage to keep governors structurally "weak." Supporters of this system argue that it is relatively graft free, nonburdensome to taxpayers, and more democratic than an integrated, pyramid structure with a powerful chief executive at the top.

Unlike the Texas governor, the president of the United States is a "strong" chief executive who appoints (with Senate approval) and removes (independently) the department heads who form the president's cabinet (attorney general, secretary of the treasury, and secretary of defense, among others). In Texas, executive responsibility is dispersed among several elected and appointed officials, most of whom function beyond gubernatorial control. Critics of the Texas system voice two major complaints. First, it rewards a governor's friends and financial supporters with key appointments regardless of their competence or professional qualifications. Second, it involves use of a long ballot from which voters must choose relatively unknown candidates for several executive offices.

Reconstruction Influence

Many of Texas's political traditions and institutions stem from post–Civil War experiences. Thus, today's executive structure shows the influence of anti-Reconstruction reactions against Governor E. J. Davis's administration (1870–1874).

A former Union army general and the state's first Republican governor, Davis was armed with strong executive powers provided by the Constitution of 1869. Numerous abuses of power by state officials, who reported directly to Governor Davis, explain why many Texans still distrust the "strong"

FIGURE 7.1   The Texas Executive Structure

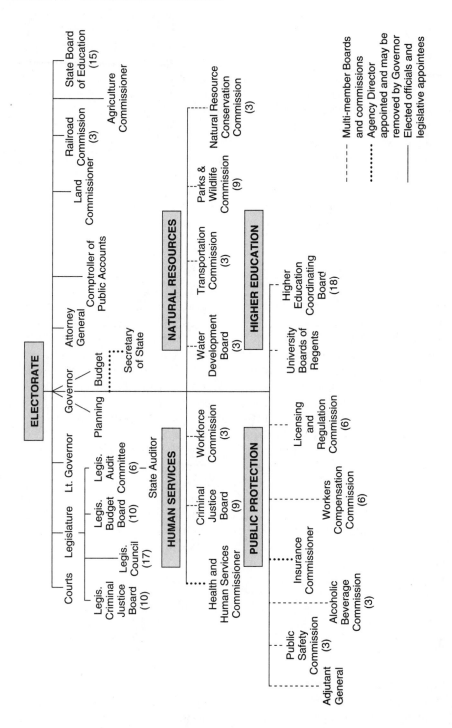

executive model of state government. Thus, the Constitution of 1876, written after the end of the Reconstruction era, provides for a governor who shares power with other elected executive officials: lieutenant governor, comptroller of public accounts, commissioner of the General Land Office, and attorney general. In 1890, the Constitution was amended to provide for election of the three-member Railroad Commission; later the legislature expanded the number of elected executive officials by creating the office of the agriculture commissioner and the 15-member State Board of Education. The secretary of state is the only constitutional executive officer who is appointed by the governor, with approval by the Senate.

What began as a nineteenth-century reaction to reconstruction policies and an unpopular governor is today a huge, bureaucratic system with several elected executive officials and about 150 boards and commissions (excluding the governing boards for state universities) that are closely tied to special interests and their lobbyists. E. J. Davis is buried in Austin's state cemetery, but the anti-Reconstruction legacy lives in Texas's biggest public enterprise: the state government that regulates and provides services for more than 19 million Texans. Unlike a private business, however, the state bureaucratic system operates with multiple chief executive officers (CEOs), some of whom are popularly elected.

Gubernatorial Politics

Heavily financed gubernatorial contests between Democratic and Republican party candidates result in powerful interest groups contributing money to both political camps. (See pages 114–116 and 137–140 on campaign finance.) With millions of dollars being pumped into a race, the victorious gubernatorial candidate is obligated to reward some heavy donors by appointing them to key policymaking positions. The practice of buying influence permeates American politics, and Texas politics is no exception.

Other factors involved in gubernatorial politics include the ways in which a Texas governor accommodates diversity—economic, ethnic, and racial. If there is a widely held perception that a governor caters to only an elite group, that official runs a high risk of defeat when seeking reelection. Because public opinion is greatly influenced by television and the press, well-orchestrated media relations are critical to the success of any governor. Lacking sufficient constitutional powers to function effectively as a "chief executive," a Texas governor must rely heavily on skills in personal relations and gentle persuasion as well as arm twisting.

Comparative Profiles

How personal styles may compensate for deficiency in constitutional power is illustrated in the profiles of two well-known Texas governors: Ann Richards and George W. Bush.

Style Interpersonal relations play pivotal roles in determining gubernatorial success. For Texas governors, *success* translates into legislative accomplishments because, as discussed in Chapter 6, the legislature dominates policymaking in the Lone Star State. Governors Richards and Bush offer contrasting styles in how to "work the legislature."

Overcoming personal problems of alcoholism and divorce, Richards brought a unique style to Texas politics by appointing to public office record numbers of women (1,041), Hispanics (442), and African Americans (384).[1] To gain Senate confirmation for these appointees (other than staff assistants), her good relations with Lieutenant Governor Bob Bullock proved invaluable. Skillfully exploiting television interviews and personal appearances around Texas, the motorcycle-riding, quail-hunting governor practiced "good ol' boy" politics without alienating her liberal supporters.[2] This performance contributed to her unprecedented success in shaking up the state bureaucracy. At her urging, the legislature created two cabinet-style positions: health and human services commissioner and insurance commissioner. Both offices are filled by gubernatorial appointment with Senate confirmation. What is radically different from other state offices, however, is that the governor may remove each commissioner without legislative approval.

In November 1994, Richards lost the governor's office to George W. Bush, a young Republican bent on reshaping state policies along conservative lines. A month before Bush's electoral victory, one political commentator had noted, " . . . for every female or minority appointee, there is a white man who did not get that post. There are a lot of white men out there who don't care—or are angered—that Ann Richards has close ties with Mexico or the White House and a preponderance of these angry white men seem to support George W. Bush."[3]

After taking office, Bush displayed a conciliatory style. *Bipartisanship* and *accessibility* became his trademarks as he reached out to a legislature controlled by Democratic majorities in both the Senate and the House of Representatives. During the regular session of the 74th Legislature in 1995, his weekly breakfast meetings with House Speaker Pete Laney and Lieutenant Governor Bob Bullock facilitated passage of a program favorable to business and other conservative groups. Also successful were Bush's efforts to reform state laws concerning juvenile justice, civil liability (tort reform), and welfare programs.

Approaching his second test with lawmakers in 1997, Governor Bush sought to overhaul state tax laws, beginning with tax relief for property owners. Other policy initiatives included a public school reading program, an increase in the number of charter schools, welfare reform, and new child adoption requirements.

Bush's legislative accomplishments reflect an unwavering devotion to conservative government. In his words, "Prepare the environment so that capital feels free to come here. Government often tries to do too many things, and therefore does nothing."[4] Despite that commitment, however, Governor Bush became burdened with new responsibilities due to **devolu-**

tion of government. This means the federal government is returning to the states many responsibilities, such as providing social services.

Power Ranking With a steady influx of "new" Texans from other states (such as California and New York) that have "strong" governors, many citizens are questioning whether a "weak" executive system can effectively govern Texas in such critical policy areas as education, prisons, welfare, and health care. Organizational models, however, are of little interest to out-of-state businesses in deciding where to relocate. What matters to most "old" and "new" entrepreneurs is a favorable economic climate that maximizes profits, an educational system that provides a highly skilled work force, and a cooperative state government that keeps taxes low. Limited power in the Texas governor's office elevates the legislature to a dominant position, which in turn favors wealthy interests with financial and personal ties to lawmakers. Keeping the state governor "weak" may be accepted, and perhaps encouraged, in corporate boardrooms, but this arrangement tends to be viewed with skepticism by concerned citizens. Nevertheless, Texas governors enjoy great prestige, and popular occupants of that office can do much to mold public opinion and influence policymaking.

Election

Superimposed on constitutional prerequisites for minimum age (30 years), U.S. citizenship, and Texas residency (for five years immediately preceding the gubernatorial election) are numerous extralegal restraints. Historically, a conservative-moderate mold for successful gubernatorial aspirants seemed unbreakable. William P. Clements (in 1978 and 1986) and George W. Bush (in 1994 and 1998) partially broke tradition by becoming Texas's first and second Republican governors, respectively, since E. J. Davis. (See Table 7.1 for a listing of Texas governors since 1874.) As conservative businesspeople, Clements and Bush resembled most of their Democratic predecessors in the governor's office. But their Republicanism, and the fact that they had not previously held elective public office, represented a dramatic departure from the past.[5]

With Ann Richards's election serving as an impetus for more women and minorities to enter politics, future occupants of the governor's office could be even more unconventional. What some observers refer to as "WASP" (white, Anglo-Saxon, Protestant) domination of Texas politics is being challenged by new groups, particularly Hispanics.

Compensation

Gubernatorial compensation is set by the Texas Legislature. For fiscal years 1998 and 1999, the annual salary for the governor was set at $115,345; but Bush refused the raise and continued to receive $99,122. Fringe benefits for the governor include allowances for staffing and maintaining the governor's mansion and use of a state-owned limousine.

TABLE 7.1 Governors of Texas Since 1874*

Governor	Term	Distinction
Richard Coke	1874–1876	Present constitution was written
Richard B. Hubbard	1876–1879	First governor under Constitution of 1876
Oran M. Roberts	1879–1883	First governor to come from the Tyler Gang
John Ireland	1883–1887	Ended the fence-cutting war in West Texas
Lawrence S. Ross	1887–1891	"Man of the people"—mediocrity in government
James S. Hogg	1891–1895	Railroad Commission was created
Charles A. Culberson	1895–1899	The "Quiet Era" in Texas politics
Joseph D. Sayers	1899–1903	Left U.S. Congress for the governorship
Samuel W. T. Lanham	1903–1907	Colonel Edward M. House served as his campaign manager
Thomas M. Campbell	1907–1911	First leftist in the governorship
Oscar B. Colquitt	1911–1915	Campaigned against Prohibition—led to administrative squabbles
James E. Ferguson	1915–1917	Only governor to be impeached and convicted
William P. Hobby	1917–1921	Began an amicable era in Texas's relations with Mexico
Pat M. Neff	1921–1925	First governor to emphasize high cost of winning the governorship
Miriam A. Ferguson	1925–1927	First woman elected governor of Texas
Dan Moody	1927–1931	Laid the groundwork for creation of the Board of Pardons and Paroles
Ross S. Sterling	1931–1933	Imposed martial law in East Texas oil fields for six months
Miriam A. Ferguson	1933–1935	First governor to be re-elected to a nonconsecutive second term
James V. Allred	1935–1939	Strong supporter of FDR's New Deal
W. Lee O'Daniel	1939–1941	Championed populist causes with extensive use of the radio
Coke R. Stevenson	1941–1947	First governor to break two-term tradition
Beauford H. Jester	1947–1949	First governor to initiate revision of the Texas Constitution
Allan Shivers	1949–1957	Led Texas Democrats for Eisenhower and Republican party in 1952 and 1956
Price Daniel	1957–1963	First governor to seek a fourth elective term
John Connally	1963–1969	Creation of Higher Education Coordinating Board
Preston Smith	1969–1973	Began Goals for Texas program
Dolph Briscoe, Jr.	1973–1979	First governor to be elected to a four-year term (1975–1979)
William Clements, Jr.	1979–1983	First Republican governor elected in over 100 years
Mark White	1983–1987	Led movement to reform public education
William Clements, Jr.	1987–1991	Reluctantly approved the biggest tax increase in Texas history
Ann Richards	1991–1995	Appointed a record number of women and minorities to high office
George W. Bush	1995–	First son of a former president to be governor of Texas

*See "Chief Texas Administrative Officials" in the *Texas Almanac* for a listing of all Texas chief executives from the first Spanish governor, Domingo Terán de los Rios (1691–1692), to the present.

The Texas Constitution forbids the governor and other executive officers (except the lieutenant governor) from holding any other civil or corporate office, and the governor may receive neither compensation nor the promise of pay for other employment while in office. George W. Bush, for example, placed his assets in an untouchable blind trust (a legal arrangement whereby personal assets are administered independently of the public officeholder) while serving as governor.

Succession

Should a governor die, resign, or be removed from office, or should a governor-elect refuse to take office or be unable to fill the office, the constitutional order of succession is headed by the lieutenant governor. Next in line is the president pro tempore of the Senate. After these two officials, the legislature designates the following line of succession: speaker of the House, attorney general, and chief justices of the 14 courts of appeals in ascending numerical order, beginning with the chief justice of the First Court of Appeals, which has its primary seat in Houston.

Unlike the Twenty-fifth Amendment to the U.S. Constitution, the Texas Constitution does not stipulate who is to carry out responsibilities of the office of governor in the event of physical or mental disability. The lieutenant governor, however, becomes acting governor while the governor is absent from the state. By custom, the Texas governor and lieutenant governor arrange their schedules so that, on at least one occasion, both are conveniently out of state at the same time. In such circumstances, the president pro tempore of the Senate has the honor of becoming acting governor until the governor or lieutenant governor returns. An acting governor is paid the same amount as the governor for each day the governor is absent from the state.

Removal from Office

Impeachment by the House of Representatives and conviction by the Senate constitute the only constitutionally prescribed method of forcing a Texas governor from office before the end of a term. Article XV of the Texas Constitution states, "The power of impeachment shall be vested in the House of Representatives." Each article of impeachment (similar to a grand jury's indictment) must be approved by a majority vote of the House. To remove the governor, one or more impeachment articles passed by a simple majority vote in the House must be approved by a two-thirds majority vote of the Senate membership. When a governor or lieutenant governor is tried, the chief justice of the Texas Supreme Court presides over the Senate. The penalty for conviction on an impeachment charge is removal from office and disqualification from holding any other appointive or elective public office in the state (however, such conviction does not bar the person from holding a federal office such as U.S. senator or representative). Following removal, a former governor who has been ousted after violating a law may be tried and convicted in a regular criminal trial or may be subjected to a judgment rendered in a civil court.

Although all of Texas's state constitutions have provided for impeachment and removal of the governor, only Governor James E. ("Pa") Ferguson was impeached and removed. Ferguson's troubles stemmed from a personal feud with the University of Texas. Firing of professors was one policy he tried to dictate to the university's board of regents. After Ferguson vetoed all appropriations for the university, the House Speaker called a special session of the legislature. This action was approved by the attorney general, although the Texas Constitution gives the power to call special sessions only to the governor. On September 25, 1917, the Senate convicted Ferguson on ten articles of impeachment, one of which charged him with official misconduct. The other nine articles involved violations of the state's banking laws and use of state funds for private gain. Grounds for removing governors or other officials in the executive branch are not stipulated in the Texas Constitution; rather, impeachment proceedings are highly charged political affairs with legal overtones.

Staff

Even though the Texas governor's hands are often tied when dealing with the state bureaucracy, the chief executive's personal staff continues to function directly under gubernatorial supervision. A governor's success in dealing with lobbyists, interest groups, the legislature, and the general public depends largely on staff input and support.

The **Office of the Governor** directs programs mandated by the legislature, such as statewide planning. Pressure for belt tightening in state government resulted in a reduction of staff from more than 300 at the end of Governor Ann Richards's term (1991–1995) to about 150 in the Bush administration.

The principal impetus for more personnel in the governor's office is an activist approach to statewide issues, ranging from criminal justice coordination to administration of federal funds. Furthermore, there is a nationwide trend toward personalizing this office to provide every interested citizen with access to the governor or a staff member. Also, increasing importance is being given to intergovernmental relations involving cities, councils of governments, interstate councils, federal agencies, and international affairs (particularly matters involving Mexico). The governor of Texas appoints and removes staff members without legislative approval.

To what degree informal relations among the governor's appointed assistants and unofficial advisers influence gubernatorial decisions is open to speculation. One might argue that protecting their chief is still a primary function of many staff assistants, particularly the press secretary and the assistant for board appointments. All Texas governors have placed close friends and political associates—people who can be relied on for their loyalty to the chief executive—in these positions. Despite the fact that most governors and U.S. presidents rely on a chief of staff to manage their offices, Governor Bush chose a more "direct access model". Seven directors, along with an executive assistant and general counsel, report directly to Bush without interference from a "gatekeeper."

One troublesome issue occurs when aides resign staff positions to take more lucrative jobs as lobbyists. Potential conflicts of interest arise, particularly if favorable gubernatorial treatment is given to special-interest groups, represented by former staff members, before the governor's term expires. Governor Bush barred his staff from lobbying activities for no less than one year and one full regular session of the legislature after they resign.

Powers of the Governor

Inaugurated on the third Tuesday in January of every fourth year (always the odd-numbered year before a presidential election), the governor of Texas takes an oath "to cause the laws to be faithfully executed." Herein lies the general constitutional responsibility of the office; however, the governor has few formal powers to carry out this mandate. Whatever success the governor may achieve stems less from constitutional or statutory power than from the chief executive's ability to rally public opinion behind gubernatorial programs and balance the ever-present demands of lobbyists. Powers of the governor may be classified as formal (executive, legislative, judicial) and informal.

Executive Powers

State constitutional and statutory weaknesses of the Texas governorship are apparent on examination of the governor's formal powers. Despite legal barriers, some governors transcend such restrictions by developing and using important political skills.

Appointive Power　Fundamental to effective management of any organization is the power to appoint staff assistants to whom a supervisor may look for advice and loyal service. **Appointive power** is the most significant tool given to Texas governors. Statutes creating administrative agencies have made possible the appointment of a governor's friends and political supporters to policymaking positions on some 150 boards and commissions. Department heads appointed by the governor include the adjutant general, who heads the Texas National Guard; executive directors of the Department of Housing and Community Affairs, the Office of State-Federal Relations, the commissioners of health and human services, education, insurance, firefighters' pensions, and chief administrative law judge of the State Office of Administrative Hearings (SOAH). Members of the governor's personal staff also are appointed.

Because Texas governors serve four-year terms, they have opportunities to appoint nearly 3,000 persons to such powerful boards and commissions as the Board of Human Services, the Transportation Commission, and the boards of regents for multicampus university systems and regional universities. Gubernatorial appointive power, however, is not without certain legal and political limitations.

The Texas Constitution requires that all appointees (except personal staff) be confirmed by the Senate with a two-thirds vote of senators present. "Advice and consent" is a time-honored tradition required of U.S. presidents and most governors in other states. Practical politics requires that the governor consult with a prospective appointee's state senator before sending the name to the full Senate for confirmation. **Senatorial courtesy,** therefore, involves much staff work by an appointments director in the governor's office. Background checks include how the appointee is tied to interest groups who supported the governor during the last election campaign. Embarrassment can occur if an appointee is not fully researched. As a result of such an oversight, for example, Governor Dolph Briscoe appointed a dead man to a state board.

Governors may try to circumvent the Senate by making **recess appointments** while the Senate is not in session. However, the Texas Constitution requires that all recess appointments be submitted to the Senate for confirmation within ten days after it convenes for a regular or special session. Failure of the Senate to confirm a gubernatorial recess appointment prevents the governor from reappointing that person to the same position.

Another limitation results from the fact that most state boards and commissions are composed of members who serve for six years with overlapping terms of office. Thus, a first-term governor must work with carryovers from previous administrations even if such carryovers are not particularly supportive of the new governor.

Due to the elective status of the 3-member Railroad Commission (elected statewide) and the 15-member State Board of Education (elected from districts drawn by the legislature), the governor has no direct control over these agencies. A State Board of Education member who dies or resigns is replaced by board appointment, whereas a Railroad Commission vacancy is filled by gubernatorial appointment with Senate confirmation.

Appointive power of the governor extends to filling vacancies for elected heads of the executive departments, members of the Railroad Commission, and judges (except those for county, municipal, and justice of the peace courts). Also, when a U.S. senator from Texas dies, resigns, or is removed from office before his or her term expires, the governor fills the vacancy with an interim appointee. That appointee serves until a successor is elected in a special election called by the governor. A vacancy in either house of the Texas Legislature or in the Texas delegation to the U.S. House of Representatives does not result in an interim appointment. Instead, the governor must call a special election to fill the position until the next regularly scheduled election.

By 1998, Bush's appointments weighed heavily in favor of Anglo males, with some notable exceptions, including Budget Director Albert Hawkins and Adjutant General Daniel James, both African-American males. In 1998, in a move that was interpreted by some observers as trying to woo Hispanic voters, Bush appointed Al Gonzales to succeed Tony Garza as secretary of state.

Removal Power   In creating numerous boards and commissions, the legislature gives the governor extensive appointive power but no independent **removal power** over most state agencies. Lack of effective removal power greatly limits gubernatorial control over the state bureaucracy. The governor's independent removal power extends to members of the governor's staff and three statutory officials: the executive director of the Department of Housing and Community Affairs, the health and human services commissioner, and the insurance commissioner. This removal power is rarely exercised.

Elected department heads and their subordinates are not subject to the governor's removal power. The governor may informally pressure a board member to resign or accept another appointment, but this is not as effective as the power of direct removal. Governors may remove their own appointees with the consent of two-thirds of the state senators present, but this authority still falls short of independent removal power. Of course, the governor, other elected state officers, and state judges may be removed through the impeachment process involving the House and the Senate. (See page 162). State judges also may be removed by the governor on *address* of two-thirds of each house, and the attorney general may initiate *quo warranto proceedings* leading to the removal of public officials found guilty of official misconduct. These state constitutional removal procedures are rarely used, however. The usual practice is for resignations to occur following highly publicized scandals or alleged wrongdoing by gubernatorial appointees.

Military Power   The governor of Texas is commander-in-chief of the state's military forces, which include both air and ground units (except when the president of the United States calls the Texas National Guard into federal service). Acting under gubernatorial direction, the adjutant general (the state's highest-ranking military officer) may mobilize the Texas National Guard to enforce state law, repel invasion, curb insurrection and riot, and maintain order in times of natural disasters, such as those resulting from destructive tornadoes and floods. The governor may declare **martial law** (temporary rule by the state's military force and suspension of civil authority) if deemed necessary because of civil disorder, such as a riot that local authorities cannot handle.

Law Enforcement Power   Some control over state law enforcement accrues to the governor through power to appoint, with Senate approval, the three members of the Public Safety Commission. The commission-appointed director of public safety oversees a staff of nearly 5,000 members in the Department of Public Safety (DPS). Included among the department's responsibilities are highway traffic supervision, driver licensing, motor vehicle inspection, and criminal law enforcement in cooperation with local and federal agencies. If circumstances demand swift but limited police action, the governor is empowered to assume command of the Texas Rangers, a branch of the Department of Public Safety composed of more than 100 highly trained law enforcement personnel. Ranger membership (licensed officers) was exclusively male until two women joined in 1993. In 1998, Ranger officers included 103 males (83 Anglo, 14 Hispanic, 5 African-American, 1 Asian-American) and 2 females (1 Anglo, 1 African-American). In Texas, as in other states, law enforcement is primarily a city and county responsibility rather than a state function.

Budgetary Power Gubernatorial **budgetary power** is subordinated in part to the legislature's prerogative of controlling the state's purse strings. Thus, a duality exists in preparing the Texas state budget. By statutory requirement, the governor and the Legislative Budget Board should prepare separate budgets for consideration by the legislature; however, governors failed to submit a budget in 1989, 1993, and 1995. Traditionally, both houses are inclined to give greater respect to the board's spending proposals. The governor's only constitutional control over state spending lies in the power to veto an entire appropriations bill or individual budget items. For example, Governor Bush used the item veto to cut $48.4 million from the $86.2 billion budget for fiscal years 1998 and 1999. Recognizing that the governor's hand needed strengthening in managing the budget, the legislature has relinquished some of its budgetary control. (See p. 273.)

Legislative Powers

Perhaps the most stringent test of a Texas governor's capacity for leadership involves handling of legislative matters. The governor's **legislative power** is exercised through three major functions authorized by the Texas Constitution: delivering messages to the legislature, vetoing legislation, and calling special sessions of the legislature. However, the success of a legislative program depends heavily on a governor's ability to use informal persuasion with influential lobbyists, legislative leaders (particularly the Speaker of the House of Representatives and the lieutenant governor), the press, and, occasionally, the general public.

Message Power The Texas Constitution requires the governor to deliver a State of the State address at the beginning of each regular session of the legislature. On occasion, special messages may be presented either in person or in writing. By custom, the governor delivers a farewell message at the conclusion of a term of office, but Ann Richards did not deliver such an address when she stepped down in January 1995. Successful use of the **message power** in promoting a harmonious relationship between the governor and the legislature depends to a large degree on variables such as timing of special messages concerning volatile issues, support of the governor's program by chairs of powerful legislative committees, and the personal popularity of the governor.

Veto Power The most direct legislative tool of the governor is the power to veto legislation. This is done by returning a bill unsigned (with written reasons for not signing) to the house in which it originated. If the legislature is no longer in session, the vetoed bill is filed with the secretary of state. **Veto power** takes different forms. For example, the governor may veto an entire bill or any line item in an appropriation bill while permitting enactment of the remainder of the bill. Hence, the **item veto** places the governor in a powerful bargaining position with individual legislators in the delicate game of pork-barrel politics. That is, the governor may strike a bargain with a senator or representative in which the chief executive promises not to deny funding for a lawmaker's pet project (the pork). In return, the legislator agrees to support a bill the governor favors. The legislature can override the governor's veto by a two-thirds majority vote in both houses, but this has occurred only once since the administration of Governor W. Lee O'Daniel (1939–1941). In 1979, the House and Senate overrode Governor Clements's veto of a local bill. Thus, the strong veto power that the Texas Constitution gives to the governor and the governor's informal power of threatening to veto a bill provide formidable weapons for dealing with uncooperative legislators.

Both the governor of Texas and the president of the United States have the prerogative of neither signing nor vetoing a bill within ten days (Sundays excepted) after its passage, thus allowing the measure to become law without executive signature. But if the president "pockets" a bill that is passed within ten weekdays before congressional adjournment, such failure to act kills the measure. Although not possessing pocket-veto power, the governor of Texas may exercise a **postadjournment veto** by rejecting any pending legislation within 20 days after a session has ended. Since most bills pass late in a legislative session, the postadjournment veto is a powerful tool for the governor.

Calling Special Sessions Included among the governor's powers is the authority to call **special sessions** of the legislature. No constitutional limitation is placed on the number of special sessions that may be called, but a special session is limited to 30 days. During a special session, the legislature may consider only those matters the governor specifies in the call or subsequently presents to the legislature. Confirmation of appointments and impeachment proceedings may be considered by the legislature without gubernatorial approval. Effective use of the power to call special sessions depends to a large extent on the governor's timing and rapport with legislative leaders. From 1991 through 1994, Governor Richards called four special sessions, but Governor Bush did not summon lawmakers back to Austin in his first term as governor.

Judicial Powers

Though possessing few formal judicial powers, the governor of Texas may fill vacancies on many courts and perform acts of clemency to lighten the sentences given to some convicted criminals.

Appointment and Removal of Judges and Justices More than half of Texas's state judges and justices first serve on district courts and higher appellate courts after gubernatorial appointment to fill a vacancy caused by a judge's death, resignation, or removal. According to Article XV, Section 8, of the Texas Constitution, the governor may remove any jurist "on address of two-thirds of each house of the legislature for willful neglect of duty, incompetency, habitual drunkenness, oppression in office, or other reasonable cause which shall not be sufficient ground for impeachment." Governors rarely resort to such action, however, leaving removal of state jurists to other proceedings and to the voters.

Acts of Executive Clemency The 18-member Board of Pardons and Paroles is a division of the Texas Department of Criminal Justice. **Parole** involves release from prison before completion of a sentence and is conditioned on the parolee's good behavior. It is granted by the board without action by the governor, but the governor may perform various acts of **executive clemency** that set aside or reduce a sentence. For example, a **full pardon** or a **conditional pardon** may be granted by the governor on recommendation of the board. Restoration of all civil rights, including the right to vote, distinguishes a full pardon from a conditional pardon. Acting independently, the governor may revoke a conditional pardon and may grant one 30-day reprieve in a death-sentence case. A **reprieve** temporarily suspends execution of the penalty imposed by a court. Ann Richards refused all requests for reprieve from the 48 condemned men who were executed during her four years as governor, and George W. Bush had granted no such requests by mid-1998.

Despite anguished pleas not to execute convicted murderer Karla Faye Tucker in February 1998, Bush refused to grant her a reprieve. She was executed by lethal injection and became only the second woman in Texas history to be put to death by the state. Aside from the single reprieve the governor may grant independently in a capital punishment case, the chief executive may grant others only on recommendations of the board. If recommended by the Board of Pardons and Paroles, a governor may also reduce a penalty through **commutation** (reduction) **of sentence** and may remit fines and forfeitures. On June 26, 1998, in the much-publicized case of serial killer Henry Lee Lucas, Governor Bush commuted his death sentence to life imprisonment.

Informal Powers

Any description of gubernatorial powers would be incomplete without noting executive involvement in ceremonial functions. In the eyes of most Texans, the governor's impressive office in the Capitol holds center stage. Although this room is used primarily for press interviews and public ceremonies, its occupant is a symbol of the government of Texas. Of course, a governor cannot accept all invitations to deliver speeches or participate in dedications, banquets, and other public events. Within the limits of time and

Governor George W. Bush (right) greets State Senator Carlos Truan (D-Corpus Christi) and a group of Texas high school students in front of the State Capitol. (Senate Media Services)

priorities, however, every governor does attempt to play the role of **chief of state**. The breadth and depth of this role cannot be fully measured, but its significance should not be underestimated in determining a governor's effectiveness.

Media relations are also important to the governor's ability to overcome constitutional weaknesses of the office. Handling the press requires not only an able press secretary but support from gubernatorial family members.

The Plural Executive

Politically, the governor of Texas is the state's highest-ranking officer, but in practice executive power is shared with various state officers. Although millions of Texans cannot readily identify them, the attorney general, comptroller of public accounts, land commissioner, and agriculture commissioner oversee large departments with multimillion-dollar budgets. Their 1998–1999 salaries were set by the legislature at $92,217 for each officer. Along with the governor, lieutenant governor, and appointed secretary of state, these state officials are referred to collectively as the **plural executive**. This structural arrangement contributes significantly to the state's long ballot because these executive officials (except the secretary of state) are popularly elected to four-year terms with no limit on their re-election. There is no restriction on the number of terms a secretary of state may serve, although each new governor appoints his or her own. Elected department heads are largely independent of gubernatorial control; however, the governor makes appointments to fill vacancies in these offices without senatorial confirmation. Unlike department heads in the federal government, those in Texas do not form a cabinet to advise the governor.

Lieutenant Governor

Considered by some political observers to be the most powerful official in Texas government, the lieutenant governor functions more in the legislative area than in the executive branch. A 1984 amendment to the Texas Constitution requires the Texas Senate to convene within 30 days whenever a vacancy occurs in the lieutenant governor's office; that body then elects a state senator to fill the office until the next general election. This elected senator wears two hats: lieutenant governor and state senator. The annual state salary for the office of lieutenant governor is only $7,200, the same as that paid members of the legislature.

As president of the Senate, the lieutenant governor is the presiding officer for that chamber and exercises great influence on legislation. Also, because the lieutenant governorship is regarded as a possible steppingstone to the governorship or other high positions, intense competition exists among candidates for that office.

Following the record-shattering five terms of William P. Hobby, Jr., Bob Bullock was elected lieutenant governor in 1990 and reelected in 1994. Profiting from strong name recognition, Democrat Bullock easily outdistanced his Republican rivals, Rob Mosbacher, Jr., and Tex Lezar, in 1990 and 1994, respectively. One veteran political analyst concluded:

> Perhaps what's most definitive about Bob Bullock is that he is at ease with the light and dark sides of power, where carrots and sticks exist. That's perhaps more true of him than any Texas politician since Lyndon Johnson. In fact, to understand Bob Bullock one should start with the equally complex L.B.J. The personalities of each Texan provide a playground for political psychology.[6]

In 1997, shortly after the end of the regular 75th legislative session, Bullock shocked the state by announcing that he would not seek reelection in 1998. In that year Republican Rick Perry won the office by defeating Democrat John Sharp. Perry and Sharp were finishing second terms as commissioner of agriculture and comptroller, respectively.

Attorney General

Increasingly, one of Texas's most visible and powerful officeholders is the attorney general. Whether suing tobacco companies, arguing affirmative action questions, or trying to resolve redistricting disputes, the state's chief lawyer is on the cutting edge of many public policy debates. This officer gives advisory opinions to state and local authorities and represents the state in civil litigation.

Overseeing more than 3,500 employees, the attorney general's office is consulted for advice concerning the constitutionality of pending bills. The governor, heads of state agencies, and local government officials also request attorney general opinions on the scope of their jurisdiction and interpretations of vaguely worded laws. Although neither judges nor other officials are bound by these opinions, such rulings are considered authoritative unless overruled by a court decision or legislation. Another power of the attorney general is to initiate *quo warranto* proceedings involving the trial of a state official who, if found guilty of some official misconduct, may be removed from office.

Election as the Democratic candidate in 1990 gave Attorney General Dan Morales the distinction of being the first Hispanic elected to head an executive department under the Texas Constitution of 1876. Morales's low-key style stood in sharp contrast to the high-profile lawsuits (including a multibillion-dollar settlement with tobacco companies) handled by his office. In 1994, Morales won a second term by defeating his Republican rival, Don Wittig, a Houston state district judge.[7] He did not seek reelection in 1998. In that year Republican John Cornyn (a former Supreme Court justice) defeated Democrat Jim Mattox (a former attorney general) to become the first GOP attorney general since Reconstruction.

Commissioner of the General Land Office

Although less visible than other elected executives, the commissioner of the General Land Office has emerged as a major policy player in Texas politics. Since the creation of the General Land Office under the Constitution of the Republic of Texas (1836), the commissioner's duties have expanded to include awarding oil, gas, and sulfur leases on state-owned land, serving as chair of the Veterans Land Board, and sitting as an *ex officio* (holding another office) member of other boards. With nearly 700 employees, the General Land Office also oversees the growth of the Permanent School Fund, which is financed by oil and gas leases, rentals, and royalties (involving state-owned land) that provide about $170 million for public school funding each year.

After serving as land commissioner for 16 years, Garry Mauro failed in his attempt to win the governorship in 1998.[8] In that year Republican David Dewhurst won the office of land commissioner by defeating Democrat Richard Raymond.

Commissioner of Agriculture

By law, the commissioner of agriculture is supposed to be a "practicing farmer," but this criterion is vague enough to allow anyone who owns or rents a piece of agricultural land to qualify. The political reality of winning the office stems principally from name identification among the state's voters. In 1998, Republican Susan Combs became the first woman agriculture commissioner by defeating Democrat L. P. "Pete" Patterson.

Speaking before the 80th annual convention of the Panhandle Grain and Feed Association, Rick Perry declared, "We need to look at government and see how we can reduce it, not reinvent it. Then, when it rains, we can start to look at where agriculture is going to go and not worry about running into roadblocks."[9] Such is the conservative philosophy of Texas's former commissioner of agriculture, who, like Governor Bush, was being touted for higher office by Republican supporters at the time of his election, in 1994.

The agriculture commissioner's control over often controversial pesticides is exercised through the department's Pesticide Programs Division. It restricts use of high-risk chemicals, issues licenses to dealers, commercial applicators, and private applicators (who use pest control chemicals on their own farms and ranches). Additional responsibilities include enforcing agricultural laws and providing service programs for Texas farmers, ranchers, and consumers. Enforcement powers of the department include inspections to determine the accuracy of commercial scales, pumps, and meters.

As Texas continues to expand its international markets, the commissioner is a key officeholder in promoting Texas agricultural products abroad. Annually, Texas agribusiness reaps nearly $3 billion from international agricultural sales.

Comptroller of Public Accounts

One of the most powerful elected officers in Texas government is the comptroller of public accounts, the state's chief accounting officer and tax collector. According to the Texas Constitution, before the legislature can pass an appropriation bill by a simple majority vote in the House and Senate, the comptroller must certify that revenue is expected to be available to cover all proposed expenditures. Otherwise, an appropriation must be approved by a four-fifths majority vote in both houses.

Bob Bullock left the comptroller's post in 1990 to become lieutenant governor. He was succeeded by Democrat John Sharp, a former state legislator and member of the Texas Railroad Commission. Sharp won a second term in 1994. Having earned a high level of respect for his cost-cutting efforts and proposals for increasing the efficiency of state agencies, Sharp became a candidate for lieutenant governor in 1998. In that year Republican Carole Keeton Rylander became the first woman to be elected as comptroller. Her Democratic opponent was Paul Hobby, son of former Lieutenant Governor Bill Hobby.

When Texas voters abolished the office of state treasurer by constitutional amendment in November 1995, the state comptroller's duties expanded to include receiving state revenues and administering deposits of state funds in some 500 banks, savings and loan associations, and credit unions approved by the State Depository Board. The comptroller, the banking commissioner, and another person appointed by the governor are members of this board.

The comptroller is also an *ex officio* member of the State Banking Board. Because all state-regulated banks must be chartered by the board, the comptroller is in a position to reward political supporters by influencing the awarding of charters for new banks.

Secretary of State

The only constitutional executive officer appointed by the governor of Texas is the secretary of state. To be effective, this appointment must be confirmed by the Senate. The secretary of state serves a four-year term with no limitation on the number of reappointments. When Secretary of State John Hannah resigned to become a federal judge in 1994, Governor Richards appointed Dallas attorney Ron Kirk to that office. Kirk was the second African American to hold the office of secretary of state and later was elected mayor of Dallas. Tony Garza, a former Cameron County judge (Brownsville), was Governor Bush's first appointment in 1995. When Garza ran for railroad commissioner in 1998, Bush appointed Al Gonzales, a Houston attorney, who previously served as the governor's general counsel.

Overseeing a staff of more than 200 people, the secretary of state is the chief election officer of Texas. Principal duties include the following:

- Administering state election laws in conjunction with county officials
- Tabulating election returns for state and district offices
- Granting charters to Texas corporations
- Issuing permits to outside corporations to conduct business within Texas
- Processing requests for extradition of criminals to or from other states for trial and punishment

With these diverse duties, the secretary of state is obviously more than just a recordkeeper. How the office functions is determined by the occupant's working with the governor.

The Bureaucracy

Knowledge concerning the state personnel system and the **board-commission system** of administrative agencies is essential to an understanding of how Texas politics is practiced. This complex governmental machine operates within a network of gubernatorial appointments, legislative appropriations, and state tax laws, but its levels of efficiency affect the quality of life for all Texans.

Public schools and state universities, health care programs, consumer protection, and environmental protection raise important issues and require the expenditure of billions of dollars in public funds. Thus, every Texas teacher, health professional, businessperson, laborer, and farmer is touched in some way by the state's public policies and its administrative machinery. Likewise, the influence of public policy and administration extends to all who pay taxes, study for diplomas and degrees, purchase goods and services, and consume air and water. In short, all of us are beneficiaries or victims of bureaucratic politics.

Texas public policies, usually generated by governors and legislators, are implemented by the state's bureaucrats. These public employees work in government organizations with many different names, including "agency," "board," "commission," and "department."

Size

State government is the biggest employer in Texas. When state college and university personnel are included, more than 300,000 Texans (full and part time) draw a state paycheck for their labor. Texas operates with neither a central personnel office nor a state-required merit selection system (civil service) for most state jobs. Each state agency determines its own personnel policies, but salaries, wage scales, and other benefits are set by the legislature.

After a 20-year pattern of bulging payrolls, Texas state employment began to decline somewhat in 1996. Spurred by State Comptroller John Sharp's cost-cutting incentives and budgetary cuts by the legislature, state agencies are being forced to trim personnel. Compared to the extensive downsizing of many private businesses and corporations in 1995–1996, however, Texas's reduction of 2,919 state positions (1.1 percent of the state government's work force) appears paltry. Houston-based Shell Oil Company reduced its work force from 32,000 to 25,000 over a two-year period in the early 1990s due to declining oil prices and lessening worldwide dependence on Texas's petroleum industry.[10]

Reduction-in-force (RIF) policies always present a formidable challenge to administrators. Attrition, caused mostly by employees' resignations and/or retirements, is relatively painless. Such vacant positions are simply left unfilled. Involuntary termination (firing), in contrast, poses more serious problems. There are low percentages of women and minorities in state employment, particularly at the managerial level. The domination of executive positions by white males heading major state agencies is another issue that is growing more acute as women, African Americans, Hispanics, and Asian Americans aspire to higher-paying positions.

Staff reductions, coupled with gender, ethnic, and racial issues, highlight an underlying issue that affects every facet of policymaking and administration—specifically, how to employ and retain a diversified public work force to serve Texas's increasingly multicultural population. Serving as advocates for state employees are two lobbying groups, the Texas State Employees Association (more than 15,000 members) and the Texas State Employees Union (nearly 10,000 members).

Customer Service

What people want most from their governments at every level is *service*. State of Texas customers are no exception. Recognizing that individuals are easily angered and frustrated with a lack of responsiveness from state agencies, former governor Ann Richards created a **state ombudsman** office. Perpetuated by Governor George W. Bush, the Citizen's Assistance Hotline is a link between state government and its customers, the taxpayers. By dialing a toll-free number (1-800-843-5789), individuals may receive assistance from the governor's office in coping with state bureaucratic hassles.

Education

Pressured students, beleaguered taxpayers, frustrated policymakers, and concerned journalists are embroiled in heated debates over education at all levels. "Can Johnny read?" is part of a more contentious issue: "What is Johnny reading?" Led by the Christian Coalition and other interest groups (see pages 133–135), conservative forces wage a relentless campaign to monitor textbook content, enforce tougher student discipline policies, and impose local controls. Responsibility for delivery of educational services from kindegarten through high school rests primarily with more than 1,000 independent school districts (ISDs). (See page 73.) Despite recent efforts to decentralize administration and free local schools from state supervision, policy directives from Texas lawmakers and state bureaucrats continue to control public school administration and classroom instruction. Such control is extended also to Texas's public colleges and universities.

Public Schools

Most Texans possess an inherent belief in public education. Mirabeau B. Lamar, third president of the fledgling Republic (1838–1841), spearheaded a drive to set aside land in each county for the support of public schools and "50 leagues for a state university."[11] Remembered as the "Father of Education in Texas," Lamar set the Lone Star State on an irreversible course. Today, the state's commitment to both funding and administrative support for public schools is clear. But how much authority should local school districts exercise? Even more controversial is the issue of how to fund education adequately with taxes that are fairly apportioned. (See page 285 for a discussion of Texas school finance issues.)

Texas Education Agency
With more than 1,000 local school districts administering nearly 6,200 public schools, many concerned citizens question whether additional layers of educational bureaucracy are needed. Already in place at the federal level is the U.S. Department of Education, with more than 4,500 employees. In the Lone Star State, the **Texas Education Agency (TEA),** headquartered in Austin, is staffed with more than 500 full-time employees.

Created by the legislature in 1949, TEA today is organized into five administrative units: office of the commissioner, instruction, finance, reading initiative, and chief counsel. The agency is headed by the commissioner of education, who is appointed by the governor to a four-year term with Senate confirmation.[12] Working under policies set by the State Board of Education, TEA sets teacher certification standards, accredits schools, oversees the Texas Assessment of Academic Skills (TAAS) in testing of elementary and secondary school students, grants waivers to schools seeking "charter" status and exemptions from certain TEA regulations, administers the Permanent School Fund, and supervises the Foundation School Program that allocates state money to independent school districts. Whenever a local school district fails to meet state standards, TEA officials are permitted by law to assume control of that district temporarily until acceptable reforms are instituted.

State Board of Education Holding center stage for statewide policies affecting more than 3.5 million students is an elective board. First created in 1929 as an appointive body, the **State Board of Education (SBOE)** is currently composed of 15 nonsalaried members, elected to four-year overlapping terms from legislatively drawn districts. Appointed as chair is a board member nominated by the governor and confirmed by the Senate.

Controversies surrounding board policies stem from an intensely heated ideological debate. Liberals argue for more academic freedom for teachers to advance experimental teaching strategies, sex education programs, and multicultural curricula. Conservatives, on the other hand, take issue with how the TEA is administering the Texas Essential Knowledge and Skills (TEKS) curriculum re-write, school-to-work initiative, and investments in Texas's Permanent School Fund. One point of contention is who should be responsible for textbook selection. As part of a massive educational reform package enacted in 1995, local school districts are permitted to select their own textbooks from a state-approved list. The SBOE cannot overturn local adoptions of books paid for with state money. Following an attorney general's opinion, local school districts remain the final authority in textbook selection after the SBOE has approved an adoption list.

Colleges and Universities

Higher education in Texas is a mammoth enterprise. State policymakers are often baffled by academicians' seemingly insatiable demands for more tax dollars. Presidents of public colleges and universities insist, however, that more money is needed if Texas is to compete successfuly with other states in recruiting and retaining the best professors and attracting and developing job-providing industries. Unlike public schools with their local property taxes, state-supported four-year institutions, officially termed "universities," must rely on state appropriations, student tuition and fees, and privately funded scholarships and gifts, along with government and corporate research funding, for their financial support. Community or junior college districts also compete with universities for state money, although two-year schools are partially funded from their own districtwide property taxes.

Texas Higher Education Coordinating Board In an effort to provide some semblance of statewide direction for all public colleges and universities, including two-year institutions, then governor John Connally proposed a new state board to the legislature in 1965. State lawmakers responded with creation of the 18-member **Texas Higher Education Coordinating Board**. Members are appointed by the governor to six-year terms with Senate approval. The board approves requests for new universities, more degree offerings, and creation of community college districts.

Boards of Regents The heaviest hitters in Texas's higher education conflicts are well-paid lobbyists representing four university systems: the University of Texas, Texas A&M University, the University of Houston, and Texas State University (which does not have a central campus). Boards of regents for each system are gubernatorially appointed with Senate approval. In each legislative session, these institutions wage turf wars to merge smaller universities with one of the "Big Four."

Policy Issues Aside from playing the numbers game of expanding campuses and enrollments, Texas colleges and universities face some complex problems. How they resolve sensitive issues of admissions policies, minority student scholarships, faculty salaries, class sizes, and graduation rates will go a long way toward determining whether the Lone Star State will compete successfully in national and global economic arenas. Here are some of the problems state legislators and university administrators face:

- How to establish admissions policies that will not conflict with the federal court ruling in *Hopwood* v. *Texas* that eliminated race-based admission policies as then practiced by the University of Texas law school. This ruling was extended by the Texas attorney general to eliminate race-based financial aid decisions.
- How to narrow the faculty salary gap between men and women
- How to increase funding for remedial education to prepare students for college credit courses and successful completion of the state-mandated Texas Academic Skills Program (TASP), a set of basic skills tests for entering freshmen students
- How to increase retention and graduation rates without "watering down" courses and degree requirements

With nearly 50 percent of Texas college students failing TASP since its inception in the 1992–1993 school year, legislators have demanded greater accountability from colleges and universities. At the same time, administrators have sought funding from businesses and individual donors to compensate for state spending cuts. Compounding these difficulties are other issues, headed by Congress's overhaul of the nation's welfare programs, that promise to challenge Texas policymakers as the twenty-first century unfolds.

Social Services

Through the 1990s there has been a growing trend toward devolution, a process whereby states (rather than the federal government) assume primary responsibility for administering and financing programs such as welfare. Social services include much more than governments handing out money. Politicians' most underserved constituencies include elderly persons suffering from age-related infirmities, inadequate health care, malnutrition, physical disabilities, mental illness, and life-threatening diseases such as AIDS. But most needy individuals are not organized to compete with special-interest groups and their high-powered lobbyists. Nevertheless, the Lone Star State has responded with social service agencies that provide assistance for millions of needy Texans. (See Table 7.2.)

Although the legislature created an umbrella office responsible for coordinating social service policies, this arrangement falls far short of centralizing policymaking. The **health and human services commissioner** is appointed by the governor (with Senate confirmation) and can be removed by the governor. This official oversees policy planning previously carried out by 11 separate agencies.

Human Services

Central to the ongoing debate about government dependency is how to provide *workfare* instead of welfare. Removing people from public assistance programs without adequate financial and emotional support only invites more crime, family violence, and other social problems that are even harder to resolve (financially and otherwise). What Governor Bush and the legislature (working from former State Comptroller John Sharp's recommendations) began in 1996 will require more education dollars if Texas's welfare reforms are to succeed.

After receiving approval by the U.S. Department of Health and Human Services, Texas launched its most drastic overhaul of welfare policies since

TABLE 7.2 Governing Bodies for Texas State Social Service Agencies

	Membership*	Term Length
Board of Health	6**	6 years
Human Services Board	6***	6 years
Mental Health and Mental Retardation Board	9***	6 years
Protective and Regulatory Services Board	6***	6 years
Workforce Commission	3**	6 years

*Members are appointed by the governor with Senate approval.
**Chairperson is selected on a rotation basis.
***Governor designates chairperson.

Source: *Guide to Texas State Agencies*, 9th ed. (Austin: Lyndon B. Johnson School of Public Affairs, University of Texas at Austin, 1996).

establishing the State Department of Public Welfare in 1939. Known today as the **Texas Department of Human Services (TDHS)** and employing more than 17,000 people, TDHS is charged with administering the following policies:

■ Individuals receiving cash assistance under the federally funded **Temporary Assistance for Needy Families (TANF)** program must sign a "personal responsibility agreement" requiring them to either work or enroll in a job-training program. Recipients are limited to three years of benefits under the agreement. Children of welfare recipients would continue to receive benefits if their parents tried, but failed, to find employment. Typical TANF recipients are single mothers with at least two children receiving $188 monthly. Federal block grants allow states to supplement state funds or find more innovative ways to help jobless persons with children.

■ When the three-year time limit expires, welfare recipients receive no benefits for five years, after which they can return to the welfare rolls. Federal policy places a five-year limit on benefits, without the lifetime chance to return to welfare rolls, forcing Texas to secure a waiver so that federal policy can be preempted.

When Medicaid and food stamp benefits are included, TANF recipients' average monthly cash assistance amounts to only $800. That sum could also be reduced, given congressional changes. Beginning in 1997, federal law replaced the national-state funding of Medicaid with block grants to the states. To comply with Congressional overhaul of welfare policy, the Texas Legislature changed Medicaid funding in 1997. Designed to provide medical care for persons falling below the poverty line (in 1997, a family of 3 with $13,333, in assets), **Medicaid** is not to be confused with Medicare. Also part of President Lyndon B. Johnson's Great Society initiatives in the 1960s, **Medicare** is administered by the U.S. Department of Health and Human Services without use of state funds. This federal program provides medical assistance to qualified applicants age 65 and older.

Congressional changes in the food stamp program also drastically affected Texans. As with welfare policies, state officials try to set their own rules. Beginning in 1995, the "Lone Star Card" requires food stamp recipients to use plastic cards rather than paper coupons for purchases. After only two years of card usage, Texas led the nation in reducing the total number of state food stamp recipients from 2.79 million in 1994 to 1.9 million in 1995.[13] By 1998, the average number of Texans on receiving cash assistance had shrunk by 20 percent to 219,579.[14]

Health

With more than 5,000 full-time employees, the Texas Department of Health (TDH) performs a wide variety of functions that include public health planning and enforcement of state health laws. TDH administers the following programs for needy persons: acute care, reimbursement of hospitals, prescription medicines, and transportation of patients to health care appointments.

Headed by a board-appointed commissioner, who must be a licensed physician, TDH is responsible for educating Texas's growing population about infectious diseases. As the principal killer of men in their thirties, no other public health problem rivals that of **acquired immunodeficiency syndrome (AIDS)**. Commonly transmitted by sexual contact and contaminated needles used by drug addicts, the deadly human immunodeficiency virus (HIV), which leads to full-blown AIDS, is an international epidemic. Texas trails only New York, California, and Florida in number of victims. By mid-1998, TDH officials reported 46,924 cumulative AIDS cases since 1980. More than 26,000 Texans have died as a result of HIV.

Mental Health and Mental Retardation

For individuals unable to afford private therapy, public mental health programs are available. Although Texas continues its massive mental health bureaucracy (more than 24,000 employees) known as the Texas Department of Mental Health and Mental Retardation (MHMR), legislative spending cuts are downsizing operations.

Usually administered by county commissioner–appointed boards, 35 mental health community centers carry the brunt of mental illness casework. Although local mental health units receive some state funding, more than 50 percent of their operations is financed from budgets of county governments.

Two other public policy issues apply to Texas's growing populations of individuals suffering from mental health problems (nearly 154,000) and mental retardation (more than 43,000) who are served by MHMR: overcrowding of facilities and state regulation of private psychiatric hospitals.

Employment

In 1995, the legislature abolished the Texas Employment Commission (TEC) and consolidated 29 job-training programs (administered by eight state agencies) under the new **Texas Workforce Commission (TWC)**. Directed by three salaried commissioners, TWC continues to collect a payroll tax that provides revenue used for weekly benefit payments to unemployed workers who are covered by the Texas Unemployment Compensation Act. TWC helps to coordinate the congressionally funded Job Corps program and programs under the Job Training Partnership Act. Therefore, TWC is subject to federal policies for hiring, promoting, and dismissing its employees.

Economic Policies

Have you ever complained about a high telephone bill, automobile insurance premium, or fishing license fee? Welcome to Lone Star State regulatory politics! Lobbyists spend millions of dollars each legislative session to protect special interests. For businesses seeking to boost profits or professional groups trying to bolster their licensing requirements, big money drives Texas's political process. Left behind are unorganized consumers, who often are forced to pick up the tab with higher bills and fees, and, on occasion, inferior service. Whether grappling with lobbying pressures or consumer demands, decisions of the Texas Railroad Commission, the Public Utility Commission, the commissioner of insurance, and other state officials affect not only corporate profits but also standards of living for millions of Texans.

Business Regulation

Two state agencies, the Texas Railroad Commission (TRC) and the Public Utility Commission (PUC), exemplify what is happening to regulatory policies nationwide. One industry-backed policy is **deregulation,** whereby business practices are governed by market conditions rather than governmental rules.

Oil and Gas Texas does not have an energy department, much less a state-funded agency with a title that identifies it as a regulator of either the oil or natural gas industry. Instead, the **Texas Railroad Commission (RRC)** functions in several capacities, most of which have nothing to do with railroads. Today, rather than "busting" railroad monopolies, as was the practice throughout much of the commission's history dating from 1890, commission members engage primarily in oil and gas politics, in addition to performing other regulatory duties thrust on them by the legislature. For example, appeals of municipally set gas rates for residential and business customers must be heard by the commission. Despite a decline in influence since oil prices collapsed in the 1980s, Texas's oil and gas corporations carry substantial clout in commission politics.

Sometimes federal policies preempt Railroad Commission powers. Examples include deregulation of trucking by the U.S. Congress and approval of a merger of the Union Pacific and Southern Pacific railroads by the U.S. Transportation Board.

Traditions die hard in conservative Texas. Abolishing or significantly overhauling the Lone Star State's oldest regulatory body, so closely tied to oil and gas interests, is unlikely to occur until aroused citizens are made aware of possible savings to their pocketbooks. Regulation of **intrastate commerce,** whereby states control transportation within their borders, is a long-standing, cherished state right reserved by the U.S. Constitution's Tenth Amendment. Whether a misnamed Texas Railroad Commission should continue to perform intrastate duties will be debated by reformers for years to come.

Public Utilities State regulation of Texas's utility companies first began in 1975 with the creation of the **Public Utility Commission (PUC),** whose three members are appointed by the governor to overlapping, six-year terms following Senate approval. Each commissioner receives an annual state salary of $90,071. From PUC's inception, consumers grumbled that they were being outspent and outmaneuvered by giant corporations (for example, Texas Utilities and Southwestern Bell Telephone) in complex proceedings to set electrical power and telephone rates. Since 1983, the state-funded Office of Public Utility Counsel represents consumers and small businesses at PUC hearings.

Insurance Beginning in 1993, the legislature replaced the three-member state insurance board with a full-time, state-salaried **commissioner of insurance.** Representing consumers in setting rates for automobile, homeowner, and liability coverage is the Office of Public Insurance Counsel. This official is appointed by the governor, with Senate approval, to serve a two-year term, the commissioner of insurance can also be removed by the governor without senatorial consent.

Skyrocketing costs of automobile ownership and maintenance probably draw more consumer reaction than any other public policy topic except taxes. How much to charge for automobile insurance is determined by state policies. Insurance companies are free to set their rates 30 percent above or below a benchmark determined by the insurance commissioner. Benchmarks are established following public hearings and are based on input from insurance companies and the Office of Public Insurance Counsel. The state is divided into 52 regions and the commissioner sets a different benchmark for each region. Consumers may shop for automobile and homeowner insurance by calling a toll-free number outside of Austin (1-800-599-SHOP) or 305-7211 within the Capital City.

Business Promotion

Cynics contend that the business of Texas government is *business*. Closer examination, however, reveals that in three policy areas—transportation, tourism, and licensing—the public interest, as well as private profit, is considered by policymakers.

Highways Nearly 77,000 miles of state highways have been constructed and are maintained by the Texas Department of Transportation (TXDOT). This department is headed by a three-member commission appointed by the governor to six-year, overlapping terms with Senate concurrence. Drawing no state salary, each commissioner must be a "public" member, without financial ties to any company contracting with the state for highway-related business.

Texans, like most Americans, are in love with their personal vehicles. Despite mass transit initiatives in some large cities (see page 75), the difficulty of getting people out of cars and pickup trucks and into buses or trains confounds policy planners at every level of government. The consequences of heavy highway use are accident-caused injuries and deaths as well as increasingly rough roads and bridges in need of structural repairs or replacement. Ranked third behind education and social services, highway maintenance will continue to command a high but steadily declining percentage of tax dollars in Lone Star State spending priorities.

Tourism and Trade Responsibility for preservation of Texas's natural habitats, along with providing recreational areas, lies with the Texas Parks and Wildlife Commission. Its nine members are gubernatorially appointed from statewide candidates, as with most other gubernatorially named boards and commissions. The chair of the commission is also designated by the governor. Fees for fishing and hunting licenses and entrance fees for 125 state parks are set by the commission.

Tourism is big business in the Lone Star State. It involves not only outdoor recreation for Texas residents but also strategies for attracting national and foreign visitors. Increasingly, global economics is creating linkages between state policymakers and private interests.

The Texas Department of Economic Development, which was created by the legislature, is attempting to find international markets for Texas products and to promote tourism. (See the reading on pages 222–224.) In restructuring the former Texas Department of Commerce, state lawmakers created a nine-member governing board. Appointed by the governor with Senate confirmation, four board members must represent the following interests: rural, small business, tourism, and international trade. Managed by an executive director who is appointed (with Senate approval) and can be removed by the governor, the department employs more than 200 full-time employees.

Certification of Trades and Professions More than 40 occupational groups are certified (licensed) to practice their respective skills by state boards and commissions.[15] Among trades included are those of plumbers, electricians, barbers, cosmetologists, and well drillers. Fifty percent of certifying agencies are health-care related, including vocational nurses, dental hygienists, physical therapists, and psychologists. As a result of combined legislative and public pressure, each licensing board and commission now includes at least one "public" member (an individual who does not work in the regulated occupation). All members are appointed to six-year terms by the governor, with approval by the Senate. From accountants to vocational nurses, board-commission standards for persons who perform myriad services stem from the politics of gubernatorial appointments and senatorial confirmations or rejections.

Environmental Issues

Among Texas's many public policy concerns, none draws sharper lines of disagreement than *how* to maintain and nurture all forms of life while advancing business and agricultural development. No arguments exist over *why* more action is needed to combat pollution. Texas industries produce more toxic contaminants (chemical waste) than those of any other state.

That grim reality is part of an increasingly complex political web that ensnares local, state, and national policymakers.[16]

Conservative Texas business interests, always angered by governmental "red tape," advance state policies to forestall federal regulations. Tracking corporate Texas's every step, however, is a growing army of public "watchdogs" (such as the Sierra Club) that are quick to expose polluting industries. One scathing report cited 1,070 active industrial plants in Texas operating without pollution control permits. Located in 172 of the Lone Star State's 254 counties, these "nonpermitted" industries were operating pre-1971, the year of Texas's first Clean Air Act. Therefore, 172 plants in 1998 were "grandfathered or exempted from pollution regulation."[17]

Power politics results from campaign contributions and other favors bestowed on environmental policymakers. Texas governors and legislators, along with locally elected officials, are intensely lobbied to protect multimillion-dollar industries ranging from Gulf Coast oil and gas refineries to out-of-state waste disposal companies.[18] Observing this political scenario is an increasingly nervous citizenry worried about whether Texas air and water will be clean enough to sustain life. Environmental issues know no political boundaries.

Air and Water

Coordination of the Lone Star State's environmental policies did not occur until 1993, when the **Texas Natural Resource Conservation Commission (TNRCC)** was created. Referred to as "Train Wreck" by some critics, supporters of Ann Richards applauded the merger of the Texas Water Commission, Air Control Board, and other environment-related state agencies into TNRCC. Commission members are appointed to six-year terms by the governor, and, unlike in its predecessor agencies, TNRCC's chair is gubernatorially chosen. Following Richards's lead, therefore, state lawmakers completely refocused Texas's environmental policymaking. Receiving full-time state salaries ($90,071 in 1998), commission members select an executive director, who oversees more than 2,700 employees.

State policymakers continually face a balancing act among federal directives, local business pressures, and environmental groups demanding swifter action. Delays in efforts by Dallas and Fort Worth to implement a regional plan for testing automobile emissions is one example of multiple agencies thwarting public policy. When TNRCC exempted Collin and Denton counties from regional testing regulations, officials in Dallas and Tarrant counties scrapped their original plan. As a result, EPA deadlines were missed and air pollution caused by automobile emissions increased in the state's most populous area.

Texas's air pollution problems are not confined to vehicles, however. Petrochemical plants, smelters, and steel mills dot cityscapes statewide. Combined, these and other waste-emitting industries put the health of millions of Texans at risk.

Water contamination is another major area of TNRCC's responsibilities. Working with local prosecutors, the commission hears disputes between alleged polluters and consumers over dumping toxic waste into state waterways. As with all regulatory bodies, TNRCC decisions can be appealed to state district courts.

Another state agency involved in water policies is the Texas Water Development Board (TWDB). Unlike the membership of TNRCC, the six members of TWDB are nonsalaried. They are appointed by the governor, who also designates the board chairperson. Along with developing strategies for water conservation in drought-ridden Texas, staff members administer other programs mandated by the legislature. With passage of a comprehensive planning bill in 1997 (S.B. 1), the legislature empowered the TWDB to work with different regions of the state and local officials in trying to meet twenty-first century water needs. S.B. 1 also allows county commissioners to consider water availability in making platting decisions—the rules under which subdivisions are developed.

Drawing statewide attention is TWDB's handling of more than $400 million of federal and state money to assist residents living in over 1,500 *colonias* along the Texas side of the Rio Grande. Polluted drinking water heads their list of pressing problems. This has drawn Texas policymakers into another debate over how to solve local problems with external funding.

Hazardous Waste

"Not in my backyard" is a rallying cry among Texans incensed over having their communities selected as storage sites for toxic materials. Some West Texas counties (noted for sparse populations, undeveloped land, and little political clout) seem to be easy prey for state and federal officials seeking to dispose of industrial and residential waste. Charged with setting policy for locating toxic dump sites is the Texas Low-Level Radioactive Waste Disposal Authority, governed by a six-member board appointed by the governor. But only TNRCC can authorize the actual dumping of toxic waste. **Low-level radioactive waste** consists of nuclear materials produced by hospitals, medical schools, nuclear power plants, and research laboratories.

Scientists and other authorities argue that when properly buried underground, low-level radioactive waste is harmless and can be reused for medical research. Local residents, such as the mostly Hispanic community of Sierra Blanca, home to fewer than 700 people, protested vigorously when their county (Hudspeth County) was selected for Texas's first low-level radioactive waste storage site. Schoolchildren from nearby Mexico, supporting their West Texas neighbors, marched in Austin to protest possible pollution of Mexican soil and water. Despite their efforts, state officials went forward with the Hudspeth County dump site in 1998.

After the legislature passed a law banning private companies from dumping low-level radioactive wastes, Waste Control Specialists Company, controlled by Dallas investor Harold Simmons, selected Andrews County (bordering New Mexico) for a dump site. Claiming exemption from state law because his company operates with federal contracts and does not dump radioactive wastes, Simmons, a wealthy contributor to Governor Bush, played "hardball" with Texas officials in getting his Andrews County dump site approved by both TNRCC and the U.S. Department of Energy.

High-level radioactive waste consists primarily of spent (used) nuclear fuel rods, liquid waste resulting from reprocessing those fuel rods, and scrap materials left after manufacturing nuclear weapons. Potentially toxic for thousands of years (compared to several hundred years for low-level radioactive material), high-level radioactive waste must be stored at sites selected by the U.S. Department of Energy (DOE). Due to intervention by two Texas politicians, then U.S. senator Lloyd Bentsen and Houston Congressman Jack Fields, Deaf Smith County residents were elated to learn in 1987 that Yucca Mountain in Nevada was the primary DOE-selected site and that their Panhandle county was off the federal list.

Generated largely by Texas's petrochemical industry, **nonradioactive hazardous waste** poses another dilemma for protecting the environment. Housing and commercial land developers covet landfill sites for their building projects. Pressured to relax guidelines for cleaning up dump sites in land-scarce cities, TNRCC has angered environmentalists with its pro-business policies.

Too Many Agencies?

If asked whether government is too costly and cumbersome, most Texans would quickly answer "yes." Counting the governing boards of state universities, more than 200 separate boards and commissions are tax funded. Determining a precise number is virtually impossible given continual restructuring by the Texas Legislature as agencies are abolished, created, or merged.

Far more difficult to answer is how to streamline the Lone Star State's bureaucracy. Beginning in 1977, responding to a nationwide movement for less governmental secrecy, the legislature passed *sunshine* laws making government meetings and records open for public view. That same year, Texas lawmakers began a **sunset process** whereby state agencies are systematically studied and then abolished, merged, or retained. Always refusing to relinquish their power, state representatives and senators must give final approval concerning which departments live or die. Herein lies the danger of perpetuating the status quo. Regulated industries (which often enjoy cozy relationships with friendly administrators) and state employees (fighting for their jobs) wage vigorous campaigns to keep business as usual.

Every 12 years, each state agency is reviewed by the Sunset Advisory Commission, composed of ten legislators (five from each chamber). Working with a staff of fewer than 30 employees, the commission makes its recommendations to the legislature as a whole. By mid-1998, only 29 minor state boards and commissions had been abolished ("sunsetted") following review of more than 260 agencies since 1979.

Looking Ahead

Three trends appear likely to continue in Texas's approach to state administration. Each transcends partisan politics, given conservative trends in both Austin and Washington, D.C.

First, *accountability* demands are forcing policymakers to require documentation of progress in education, human services, and other public policy areas. Driven by business principles of profit motive and cost effectiveness, taxpayers are sending at least one clear message to their public officials: they want "better" (at least from a business perspective) results for their money. Whether mandating schools to graduate students with marketable skills or forcing able-bodied welfare recipients to find jobs, many public policies are "bottom line" driven.

Second, and perhaps more likely to continue, regardless of who sits in Washington's White House or the governor's mansion in Austin, is *devolution*. Empowerment of grassroots (state and local) governments began not with conservative Republicans gaining control of Congress in 1994 but from an increasing realization that governments alone cannot solve all problems.

Finally, state policies will continually be shaped by *judicial decisions* when they conflict with national programs. How courts (federal and state) attempt to resolve high-stakes disputes emanating from telecommunications and environmental policies is reason enough to study politics as practiced by Texas jurists. Chapter 8 focuses on Texas's judicial system and its relationship to the bureaucracy, particularly administration of the state prison system.

Notes

1. See Celia Morris, *Storming the Statehouse: Running for Governor with Ann Richards and Dianne Feinstein* (New York: Charles Scribner's Son, 1992). Also see Mike Shropshire and Frank Schaeffer, *The Thorny Rose of Texas: An Intimate Portrait of Governor Ann Richards* (New York: Birch Lane Press, 1994).
2. See Alison Cook, "Lone Star," *New York Times,* February 7,1993, Section 6, pp. 22–27, 38–39, 42–47.
3. James Cullen, "Angry White Men and Polls," *Texas Observer,* October 28, 1994, p. 10.
4. Quoted in Caleb Solomon and Michael Totty, "Talking to the Governor: Taxes, Torts, Tobacco," *The Wall Street Journal,* May 1, 1996, p. T1.

5. See Carolyn Barta, *Bill Clements: Texian to His Toenails* (Austin: Eakin Press, 1996).

6. William McKenzie, "Bob Bullock: The New LBJ," *The Dallas Morning News,* June 15, 1993, p. 15A. For an accurate political profile of Bullock, see Robert Bryce, "The Last Don," *Texas Observer,* January 31, 1997, pp. 8–15.

7. See Robert Draper, "Dan Morales: A Heavyweight in State Politics," *Texas Monthly* (September 1996), pp. 117, 168–169.

8. Garry Mauro's experiences as land commissioner are related in his *Beaches, Bureaucrats, and Big Oil* (Austin: Look Away Books, 1997).

9. Kay Ledbetter, "Less Government Better for Agriculture," *Amarillo Daily News,* May 4, 1996, p. 1B.

10. Caleb Solomon, "Economic Focus: After Years of Expansion, State Payroll Falls (a Bit)," *The Wall Street Journal*, July 3, 1996, p. T1.

11. *Texas Almanac and State Industrial Guide, 1998–99* (Dallas: The Dallas Morning News, 1997), p. 501.

12. *Guide to Texas State Agencies,* 9th ed. (Austin: Lyndon B. Johnson School of Public Affairs, University of Texas at Austin, 1996), p. 88.

13. "Lone Star Card Succeeds," *Austin American-Statesman,* May 22, 1996, p. A14.

14. "Texas Welfare Rolls Shrinking," *Waco Tribune-Herald*, June 28, 1998, p. 3A.

15. See *Guide to Texas State Agencies* for a complete listing of licensing boards and commissions.

16. For an "Environmental Road Map" of the Lone Star State, see *Texas Environmental Almanac* (Austin: Texas Center for Policy Studies, 1995). Detailed coverage is given to water, land, air, energy, and waste.

17. See *Grandfathered Air Pollution: The Dirty Secret of Texas Industries* (Austin: Galveston-Houston Association for Smog Prevention and the Lone Star Chapter of the Sierra Club, April 1998).

18. See *Dirty Air, Dirty Money: Grandfathered Pollution Pays Dividends Downwind in Austin* (Austin: Texans for Public Justice, June 1998).

Key Terms and Concepts

devolution of government
Office of the Governor
appointive power
senatorial courtesy
recess appointment
removal power
martial law
budgetary power
legislative power
message power
veto power
item veto
postadjournment veto
special sessions
parole
executive clemency
full pardon
conditional pardon
reprieve
commutation of sentence
chief of state
plural executive
board-commission system
state ombudsman
Texas Education Agency (TEA)
State Board of Education
   (SBOE)
Texas Higher Education
   Coordinating Board

health and human services
   commissioner
Texas Department of Human
   Services (TDHS)
Temporary Assistance for Needy
   Families (TANF)
Medicaid
Medicare
acquired immunodeficiency
   syndrome (AIDS)
Texas Workforce Commission
   (TWC)
deregulation
Texas Railroad Commission
   (RRC)
intrastate commerce
Public Utility Commission (PUC)
commissioner of insurance
Texas Natural Resource
   Conservation Commission
   (TNRCC)
low-level radioactive waste
high-level radioactive waste
nonradioactive hazardous
   waste
sunset process

SELECTED READING

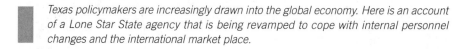

New Player Tackles Job of Selling Texas*

Bruce Hight

Texas policymakers are increasingly drawn into the global economy. Here is an account of a Lone Star State agency that is being revamped to cope with internal personnel changes and the international market place.

Rick Thrasher is something of a Canadian "good ol'boy" a man as comfortable talking slap shots as he is sales. What he's selling now is Texas, a state that doesn't know much about hockey but is stuffed full of good ol'boys. Thrasher is the new executive director of the recently reorganized Texas Department of Economic Development, an agency with a long history of political upheavals and spankings in the legislative woodshed.

Growing up in Canada taught Thrasher to slide around—or, if necessary, through—obstacles while swinging a stick. That background could come in handy as he promotes the state's economic development in a world of global competition while assuring skeptical legislators that he's not joy-skating with the state budget. . .

Troubled History

What is now the Texas Department of Economic Development can trace its bureaucratic roots back to the creation in 1959 of the Texas Industrial Commission. In 1983, it became the Texas Economic Development Commission.

In 1987, the Legislature merged the economic development commission with other state agencies, gave it additional job training duties and called it the Texas Department of Commerce. At the time, Bill Clements, a Republican, was governor.

In 1991 Ann Richards, a Democrat, took office as governor and, charging that the department had been poorly run, forced out more than 30 employees and installed her own leadership team. Some of those employees later sued to get their jobs back, but lost.†

---

*From the *Austin American-Statesman*, March 15, 1998. Bruce Hight is a staff writer for the *American-Statesman*. Reprinted by permission.

†Editor's note: Although they lost in two federal court cases, late in 1997 eight former Texas Department of Commerce workers were informed by the U.S. Department of Labor that they should recover their jobs, lost wages and benefits, and interest. See Denis Ganis, "Ruling Backs 8 Ex-State Workers," *Austin-American Statesman,* March 15, 1998.

Then in 1993 George W. Bush, a Republican, took office. He appointed a Houston businesswoman, Brenda Arnett, who promised to improve relations with state lawmakers who felt the agency was ineffective. But within months Arnett, too, came under fire for overseas travel to South Africa, Chile, Argentina, and Germany, as well as taking dozens of trips within Texas on state airplanes instead of less expensive commercial flights.

Last year the Legislature, deciding a house cleaning was not enough, embarked on a major renovation under the direction of Senator David Sibley, R-Waco, chairman of the Senate Economic Development Committee. "The Department of Commerce had become somewhat of a trash can," Sibley said. "Every time we had some kind of function we weren't sure where it went, we just stuck it over in Commerce. They ended up, I believe, being unfocused." Sibley said he wanted to depoliticize the agency by giving it some insulation from the comings and goings of governors. So lawmakers, with Bush's cooperation, took away the governor's power to appoint the executive director and gave it to a reorganized nine-member board. The new approach conforms with the way most state agencies are organized.

By having the nine board members serve six-year staggered terms, an agency is seldom turned upside down upon the arrival of a new governor elected to a four-year term. Of course, this being a new board, Bush was able to appoint all its members. The Legislature also stripped away several jobs the agency had accumulated over the years. (In one case lawmakers goofed, though many in Austin weren't complaining. In rewriting the law governing the agency, they inadvertently killed language that had blocked some of the city of Austin's strict land development ordinance.)

Political Background

While Thrasher is a professional in economic development, he was born and bred in a political world. His father. a lawyer, served in the Canadian Parliament from Ontario for five years and then was an executive assistant to Prime Minister John Diefenbaker. And though Thrasher has known professional success, he's no stranger to political body checks. In 1995 he was hired by Wichita/Sedgwick County Partnership for Growth of Wichita, Kansas, to promote economic development in that area. The partnership was a joint effort of the local chamber of commerce and city and county governments. But the Wichita-area partnership split as a new mayor took office and a dispute arose over shifting funds from established programs into new ones, according to newspaper reports by the *Wichita Eagle*. In September 1996 the partnership's board voted to dissolve. Thrasher was paid his $115,000-a-year salary under his contract through 1997.

Last year [1997] a search firm hired by the new economic development board in Texas sought Thrasher for advice on hiring a new executive director, then got interested in hiring him for the job. The board couldn't pay him more than $89,500 under the state budget, but he said he took the job anyway because of the emphasis on local economic development, and the chance to rebuild a problem agency as well as Bush's reputation. But, he said, changes at the agency will not involve wholesale dismissals and will come as an evolution, not revolution. Texas he said, has been smart in developing its high technology industry and learning how to use that technology. But the state needs to raise its profile globally, he said.

Beyond the Border

Texas's only foreign office is in Mexico City. It has had representatives in other overseas cities before, but the offices were closed after questions were raised about their cost and effectiveness. Still, Thrasher said, Texas communities are competing with cities worldwide, and other states have been much more aggressive in reaching out. For example, he said, 36 states have offices in Tokyo and about 20 have offices in Canada, which, like Mexico, is a partner with the United States in the North American Free Trade Agreement. Thrasher said he does not have a specific plan yet for an overseas commerce initiative, but that a high priority is beefing up the Mexico City office.

Chapter 8

★

LAWS, COURTS, AND JUSTICE

Outlook

Thadeus & Weez   **by Charles Pugsley Fincher**

Copyright © 1998 by Charles Pugsley Fincher.

*A*s Weez auctions judges to the highest bidder in the accompanying cartoon, he highlights a controversial issue: popular, partisan election of judges and justices of Texas courts. Only nine states select all trial court judges by partisan election (identifying the political party of the judicial candidate on the ballot), and only twenty-two states elect appellate judges and justices.

In February 1998, Texans for Public Justice, a nonpartisan organization, released a report indicating that 40 percent of campaign contributions to Supreme Court justices were donated by lawyers and litigants with cases before that court.[1] Except for the identity of the contributors, the study mirrored complaints raised in a 1987 report on the CBS show, *Sixty Minutes*. In an episode entitled "Justice for Sale," reporters alleged that Texas Supreme Court justices were influenced by campaign contributions from plaintiffs' attorneys. CBS returned to the Lone Star State in 1998 to film a sequel claiming that now contributions from defense lawyers and businesses affected judicial decisions. Justices on the Texas Supreme Court argued that their critics were not able to link a campaign contribution with any specific court decision. This chapter deals with issues involving both civil law and criminal justice and describes how the practice of Texas politics influences our laws, courts, judges, lawyers, and institutions of correction and criminal rehabilitation.[2]

An Introduction to Texas's Justice System

Significant connections between politics and justice in Texas result from state constitutional requirements that judicial officials (except municipal court judges) be popularly elected. This means campaigning for nomination in a party primary; running as a Democratic, Republican, or third-party candidate in a general election; and soliciting campaign contributions from lawyers and other individuals who have an interest in judicial politics. Many Texas judges obtain their offices initially when they are appointed to fill a vacancy caused by a judge's death or retirement before the end of a term of office. Such appointments are usually influenced by political party affiliation. Although judges are involved in the policymaking process, they attract less public attention than do state legislative and executive officials.

Some Important Questions

With almost 3,000 judges and justices and almost the same number of courts, Texas has one of the largest judicial systems in the country. Counting traffic violations dealt with by lower courts, millions of cases are handled each year. Some of these are civil cases involving disputes over money and property; others concern crimes that may lead to fines and/or jail and prison sentences for convicted persons. Texans participate in the judicial system in many ways. As voters, they elect judges, prosecuting attorneys, sheriffs, and constables. Sooner or later, most Texans will be called to serve as jurors and participate directly in the judicial process. In addition, many citizens are sued or sue others, or are charged with criminal conduct. Consequently, every Texan should ask, "Do we have adequate laws? Fair courtroom procedures? Honest judges? Diligent prosecutors? Competent defense attorneys? Efficient courts? Modern correctional institutions? Effective rehabilitation programs that promote public safety while re-educating and reforming convicted criminals?"

A Changing Focus

As the number of prison and jail inmates has increased in Texas and throughout the nation in recent years, criminologists debate whether imprisonment is a significant deterrent to crime.[3] Proponents of tougher prison sentences argue that lengthy incarceration is needed to incapacitate prisoners—in other words, to keep prisoners from committing additional crimes against the general public. Opponents stress that many prisoners are guilty of low-level drug offenses and other nonviolent crimes, and therefore are not a serious threat to the public. Further, citing Texas as an example, experts note that the state with the second-highest number of death-row inmates (more than 425) and the highest incarceration rate in the country also has a homicide rate that is about 30 percent above the national average and one of the highest overall crime rates in the nation. They insist that any reduction in crime is attributable to a decline in the crime-prone population (males between ages 13 and 24), not to confinement. Critics further contend that imprisonment is costly and diverts funds from crime prevention programs. Experts have clearly not reached a consensus on the causes of or deterrents to crimes.[4]

Policymakers have become increasingly concerned about the need for crime prevention and alternative-to-prison programs. In recognition that taxpayers lack infinite resources to build and fund prisons, emphasis has begun shifting to programs intended to deter young Texans from criminal activity. Prison officials have recognized a need to teach work and academic skills to inmates so they can hold jobs upon their return to the community. Criminologists and lawmakers agree that incarceration cannot be the sole solution to deterring crime in Texas.[5]

State Law in Texas

Courts of the state of Texas deal with cases involving **criminal law** (proceedings in which an individual is accused of having committed a crime) and cases dealing with **civil law** (any noncriminal matter). A court's authority to hear a particular case is defined as its **jurisdiction**. The law creating a particular court fixes the court's jurisdiction; it may be civil, criminal, or both. In addition, some courts have **original jurisdiction** only, meaning they are limited to trying cases being heard for the first time. Other courts are restricted to hearing appeals from lower courts and thus have only **appellate jurisdiction**. Still other courts exercise both original and appellate jurisdiction.

Regardless of their jurisdiction, Texas courts are responsible for interpreting and applying state law. These laws include statutes enacted by the legislature, the provisions of the Texas Constitution, and judge-made common law that is based on custom and tradition dating back to the days of medieval England.

Code Revision

Newly enacted laws passed in each legislative session are compiled by the Office of the Secretary of State and published under the title *General and Special Laws of the State of Texas*. For easier reference, these laws are arranged by subject matter. Many of these statutes may be found in *Vernon's Annotated Texas Civil Statutes*. In recent years, the legislature has reorganized and revised a number of Texas laws related to specific topics (such as education or taxes) into a systematic and comprehensive arrangement of legal codes; these are found in *Vernon's Texas Codes Annotated*.

In addition to piecemeal changes resulting from routine legislation, pressure occasionally mounts for extensive revision of an entire legal code. Thus, in 1991 the 72nd Legislature created the 25-member Texas Punishment Standards Commission. The commissioners drafted Penal Code recommendations to be considered by the state's senators and representatives when they convened for the legislature's 73rd regular session in January 1993. As a result, Texans were given a revised Penal Code featuring important changes in definitions of crimes, periods of imprisonment, and conditions for parole and community supervision. Subsequent modifications have been necessary to resolve problems not addressed by the original revisions, such as increasing punishment for state jail felons who are repeat offenders and creating a new felony for crimes committed by inmates of privately owned jails. The state's juvenile justice system was reformed by the 74th Legislature's revisions to the Family Code (see pages 254–257).

Criminal Law

Features of the Texas Penal Code include **graded penalties** for noncapital offenses and harsher penalties for repeat offenders. Also provided is a two-step procedure for establishing whether a crime punishable by death (a **capital felony**) has been committed and, if so, whether a death sentence should be ordered.

Graded Penalties There are first-, second-, and third-degree **felonies** for which imprisonment and fines may be imposed in cases involving the most serious noncapital crimes. Some lesser offenses (especially those involving alcohol and drug abuse) are defined as **state jail felonies** (so-called fourth-degree felonies) and are punishable by fines and confinement in jails operated by the state. If a deadly weapon is used, the offense is punished as a third-degree felony. There are also three classes of **misdemeanors** (A, B, and C) for which county jail sentences and/or fines are levied. (See Table 8.1 for categories of offenses and ranges of penalties.)

Enhanced Punishment A second conviction for a second- or third-degree felony or a third conviction for a state jail felony may result in **enhanced punishment,** meaning repeat offenders are punished as though they had committed the next higher degree of felony. Enhancement of a first-degree felony raises the minimum sentence from 5 years to 15 years. A third felony conviction for a first-, second-, or third-degree felony allows a sentence of imprisonment ranging from 25 to 99 years or life. A second conviction for a sex-related felony automatically results in a sentence of life imprisonment, with no opportunity for parole for 35 years. Although enhancement does not apply to Class C misdemeanors, repeated Class B and Class A misdemeanor convictions result in minimum jail sentences of 30 days and 90 days, respectively. If a court decides that a criminal was motivated by hatred toward a particular group, enhancement results.[6] In addition, a wide range of organized criminal activities, including those of street gangs, are given penalties one category higher than those for criminal activities involving only two persons.

Capital Punishment Texas leads the nation in the number of convicted felons executed since 1982 (157 through September 1998) and is second only to California in the number on death row. Although a majority of Texans continue to express support for the death penalty as a way to deal with violent crime, there has been a decline in support since the execution of Karla Faye Tucker in early 1998. She was the first woman put to death by Texas since 1863.

Under the Texas Penal Code, eight crimes are categorized as capital felonies for which the death penalty may be applied. Conviction requires evidence indicating an intent to murder or cause serious bodily harm to the victim or evidence that a murder occurred while another felony, such as a robbery, was being committed. An individual who aids a murderer may also be convicted of capital murder if the accomplice intended to murder a victim or contemplated that death could occur as a result of the crime. Murders of particular categories of people, such as young children and officials performing their jobs (including peace officers [whether on-duty or off-duty], prison employees, and firefighters) are classified as capital murders. In addition, murders that occurred in particular circumstances are capital murder felonies, including those committed during an attempted or a successful escape from prison; those committed for pay (the person hiring the murderer is also guilty of capital murder); those committed for retaliation, such as against a juror or witness; and serial murders. Murders committed by imprisoned felons are also categorized as capital murder felonies.

TABLE 8.1 Selected Noncapital Offenses, Penalties for First Offenders, and Courts Having Original Jurisdiction

Selected Offenses	Offense Category	Punishment	Court
Murder Theft of property valued at $200,000 or more	First-degree felony	Confinement for 5–99 years/life Maximum fine of $10,000	District court
Theft of property valued at $100,000 or more but less than $200,000 Aggravated assault, including a spouse	Second-degree felony	Confinement for 2–20 years Maximum fine of $10,000	District court
Theft of property valued at $20,000 or more but less than $100,000 Unlawfully taking a weapon to a school	Third-degree felony	Confinement for 2–10 years Maximum fine of $10,000	District court
Theft of property valued at $1,500 or more but less than $20,000 Illegal recruitment of an athlete if the value of any benefits are more than $1,500 but less than $20,000	State jail felony	Confinement for 180 days–2 years Maximum fine of $10,000	District court
Theft of property valued at $500 or more but less than $1,500 Burglary of coin-operated machines Stalking with threat of bodily harm	Class A misdemeanor	Confinement for 1 year Maximum fine of $4,000	Constitutional county court and county court at law
Theft of property valued at $20 or more but less than $500 Possession of four ounces or less of marijuana Driving while intoxicated	Class B misdemeanor	Confinement for 180 days Maximum fine of $2,000	Constitutional county court and county court at law
Theft of property valued at less than $20 Advertising, preparing, or selling term papers and reports for use by others Belonging to a sorority, fraternity, or gang in a public school	Class C misdemeanor	No confinement Maximum fine of $500	Justice of the peace court and municipal court (if offense commited within city limits

After a jury has found a defendant guilty of a capital offense, it must answer two questions:

- Is there a probability that the defendant will commit criminal acts of violence that would constitute a continuing threat to society?
- Is there mitigating evidence in the defendant's background, such as child abuse or mental retardation, that warrants a sentence of life imprisonment rather than death?

The jury must unanimously answer "yes" to the first question and "no" to the second question to impose the death penalty. Victim impact evidence concerning suffering (physical, emotional, and financial) experienced by relatives of the murdered person may also be considered by jurors in determining punishment. In the event the jury cannot reach a unanimous decision to assess the death penalty, the convicted felon receives life imprisonment. Anyone receiving a life sentence for a capital felony must be imprisoned for a minimum of 40 calendar years, without credit for good conduct, before becoming eligible for release on parole. An affirmative vote of two-thirds of the 18-member Board of Pardons and Parole is required for granting such release. Texas jurors are not advised of the minimum 40-year term before deliberation. This failure has been criticized by the U.S. Supreme Court.

If the death penalty is assessed, the prisoner has an automatic right of appeal directly to the Texas Court of Criminal Appeals, the highest Texas court to hear criminal matters. In this proceeding, the Court of Criminal Appeals reviews the record of the trial to determine whether any errors occurred in the handling of the trial. Fewer than 15 percent of convictions are overturned on appeal. Overturning a conviction does not mean charges are dismissed. Rather, a new trial is usually scheduled and the defendant is retried. In a separate proceeding a convicted capital felon may also file a writ of habeas corpus to challenge the constitutionality of a conviction.

Prisoners who receive the death penalty cost the county and state taxpayers about $2.3 million on average for trial and appeal. Imprisonment for 40 years in a single cell, on the other hand, would cost about one-third of this amount. Despite the economic cost, the number of capital murder trials and death penalty convictions continues to increase.

For nearly a century, death by hanging was the means of capital punishment in Texas. Then, between 1924 and 1964, a total of 361 persons were put to death in "Old Sparky," the state's electric chair, now on display in a museum in Huntsville. Subsequently, because of federal court rulings, no executions occurred in Texas until December 1982, when the first condemned murderer to receive an intravenous lethal injection was put to death. By late 1998, almost 160 additional murderers had been executed.

Civil Law

As used in Texas, the term *civil law* generally refers to matters not covered by criminal law. The following are important subjects of civil law: **torts** (for example, unintended injury to another person or that person's automobile resulting from a traffic accident), contracts (for example, agreements to deliver property of a specified quality at a certain price), and domestic relations or family law (such as marriage, divorce, and care of children by parents). Civil law disputes usually involve individuals or corporations. In criminal cases, an individual is prosecuted by the state. Nevertheless, a single incident may result in prosecution on a felony or misdemeanor charge and a civil suit for personal damages. Limiting recovery amounts by injured parties, who claim they had been damaged by some type of tort, is one of the most important changes in civil law in recent years.

Courts, Judges, and Lawyers

Article V of the Texas Constitution is titled "Judicial Department." This article provides that all state judicial power "shall be vested in one Supreme Court, in one Court of Criminal Appeals, in Courts of Appeals, in District Courts, in County Courts, in Commissioners Courts, in Courts of Justice of the Peace and in such other courts as may be provided by law." In exercising its constitutional power to create other courts, the Texas Legislature has created municipal courts, county courts-at-law, and probate courts. These courts are referred to as *statutory courts.*[7]

The Texas judicial system is complex. (See the structure of the current judicial system presented in Figure 8.1.) A court may have both exclusive and concurrent jurisdiction. A court that has **exclusive jurisdiction** is the only court with the authority to decide a particular type of case. **Concurrent jurisdiction** means that more than one court has authority to try a specific dispute. In that instance, a plaintiff selects the court in which to file the case. The same court may have original and appellate jurisdiction. Further distinctions are made regarding whether a court resolves criminal matters, civil cases, or both. Qualifications for judges also vary among the different courts as shown in Table 8.2.

Local Trial Courts

The courts with which Texans are most familiar are municipal courts and justice of the peace courts. Together these local trial courts handle, among other types of cases, charges involving Class C misdemeanors, the least serious category of criminal offenses. Both municipal judges and justices of the peace serve as magistrates of the state. In this capacity, they issue warrants for arrest of suspects and conduct hearings to determine whether a person charged with a criminal act will be jailed pending further court action or released on bail.

Municipal Courts Judicial bodies in about 850 incorporated cities, towns, and villages in Texas are known as *municipal courts*. The mayor of a general-law city serves as municipal judge, unless the city council provides for election or appointment of someone else to perform this function. Usually

FIGURE 8.1   Court Structure of Texas

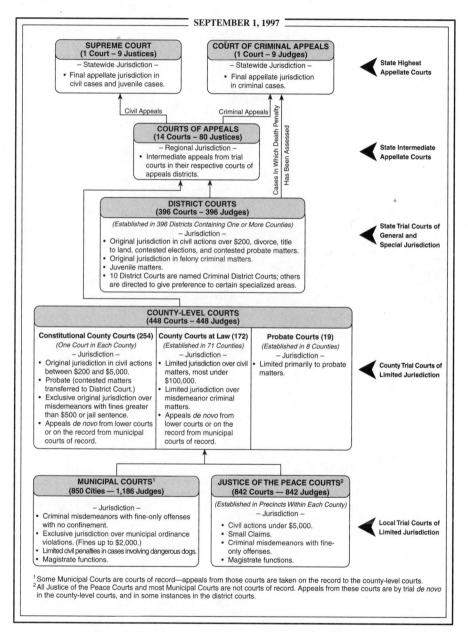

Source: Reprinted courtesy of the Office of Court Administration

TABLE 8.2 Judges and Justices of Texas

Court	Judicial Qualifications	Term of Office	Annual Salary*	Method of Selection	Unexpired Terms Filled by
Local Courts					
Municipal courts	Vary, set by each city	Varies, set by each city	Paid by the city; highly variable	Appointment or election, as determined by city charter	Determined by city charter
Justice of the peace courts	None	4 years	Paid by the county; highly variable	Partisan precinctwide elections	Commissioners court
County Courts					
Constitutional county courts	Must be "well informed" in Texas law, but not required to have a law degree	4 years	Paid by the county; highly variable	Partisan county-wide elections	Commissioners court
Statutory county courts (courts at law and probate courts)	At least 25, licensed attorney with minimum of 4 years' experience, resided in county for 2 years	4 years	Paid by the county; highly variable	Partisan countywide elections	Commissioners court
State Courts					
District courts	Licensed attorney with minimum of 4 years' experience, resided in district for 2 years	4 years	$101,700; county salary supplements; must be $1,000 less than court of appeals justices' salaries	Partisan districtwide elections	Governor with advice and consent of the Senate
Courts of appeals	At least 35, licensed attorney with minimum of 10 years' experience	6 years	$107,350 (justices); $107,850 (chief justices); county salary supplements; must be $1,000 less than Supreme Court Justice's salaries	Partisan districtwide elections	Governor with advice and consent of the Senate
Court of Criminal Appeals	At least 35, licensed attorney with minimum of 10 years' experience	6 years	$113,000 (judges); $115,000 (presiding judge)	Partisan statewide elections	Governor with advice and consent of the Senate
Supreme Court	At least 35, licensed attorney with minimum of 10 years' experience	6 years	$113,000 (justices); $115,000 (chief justice)	Partisan statewide elections	Governor with advice and consent of the Senate

*Fiscal year 1999.

Source: Office of Court Administration.

municipal court judges of home-rule cities are named by city councils for two-year terms. Although they are not required to be licensed attorneys (unless presiding over a municipal court of record), more than one-fourth of Texas's 1,150 municipal judges have this professional qualification. The city council determines the number of judges and sets judicial salaries.

Municipal courts have neither civil nor appellate jurisdiction. Their original and exclusive criminal jurisdiction extends to all violations of city ordinances, and they have criminal jurisdiction concurrent with justice of the peace courts over Class C misdemeanors committed within city limits. Municipal court judges are authorized to impose maximum fines of $2,000 in cases involving violations of some municipal ordinances (for example, regulations governing fire safety and public health). The maximum fine for violations of other city ordinances and state criminal laws is $500. If an individual is dissatisfied with the result of a municipal court ruling, the case can be appealed to the county court or a county court-at-law. Appeals are filed only in about 1 percent of municipal court cases.

If a city has a municipal **court of record** (a court with a court reporter to record the testimony and proceedings), a transcript of the municipal trial is made and the appeal at the county level is based on that record of the case. Otherwise, cases that are appealed are given a **trial de novo** (a completely new trial). Since 1987, the legislature has authorized all incorporated cities to maintain municipal courts of record. Because of the expense involved, fewer than 30 Texas municipalities have a municipal court of record.

Justice of the Peace Courts A justice of the peace, often called the JP, is elected for a term of four years by voters residing in a precinct whose boundaries are created by the county commissioners court. The number of precincts per county (one to eight) and the number of JPs per precinct (one or two) are mandated according to population by the Texas Constitution. Texas has more than 840 justices of the peace, most of whom serve on a part-time basis. Annual salaries are set by county commissioners courts and range from a token $1 to more than $80,000.

Neither previous legal training nor experience is required for the position, but about 5 percent of Texas's JPs (usually in large cities) are lawyers and may engage in private legal practice while serving as a justice of the peace. Within a year after election, a justice of the peace who is not a lawyer is required by law to complete a 40-hour course in the performance of the duties of that office. Thereafter, 20 hours of instruction are supposed to be received annually. Since failure to complete the courses is a violation of a JP's duties under the law, arguably a noncomplying JP could be removed from office for official misconduct. However, such removal is highly unlikely.

Judicial duties of justices of the peace in urban areas constitute a full-time job, whereas in many rural precincts very few cases are tried. In addition to presiding over the justice court, a justice of the peace serves as an ex officio notary public and, like other Texas judges and justices, may perform marriages. A JP also functions as a coroner, who determines the cause of death when the county commissioners court has not named a county medical examiner. Justice of the peace courts have both criminal and civil jurisdiction. In all cases, their jurisdiction is original. In criminal matters, these local courts try Class C misdemeanors, but any conviction may be appealed to the county court or a county court at law for a new trial.

A justice of the peace depends on the precinct constable to handle any courtroom violence. A constable, who is a peace officer with full law enforcement authority, is elected for a four-year term in each JP precinct. Most constables, however, leave law enforcement and crime detection to local police and the county sheriff's department. The principal function of constables is to serve writs (for example, a subpoena requiring appearance in court) and other processes issued by JPs. In a precinct with a large population, the constable is usually assisted by one or more deputy constables.

Exclusive civil jurisdiction of JP courts is limited to cases in which the amount in controversy is $200 or less, not including interest. Concurrent civil jurisdiction is shared with county courts and district courts if the amount in controversy exceeds $200 but is not more than $5,000. Appeals from a JP court are taken to the county level, where cases are tried de novo.

Small Claims Courts Presided over by the justice of the peace, a **small claims court** can hear almost any civil dispute in which the damages claimed are for $5,000 or less, except for divorces, slander, or suits affecting title to land. Plaintiffs must pay a fee of up to $65 to bring a case. Because these proceedings are informal, parties to the suits often represent themselves. When the amount in controversy exceeds $20, the losing party may appeal to a county-level court.[8]

County Trial Courts

Every Texas county has a county court as prescribed by the state Constitution, and some have one or more additional county-level courts. All are courts of record, and each is presided over by a single judge, who is elected on a countywide basis for a term of four years. A vacancy on a county-level court is filled by the county commissioners court. Annual salaries are set by the commissioners court of each county and vary from a few thousand dollars in sparsely populated rural counties to more than $100,000 in heavily populated urban counties.

Constitutional County Courts Under the Texas Constitution, each of the state's 254 counties has a county judge who is supposed to be "well informed in the law of the State." County judges performing judicial functions—along with judges of county courts at law, district courts, and appellate courts—must take Supreme Court–approved courses in court administration, procedure, and evidence. Only one-fourth of Texas's constitutional county court judges are licensed attorneys.

Most of the 254 constitutional county courts have original and appellate jurisdiction as well as probate, civil, and criminal jurisdiction. In some instances, however, the legislature has established county courts at law to exercise such jurisdiction. **Probate** matters include establishing the validity of wills, guardianship proceedings, and mental competency determinations.

Original civil jurisdiction of a constitutional county court is limited to cases involving between $200 and $5,000. Original criminal jurisdiction includes all Class A misdemeanors and Class B misdemeanors.

Appellate criminal jurisdiction extends to cases originating in JP courts and municipal courts. A constitutional county court's appellate jurisdiction is final with regard to criminal cases involving fines of $100 or less. For cases in which greater fines are imposed, appeal may be taken to a court of appeals. Civil cases are heard on appeal from JP courts when the amount in controversy is greater than $20. Civil jurisdiction is final with regard to those cases in which the amount in controversy does not exceed $100.

County Courts at Law In counties with large populations, the burden of presiding over the county commissioners court and handling many administrative responsibilities has left the judges of constitutional county courts with little or no time to try civil, criminal, and probate cases. Thus, the legislature had authorized more than 175 statutory courts through 1998 that are most commonly called *county courts at law*. Statutory court judges, who must be licensed attorneys, relieve constitutional county court judges of some or all courtroom duties in more than 70 counties. With few exceptions, the criminal jurisdiction of county courts at law is limited to misdemeanors. Civil jurisdiction of most county courts at law is limited to controversies involving amounts of $200 to $100,000. Annual salaries for judges vary. Multicounty statutory courts are authorized.

Probate Courts Some constitutional county courts share probate jurisdiction with county courts at law. In a few heavily populated counties, the legislature has established one or more county-level probate courts to hear probate cases only. For example, Tarrant County has two probate courts, Dallas County has three, and Harris County has four. Contested matters in probate cases are taken to district courts.

State Trial Courts

Texas's principal trial courts are composed of nearly 400 district-level courts of general and special jurisdiction as of 1998. Each has one judge, who is elected to serve for a term of four years. For fiscal year 1999, the minimum state salary for a district judge was set at $101,700 per year. Counties within a district may pay salary supplements.

Most state trial courts are designated simply as *district courts*, but a few are called *criminal district courts*. Each district-level court has jurisdiction over one or more counties, but a heavily populated county may have several district courts with countywide jurisdiction.

Qualifications for judges of district-level courts include U.S. citizenship, residence in the district for two years immediately before election or appointment, and a license to practice law in Texas. As a guarantee of practical legal experience, a district-level judge must have been a practicing lawyer, a judge of a court of record, or both for at least four years prior to election. As in the case of Texas judges in other state courts, a vacant judgeship (resulting from death, resignation, retirement, removal, or the creation of a new court) is filled by gubernatorial appointment with the advice and consent of the Senate.

More than half of the judges in district-level courts initially reach the bench as a result of appointment. Historically, having the political advantage of running as incumbents, they retained their positions by winning subsequent elections. In recent elections, however, incumbent Democratic judges have been defeated in increasing numbers as party affiliation has become more important than incumbency.

District Courts Most district court judges are authorized to try both criminal and civil cases, although a statute creating a court may specify that the court give preference to one or the other. All criminal jurisdiction is original. Except for cases transferred from constitutional county courts, misdemeanor jurisdiction is limited to offenses involving misconduct by government officials while acting in an official capacity. Felony jurisdiction extends to capital felonies; felonies of the first, second, and third degree; and state jail felonies. Appeal following a capital felony conviction is taken directly to the Court of Criminal Appeals. Other criminal convictions are appealed to one of the state's 14 intermediate appellate courts.

District courts have exclusive original jurisdiction over civil cases involving divorce, land titles, contested elections, slander, and defamation of character. They have original civil jurisdiction in controversies involving $200 or more. Thus, concurrent jurisdiction with lower courts begins at this level; above the maximum "dollar-amount" jurisdiction of those courts, district courts exercise exclusive civil jurisdiction. Appeals of civil cases go to a court of appeals.

Criminal District Courts Five courts in Dallas County, four in Tarrant County, and one in Jefferson County have been designated as criminal district courts. Nevertheless, each of these courts has general jurisdiction that extends to civil cases. More confusing, however, is the fact that some courts designated as district courts with general jurisdiction have been instructed by the legislature to hear criminal cases only, and others have been instructed to "give preference to" criminal cases. Such a hodgepodge of jurisdictions is but one indication that reorganization and simplification of the Texas judicial system are needed.

Appellate Courts

The Lone Star State's appellate courts consist of 14 courts of appeals, the Court of Criminal Appeals, and the Supreme Court of Texas. Each of these courts has three or more judges or justices, and all members are popularly elected for terms of six years. Terms are staggered so that one-third of the members are elected or re-elected every two years. This arrangement helps to ensure that at any given time, barring death, resignation, or removal from office, each appellate court will have two or more judges with prior experience on that court.

Justices of courts of appeals, judges of the Court of Criminal Appeals, and justices of the Supreme Court of Texas must be at least 35 years of age and have had ten years of experience as a practicing lawyer or ten years of combined experience as a practicing lawyer and judge of a court of record. Decisions are reached by majority vote of the judges assigned to the case after their examination of the written record of the case; their review of written briefs, or arguments, prepared by the parties' attorneys; and their hearing of oral argument by the attorneys. The Supreme Court of Texas and the Court of Criminal Appeals are authorized to answer questions about Texas law asked by federal appellate courts (for example, the U.S. Supreme Court).

Courts of Appeals   The legislature has divided Texas into 14 state court of appeals districts and has established a court of appeals in every district. Each of these intermediate appellate courts is composed of a chief justice and from 2 to 12 justices. A court of appeals justice receives a state salary that is 95 percent of the salary of a Supreme Court justice. Thus, in fiscal year 1999, the state salary for members of courts of appeals was $107,350. County governments in a district may provide salary supplements.

Courts of appeals hear appeals of civil and criminal cases (but not those involving capital punishment) from district courts and county courts. Final jurisdiction includes cases involving divorce, slander, boundary disputes, and elections held for purposes other than choosing government officials (for example, bond elections). Courts must hear appeals in panels of at least three justices. A majority vote of a panel of justices is required for a decision.

Court of Criminal Appeals   Texas and Oklahoma are the only states in the union that have bifurcated (divided) court systems for dealing with criminal and civil appeals. In Texas, the highest tribunal with criminal jurisdiction is the Court of Criminal Appeals. This nine-judge court hears criminal appeals exclusively. Noncapital criminal cases are appealed from the 14 courts of appeals. Capital punishment cases are appealed directly to the Court of Criminal Appeals from district courts.

Members of the Court of Criminal Appeals, including one whom voters elect as presiding judge, are popularly elected in partisan elections on a statewide basis for six-year terms. Annual salaries of judges of the Court of Criminal Appeals were set at $113,000 for fiscal year 1999. The presiding judge was authorized to receive $2,000 more because of his administrative responsibilities.

Supreme Court   Officially titled the Supreme Court of Texas, the state's highest court with civil jurisdiction has nine members elected statewide on a partisan basis: one chief justice and eight justices. Annual salaries for the justices and the chief justice are the same as those for the judges and the presiding judge of the Court of Criminal Appeals.

With no criminal jurisdiction, this high court is supreme only in cases involving civil law. Because it has very limited original jurisdiction (for example, issuing writs and hearing cases involving denial of a place on an election ballot), nearly all of the Court's work involves appeals of cases that it determines it must hear based on statutory provisions. Much of the Supreme Court's work involves handling applications for a writ of error, which can be requested by a party who argues that a court of appeals made a mistake on a question of law. If as many as four justices favor issuing the writ, the case is scheduled for argument in open court.

In addition to hearing motions and applications and deciding cases, the Supreme Court performs other important functions. It is responsible for formulating the rules of civil procedure, which set out the manner in which civil cases are to be handled by the state's trial courts and the appellate courts. The Supreme Court also has the authority to transfer cases for the purpose of equalizing the workloads (cases pending on the dockets) of courts of appeals. The chief justice can temporarily assign district judges outside their administrative judicial regions and assign retired appellate justices (with their consent) to temporary duty on courts of appeals. Early in each regular session of the Texas Legislature, the chief justice is required by law to deliver a "State of the Judiciary" message, either orally or in written form, to the legislature.

Disciplining and Removing Judges and Justices

Each year, a few of Texas's judges and justices commit acts that warrant discipline or removal. Traditionally the most common method of dealing with erring judges was to vote them out of office at the end of a term, but situations involving the most serious judicial misconduct were handled through trial by jury for judges at all levels and by legislative address or impeachment for state court judges. Although all of these methods are still available, the State Commission on Judicial Conduct now plays the most important role in disciplining the state's judiciary at all levels. It investigates about 900 complaints a year against judges. This 11-member commission is composed of five judges, each from a different-level court; two attorneys; and four nonattorney private citizens.

The State Commission on Judicial Conduct may suspend from office any judge (or justice) who has been indicted by a grand jury for a felony or who has been charged with a misdemeanor involving official misconduct; privately or publicly admonish, warn, or reprimand a judge; require a judge to obtain additional judicial training or education; order a formal hearing concerning public censure, removal, or retirement of a judge; or request the Supreme Court to appoint a master to hear evidence and then report to the commission.

Lawyers

Both the Supreme Court and the State Bar of Texas play a role in regulating legal practice in the state. The Supreme Court is involved with issues relating to the training and licensing of lawyers. Although accreditation of law schools is largely a responsibility of the American Bar Association, the

Supreme Court appoints the eight-member Board of Law Examiners. That board supervises administration of the bar exam for individuals seeking to become licensed attorneys, and it certifies the names of successful applicants to the court.

To practice, a licensed attorney must be a member of the State Bar of Texas and pay dues for its support. Although the State Bar is well known for its high-pressure lobbying activities, it promotes high standards of ethical conduct for Texas lawyers and conducts an extensive program of continuing legal education. To maintain their active status, practicing attorneys must complete at least 15 hours of continuing education each year, of which at least 3 hours must be devoted to legal ethics.

As an administrative agency of the state, the State Bar is authorized to discipline, suspend, and disbar attorneys. Investigations and hearings involving professional misconduct by attorneys are conducted by local grievance committees composed of lawyers and individuals outside the legal profession. Even without the filing of a complaint, the bar may take action to police its membership.

Although there is an abundance of lawyers in the Lone Star State, legal services are still not available to many Texans. About 80 percent of the state's lawyers provide some form of charity legal work in 1997, but many impoverished Texans who need legal assistance can not obtain it. Attorneys are encouraged to provide low-cost and **pro bono** (cost-free) assistance to indigent individuals. Under the Sixth Amendment to the U.S. Constitution and the Bill of Rights in the Texas Constitution, individuals accused of a crime are entitled to be represented by an attorney. Courts must appoint attorneys for criminal defendants who establish that they are indigent. These attorneys are paid by the county. No assistance is available for habeas corpus proceedings brought by prisoners, except for defendants who have been sentenced to death.

If these same individuals were trying to get legal help for a civil matter, little or no free assistance would be available. As the U.S. Congress has reduced funding for the Legal Services Corporation, a federal program begun during the administration of Richard Nixon to provide legal services for civil matters to poor people, the State Bar has worked to fill the gap through attorney volunteers. Recommending that attorneys donate 50 hours per year to assisting needy clients, the State Bar asks attorneys to report their volunteer hours annually when paying their dues. Pro bono work by attorneys is not limited to helping indigent individuals. From 1994 through 1998, the prestigious Houston law firm Vinson & Elkins, donated more than $2 million in legal services representing the University of Texas Law School in the case of *Hopwood* v. *Texas*.

Juries

A jury system enables citizens to participate directly in the administration of justice. Texas has two types of juries: grand juries and trial juries. The state's Bill of Rights guarantees that individuals may be charged with a felony only by grand jury indictment. It also guarantees that anyone charged with either a felony or a misdemeanor has the right to trial by jury. Jury trials are required in civil cases if requested by either party.

Grand Jury

A **grand jury** is composed of 12 citizens who may be chosen at random or selected by a judge from a list of 15 to 20 county residents recommended by a judge-appointed grand jury commission. Members of a grand jury must have the qualifications of trial jurors and are paid like trial jurors. (See pages 243–244.) As required of a trial juror, a grand jury member must not be under indictment for a felony or charged with a misdemeanor theft at the time of selection. The district judge appoints one juror as foreman or presiding juror to preside during jury sessions. A grand jury's life extends over the length of a district court's term, which varies from three to six months. During this period, grand juries have authority to inquire into all criminal actions, but devote most of their time to felony matters.

The work of a grand jury is conducted in secrecy. Jurors and witnesses are sworn to keep secret all they hear in grand jury sessions. If, after investigation and deliberation (often lasting only a few minutes), at least nine grand jurors decide there is sufficient evidence to warrant a trial, an indictment is prepared with the aid of the prosecuting attorney. The **indictment** is a written statement accusing some person or persons of a particular crime (for example, burglary of a home). An indictment is referred to as a **true bill**; failure to indict constitutes a **no bill**.

For misdemeanor prosecutions, grand jury indictments are authorized but not required. Any credible person may file a **complaint,** a sworn statement asserting that there is good reason to believe a person has committed a particular offense. On the basis of this complaint, the district or county attorney may prepare an **information,** a document that formally charges the accused with a misdemeanor offense.

Trial Jury

Although relatively few Texans ever serve on a grand jury, almost everyone can expect to be summoned from time to time for duty on a trial jury (**petit jury**). Official qualifications for jurors are not high, and many thousands of jury trials are held in the Lone Star State every year. To ensure that jurors are properly informed concerning their work, they are provided with brief printed instructions (in English and Spanish) that describe their duties and explain basic legal terms and trial procedures.

Qualifications of Jurors To be considered qualified, a Texas juror must be

- A citizen of the United States and of the state of Texas
- Eighteen years of age or older
- Of sound mind

- Able to read and write (with no restriction on language), unless literate jurors are unavailable
- Neither convicted of a felony nor under indictment or other legal accusation of theft or of any felony

Qualified persons have a legal responsibility to serve when called, unless exempted or excused. Exempted from jury duty are individuals who

- Are age 70 or older
- Have legal custody of a child or children under age 10
- Are enrolled and attending a college or secondary school

Nevertheless, judges retain the prerogative to excuse others from jury duty in special circumstances. A person who is legally exempt from jury duty may avoid reporting to the court as summoned by filing a signed statement with the court clerk at any time before the scheduled date of appearance.

Selection of Jurors   A **venire** (jury panel) is chosen by random selection from a list provided by the secretary of state. The list includes the county's registered voters, licensed drivers, and persons with identification cards issued by the Department of Public Safety. A trial jury is composed of 6 or 12 individuals: 6 in a justice of the peace court, municipal court, and county court or 12 in a district court. A jury panel generally includes more than the minimum number of jurors.

Attorneys are allowed to question jurors through a procedure called **voir dire** (which literally means "to speak the truth") to identify any potential jurors who cannot be fair and impartial. An attorney may challenge for cause any venire member suspected of bias. If the judge agrees, the prospective juror is excused from serving. An attorney challenges prospective jurors either by **peremptory challenge** (up to 15 per side, depending on the type of case, without having to give a reason for excluding the venire members) or by **challenge for cause** (an unlimited number). Jurors may not be excluded on the basis of race or ethnicity. Many individuals try to avoid jury duty by failing to appear (punishable as contempt for ignoring the court's order) or answering voir dire questions in a way that makes them appear biased.

For a district court, a trial jury is made up of the first 12 venire members who are neither excused by the district judge nor challenged peremptorily by a party in the case. For lower courts, the first six venire members accepted form a jury.

When jurors are empaneled, a district judge may direct the selection of four alternates, and a county judge may require the selection of two alternates. If for some reason a juror cannot finish the trial for either a civil or a criminal case, an alternate juror may be seated as a replacement.

Compensation of Jurors   Daily pay for venire members and jurors varies from county to county. In 1997, the legislature authorized each county commissioners court to authorize payment at an amount not to exceed $50 per day, but most counties set payment for venire members (those who are summoned for jury duty) at only $6 per day and pay for jurors at a mere $10 for each day of jury service. Amounts in excess of payments set by the county may be paid by the parties to the case if they agree to do so. Employers are prohibited by law from discharging permanent employees because they have been summoned as prospective jurors or selected as jurors.

Judicial Procedures

Many Texas residents, as well as people from outside the state, appear in court as litigants or witnesses. As a litigant, for example, a person becomes a party to a civil case arising from an automobile accident or from a divorce or child custody matter. A person would become a party in a criminal case when accused of a crime such as robbery. Witnesses may be summoned to testify in any type of case brought before the trial courts of Texas, but a court pays each witness only $10 per day for court attendance. In still another capacity, a citizen (even someone without legal training) may be elected to the office of county judge or justice of the peace. For these reasons, Texans should understand what happens in the courtrooms of their state.

Civil Trial Procedure

Rules of civil procedure for all courts with civil jurisdiction are made by the Supreme Court of Texas, but these rules cannot conflict with any general law of the state. Rules of civil procedure are enacted unless they are rejected by the legislature.

Pretrial Actions Civil cases normally begin when the **plaintiff** (injured party) files a **petition,** a written document containing the plaintiff's complaints against the **defendant** and the remedy that is sought—usually money damages. This petition is filed with the clerk of the court in which the lawsuit is contemplated, and the clerk issues a **citation**. The citation is delivered to the defendant, directing that person to answer the charges. If the defendant wants to contest the suit, he or she must file a written answer to the plaintiff's charges. The **answer** explains why the plaintiff is not entitled to the remedy sought and asks that the plaintiff be required to prove every charge made in the petition.

Before the judge sets a trial date (which may be many months or even years after the petition is filed), all interested parties should have had an opportunity to file their petitions, answers, or other pleas with the court. These written instruments constitute the pleadings in the case and form the basis of the trial.

Either party has the option to have a jury determine the facts. If a jury is not demanded, the trial judge determines all facts and applies the law. When a jury determines the facts after receiving instructions from the judge, the judge's only duty is to apply the law to the jury's version of the facts.

Trial of a Civil Case   As a trial begins, lawyers for each party make brief opening statements. The plaintiff's case is presented first. The defendant has the opportunity to contest the relevance or admissibility of all evidence introduced by the plaintiff and may cross-examine the plaintiff's witnesses. After the plaintiff's case has been presented, it is the defendant's turn to offer evidence and the testimony of witnesses. This evidence and testimony may be challenged by the plaintiff. The judge is the final authority as to what evidence and testimony may be introduced by all parties, though objections to the judge's rulings can be used as grounds for appeal.

After all parties have finished their presentations, the judge writes a **charge to the jury,** submits it to the parties for their approval, makes any necessary changes they suggest, and reads the charge to the jury. In the charge, the judge instructs the jury on the rules governing their deliberations and defines various terms. After the charge is read, attorneys make their appeals to the jury, at which point the jury retires to elect one of its members as the foreman (presiding juror) and to deliberate. The jury will be given a series of questions to answer that will establish the facts of the case. These questions are called **special issues**. The judgment will be based on the jury's answers to these special issues. The jury will not be asked directly whether the plaintiff or the defendant should win. To decide a case, at least ten jurors must agree on answers to all of the special issues in a district court, and five must agree in a county court or JP court. If the required number of jurors cannot reach agreement, the foreman reports a **hung jury**. If the judge agrees, the jury is discharged. Either party may then request a new trial which will be scheduled; otherwise, the case is dismissed.

A jury's decision is known as a **verdict**. On the basis of a verdict, the judge prepares a written opinion, known as the **judgment** or *decree of the court*. Either party may then file a motion for a new trial based on the reason or reasons the party believes the trial was not fair. If the judge agrees, a new trial will be ordered; if not, the case may be appealed to a higher court. In each appeal, a complete written record of the trial is sent to the appellate court.

Appeal of a Civil Case   In a court of appeals or in the Supreme Court, a case is heard by justices without a jury. The appellate court proceeds on the basis of the record sent up from the lower court and written and oral arguments by the lawyers. After the appeal has been heard in open court, the judges take the case to conference. There they discuss it among themselves and arrive at a decision by a majority vote. The usual route of appeals is from a county or district court to a court of appeals and then, in some instances, to the Supreme Court of Texas.

Criminal Trial Procedure

Rules of criminal procedure are made by the legislature. The Texas Code of Criminal Procedure was substantially revised in the 1960s to bring Texas procedures into line with the U.S. Supreme Court's rulings regarding confessions, arrests, searches, and seizures. Other changes resulted from pressure by the State Bar of Texas. Since 1967, additional rules of procedure have been adopted by the legislature to promote fairness and efficiency in handling criminal cases.

Pretrial Actions Probably millions of illegal acts are committed daily in Texas. For example, many people drive automobiles faster than official speed limits allow or drive while under the influence of alcohol. After an arrest is made, but before questioning, a suspect must be informed of the right to remain silent, of the possibility that any statement may be used as evidence by the state, and of the right to consult with counsel (a lawyer). When charges are filed by a prosecuting attorney, a suspect must be taken before a judicial officer (usually a justice of the peace) who names the offense or offenses charged and provides information concerning the suspect's legal rights. A person who is charged with a noncapital offense may be released on **personal recognizance** (promising to report for trial at a later date), released on bail by posting personal money or money provided for a charge by a bail bond service, or denied bail and be jailed. People who cannot afford to hire a lawyer must be provided with the services of an attorney in any felony or misdemeanor case in which conviction may result in a prison or jail sentence.

Under Texas law, the right to trial by jury is guaranteed in all criminal cases, even those involving the most minor misdemeanors. Except in a capital felony case where the district attorney is seeking the death penalty, however, defendants may waive jury trial (if the prosecuting attorney agrees) regardless of the plea—guilty, not guilty, or **nolo contendere** (no contest). To expedite procedures, prosecuting and defense attorneys may engage in **plea bargaining,** in which the accused pleads guilty in return for a promise that the prosecutor will seek a lighter sentence or will recommend community supervision. Usually a judge will accept a plea bargain. If the defendant waives a trial by jury and is found guilty by a judge, that judge also determines the form and amount of punishment to be imposed.

Trial of a Criminal Case After the trial jury has been selected, an indictment or an information is read by the prosecuting attorney. The jury is thus informed of the basic allegations of the state's case, and the defendant enters a plea.

As plaintiff, the state begins by calling its witnesses and introducing any evidence supporting the information or the indictment. The defense may challenge the truth or relevance of evidence presented and is allowed to cross-examine all witnesses. Next, the defense may present its case, calling witnesses and submitting evidence that in turn is subject to attack by the prosecution.

After all evidence and testimony have been presented, the judge charges the jury, explaining the law applicable to the case. Both prosecuting and defense attorneys are then given an opportunity to address final arguments to the jury before it retires to reach a verdict.

Verdict and Sentence A unanimous decision is required for the jury to reach a verdict of guilty or not guilty. If jurors are hopelessly split and the result is a hung jury, the judge declares a mistrial, discharges the jurors, and, if requested by the prosecuting attorney, orders a new trial with another jury.

When a jury brings a verdict before a court, the judge may choose to disregard it and order a new trial on grounds that the jury has failed to arrive at a verdict that achieves substantial justice. In a jury trial, the sentence may be fixed by the jury if the convicted person so requests; otherwise, the judge determines the sentence. In either event, a separate hearing on the penalty is held, at which time the person's prior criminal and/or juvenile record, general reputation, and other relevant factors may be introduced—such as facts concerning the convicted person's background and lifestyle as determined by a presentence investigation.

Appeal of a Criminal Case A convicted defendant has the right to appeal on grounds that an error in trial procedure occurred. When an appeal is made, the court clerk forwards the attorneys' briefs and the trial record to the appropriate appellate court. All capital punishment cases and a limited number of other criminal cases are taken directly to the Court of Criminal Appeals. Habeas corpus appeals that challenge the constitutionality of a conviction may be filed in state and federal courts. Under recent "speedy execution laws" at both levels of government, death row inmates are restricted in the number and timing of habeas corpus appeals.

Prosecutors have a limited right of appeal in criminal cases. They may challenge court actions such as a court's dismissal of an indictment, a modification or change in a judgment, or the granting of a new trial. An appeal must be filed by the state within 15 days of the close of a trial. During the trial, the prosecution may obtain a stay (delay) of proceedings until a court of appeals acts on an appeal related to a ruling by the trial judge.

Correction and Rehabilitation

Confinement in a prison or jail is designed to punish lawbreakers, deter others from committing similar crimes, and isolate offenders from society, thus protecting the lives and property of citizens who might otherwise become victims of criminals. Ideally, while serving a sentence behind bars, a lawbreaker will be rehabilitated and, after release, will obey all laws, find employment, and make positive contributions to society. In practice, almost 50 percent of convicted criminals violate the conditions of their release or commit other crimes after being released.

The number of Texans who are either imprisoned or supervised by the Texas Department of Criminal Justice has continued to increase. By early 1998, Texas prison officials became concerned that the inmate population would exceed 144,600, the total number of available beds in the state prison system. New construction and agreements with counties to house convicted felons in county jails helped solve the overcrowding problem. In addition, more than 315,000 convicted felons were free but serving sentences under **community supervision** (formerly termed *probation*) or on parole. Longer sentences, fewer paroles, and more parole revocations have resulted in an accelerated increase in the prison population.

The Texas Department of Criminal Justice

The principal criminal justice agencies of the state are organized within the Texas Department of Criminal Justice (TDCJ). This department is headed by the nonsalaried Texas Board of Criminal Justice, composed of nine members appointed by the governor (with advice and consent of the Senate) for overlapping six-year terms. The governor selects one member to chair the board, which employs a full-time executive director who hires directors of the department's divisions. Each division director is responsible for hiring division personnel. A total of 40,000 Texans were employed by TDCJ in 1998, making it the largest employer in the state.

The Community Justice Assistance Division establishes minimum standards for county programs involving community supervision and community corrections facilities (such as a "boot" camp or a restitution center). Programs that meet the division's standards are certified for state funding.

Operation and management of the state prison system, composed of 108 units (as of 1998), is the responsibility of the Institutional Division. Older units are located largely in East Texas, but recent construction programs have established several new prison units throughout the state.

The State Jail Division operates facilities for incarcerating individuals who have been convicted of state jail felonies. These institutions are designed for nonviolent offenders, most of whom undergo treatment for drug and alcohol abuse and other rehabilitative programs.

The Pardons and Paroles Division manages Texas's statewide parole and mandatory supervision system for convicted felons. The 18-member Board of Pardons and Paroles recommends acts of clemency (such as pardons) to the governor and grants or revokes paroles.

Criminal Justice Policy Council

The Criminal Justice Policy Council is responsible for conducting research, evaluating programs, and making recommendations for improving Texas's criminal justice system. It consults with legislative and executive officials to set priorities for its research projects. Among these officials are the governor, the lieutenant governor, the Speaker, the chairs of the House and Senate committees with primary responsibility for criminal justice matters, and the chairs of the House and Senate committees responsible for appropriations.

As a result of legislative action in 1997, the Council is under the direct supervision of an executive director, who is appointed by the governor with the advice and consent of the Senate.

State Institutions of Corrections for Adults

Adult offenders who are sentenced to confinement on misdemeanor convictions are housed in a county jail or another type of community corrections facility. When sentenced to confinement after a felony conviction, an adult is supposed to be incarcerated in a state prison unit or state jail within 45 days. When Texas prisons become overcrowded, they are unable to accept convicted felons in a timely manner. This has sometimes resulted in overcrowding in county jails.

Prison System Huntsville is the headquarters of the Institutional Division of the Texas Department of Criminal Justice (TDCJ), which is the administrative successor to the former Texas Department of Corrections (TDC). Correcting or modifying the behavior of convicted felons is a goal of TDCJ's Institutional Division. Through programs of training and instruction, efforts are made to rehabilitate inmates and equip them with a means for self-support after their release. Discipline and education are the primary means of combating **recidivism** (criminal behavior resulting in reimprisonment after release). Every prisoner must be given a job but may elect not to work. The work these prisoners perform saves the state money and, in some instances, generates revenue for the state. Prisoners repair engines; make laundry detergent, and bath and dishwashing soaps; and perform all types of agricultural labor. Many are enrolled in vocational programs. About 76,000 inmates attend vocational and academic classes offered through the prison system's Windham Independent School District. College-level courses are also available. More than 90 percent of the prisoners have less than a high school education, and nearly half are illiterate. According to estimates by TDCJ officials, between 85 and 90 percent committed crimes while under the influence of narcotics, were drug users, or were convicted of drug-trafficking crimes. For a description of life in the Texas prison system, see the reading on pages 263–265.

Prison Problems During the 1980s, much controversy and litigation surrounded the Texas prison system. U.S. District Court Judge William Wayne Justice's ruling in *Ruiz* v. *Estelle* (1980) established the framework for a complete reorganization and expansion of the Texas penal system. He condemned the overcrowded, understaffed, substandard facilities and ordered sweeping changes in policies and operations. Justice returned most of the control of the prison system to the state under court supervision in a settlement entered in 1992. Attorney General Dan Morales filed suit in 1996 requesting that the settlement be vacated (or eliminated) so that full control of the Texas prison system could be returned to the state with no further supervision by the federal court.

In the ten-year period between 1985 and 1995, Texans constructed facilities for 110,000 new prison beds at a cost of more than $2.5 billion. Prior to the completion of construction of these units, many county jails throughout

Prisoners congregate in a common area of the Coffield Prison Unit in 1984 when Texas was under a federal court order to eliminate overcrowding. (Copyright 1984 Alan Pogue).

Texas were jammed to overcapacity because much of their cell space was occupied by more than 10,000 convicted felons (including about 1,700 women) awaiting transfer to state prison units. In an effort to free prison beds, nonviolent offenders were released through grants of unearned, good-time (good behavior) credits ranging from 30 to 180 days. As a result, convicted felons actually were serving only about one month for each year of their prison sentences.

Some counties sued the state in an attempt to recover funds spent to incarcerate these convicted felons in county jails. When the 73rd Legislature convened in January 1993, funds were appropriated to pay counties to house convicted felons. This practice continued until August 31, 1995, costing the state more than $635 million in reimbursement payments to the counties.

State Felony Jails As revised in 1993, the Texas Penal Code provides for a system of state jails to house people convicted of state jail felonies. Such a system is designed to accommodate nonviolent offenders, thus leaving space for violent criminals in the more expensive prison units and at the same time relieving the overcrowding in county jails. State jails are rehabilitation oriented. Allowing judges to sentence offenders to "up-front" time (a period of incarceration preceding community supervision), the law also provides for substance abuse and other support programs. Some judges have been reluctant to utilize this new sentencing mechanism, however, because they do not believe there is enough incarceration time for prisoners.

Local Government Jails

Unlike the state felony jails that are funded through appropriations made by the Texas Legislature, county and city jails are financed largely by county and municipal governments, respectively. Like penal institutions of the TDCJ, however, these local jails are used to control lawbreakers by placing them behind bars.

County Jails All but about a dozen Texas counties maintain a jail. Some counties have contracted with commercial firms to provide "privatized" jails, but most counties maintain public jails operated under the direction of the county sheriff. These penal institutions were originally established to detain persons awaiting trial (if not released on bail) and to hold individuals serving sentences for misdemeanor offenses. Jail facilities vary in quality and usually do not offer rehabilitation programs.

The Texas Commission on Jail Standards is responsible for establishing minimum standards for county jails, requiring an annual jail report from each county sheriff, reviewing jail reports, and arranging for inspection of jails. In case of failure to comply with commission rules, a jail may be closed or the commission, represented by the attorney general, may take court action against the county.

During the period in which the state had inadequate facilities to house convicted felons, counties were paid a per diem while prisoners awaited transfer to state prisons. The resulting overcrowding of county jails led to prisoner lawsuits and federal mandates to counties to eliminate the overcrowded conditions. As Texas's prison building program was completed, state facilities were able to accommodate all of Texas's convicted felons. Today, some counties lease their jails to private companies. Others contract to accept inmates from other states for a fee of $30 to $45 per diem. Evidence of prisoner abuse by Texas's jail guards has resulted in the cancellation of some of these contracts.

Municipal Jails Although a Texas city is not required by law to have a municipal jail, there are more than 300 in the state. Some are used primarily as "drunk tanks" in which to detain people for a few hours after they have been arrested for public intoxication. Other municipal jails in large cities house hundreds of inmates who have been arrested for a variety of Class C misdemeanors or violations of city ordinances. Some inmates may "lay out" a fine for a traffic violation because they are unable or unwilling to pay; others may have committed violent crimes and are held temporarily until they can be transferred to a more secure county jail. The quality of municipal jail facilities varies greatly, and they are not subject to regulation by the Texas Jail Standards Commission.

Private Prisons

Texas also dealt with its prison crisis by contracting with private prison operators to construct and operate prisons and prerelease programs. Some counties privatized their facilities. Texas has more privately operated facilities than any other state. Some private operators contract with the federal government and other states to provide prisoners. States housing prisoners in private correctional units in Texas must contract with the local county or city for this service. The governmental entity then contracts with the private facility. This procedure transforms the private unit into a county or city jail which is then subject to regulation by the Texas Commission on Jail Standards. The Commission oversees all local jails that house out-of-state inmates. In addition, operators of private facilities must reimburse the state if state assistance is required to deal with an emergency such as catching an escaped inmate or quelling a riot.

Supervision of Released Offenders

Although Texas prisons and jails are usually successful in isolating lawbreakers, these institutions have left much to be desired in the area of rehabilitation. Confinement is expensive for taxpayers and often produces embittered criminals rather than rehabilitated, law-abiding citizens. Thus, criminal justice reform measures in recent years have placed a strong emphasis on supervision of released offenders and effective rehabilitation.

Community Supervision In cases involving adult first-time offenders convicted of misdemeanors and lesser felonies, jail and prison sentences are commonly commuted to community supervision, which until recently was termed *adult probation*. Thus, convicted persons are not confined if they fulfill certain court-imposed conditions. Judges are allowed to be creative in setting probation terms. In an effort to deter crime (and, coincidentally, attracting significant media attention), judges have used public humiliation techniques such as requiring a child molester to post a warning sign on the front door of his home or directing a thief to carry a sign advertising his guilt in front of a store from which he had stolen. Despite these efforts, 30 percent of probated felons violate their probation conditions and serve time in prison.

The district judge or judges trying criminal cases within a district must establish a community supervision and corrections department and hire personnel to conduct presentence investigations, supervise and rehabilitate defendants placed under community supervision, enforce community supervision rules, and employ personnel to staff corrections facilities. Judges of county courts at law that try criminal cases may participate in managing the department. A county commissioners court may establish a county correctional center under the operational direction of the sheriff.

Parole Prisoners who have been incarcerated for some portion of their sentence may be eligible for **parole**. Murderers, armed robbers, and other violent offenders must serve half of a prison sentence or 30 years (whichever is less) before they can be considered for release on parole. Persons receiving a life sentence for aggravated kidnapping, aggravated sexual assault, or indecency with a child must serve at least 35 years, and those receiving a life sentence for capital murder must serve at least 40 years. These are periods of "flat time" (without the possibility of having prison time reduced for good behavior). Other offenders may apply for parole after serving one-fourth of a sentence (one-third if convicted before September 1987) or 15 years, whichever is the lesser (minus good-time credit, time off for good behavior). Good-time credit is used to discourage prisoners' frivolous lawsuits. Prisoners who file two or more frivolous lawsuits in a year, as determined by a court, can lose up to six months of good-time credit, thus lengthening the period until they are eligible for parole.

Application for parole is made to the Board of Pardons and Paroles. This board is composed of 18 full-time salaried members appointed by the governor with advice and consent of the Senate to serve for six-year terms. A panel of three parole board members reviews applications and recommends granting or denying parole for felons who are imprisoned or in jail. In the case of a person serving a capital felony sentence, a two-thirds vote of the entire membership of the board is required for granting parole. A panel of board members conducts hearings to determine whether parole or release to mandatory supervision (such as residence in a halfway house) should be revoked. In addition to requiring that a parolee report periodically to a local parole officer, the board may specify that a parolee must submit to drug testing and/or electronic monitoring. Before release, arrangements must be made for the parolee's employment or maintenance and care.

A parolee's status is similar to that of a person under community supervision. Thus, a parolee is expected to report regularly to a parole officer, refrain from all illegal conduct, and fulfill other conditions imposed by the board, such as making reparation or restitution to the victim of the parolee's crime. Parolees also pay a monthly administrative fee of $8. Paroled sexual offenders must register with a local law enforcement agency in any county where they will reside for more than seven days. Notice must be published in Spanish and English in a local newspaper at the expense of the felon. This notice must include the street and zip code in which the offender resides. Failure to comply with conditions of parole may result in revocation of parole, and the parolee will be imprisoned to serve out the full sentence.

In 1997, Texas legislators, concerned about the early release of a number of violent felons from Texas prisons, devised a new category of parole. This super-intensive classification allows the Board of Pardons and Paroles to order a released offender to stay in secure lock-ups, to be electronically monitored by satellites, or to report more frequently to a parole officer who has a reduced caseload. The effectiveness of this program was monitored by the Senate's Interim Committee on Criminal Justice beginning in mid-1997. Half of the superintensive paroles had been revoked by mid-1998.

Rehabilitation Concern about recidivism rates that remained above the national level and were increasing as costs for prison operations continued to rise caused Texas legislators to demand accountability of prison officials. Emphasis shifted to providing rehabilitation programs for prisoners within two years of exiting the system. The first effort to alter this system occurred when Prison Fellowship Ministries opened at the Jester II unit near Houston. Prisoners within two years of release who volunteered for the program were transferred to Jester, where they enrolled in the intensive prerelease project. Provided free to the prison system, the program includes life-planning activities, seminars to restore family relationships, and Bible study courses.

In 1997, Texas became the first state in the nation to authorize voluntary surgical castration for repeat sex offenders who have molested children. Although criticized by opponents as a barbaric practice, supporters argued that the procedure is used successfully in European countries to reduce recidivism among pedophiles. Neither courts nor the Board of Pardons and Paroles may condition punishment or release on the offender's willingness to be castrated. Another remedy used in other states and supported by many Texas legislators is **civil commitment**. This procedure requires inmates who have been identified as sexual predators to be committed to mental institutions after they have served their prison terms.

Juvenile Justice

In response to a rapidly rising crime rate among Texas youth in the 1990s, the legislature overhauled the state's juvenile justice laws in 1995. Creating a juvenile justice system that clearly distinguishes between youthful pranks and violent, predatory behavior, legislators stiffened punishment for violent youth, created more detention bed space, and provided for counseling and other services for children (including those as young as seven) who are considered to be at risk for developing behavioral problems. The law also allows the photographing and fingerprinting of juveniles arrested for a Class B misdemeanor or a more serious offense, requires that a database of juvenile records be maintained by the Texas Department of Public Safety for use by state and local law enforcement agencies, holds parents liable for the conduct of their children, and authorizes state funding for the construction of county detention facilities.

Generally, young Texans who are at least 10 years of age but under 17 years are treated as "delinquent children" when they commit acts that would be classified as felonies or misdemeanors if committed by adults. Designated as "status offenders" are children who commit noncriminal acts such as running away from home, failing to attend school, or violating a curfew established by a city or county.

State and Local Agencies

Under Texas law, each county is required to have a juvenile probation board that designates one or more juvenile judges, appoints a chief juvenile probation officer, and makes policies that are carried out by a juvenile probation department. Some boards and departments serve more than one county. Overseeing these county departments is the Texas Juvenile Probation Commission (TJPC). Its nine members are appointed by the governor with the consent of the Senate. The TJPC allocates state funds to county juvenile boards, trains and certifies juvenile probation officers, and sets standards for local detention and probation facilities.

Supervising the rehabilitation and training of delinquent youths is the responsibility of the Texas Youth Commission (TYC). The six members of the TYC are appointed by the governor with Senate approval.

Procedures and Institutions

Although juvenile offenders are arrested by the same law enforcement officers who deal with adult criminals, they are detained in separate facilities. Counseling and probation are the most widely used procedures for dealing with juvenile offenders. An increasing number of delinquent youths, however, are placed on probation in local boot camps and residential treatment centers or committed to facilities operated by the TYC.

Referral An arresting officer has the discretion to release a child or refer the case to a local juvenile probation department, which may place the child in detention. Other children may be referred to such a department by school officials, crime victims, and even parents. Thus, in one way or another, more than 135,000 Texas youths enter the state's juvenile justice system each year. While juvenile probation officials decide what should be done with a referral, a youth may be detained in a local juvenile detention facility for from one day to six months. Nevertheless, within 48 hours of a juvenile's being taken into custody, a court must verify that there is probable cause for the arrest and that grounds for detention exist. A detention hearing must then be conducted every 10 days, unless waived by the juvenile's lawyer.

Court Procedures Each county juvenile board designates one or more courts as a juvenile court. It may be a constitutional county court, a county court at law, a criminal district court, or a district court. A trial in a juvenile court is termed an **adjudication hearing**. The county or district attorney represents the state, and the youth may be represented by a lawyer, question witnesses, and testify or remain silent. A jury will hear the case if requested, but most adjudication hearings do not involve a jury. These proceedings must be open to the public, unless the judge has good cause for not allowing it. In all cases, the victim has the right to be present. Juvenile courts are civil rather than criminal courts; therefore, any appeal of a court's ruling will be made to the appropriate court of appeals and ultimately (in a few cases) to the Texas Supreme Court.

If the court finds that a youth needs rehabilitation or the public must be protected from the juvenile, a **disposition hearing** is held. A child is not entitled to a jury for a disposition hearing; thus, that hearing is conducted by the juvenile judge hearing the case. The state's attorney introduces into evidence a social history prepared by the probation officer; the social history describes the youth's background, record of behavior, and formal education. Then the court decides whether to dismiss the case, put the youth on probation, or commit the youth to a TYC facility.

A Juvenile Determinate Sentencing Law is available for about 20 different offenses. This sentencing provision allows incarceration in an adult prison for as long as 40 years for juveniles who commit offenses such as capital murder and aggravated sexual assault. First, a person sentenced under this law is committed to a TYC facility. Once the juvenile turns 18, a release hearing is conducted. At the hearing the court decides whether the offender will be released on parole, retained in a TYC facility until 21 years of age, or transferred to the Institutional Division of the TDCJ. From 1987, the year of the law's enactment, through August 1998, a total of 1,250 juveniles were assessed determinate sentences, and nearly 300 of those offenders were ultimately sent to adult prisons.

Juvenile courts may waive their exclusive original jurisdiction and transfer a child to the appropriate district court for criminal proceedings if the child is 14 or older and committed a capital or first-degree felony or is 15 or older and committed a capital, first-, second-, or third-degree felony. Reacting to the murder of four students and a teacher by an 11-year-old and a 13-year-old in Jonesboro, Arkansas, Representative Jim Pitts proposed that offenders as young as 10 be eligible for adult certification and the imposition of the death penalty. Under his proposal a convicted youth would not be executed until the age of 17, however.

Texas Youth Commission Facilities   Juveniles who violate terms of probation or are found delinquent for a serious criminal offense may be confined to TYC training schools and boot camps located across the state. (For the location of TYC facilities and offices see Figure 8.2.) Having built adequate space to house adult offenders, Texas has now turned to increasing available facilities for juveniles. It is anticipated that by the year 2000 over 6,000 offenders will be housed in TYC facilities, a fourfold increase since 1994.

Also, TYC operates halfway houses for juveniles who need minimum supervision. It contracts with privately operated, community-based residential programs that provide vocational training, drug treatment, GED preparation, and other services. Nearly 20 percent of the average daily population of juvenile offenders resided in private contract facilities in 1998.

Prevention   Recidivism rates for juvenile offenders who have been incarcerated remain high. In a 1996 study conducted by the Rand Institute, researchers determined that programs encouraging high-risk students to complete school or teaching parenting skills are much more effective than juvenile incarceration in lowering crime rates. Changes to the juvenile justice system in 1997 mandated the creation by school districts of alternative schools to educate students with behavioral problems. The Texas Mediation

FIGURE 8.2 Service Areas and Facilities of the Texas Youth Commission.

Source: Texas Youth Commission.

Initiative, directed by the attorney general's office, is available to teach offenders and public school students conflict resolution techniques as alternatives to settling disputes with violence.

In an effort to increase parental involvement, the Family Code requires attendance by parents at all juvenile court proceedings and allows a judge to order parents to perform community service obligations with their children, pay restitution to victims, pay child support to offset their children's incarceration costs, and continue paying health insurance premiums for their children during incarceration. Judges can also order parents to attend parenting classes. Some critics have labeled these efforts "designer justice" and argue that parental responsibility is only a fad that will have no effect on juvenile crime rates. As the cost of incarceration has increased and the fear that youths are becoming more violent has escalated, alarmed Texans have become receptive to almost any ideas that embrace accountability, responsibility, and punishment.

Problems and Reforms: Implications for Public Policy

Throughout the 1980s and into the 1990s, Texas's criminal justice system experienced a series of crises resulting from an increase in violent crimes and stiffer sentences for criminals. The legislature responded (often slowly) with authorizations for more courts and judges, increased appropriations for correctional institutions and facilities, changes in probation and parole systems, new punishment and sentencing alternatives, and expanded programs for the rehabilitation of offenders. This section describes ongoing efforts to deal with other policy areas.

Coping with Crowded Dockets

Few people will dispute the adage "Justice delayed is justice denied." Yet one of the most common problems facing Texas's courts is that of court dockets swelling with cases awaiting trial. One solution to the problem of overloaded dockets is to provide more judges. Thus, from session to session, the legislature has established a growing number of courts. Lawmakers have also responded to an ever-increasing volume of litigation by providing for the movement of cases from an overworked court to another court with a lighter docket (that is, a short list of pending cases). In addition, the Texas Legislature has authorized the temporary assignment of active and retired judges to courts with crowded dockets. Furthermore, for more than a decade, litigants have been encouraged to use one of the alternative dispute resolution procedures.

To reduce court workloads, speed the handling of civil disputes, and cut legal costs, each county is authorized to set up a system for **alternative dispute resolution (ADR)**. Such a system is defined by law as "an informal forum in which mediation, conciliation, or arbitration is used to resolve disputes among individuals, including those having an ongoing relationship such as relatives, neighbors, landlords and tenants, employees and employers, and merchants and consumers." Courts also refer many pending civil lawsuits to **mediation** (in which an impartial mediator facilitates communication between the parties in a conference designed to allow them to resolve their dispute) or **arbitration** (in which impartial arbiters hear both sides and make an award that is binding or nonbinding, depending on the parties' previous agreement) and other ADR processes.

Judicial Selection

Late in August 1987, Chief Justice John Hill announced that as of January 1, 1988, he would resign from the Supreme Court of Texas to fight for reform of the state's judicial selection system. To some observers, tightly contested Supreme Court electoral races and split-ticket voting suggest that Texas voters have been well informed and discriminating in their support of judicial candidates. Thus, it is argued that the system of partisan election by popular vote has produced good results. On the other hand, many Texans agree with John Hill's principal criticisms of the state's judiciary: that judges are elected as candidates of political parties and the expensive election campaigns of judicial candidates are financed largely with contributions from lawyers who practice in their courts.

Critics of partisan election of judges tend to favor a merit selection model such as those used in Missouri and most other states. The **Missouri Plan** features a nominating commission that recommends a panel of names to the governor whenever a judicial vacancy is to be filled. The appointee then serves for a year or so before the voters decide, on the basis of his or her record of judicial performance, whether to give the new judge a full term or allow the nominating commission and the governor to make another appointment on a similar trial basis.

Efforts to change the way judges are selected in Texas have consistently failed in the legislature. In 1995, a proposal to choose state judges through a combination of gubernatorial appointments, popular elections, and **retention elections,** in which voters have an opportunity to approve or disapprove an appointee, failed to gain support. A similar proposal, which was limited to the selection of appellate judges, failed in the 75th Legislature. During the interim period between the 75th and 76th legislative sessions, the Senate Jurisprudence Committee continued to study the issue.

Fund raising limits have been set for judicial candidates, however. The amount any individual or law firm can now donate to a judge's election campaign is restricted to $5,000 and $30,000, respectively, in statewide races and lesser amounts in district elections. Although a number of other reforms were proposed to the 75th Legislature by the Texas Commission on Judicial Efficiency, the only significant change affecting the judiciary was a pay increase.

Rights of Crime Victims

Traditionally, Texas law has given more attention to correcting and rehabilitating criminals than to the rights of crime victims. With enactment of the Crime Victim Compensation Act of 1979, however, the Texas Legislature took an important step to aid people who lose wages and incur expenses (for example, the costs of medical and legal services) as a result of injuries inflicted by adult criminals or juveniles. Victims and their families are entitled to up to $50,000 to cover costs such as funeral expenses, medical treatment, counseling, and lost wages. Administered by the Texas attorney general since 1991, this compensation program is financed through monthly fees paid by parolees, other fees collected by district courts, and payments made by individuals convicted of felonies and misdemeanors, including traffic violations. At the end of 1996, this fund had almost $105 million on deposit. By a constitutional amendment approved by Texas voters in 1997, the fund can never be used for any purpose other than helping crime victims.

Texas has expanded protection for past and potential victims through constitutional amendment and statutory law. The Texas Constitution guarantees throughout the criminal justice process that the victim will be treated with fairness and respect, and it secures the victim's "right to be reasonably protected from the accused." Through either the Texas Constitution or statutory law, victims have the following additional rights:

- To be notified of court proceedings
- To be present at all public court proceedings, unless a judge decides that testimony by the victim might be materially affected
- To confer with a representative of the prosecutor's office
- To receive restitution
- To obtain information concerning conviction, sentencing, imprisonment, and release of the accused criminal
- To appear in person before the Board of Pardons and Paroles to challenge a parole of the assailant
- To receive automatic notification if the assailant escapes, is placed on community supervision, or undergoes any other change in his or her status

Particular categories of criminals are now treated in a way that allows protection for potential victims. The public has the right to know if a convicted child molester is residing in the community. Information that must be published in a newspaper of general circulation includes the offender's age, gender, zip code, and street name; the type of offense committed; and the victim's gender. Notice is also furnished to schools in the area. Lifetime registration is required of some sex offenders. Victims of domestic violence now have additional protection through antistalking laws and a right to emergency protective orders to keep abusers away from them. Stricter punishment of abusers became a part of the law in 1995. All of these changes reflect a national trend toward protecting victims more than criminals, a change in which Texas has often been the leader.

Looking Ahead

The Texas legal system is indeed confusing and difficult. From deciding which court should hear a case because of overlapping court jurisdiction to identifying its presiding elected officials—the judges and justices of the courts—the system appears to be shrouded in mystery and anonymity. Often understood only by those who use the system on a daily basis—Texas lawyers—the decisions of criminal and civil court judges affect every Texan. It is therefore critical that citizens understand this expensive, confusing system that governs their lives and receives support from their tax dollars. The Texas Legislature will continue to deal with issues related to teen-age gangs, safety and medical conditions in prisons, prison capacity, and the civil commitment of sex offenders. In the 21st century, Texans will need to resolve the problems of judicial selection, simplification of the court structure, achievement of racial and ethnic diversity in the judiciary, and the special needs of an aging prison population. Financing these services will also be a concern. The following chapter discusses how Texas raises the revenue to fund government services such as the courts and the criminal justice system, as well as how Texas budgets its money to cover the cost of these programs and the many other activities of state government.

Notes

1. Bill Medaille and Andrew Wheat, *Payola Justice: How Texas Supreme Court Justices Raise Money from Litigants* (Austin: Texans for Public Justice, February 1998).
2. Of special interest to young college and university students is lawyer L. Jean Wallace's *What Every 18-Year-Old Needs to Know about Texas Law* (Austin: University of Texas Press, 1992). A former students' attorney at Texas Tech University, Wallace includes criminal offenses of special interest to college students. Two other easy-to-understand books that explain Texas law are Richard Alderman's *Know Your Rights: Answers to Texans' Everyday Legal Questions,* 4th ed. (Houston: Gulf Publishing Company, 1994), and Charles Turner and Ralph Walton's *Texas Law in Layman's Language,* 5th ed. (Houston: Gulf Publishing Company, 1995).
3. Ellen K. Coughlin, "Throwing Away the Key," *The Chronicle of Higher Education*, April 26, 1996.
4. Fox Butterfield, "Reasons for Dramatic Drop in Crime Puzzles the Experts," *New York Times*, March 29, 1998.
5. David Zane and Mary Jo Preece, "Homicide in Texas—1994," *Disease Prevention News,* Texas Department of Health, September 16, 1996. Identifying violence as a public health issue, the authors advise that techniques that have been used to promote other health issues should be implemented in violence prevention, including evaluating the effectiveness of prevention tactics, identifying and focusing prevention efforts on target populations such as youth, and treating possible causes of crime such as poverty and undereducation.
6. A report in 1996 by the Texas Civil Rights Project indicated that the number of racially motivated hate crimes had decreased since the enactment of this law, but assaults against gays and lesbians had actually increased through 1994, the last year for which data were available.
7. Annual statistics and other information on the Texas judicial system are available from the Texas Judicial Council and the Office of Court Administration. In addition to compiling information on all levels of courts, the Texas Judicial Council studies court operations.
8. The State Bar of Texas (P.O. Box 122487, Austin, TX 78711) publishes a "how-to" manual for prosecuting a claim in small claims court entitled *How to Sue in Small Claims Court.*

Key Terms and Concepts

criminal law
civil law
jurisdiction
original jurisdiction
appellate jurisdiction
graded penalties
capital felony
felony
state jail felony
misdemeanor
enhanced punishment
tort
exclusive jurisdiction
concurrent jurisdiction
court of record
trial de novo
small claims court
probate
pro bono
grand jury
indictment
true bill
no bill
complaint
information
petit jury
venire
voir dire

peremptory challenge
challenge for cause
plaintiff
petition
defendant
citation
answer
charge to the jury
special issues
hung jury
verdict
judgment
personal recognizance
nolo contendere
plea bargaining
community supervision
recidivism
parole
civil commitment
adjudication hearing
disposition hearing
alternative dispute resolution
    (ADR)
mediation
arbitration
Missouri Plan
retention election

SELECTED READING

---★---

*Texas Prisons: Myths . . . and Realities**

Many Texans believe that inmates in the Texas prison system enjoy lives of leisure spent watching television and lifting weights. In the following article, Glen Castlebury, Director of Public Information for the Texas Department of Criminal Justice, describes what life is really like for inmates.

The Texas prison system is unique in many important ways, but it still attracts certain "myths" that inmates might wish were true and taxpayers hope aren't true. Let's dispel some of those myths.

TV and AC

At the top of the myth list is the air conditioning and television—and more particularly, color television. Yes, prisoners do watch TV and, yes, it is color TV. But it does not come at taxpayer expense. All TV sets are purchased with inmates' own money because they are purchased with the profits from the inmate commissaries, the in-prison stores where inmates can buy snack foods, toiletry items, and approved magazines and books.

Once the TV is in the prison, only the basic networks, sports and educational channels are permitted, and what's viewed is regulated by the guards who keep the remote controls. Television sets are usually located in dayrooms where from 60 to 90 prisoners may watch one set. The dayrooms are typically outfitted with metal benches bolted to the floor. No kicking back in the old recliner!

Prison administrators consider the TV sets the least expensive form of occupying prisoners' time and keeping them out of mischief during off hours. And when watching TV in the heat of Texas summers, prisoners don't enjoy the luxury of air conditioning. Texas prisons have heat but they are not air conditioned. Summer daytime temperatures can soar into the 90s in the cell blocks and much of the daytime heat lingers during the overnight hours. The prisons have forced air systems that keep inside air moving and fresh air coming in. That is a health measure as prisons stay on constant alert for airborne contagious diseases when so many people are housed so densely, particularly in humid areas.

*From the *Beaumont Enterprise*, January 4, 1998. Reprinted with permission.

Lots of Work and No Pay

The mention of "off hours" brings up the myth about prisoners sitting on their duffs all day. Most citizens are surprised to learn that in Texas prisons, the day starts with wake-up call at 3:30 A.M. Breakfast starts at 4:30 A.M. and work starts at 6 A.M.

The largest majority of Texas inmates work in prison support jobs—cooking, cleaning, laundry, and maintenance of the system's 107 prison units. Texas prisons have won national acclaim for their cleanliness, the product of constant elbow-grease by inmate crews. With the system as large as it is, many prison support functions must run 24 hours a day.

About 10,000 inmates work in the system's agriculture jobs which last year produced almost $50 million worth of edible crops, livestock, and cotton for the prison system on 139,000 acres in farm and ranch land. (Prison units that don't have enough land to be in the agricultural program still provide several million pounds of fresh vegetables each year to local food banks for the needy.)

About 8,000 inmates work in the prison industries program, a system of 46 factories that last year produced $100 million worth of products—all inmate and guard clothing, mattresses, cleaning supplies and equipment, furniture, stainless steel, school bus and dump truck repair, license tags, highway signs and microfilming for state agencies, just to name a few. Prison industry products are sold to other state agencies, cities, counties, and school districts.

Inmates work in many states but what is different about the Texas system is that no inmate is paid a penny. Work is the basis for all privileges in Texas prisons. No work, no play. An inmate who refuses to work loses all privileges. He is put on "cell restriction," meaning he is moved to a two-man cell where he stays 24 hours a day. He cannot watch TV, go to the commissary, go to the recreation yard and his meals are shoved through a slot in the door so he doesn't even get a trip to the mess hall. Any personal property he owns such as family pictures or a radio is taken away. Only a small percentage of inmates refuse to work.

Community Service

As the prison population has grown so much so quickly, a new form of work has been developed to keep inmates productively employed—community public service jobs for the state and local governments. This year Texas inmates have done more than 3 million hours of public projects worth millions of dollars in tax savings to local governments. The service jobs range from removing asbestos in public schools to cleaning storm damage from creeks and rivers to building homes for Habitat for Humanity. Again, there is no pay for this work.

While other states make headlines for using inmate chain gangs, Texas has had inmates cleaning highways and state parks for years. But Texas inmates aren't chained because prison officials say, "If an inmate is so dangerous you have to chain him, then he shouldn't be out on a work gang, and besides, you can't get any good work done in chains."

Sick Call

Under a new law passed in 1997, any inmate who has any money in his inmate trust account must pay $3 when he asks to see a prison doctor. This "co-pay" system is expected to bring in nearly $1 million a year to help offset the cost of prison health care. However, no inmate will be denied medical attention for lack of money and the $3 co-payment is not charged for emergencies, follow-up calls, and sick call complaints handled by medical staff.

All prison medicine is handled as a managed health care program operated by a consortium of the University of Texas Medical Branch, Texas Tech Health Sciences Center and the University of Houston College of Pharmacy. Prison officials estimate that the managed health care system is 20 percent cheaper than having the prison system itself provide medical services.

Dress Code

All Texas men inmates are required to have very short haircuts and no facial hair. No free-world clothing is allowed; all inmates dress in prison-made white uniforms.

Chow Time

Even though the prison system raises fine beef cattle (including a winner in last year's [1997] Houston livestock show), prisoners don't eat steak. Prison-raised cattle are sold at auction, usually in cow-calf combinations, and the proceeds are used to buy packer beef trimmings that are made into ground beef at the prison's own packing houses. Ground beef dishes form the heart of the prison menus.

School Bells

Any inmate coming into prison with less than a seventh-grade education is required to attend in-prison school and work toward a General Equivalency Diploma (for high school), because the Texas Legislature and prison administrators believe that education is a major factor in rehabilitation.

The prison system's Windham School District is unique as the nation's only fully accredited school system within a prison. Currently more than 60,000 inmates are working on academic courses and 16,000 on vocational courses. Windham awards about 9,000 GEDs and 8,000 Vocational Certificates a year.

The Texas prison system, with 141,000 inmates, is second in size only to the California system and both systems are larger than any other penal systems in the free world. Texans can be proud that their state prison system's operating costs are fully 27 percent less than the national average. Even so, at $39.50 per day per inmate, the total bill is $1 billion a year to run the state's 107 prison units.

Chapter 9

★

Revenues, Expenditures, and Fiscal Policy

Copyright © 1998 by Charles Pugsley Fincher.

*F*acing a possible taxpayers' revolt in 1997, Texas's governor and the 75th Legislature undertook yet another examination of the state's fiscal (money) policy. As suggested by Charles P. Fincher's cartoon strip that begins this chapter, the focal point of that survey was the prevailing state and local tax system. Escalating property tax levies by local governments and mounting sales and business-related tax collections at the statewide level provoked increasing taxpayer dissatisfaction. This in turn prompted an unsuccessful demand for changes in the Lone Star State's tax laws.

Fiscal policy is public policy that concerns taxes, government spending, public debt, and management of government money. Since the adoption of the Texas Constitution of 1876, state fiscal policy has been dominated by the notion of a balanced budget achieved by low tax rates and low-to-moderate levels of government spending. After **fiscal year** 1992 (beginning September 1, 1991, and ending August 31, 1992), Texas state government was still able to function by using this traditional formula in its financial operations. The only significant departure took place in 1987, when the 70th Legislature enacted the largest state tax increase in U.S. history. This formula, however, does not take into account property taxes levied by counties, cities, and special districts.

The Texas Economy: Two Decades of Change

When the Lone Star State entered the decade of the 1980s, its economy was prosperous and its century-old fiscal policy seemed more than adequate to meet current needs. That economic stability was grounded in a booming oil industry and related business enterprises. On March 31, 1986, however, the price of West Texas light sweet crude oil fell below $10 a barrel and precipitated a severe economic crisis. Accompanying the collapse of the petroleum industry were three other disastrous effects on the economy:

▪ Breakdown of the Texas banking and real estate industries
▪ Cratering of (a decline in) real estate values
▪ Losses and subsequent defaults on debts incurred by investors caught up in speculation in land values

By mid-1995, a broader-based and healthier economy had emerged, primarily as a result of two factors:

▪ A reduced dependency on oil and gas
▪ An increased reliance on high-technology manufacturing, export trade, and diverse service industries[1]

Throughout the 1990s, national government funding for social services and economic development decreased. This fiscal change forced more

Texans to turn to state and local governments for help. At the same time, however, those governments had fewer resources with which to provide assistance. Texas state government in particular was forced to cope with the following problems:

- Continuing growth in population
- Increasing numbers of poor families needing assistance
- Swelling costs of education, medical care, and prisons
- Spending mandates from state courts, the U.S. Congress, national courts, and various administrative agencies of the national government
- Continuing revenue shortfalls resulting from a tax system tied to stagnant or shrinking economic sectors (particularly oil production)

Despite these troublesome problems, midway through the decade of the 1990s Texas was steadily regaining some of its financial health, enabling the state comptroller of public accounts to report cash balances for the following fiscal years: $2.2 billion, 1994; $4.9 billion, 1995; $4.2 billion, 1996; and $7 billion, 1997. This favorable fiscal turnaround was attributed to

- Healthy growth in employment
- Increases in corporate profits and personal income
- Growth in tax revenue from sales of durable goods, especially furniture and automobiles
- Significant surges in lottery and other gambling revenues[2]

Enduring Policy Issues

In the 1990s, Texas's major fiscal problems involved spending needs for schools, highways, prisons, and welfare reform programs.

Public School Pressures

Pressure for more spending on education was a result of changes recommended in 1983 by the Select Committee on Public Education (SCOPE) headed by Ross Perot and a 1989 Texas Supreme Court decision ordering the legislature to correct funding inequities between the state's richest and poorest school districts. In 1991 and 1993, the same court twice invalidated Texas's system for raising public school revenue. The 73rd Legislature, in its 1993 session, attempted to comply with the court's mandate by proposing a constitutional amendment that would have required the state's richest school districts to share $400 million in revenues with its poorest districts. In a special election on May 1, 1993, however, voters emphatically rejected that proposed solution.

Thus, very near the end of its 1993 session, the legislature enacted a "multiple-choice" plan that it hoped would satisfy both the Texas courts and the state's voting public. That plan called for the 109 richest school districts to choose one of five options for helping poor districts. Failure to comply would result in compulsory consolidation with poorer districts.

Highway Demands

Highways are usually designed to last 20 years. The average Texas highway was 18 years old in 1984. That same year, state highway officials projected a maintenance and construction cost of more than $60 billion over the following 20 years. These projections were based on highway deterioration resulting from excessive use and old age, replacement and repair costs increasing at a rate exceeding the rate of inflation, and new construction needed to accommodate a growing population. Some $25.5 billion would be needed for the 1990s, but highway revenues at 1996 rates fell short of these needs. Anticipated revenues, mostly from the gasoline tax, would produce only $11 billion (43 percent) for the decade. As late as the 1997 fiscal year, only $2.1 billion had been appropriated for highway construction and maintenance. Appropriations for 1998–1999 were not significantly increased, but in 1998 the U.S. Congress made considerably more highway money available for Texas.

Prison Stresses

A federal court decision in 1980 condemned the overcrowded, substandard conditions within Texas's prison system. This decision made prison reform an important policy issue. (See pages 249–250 for details of *Ruiz* v. *Estelle* and its consequences.) Housing a rapidly growing prison population while keeping within court guidelines required sharp increases in spending for institutions of correction and criminal rehabilitation. Thus, the 73rd Legislature proposed a constitutional amendment authorizing a $1 billion bond issue for new prisons and state felony jails. Voters approved that amendment by a margin of more than 250,000 votes in November 1993. Approximately $5 billion was budgeted for the 1996–1997 biennium. Prison costs for more than 144,000 prisoners increased more than 27 percent, or approximately $1 billion, in the 1996–1997 biennium.

Welfare Strains

A constitutional amendment adopted in 1982 mandated a ceiling of 1 percent of the total state budget for Aid to Families with Dependent Children (AFDC), now known as Temporary Assistance for Needy Families (TANF). In 1997–1998, aid was fixed at approximately $424 million. For several years, the human services budget has continued to decline. For example, spending for child care, education for women with children, and employment services for women left Texas ranking near the bottom (48th) of the 50 states in support for needy residents. Welfare reform legislation enacted by the Texas Legislature and by the U.S. Congress created confusion in welfare funding and payments.

Traditional Fiscal Policies

Historically Texas's fiscal policies have been shaped by dedication to a set of basic principles: hostility to state indebtedness (deficit financing), opposition to taxes, and insistence on limited spending for most public services.

Budget Policy

Hostility to public debt is demonstrated in constitutional and statutory provisions designed to force the state to operate on a pay-as-you-go **balanced budget**. The Texas Constitution prohibits the state government from borrowing money "except to supply casual deficiencies of revenue, repel invasion, suppress insurrection, and to defend the state in war." The comptroller of public accounts must submit to the legislature in advance of each regular session a sworn statement of cash on hand and revenue anticipated for the succeeding two years. Appropriation bills enacted at that particular session and any subsequent special session are limited to not more than the amount certified unless passed by a four-fifths majority in both houses or unless new revenue sources are provided.

Despite these constitutional provisions, **casual deficits** (unplanned shortages) occur periodically. These deficits usually arise in the **General Revenue Fund** (the fund available to the legislature for general appropriations). Although only one of almost 900 funds in the state treasury, it is the critical fund in that maze of accounts. Like a thermometer, the General Revenue Fund measures the state's fiscal health. If the fund shows a surplus, fiscal health is good; if it shows a deficit, fiscal health is poor. Less than one-half of the state's expenditure comes from the General Revenue Fund. The remainder comes from the other funds and is restricted to specific uses designated by the Texas Constitution, state statutes, or federal requirements.

A second factor influencing budget policy is the constitutional mandate that state budgets be prepared and enacted on a biennial basis. Thus, state agencies, legislators, and the state's comptroller are forced to estimate governmental revenues and spending needs more than two years in advance.

Taxing Policy

Given traditional opposition to taxes, Texas residents have pressured their state government to maintain a low level of taxation. When additional revenues have been needed, Texans have indicated in poll after poll their preference for **regressive taxes** that favor the rich and fall most heavily on the poor. Under such taxes, the burden decreases as personal income increases.

Accordingly, Texas lawmakers have developed a strongly regressive tax structure that is the second most regressive in the nation.[3] A general sales tax and selective sales taxes have been especially popular. **Progressive taxes** (taxes whose impact increases as income rises) have been unpopular. Thus, Texas does not have a personal income tax; moreover, a constitutional amendment approved in 1993 requires a popular referendum before an income tax can be levied.

Because Texas is one of only seven states without a personal income tax, it depends heavily on property and sales taxes, which rank among the highest in the nation. In addition, the Lone Star State has a dizzying array of other taxes. For example, Texas imposes taxes on bingo games, imported cement, sulfur production, and oil and gas well servicing. As a result of this tax policy, Texans whose annual income places them in the lowest 20 percent among the state's residents pay more than five times as much of that income in taxes than Texans in the top one percent in annual income.

Spending Policy

Historically Texans have shown little enthusiasm for state spending. Consequently, public expenditures have remained low relative to those of other state governments. In 1997, for example, state spending in Texas was $2,384 per capita, ranking the Lone Star State 49th among the 50 states. Traditionally Texans have indicated their willingness to spend for highways, roads, and other public improvements; but they have demonstrated much less support for welfare programs, recreational facilities, and similar social services.

Politics of Budgeting and Fiscal Management

The state's **fiscal management process** begins with a budget and ends with an audit. Other phases of the process include tax collection, investment of public funds, purchasing, and accounting. Each activity is important if the state is to derive maximum benefit from the billions of dollars it handles each year.

Budgeting

A plan of financial operation is usually referred to as a *budget*. In modern state government, budgets serve a variety of functions, each important in its own right. A **budget** is a plan for spending that serves as a statement of a government's financial condition at the close of one fiscal year and the anticipated condition at the end of the next year. It also makes spending recommendations for the coming fiscal year.

Legislative Budget Board In 1949, the Texas Legislature created the **Legislative Budget Board (LBB)** and required the director and staff to prepare a biennial (two fiscal years) current-services-based budget. The board also helps draft general appropriation bills for introduction at each regular session of the legislature. During the 1970s, attempts were made to require state appropriations on an annual basis; however, voters rejected each of the proposed constitutional changes.

Office of Budget and Planning Headed by an executive budget officer who works under the supervision of the governor, the **Office of Budget and Planning (OBP)** is required by statute to prepare and present a biennial budget to the legislature within five days after the opening of each regular session. Traditionally the governor's plan has been policy based. It has presented objectives to be attained and a plan for achieving them. As a result of this dual arrangement, two budgets, one legislative in origin and the other executive, should be prepared every two years. The two twentieth-century Republican governors (Bill Clements and George W. Bush) chose not to submit separate budgets in 1989, 1995, and 1997. Democrat Ann Richards did not submit a budget in 1993.

Budget Preparation Compilation of each budget begins with the preparation of forms and instructions by the Legislative Budget Board and the Office of Budget and Planning. These materials are sent to each spending agency early in every even-numbered year. For some six months thereafter, representatives of the budgeting agencies work closely with operating agency personnel to prepare departmental requests. By early fall, departmental estimates are submitted to the two budgeting agencies. These agencies then carefully analyze all requests and hold hearings with representatives of spending departments to clarify details and supply any additional information needed. At the close of the hearings, usually in mid-December, budget agencies traditionally compile their estimates of expenditures into two separately proposed budgets.

Each state agency requesting appropriated funds must submit a six-year strategic operating plan to the Office of Budget and Planning in the governor's office and to the Legislative Budget Board. Agency plans are then combined by OBP and LBB into a long-term strategic plan composed of three phases:

■ Statewide goals (for example, higher education for students with disabilities) and proposed measures of specific government performance
■ Strategic priorities (for example, a commitment to achieve the goal in the immediate future) and external and internal factors that might affect state government during the six-year period
■ Strategic policies (for example, installation of elevators in all buildings at the agency and other levels where state services are provided)

An agency's request must be organized according to the strategies the agency intends to use in implementing the next two years of its strategic plan. Each strategy, in turn, must be listed in order of priority and tied to a single statewide functional goal.

Thus, at the beginning of each regular session, legislators normally face two sets of recommendations for all state expenditures for the succeeding biennium. Since the inception of the **dual budgeting system,** however, the legislature has shown a marked preference for the recommendations of its own budget-making agency over those of the Office of Budget and Planning and the governor.

In most state governments, the Governor's Office or an executive agency responsible to the governor supervises **budget execution** (the process by which a central authority in government oversees implementation of a spending plan approved by the legislative body). The governor of Texas may prevent an agency from spending part of its appropriation, transfer money from one agency to another, and suggest timing for particular expenditures. There are some limits on the governor's authority, such as a maximum 5 percent increase or 10 percent decrease in an agency's appropriation. A proposal by the governor must be made public, after which the Legislative Budget Board may ratify it, reject it, or recommend changes. If the board recommends changes in the governor's proposals, the chief executive may accept or reject the board's suggestions.

In November 1991, the Legislative Budget Board adopted a policy substantially increasing its authority to monitor and direct how the state spends its money. The plan authorizes the board to set performance and achievement goals for state agencies, review how effectively those goals are being met, and adjust the budget between legislative sessions.

Tax Collection

As Texas's **chief tax collector,** the comptroller of public accounts collects more than 90 percent of state taxes, including those on motor fuel sales, oil and gas production, cigarette and tobacco sales, and franchises. (A franchise is a special privilege granted by governments, such as a monopoly granted to a utility company operating in one city or region.) The Department of Transportation collects motor vehicle registration and certificate-of-title fees; the State Board of Insurance collects insurance taxes and fees; and the Department of Public Safety collects driver's license, motor vehicle inspection, and other such fees. The Texas Alcoholic Beverage Commission collects state taxes on beer, wine, and other alcoholic beverages.

Lottery Supervision

The State Lottery Commission administers the Texas lottery and oversees bingo games. This three-member commission determines the amounts of the prizes and oversees the printing of tickets, advertising of ticket sales, and awarding of prizes.

Investment of Public Funds

Working under relatively restrictive state money management laws, the Texas state comptroller invests any surplus funds so as to earn interest. Some state funds are placed in interest-bearing negotiable order withdrawal (NOW) accounts. The comptroller is authorized to buy Treasury bills (promissory notes in denominations of $1,000 to $1 million) from the U.S. Treasury and repurchase agreements (arrangements that allow the state to buy back assets such as state bonds) from banks. Income from interest and other investments amounted to nearly $2 billion in 1997.

Purchasing

Agencies of state government must make purchases through or under the supervision of the **General Services Commission**. This commission places greater emphasis on serving state agencies for which it purchases goods than on controlling what they purchase. The commission's six members are appointed by the governor, with the advice and consent of the Senate, to six-year overlapping terms.

An agency making purchases over $15,000 must solicit written bids from at least three eligible vendors (sellers) on its competitive bidding list. Purchases of more than $1,000 but less than $5,000 require three telephone bids, at least two of which must come from minority vendors on the approved list. Competitive bidding is not required for purchases under $1,000. The Council on Competitive Government is required to determine exactly what kinds of services currently provided by the state might be supplied at less cost by private industry or other state agencies.

Accounting

The comptroller of public accounts oversees the management of the state's money. This elected official is held responsible by Texas law for maintaining a double-entry system with such ledgers and accounts as are deemed necessary. Other statutes narrow the comptroller's discretion by creating numerous **special funds,** or accounts that essentially designate revenues to be used for financing specified activities. Included are constitutional trust funds, such as the Permanent School Fund and the Permanent University Fund; retirement and other trust funds, such as the Teacher and State Employee Retirement Funds; constitutionally dedicated funds, such as the State Highway and Available School Funds; and nearly 900 other special funds. Because this money is usually earmarked for special purposes, it is not subject to appropriation by the legislature.

Major accounting tasks of the comptroller's office include preparing warrants (checks) used to pay state obligations, acknowledging receipts from various state revenue sources, and recording information concerning receipts and expenditures in ledgers and other account books. Contrary to usual business practice, state accounts are set up on a cash rather than an accrual basis. **Cash accounting** means expenditures are entered when the money is actually paid rather than when the obligation is incurred. This practice permits the state to create obligations in one fiscal year and pay them in the next. Unfortunately, it complicates the task of fiscal planning by failing to reflect an accurate picture of current finances at any given moment. The comptroller issues annual and quarterly reports that include operating statements for the various funds of the state treasury. These reports do not comprise a series of balance sheets (statements of the financial position of the state treasury funds at a given date); they are only general statements of revenues and expenditures.

Auditing

State accounts are audited (examined) under direct supervision of the **state auditor,** who is appointed to a two-year term by the Legislative Audit Committee with approval by two-thirds of the Senate. The auditor may be removed by the committee at any time without the privilege of a hearing. With the assistance of a sizable staff, the auditor checks financial records and transactions on a random basis after expenditures have been made. Auditing therefore involves reviewing the records and accounts of disbursing officers and custodians of all state funds.

Monitoring accounts constitutes a check by the legislative branch of government on the integrity and efficiency of the executive branch. The auditor is authorized to require changes in accounting or recordkeeping by any state agency to promote a more uniform system of accounts. Thus, this official has access to all state records, books, accounts, and reports and may demand assistance from all state officers and employees. Another important duty of the auditor is to examine the activities of each state agency to evaluate the quality of its services and determine whether duplication of effort exists. The auditor makes a written report to the head of the agency. This report includes recommendations for correcting deficiencies and suggestions for improvement.

Politics of Revenue and Debt Management

Through constitutional provisions, statutes, and public pressure, Texans have sought to force their state government to operate on a balanced budget. Nevertheless, the Texas budget has not always been balanced. Low taxation, casual deficits, and constitutional amendments that authorize borrowing have combined to produce a persistent state debt. Although not all of the state revenue is derived from taxation, taxes are clearly the principal source of state money.

The Politics of Taxation

Imposed by governmental authority, a **tax** is a compulsory contribution for a public purpose rather than for the personal benefit of an individual. According to generally accepted standards, each tax levied and the total tax structure should be just and equitable. Of course, there are widely varying notions of what kinds of taxes and what types of structures meet these standards.

Current Trends in Texas Taxation

In the 1970s and 1980s, five trends shaped the state's tax pattern. Foremost among these was the sharp increase in revenue from taxes on oil and natural gas production brought about by frequent increases in oil and gas prices. A second trend was the variable pattern of growth in revenues from oil and gas. Surges and slowdowns in the domestic production of oil and gas resulted in erratic behavior of revenues from those taxes. A third significant trend was the strong, stable growth of the sales tax as the dominant tax in the Texas system. A fourth key trend was the steadily declining importance of the state's quantity-based consumption taxes on motor fuels, alcoholic beverages, and tobacco—sometimes referred to as *selective* sales taxes. A fifth trend was the increased importance of taxes tied to businesses' gross receipts. Included in this category are the franchise tax, the insurance company tax, and a variety of taxes on public utilities.

Sales Taxes By far the most important single source of tax revenue in Texas is sales taxation. (See Figure 9.1 for the distribution of state income from all sources.) Altogether, **sales taxes** account for almost 54 percent of all state tax revenue. The burden that sales taxes impose on individual taxpayers varies with their particular patterns of spending. Moreover, the effective rate of taxation declines as personal income rises. For example, a sales tax of 6.25 percent on furniture selling for $10,000 amounts to $625, which would be 2.5 percent of a $20,000 annual income for a beginning school teacher but only about 0.3 percent of a $200,000 income for a business executive. As previously noted, the Texas tax system tends to be regressive,

FIGURE 9.1 Net Texas State Revenue by Source, Fiscal Year 1997, (billions of dollars)

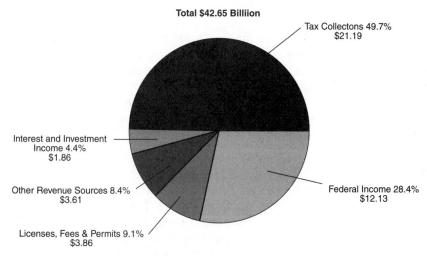

Total $42.65 Billiion

Tax Collectons 49.7% $21.19

Interest and Investment Income 4.4% $1.86

Other Revenue Sources 8.4% $3.61

Licenses, Fees & Permits 9.1% $3.86

Federal Income 28.4% $12.13

Source: Comptroller of Public Accounts, *Annual Cash Report, State of Texas, 1997*, Vol. I (Austin, 1997), p. 18.

drawing a greater percentage from the incomes of individuals in lower-income brackets than from those in higher-income brackets or from businesses and corporations. Whether a **regressive tax system** is just and equitable depends on the viewer's perspective.

For more than 35 years, the state has levied and collected two kinds of sales taxes: a general sales tax and a number of selective sales taxes. First imposed in 1961, the limited sales, excise, and use tax (commonly referred to as the **general sales tax**) has become the foundation of the Texas tax system. The current statewide rate of 6.25 percent is one of the nation's highest (ranking fifth among the 50 states).Detailed information about state and local taxes is available on the World Wide Web <http://www.window.state.tx.us/taxinfo/salestax.html>.

The base of the tax is the sale price of "all tangible personal property" and "the storage, use, or other consumption of tangible personal property purchased, leased, or rented." Exempted items include the following: receipts from water, telephone, and telegraph services; sales of goods otherwise taxed (for example, automobiles and motor fuels); food and food products (but not restaurant meals); medical supplies sold by prescription; and animals and supplies used in agricultural production.

Since 1931, when the legislature first imposed a sales tax on cigarettes, many items have been singled out for **selective sales taxes**. For convenience of analysis, these items may be grouped into three categories: highway user taxes, "sin" taxes, and miscellaneous sales taxes. Road-user taxes include taxes on fuels used to propel motor vehicles over public roads and registration fees imposed for the privilege of operating those vehicles. The principal sin taxes are those levied on cigarettes and other tobacco products, alcoholic beverages, and mixed drinks. Additional items subject to selective sales taxes include hotel and motel room rentals and retail sales of boats and boat motors.

Business Taxes   As is the case with sales taxes, Texas imposes both general and selective business taxes. Corporations and other commercial enterprises operating in this state pay three **general business taxes**:

- Sales taxes, because businesses are consumers
- The franchise tax, because most businesses operate in corporate form
- The unemployment compensation payroll tax, because most businesses are also employers

The most important of the state's **selective business taxes** are levied on the following:

- Oil and gas production
- Insurance company gross premiums
- Public utilities gross receipts

These selective business taxes account for almost 10 percent of the state's tax revenue.

Another important general business tax is the **corporate franchise tax,** which has been levied on business for more than 90 years. It is imposed on corporations for the privilege of doing business in the state. The tax is levied on the capital, surplus, and undivided profits of most corporations or on a corporation's annual income generated within the state if that amount is greater. Exempted from the franchise tax are banks, insurance companies, nonprofit corporations (such as churches and schools), and certain transport companies (mainly railroads and oil pipelines). This tax produced $2.1 billion in state revenue for the 1997 fiscal year.

All states have unemployment insurance systems supported by payroll taxes. The **payroll tax** is levied against a portion of the wages and salaries paid to individuals insured against unemployment. In Texas, rates vary from 8 percent for a business with a high turnover of workers to less than 3 percent for a business that provides steady employment for its employees.

Selective business taxes are those levied on businesses engaged in specific or selected types of commercial activities, in contrast to a general business tax, which is levied against a wide range of such operations. Because of a long history of reliance on oil and natural gas taxes, Texas has depended far more than other states on severance taxes, which currently account for about 5 percent of all tax collections. A **severance tax** is an excise tax levied on a natural resource when that resource is severed (mined, pumped, or otherwise removed) from the earth. Texas severance taxes are based on the quantity of minerals produced or on the value of the resource when removed.

The Texas **crude oil production tax** was designed with two objectives in mind: to raise substantial revenue and to help regulate the amount of oil produced. A rate of 4.6 percent of the market value of the crude oil produced generates more than $400 million in state revenue annually.

As in the case of oil, the severance tax on natural gas has produced much revenue. The **gas gathering tax** currently provides more money to the state than the crude oil tax. A rate of 7.5 percent of the value of gas produced generates more than $700 million in tax revenue each year.

Texas levies a **gross receipts tax**, which is a selective business tax, on electric, gas, gas pipeline, telephone, telegraph, and water utilities that are privately owned and operated for profit. The **gross premium tax** on insurance companies is another form of selective business taxation. Texas discriminates against "foreign" insurance companies (those chartered in other states), but foreign life, health, and accident insurers pay gross premium tax rates that decrease as the percentage of their assets invested in Texas increases. (For example, foreign casualty insurance companies with less than 85 percent of Texas investments pay a rate of 3.5 percent of gross premium receipts while those with investments of greater than 90 percent pay a rate of only 1.6 percent.) Since 1987, the state also has collected an **insurance administration tax** of 2.5 percent of the value of administrative services.

Death Tax Texas collects a **death tax** equal to the amount that would be paid to the federal government in inheritance tax if the state did not levy such a tax. Therefore, if a federal tax is due on an estate, the amount of state inheritance tax is determined by an Internal Revenue Service computation called the *federal credit for state death taxes*. The state tax equals the amount by which the federal inheritance tax is reduced through payment of a state tax. Exemption from federal taxation has been set at $600,000 since 1986; that is, the federal inheritance tax, and therefore Texas's death tax, is charged only on estates totaling more than $600,000. For example, the state death tax on a Texas ranch valued at $2.5 million would amount to $143,600.

Tax Burden The state comptroller's office places Texas well below the national average concerning the tax burden imposed on its residents. A 1995 Texas Research League study revealed, however, that when all taxes (state and local) are combined, the Texas tax burden is higher than that of 29 states. In 1997, when state taxes alone were considered, the Lone Star State's average was $1,084 per capita, ranking it 47th among the 50 states. Texas ranks ninth among the 12 major industrial states in this regard.

A significant part of the tax load falls on Texas businesses, especially oil companies, insurance companies, and public utilities. Based on past experience, these burdens on businesses are likely to be passed on to customers.

Tax Reform Distrust of state government in collecting and managing revenues and expenditures endures. Political careers in Texas have been nurtured and prolonged by appealing to the "no new taxes" ethic. In addition, strong lobbies representing powerful business interests pressure legislators to protect the financial positions of their clients. Finally, many, if not most, Texans hold to the conventional wisdom that most tax money is squandered by uncaring public officials.

Revenue from Gambling

By 1993, Texas was receiving revenue from three types of gambling operations: horse racing and dog racing, a state-managed lottery, and bingo games. At the same time, pressure was mounting for legalization of casino gambling.

Racing Texans voted to legalize parimutuel wagering on horse races and dog races in 1988. After six years, the state comptroller's office reported that Texas had collected only $35.9 million as its share of the take. With revenues of only $6.4 million during the 1996 fiscal year, income from racing began declining at a rate of approximately 33 percent per year.

Originally income to the state resulted from a 5 percent tax on horse racing wagers and a 6 percent tax on greyhound racing wagers. Those rates were significantly lowered in 1992 at the strong urging of track promoters. Since then the state has received only 1 percent of the first $100 million in horse racing wagers and 2 percent of the first $100 million at greyhound tracks. The state's shares increase 1 percent with each successive $100 million, although as of January 1, 1998, none of Texas's racetracks had seen annual total wagers of more than $100 million.

Lottery Texas voters overwhelmingly endorsed the creation of a state lottery in 1991, when they adopted a state constitutional amendment by a margin of almost three to one. The first lottery tickets, for a "scratch-off" instant-winner game, went on sale in July 1992, and a Lotto game was launched in January 1993. First-day ticket sales exceeded $23 million, which generated much more state revenue than was produced by taxes on pari-mutuel racing bets during the entire 1992 fiscal year.

First-year Lotto sales alone exceeded $1 billion, establishing a national record for lottery game sales. Lottery revenue has increased each year since its inception in 1992, rising to some $4.4 billion in sales in the 1997 fiscal year. Treasury revenues from those 1997 sales amounted to more than $1.9 billion, or about 4.2 percent of the state's total annual revenue. Legislation enacted in 1997 dedicated all profits from the lottery to education spending, rather than to the general revenue fund.

During the last four months of 1997, lottery purchases began to decline for the first time since the inception of the lottery. By mid-1998 it was anticipated that the state's share of lottery revenue would decrease by more than $280 million for the year; and rather than the $599 million increase projected by the legislature in its 1997 session, the state would experience an $881 million shortfall in the 1998–1999 budget cycle.[4]

Bingo In 1981, the Texas Legislature authorized bingo games to benefit charities (for example, churches, veterans' organizations, and service clubs). A tax of 5 percent on bingo prizes was imposed in 1993, but the state's revenue from bingo taxes began dropping slightly because bingo receipts were declining. In recent years, a variety of games, from casinos in nearby states or on Native American reservations to lottery tickets at local convenience stores, have lured Texans from the traditional bingo games. In fiscal year 1995, tax revenue from bingo amounted to more than $1.2 billion, or about 3.1 percent of the state's total revenue. In 1997, however, total bingo receipts increased by almost $2 billion to more than $3.1 billion.

Nontax Revenues

Although about 50 percent of all Texas state revenue comes from the taxes just analyzed, nontax revenues are an important source of funds. More than half of these revenues (some 28.4 percent of the total revenue in 1997) is derived from federal grants, but state business operations (such as interagency sales of goods) and borrowing also are significant sources of revenue.

Federal Grants-in-Aid Gifts of money, goods, or services from one government to another are defined as **grants-in-aid**. In the 1960s and 1970s, federal grants-in-aid contributed more revenue to Texas than any single tax levied by the state. In 1982, when the state sales tax first exceeded federal funding, the principal losers were education, welfare, and health programs. As federal funding declined, Texas and most other states responded by reducing expenditures rather than raising taxes or redirecting expenditures. Since 1982, federal funds have been directed primarily toward three programs: health and human services, highway construction, and pollution control. Along with public education, these programs now receive some 85 percent of all federal grant funds. In 1997, grants accounted for more than $12.1 billion in revenue. These funds were allocated principally to Medicaid, transportation, and education.

State participation in federal grant programs is voluntary. States choosing to participate must

- Contribute a portion of program costs (varying from as little as 10 percent to as much as 90 percent)
- Meet performance specifications established by federal mandate

Funds are usually allocated to states on the basis of a formula. Factors commonly used in deriving a formula include lump sums (made up of identical amounts to all states receiving funds) and uniform sums (based on a number of items: population, area, highway mileage, need and fiscal ability, cost of service, administrative discretion, and special state needs).

Traditionally many Texans have been opposed in principle to federal grants, usually on the grounds that federal money tends to erode the rights and powers of the state. Nevertheless, Texas has not been reluctant to take part in programs that would provide large sums of money for projects that have popular approval (for example, highway construction).

Early in 1990, the comptroller of public accounts began distributing a series of five reports analyzing federal grants-in-aid to Texas state and local governments. Those reports contend that Texas fails to receive its fair share of federal money. In fiscal year 1988, for example, Texas ranked 49th in federal dollars received on a per capita basis. Indeed, since 1981, Texas's rank each year has been either 49th or 50th. According to the comptroller, this means that "residents of 48 other states consistently get a better return on their federal tax dollars than Texans." This situation was the result of the Lone Star State's refusal to participate in several money-sharing programs (for example, the Commodity Supplemental Food Program for indigent persons).[5]

Land Revenues Texas state government receives a substantial amount of nontax revenue (more than $214 million in fiscal year 1997) from public land sales, rentals, and royalties. Sales of land, sand, shell, and gravel, combined with rentals on grazing lands, building equipment, and prospecting permits, account for approximately 3 percent of this revenue. The remaining 97 percent is received primarily from oil and natural gas leases and royalties derived from state-owned land.

Tobacco Suit Windfall Early in 1998 the American tobacco industry settled a lawsuit filed in 1996 by Texas Attorney General Dan Morales. Over the next 25 years cigarette makers will pay the Lone Star State $17.3 billion in damages for public health costs incurred by the state as a result of tobacco-related illnesses statewide. In 1998, they will contribute $1.2 billion to public health programs earmarked primarily for children's problems. Each year thereafter, they will pay the state an average of $500 million, a sum equal to more than one percent of the 1997–1998 state budget. (See pages 293–298 for a more detailed analysis of the agreement.)

Miscellaneous Sources Fees, permits, and income from investments are major miscellaneous nontax sources of revenue. Fee sources include motor vehicle inspection fees, college tuition fees, other student fees, patient fees at state hospitals, and certificate-of-title fees for motor vehicles. The most significant sources of revenue based on permits are special truck and automobile permits; liquor, wine, and beer permits; and cigarette tax permits. Income from fees and permits currently approximates $3.8 billion per year.

At any given moment, Texas actually has on hand several billion dollars invested in securities or on deposit in interest-bearing accounts. Trust funds constitute the bulk of the money invested by the state (for example, the Texas Teacher Retirement Fund, the State Employee Retirement Fund, the Permanent School Fund, and the Permanent University Fund). In 1997, investment income from all sources accounted for more than $1.8 billion (more than 4 percent) of the state's annual revenue.

The Public Debt

When expenditures exceed income, governments finance shortfalls through public borrowing. Such deficit financing is essential to meet short- and long-term crises and to pay for major projects involving large amounts of money. Most state constitutions, however, severely limit the authority of state governments to incur indebtedness.

For more than 50 years, Texans have sought, through constitutional provisions and public pressure, to force the state to operate on a pay-as-you-go basis. Despite those efforts, five types of state bonds have been authorized by constitutional amendment. Thus, many Texas voters approve both a balanced budget and bond amendments that authorize the state to borrow money.

Growth of Bonded Debt State constitutional amendments approved since 1946 authorize the creation of **bonded debt.** According to the comptroller's office, Texas's bonded debt includes the borrowings amassed by the sale of college-issued bonds and other revenue bonds issued by various state agencies. Estimates by the comptroller placed Texas's bonded debt at more than $6.6 billion in mid-1997. The exact amount of bonded debt the state owes fluctuates daily as new bonds are issued and sold and old ones are redeemed and retired. Most of the outstanding bonded debt is in either of two forms: **self-liquidating revenue bonds** guaranteed from income produced by the activity financed (for example, veterans' land bonds and college student loan funds), or **limited obligation bonds** guaranteed by income from specific taxes or assessments (for example, college building bonds). Although veterans' land loans have produced sufficient revenue to be self-liquidating, unpaid college student loans increased as large numbers of students (more than 10,000) failed to repay the money they had borrowed.

Voters have approved the creation of two treasury funds, one from which money may be granted or loaned to encourage economic development in the state and another to establish an "economic stabilization" fund (popularly called the "rainy day" fund) to be used primarily to prevent or eliminate temporary cash deficiencies in the general revenue fund. Money from these funds is used "to aid in the development and production of new or improved products" by private businesses. It is also used "to foster and stimulate" agricultural production, processing, and marketing by small Texas businesses.

The legislature has followed the strategy of asking Texas voters to approve additional bond issues rather than submit to new or increased taxes. In effect, lawmakers have chosen to finance construction of new prison facilities, mental health and mental retardation institutions, youth correctional institutions, and statewide law enforcement facilities (as well as major repairs and renovations of such facilities) by borrowing the necessary funds.

Bond Review Specific projects to be financed with bond money require legislative approval. Bond issues also have to be approved by the Texas Bond Review Board. This board is composed of the governor, lieutenant governor, Speaker of the House, and comptroller of public accounts. The total for bonds outstanding on August 31, 1997, was $6.6 billion.

Politics of Spending

Analysts of a government's fiscal policy look at public expenditures in two ways. One method is according to function, that is, the services being purchased (for example, education, highways, welfare, health, and protection of persons and property). Figure 9.2 illustrates Texas's **functional expenditures** for fiscal year 1997. The other method is according to the object of the expenditure (goods and services purchased to render the functional services, such as wages and salaries of public employees, medical assistance to needy individuals, and supplies and materials).

For more than four decades, functional expenditures have centered on three principal functions: public education, human services, and highway construction and maintenance. Similarly, three items have led all **objective expenditures** for most of that period: salaries and wages, medical and other assistance to needy individuals, and aid to public schools.

FIGURE 9.2 Net Texas State Expenditures by Function, Fiscal Year 1997, (billions of dollars)

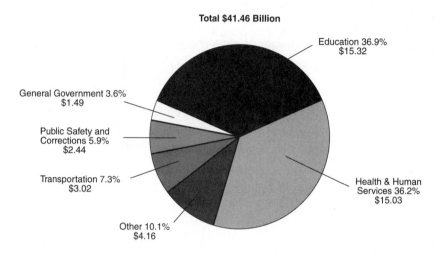

Total $41.46 Billion

Education 36.9% $15.32

General Government 3.6% $1.49

Public Safety and Corrections 5.9% $2.44

Transportation 7.3% $3.02

Health & Human Services 36.2% $15.03

Other 10.1% $4.16

Source: Comptroller of Public Accounts, *Annual Cash Report, State of Texas, 1997*, Vol. I (Austin, 1997), p. 28.

Spending to Purchase Services

Three factors are usually identified as significant reasons Texans demand more and better public services. First, changing social and economic conditions lead to increased demand for government activity. For example, increased dependence on automobiles requires expensive highways, streets, bridges, and parking facilities. Technological advances in communications, heavy industry, and energy supply have spurred demands for government regulations to protect consumers and the environment.

Second, a changing attitude toward the proper role of government contributes to public demand. Traditionally Texans and other Americans expected their governments to provide few, if any, services. Gradually, however, this attitude changed, and today citizens expect governments to take positive action to promote the general welfare. In the 1990s, however, there has been a trend toward less government involvement in the lives of individuals.

Finally, an expanded concept of democracy affects the demand for public services. For today's Texans, democracy has come to include some degree of economic equality as well as political equality. This has brought about demands for government regulation of wages and working conditions. In addition, citizens expect government to help them find jobs and to provide unemployment compensation for the jobless.

Public Schools: Kindergarten Through High School Although public education in elementary and secondary schools is a major state function, it is administered largely by locally elected school boards. Providing a basic education for all school-age children (more than 3.8 million in 1997) is the state's most expensive public service. By 1997, this activity accounted for approximately 37 percent of the state's expenditures (more than $9.5 billion per year, with more than $11.5 billion per year budgeted for the 1998–1999 biennium).

In promoting public education, Texas state government has usually confined its activity to establishing minimum standards and providing basic levels of financial support. Since 1949, state funding policy for public education has been based on three principles that underlie the **Foundation School Program**. First, the state establishes minimum, or foundation, standards for various areas of public school operations. Second, the cost of the program is funded by a combination of state and local resources channeled to the local districts on an equalized basis. Thus, rich districts pay more of the cost from local taxes and receive less state aid, whereas poor districts contribute less from local taxes and receive more state aid. Third, local districts are allowed to enrich their programs by levying higher local taxes.

The cost of three elements—salaries, transportation, and operating expenses—is shared by local districts and the state government. State aid accounts for more than 40 percent; the rest is financed locally. Each school system's local share is based primarily on the market value of taxable property within the school district, because local schools raise their share primarily through property taxes. Average daily attendance of pupils in the district, types of students (for example, elementary, secondary, or handicapped), and local economic conditions are used to determine the state's share. This share exceeds 90 percent of the amount needed to provide basic educational programs.

Funds to finance the Foundation School Program are allocated to each school system from the **Foundation School Fund**. This fund receives its money from the Available School Fund (revenue received from a variety of state taxes and income from the Permanent School Fund), the School Taxing Ability Protection Fund (money appropriated by the legislature to offset revenue reduction incurred by rural school districts), and the General Revenue Fund.

Public Higher Education Texas maintains a variety of higher education institutions, including state-supported universities and the Texas State Technical College System (with colleges in Waco, Sweetwater, and Harlingen). In addition, public community (junior) colleges are supported by local governments with assistance from the state.

State financing of public community or junior colleges is based on a "contact hour of instruction" rate for vocational-technical and academic courses. This rate concerns hours of contact between instructor and students. These two-year institutions (operated by 50 districts) use local property tax revenues, tuition fees, gifts, and state and federal grants to finance their operations. State aid currently covers more than 60 percent of the total cost.

More than 30 state universities and the Texas State Technological College System obtain basic financing from money appropriated biennially by the legislature from the General Revenue Fund. They also obtain money from fees other than tuition fees, such as student service and computer use fees (which are deposited in the General Revenue Fund), auxiliary services income (for example, rent for campus housing and food service fees), grants, gifts, and special building funds.

The University of Texas and the Texas A&M University systems share revenue from Permanent University Fund (PUF) investments, with the University of Texas System receiving two-thirds of the money and the Texas A&M University System one-third. PUF is an endowment for public higher education institutions affiliated with the University of Texas and Texas A&M University.

In the past decade, state support has declined by 24 percent, and the dollar investment per student has fallen from $3,187 in 1985 to $2,408 in 1997. To offset these financial problems, the governing boards of state-supported institutions were allowed to increase tuition and other student fees. As a result, the annual escalation of the costs of tuition and fees for the individual student has made higher education too expensive for an increasing number of Texans.

To compensate for declining enrollments brought about by increasing costs, the legislature created the Texas Tomorrow Fund in 1995. This fund enables future students to lock in the cost of tuition and other fees at public colleges and universities and also lock in the average statewide tuition and fee costs at private institutions in Texas. Tuition fees may vary from university to university, but in 1997, for example, future Stephen F. Austin State University students could fix their tuition at $100 for each semester hour regardless of the fees charged at registration. Investment earnings on the money paid into the Texas Tomorrow Fund are forecast to match much of the projected increases in cost. In effect, this scheme allows parents to pay tomorrow's tuition and fees at roughly today's prices.

During the first enrollment period (1996), the state comptroller reported that "about 40,000" Texas parents and grandparents signed contracts to begin paying for college long before the children finished high school. The comptroller estimated that parents of a baby born in 1996 or 1997 would likely have to pay $46,000 to put the child through a publicly supported college in Texas. By paying $82 a month into the Texas Tomorrow Fund for the following 18 years, parents or grandparents would have paid the child's tuition and fees, thus saving some $36,000 on college costs.

Human Services Until the 1930s, responsibility for providing financial assistance to needy individuals belonged exclusively to state governments. Public welfare services today, however, are a prime example of a state function that is shared with the federal government.

Many state governments developed **income maintenance programs** to provide support for the nonworking poor: aid for mothers with dependent children in the home, old-age assistance programs, and assistance to blind individuals. In 1935, because of rapidly growing costs, Congress came to the states' aid by passing the Social Security Act. The act established two income maintenance programs that have survived: contributory social insurance (unemployment and old-age insurance) and assistance to the needy (aid to blind, aged, and disabled persons, as well as children). With coverage expanded to include survivors and individuals with disabilities, and with health insurance added, the first of these programs came to be called Old Age, Survivors, Disability, and Health Insurance (commonly called **Social Security**). The second, widely known as **welfare,** was expanded to include aid to families in which a parent has been lost through death, disability, or absence from the home. In some states (but not Texas), human services are extended if a parent is unemployed.

Since 1972, when Congress enacted the Supplemental Security Income (SSI) Act, the U.S. Social Security Administration has been responsible for direct payments for old-age assistance, aid to blind individuals, and aid to persons with permanent and total disabilities. The cost of providing Temporary Assistance for Needy Families (TANF) is shared by state and national governments. Likewise, the state provides medical assistance to most public aid recipients, except those receiving Medicare (exclusively national) and Medicaid (shared between nation and state).

Laws enacted by the Texas Legislature in 1995 and the U.S. Congress in 1996, as noted earlier, provide for extensive modification of the responsibilities for providing welfare benefits. Two important innovations in the Lone Star State's system for implementing benefits set in motion in 1995 are a new electronic benefits transfer (EBT) system and a plastic card replacing food stamps (popularly known as the Lone Star Card). The EBT system improves the delivery of public assistance benefits and reduces the volume of such benefits lost in the black market traffic.

The *Lone Star Card* (which is similar to a bank credit card) is used to deliver food stamp assistance and Temporary Assistance for Needy Families benefits to qualified Texans. Statewide implementation allows more than 16,000 Texas retail outlets to serve some 2.7 million food stamp recipients in approximately 1.3 million Texas households.[6] After the first year's experience, administrators discovered that use of the card reduced fraud and made it easier to trace some types of abuse because of the computerized records. But they also learned that criminals (primarily drug dealers) were persuading some recipients to turn over cards in return for cash and then using the cards to obtain their own groceries. Crooked retailers also learned to ring up large but phony purchases on the cards and split the cash with the cardholders.

Welfare reform efforts at state and federal levels aim to move public assistance recipients into the work force. To succeed, this strategy depends heavily on the active involvement of community organizations (such as civic clubs and churches) and the ability of potential employers to provide jobs for the unemployed. In 1996, Governor George Bush created a 17-member task force to help churches get more involved in these programs. Composed of individuals with a wide variety of religious backgrounds, the task force was asked to encourage churches to meet human needs resulting from poverty, drug and alcohol abuse, homelessness, and AIDS.

Ranked with the other 49 states and the District of Columbia, Texas's per capita spending for human services (welfare, mental health, and treatment of mentally ill youth) ranks near the bottom. In 1996, Texas ranked 48th in expenditures for public assistance, 45th in public health expenditures, 51st in alcohol and drug rehabilitation spending, 48th in Temporary Assistance for Needy Families, 40th in Medicaid spending, and 44th in community mental retardation expenditures. Although the 74th Legislature increased appropriations for human services by some 10.4 percent (to $25.5 billion in the 1996–1997 biennium), the funds made available fell short of maintaining programs at the 1994–1995 levels.

Public Transportation Providing **public transportation services** in the United States is primarily the responsibility of state and local governments, although this function also is financed in part by the federal government. Public transportation may involve mass transit systems (for example, subways and railways), but public transportation in Texas has come to mean a system of highways and roads designed for automobiles, trucks, and busses. Thus, state transportation policy in Texas has become highway policy.

Transportation priorities have produced two important results: Texas policy encourages motor vehicle use to the detriment of other forms of transportation (especially mass transit systems), and it has favored construction of new highways and roads over the maintenance of existing ones. In the past, more than 90 percent of all highway expenditures were earmarked for new construction. Today, however, emphasis is increasingly on reconstruction and maintenance.

The pay-as-you-ride system of financing roads and highways has led Texas to transfer much of the cost to users. Principal sources of highway funds are motor fuel taxes, motor vehicle registration fees, and the federal Highway Trust Fund, to which certain federal highway user taxes are allocated. Federal aid to states is dedicated primarily to highway construction rather than to maintenance and operating expenses; the latter are the exclusive responsibility of the state. Rural roads, except those designated as farm- and ranch-to-market roads, remain the fiscal responsibility of county governments. Despite low tax rates, Texas has built one of the best highway systems in the nation, but meeting future highway needs will almost surely require more money and thus higher taxes or new taxes.

Public Health Programs Virtually all of the **public health programs** Texas provides are administered by two agencies, the Texas Department of Health and the Texas Department of Mental Health and Mental Retardation. Expenditures for the two departments exceeded $25 billion in the 1996–1997 fiscal years, and more than $36 billion was appropriated for 1998–1999. The Texas Department of Health, for example, supervises a state-mandated immunization program for children under age ten and administers the federally funded Women, Infants, and Children (WIC) program, which provides food, nutritional counseling, and health care screening for eligible Texas women and children.

Public Safety Programs Historically, responsibility for protecting persons and property and for other **public safety programs** was delegated to local governments. Today a variety of state agencies share the responsibility. The Department of Public Safety, for example, performs routine highway patrol functions, assists local law enforcement authorities in handling major crimes, and coordinates statewide efforts against lawlessness. For confinement of convicted felons, the Texas Department of Criminal Justice operates an expanding system of prison units and state felony jails. (See pages 249–251.)

In an effort to meet the prison population crisis in the 1990s, the Texas Legislature decided to pursue two strategies: significantly increasing appropriations for prisons and borrowing money to construct and staff new prisons and jails. A state constitutional amendment approved in 1991 authorized issuing $1.1 billion in bonds for the addition of 25,300 prison beds. In November 1993, Texas voters authorized a $1 billion bond issue to provide space for 22,000 more beds in prisons and in newly constructed state-felony jails. Funding was increased for operating these penal facilities. But for the first time in three decades, the 1998–1999 budget did not include money for prison construction.

Spending to Perform Services

Governments invariably spend money so that public services will be performed. Some funds, for example, must be spent to defray day-to-day costs of government operations and to assist political subdivisions with their financial needs.

Aid to Political Subdivisions State and federal **aid for Texas's local governments** is concentrated in five major program areas:

- Public safety and law enforcement
- General costs of government
- Natural resources and environmental protection
- Highways and transportation assistance
- Social services

More than 15 percent of the funds allocated come from federal grants. As previously noted, the state and federal governments also extend financial aid to school districts. Other political subdivisions, such as hospital and water districts, receive aid from the federal government but not from the state.

Administrative Costs During fiscal year 1997, the **cost of general government** at the state level was slightly more than 3.6 percent of total state expenditures. Spending for this item fell into four categories:

- Executive departments (for example, the Governor's Office)
- Business regulatory commissions (for example, the Railroad Commission)
- The legislative department (the Senate and House of Representatives)
- The judicial department (district and appellate courts)

Costs of general government in fiscal year 1997 were as follows: executive branch (all departments), $1.3 billion; legislative department (House and Senate), $95.5 million; and judicial department (all state courts), $110.6 million.

Looking Ahead

Increases in tax rates and spending totals highlighted the 1980s and 1990s in Texas. Legislators struggled to maintain public service programs at the same level while at the same time trying to respond to demands brought about by a rapidly growing population, inflation, recession, and high interest rates. Factors over which Texas had little control also added to the state's fiscal woes. Changes in federal grant policies sharply reduced available revenues in many areas, notably higher education and human services. Voter resistance to government regulation and higher taxes strengthened, while demands for funds by local governments increased. Some court decisions put added pressure on the legislature to provide costly services. Although the legislature responded by repeatedly increasing taxes and state administrators adopted strategies leading to better money management, serious problems remain.

Fiscal policies for the immediate future are likely to reflect at least four responses to changing economic and political conditions in Texas:

- Gradual but steady increases in tax rates
- Growing state responsibility for programs funded jointly with the federal government
- Deferral of capital construction, maintenance, and renovation whenever possible
- Steadily increasing public personnel costs in response to compensation demands made by state employees

These prospects have compelled Texas legislators to search for new sources of revenue. Lawmakers will also give serious consideration to a value-added tax or a personal income tax because of the need for additional revenue. "Patchwork" measures enabled lawmakers in 1991, 1993, 1995, and 1997 to meet budget crises without new taxes.

According to *Forces of Change,* a three-volume study released by the Texas comptroller of public accounts in 1994, the state's government will likely grow along with the economy and demands for public services over the next 20 years. The study concludes that although the Lone Star State has traditionally been a low-tax, low-spending state, pressures are mounting to do more to manage the economy. *Gaining Ground,* a two-volume study also produced by the comptroller of public accounts in 1994, concluded that the economic outlook for the Lone Star State was brighter than it had been in years, with the prospect of more prosperity just beyond the horizon. Thus, political forces will almost certainly cause Texas's taxing and spending to grow in relation to growth in its economy.

A 1995 study entitled *A Partnership for Independence* analyzed public assistance programs in Texas and recommended changes that would lead "assistance recipients to make smart decisions about their daily lives and how to live with the consequences of those decisions." In this study, the comptroller forecast that adoption of his welfare reform suggestions would result in a saving of more than $1 billion by 2000.

Disturbing the Peace: The Challenge of Change in Texas Government, a 1996 study by the comptroller, predicts a "brighter tomorrow" for Texas and Texans provided the state's government focuses on two "areas of primary concern": public safety and education. In all, the study makes 428 recommendations concerning changes in the way the state government operates and promises savings of more than $1 billion in forthcoming bienniums.

Notes

1. For more detailed information concerning the Texas economy during the decade of the 1980s and the early years of the 1990s, see "Theory of Devolution," *Fiscal Notes,* July 1996, pp. 1–3; "Change Looms as Texas Enters a Brave New World," *Fiscal Notes,* January 1994, pp. 1–2; "Back in Business," *Fiscal Notes,* August 1994, pp. 1, 10–12.
2. "Back in the Black," *Fiscal Notes,* December 1994, pp. 1–5.
3. Michael Trotty, "Why a State Income Tax May Make Sense for Texas," *The Wall Street Journal,* March 27, 1996.
4. See Paul Burka, "You Lose Again," *Texas Monthly* March 1998, pp. 108 and 114–117 for a detailed analysis of the lottery's decline.
5. "Paying for Federal Mandates," *Fiscal Notes,* April 1995, pp. 1–5; and "Dollars We Deserve," *A Special Financial Report* (Austin: Office of the Comptroller of Public Accounts, March 1990), p. 3.
6. "Lone Star Card Delivers Benefits for Taxpayers, Retailers, and the Needy," *Fiscal Notes,* June 1995, pp. 1, 17.

Key Terms and Concepts

fiscal policy
fiscal year
balanced budget
casual deficit
General Revenue Fund
regressive tax
progressive tax
fiscal management process
budget
Legislative Budget Board (LBB)
Office of Budget and Planning
    (OBP)
dual budgeting system
budget execution
chief tax collector
General Services Commission
special fund
cash accounting
state auditor
tax
sales tax
regressive tax system
general sales tax
selective sales tax
general business tax
selective business tax

corporate franchise tax
payroll tax
severance tax
crude oil production tax
gas gathering tax
gross receipts tax
gross premium tax
insurance administration tax
death tax
grant-in-aid
bonded debt
self-liquidating revenue bond
limited obligation bond
functional expenditure
objective expenditure
Foundation School Program
Foundation School Fund
income maintenance program
Social Security
welfare
public transportation services
public health program
public safety program
aid for Texas's local
    governments
cost of general government

SELECTED READING

---

*Texas Versus Tobacco**

Joe E. Ericson

In this original article the author analyzes the 1998 settlement of Texas's lawsuit against the tobacco industry, one of 41 suits filed by states by that year. This agreement involved by far the most money of any of those suits. Also investigated are the factors that delayed a final settlement of the lawsuit.

In January 1998, the U. S. tobacco industry, especially the manufacturers of cigarettes, suffered a major legal setback. After delaying settlement of a lawsuit that Attorney General Dan Morales had brought against them in 1996, industry officials agreed to pay the state of Texas $15.3 billion over the following 25 years. The initial payment of $1.2 billion for the first year was earmarked for public health programs primarily benefiting children.

Substance of the Agreement

During the first year following final settlement of the suit, tobacco corporations agreed to endow a public health foundation, establish insurance and education programs, and support research at four university health centers in the state. In succeeding 25 years, cigarette makers would pay the Lone Star State an average of $500 million each year—a sum equal to about 1 percent of the state's annual budget in the 1990s. Texas lawmakers would determine how to spend the money after the first year. The manufacturers also agreed to cease using billboards and reduce other advertising.[1] In addition, cigarette makers would pay as much as 90 percent of the state's legal costs, with the remainder coming from the federal government. This part of the agreement would prove to be a major point of contention in the effort to reach a final settlement.

To prevent the case from going to trial, cigarette makers agreed to pay more than $1 billion above the amount demanded by Texas. U.S. District Judge David Folsum of Texarkana had ordered the trial divided into three parts, the first phase covering only the state's charges that cigarette makers had violated federal anti-racketeering laws by concealing the risks of smoking from the public. This would give the state's attorneys opportunity to attack the industry before a jury and a national audience. Texas's original suit had asked for only $4.14 billion, including puntative damages.[2]

*This article was written especially for *Practicing Texas Politics.* Joe E. Ericson is a professor of political science, Stephen F. Austin State University.

Some Remaining Complications

Despite early celebrations by the attorney general, universities, and health organizations, some thorny complications arose almost immediately, delaying for months the final settlement. Some prominent lawmakers, among them House Appropriations Committee Chair Rob Junell (D-San Angelo) and Senate Finance Committee Chair Bill Ratliff (R-Mount Pleasant) angrily protested and sought to change the agreement. Although terms of the settlement allowed the Texas Legislature to decide how to spend more than $14 billion of the tobacco money, the protesting legislators did not want to allow Attorney General Morales any authority to commit the first year's $1.2 billion. Governor George W. Bush, Lieutenant Governor Bob Bullock, and House Speaker Pete Laney also raised questions about who would decide how the money was spent.[3]

Morales' attempt to commit the first year's payment to health care was probably based on his knowledge that Texas lawmakers have traditionally underfunded such programs, especially those aimed at benefiting poor children. He sought, therefore, to direct a spotlight on some health care areas he felt the legislature would continue to neglect or ignore: $151 million for the Children's Health Insurance Program, $428 million to create a non-profit foundation to provide grants to health care service groups, and $400 million for Texas medical schools and their research work.[4]

In the face of mounting criticism, the attorney general reluctantly agreed that state lawmakers would decide how to spend all of the tobacco settlement money. Thus, legislative leadership and gubernatorial opposition succeeded in bringing about a major change in the terms of the Texas agreement.[5]

The Washington Factor

A second complication grew out of uncertainty about the effect of the Lone Star State's settlement on a national deal pending before Congress. The tobacco industry had tried to prevent the states from trying their individual cases while Congress debated a proposed $368.5 billion national settlement. Some Washington analysts believed that an arrangement with individual states would cause Congress to abandon efforts to reach a nationwide accord, because members of Congress would then see it as unnecessary. They might argue that the issue should be settled on a state-by-state basis. Based on precedents set by Mississippi and Florida, Morales went along with a provision to allow any deal reached by Congress to supersede the Texas settlement, even if that meant the state would get less money.

The Legal Fees Issue

In mid-January, an announcement that plaintiffs' lawyers representing the state of Texas might be paid up to $2.2 billion for their part in the settlement also drew heated opposition. The state's contract with private attorneys called for a payment of 15 percent of the amount of the final settlement. The fees would initially be paid to the firms of Harold Nix of Dangerfield, John O'Quinn and John Eddie Williams, Jr., of Houston, and Wayne Reaud and Walter Umphrey of Beaumont. Those firms would then distribute the fees among the more than 120 lawyers who put in more than 1,000 hours in preparing the state's case.

Among the chief critics of the proposed legal fees were two prominent Texas Republicans: Governor George W. Bush and former Texas Supreme Court Justice John Cornyn, who was seeking to replace Attorney General Morales. They were joined by some prominent tort reform lawyers and seven prominent Democratic legislators who were smarting over Morales' attempt to control the spending of the first $1.2 billion.

After weeks of discord, in early March Governor Bush demanded that the attorney general hand over to him complete work and expense records of the private attorneys in the tobacco settlement case. The governor based his request on that section of the Texas Constitution authorizing the governor to require in writing and under oath information from other executive officers about "any subject relating to the duties, condition, management, and expenses of their respective offices."

Morales responded by asserting that he did not have such records and that they would need to be secured from the lawyers themselves. However, he did agree to furnish Governor Bush with an accounting of expenses incurred by the Office of the Attorney General and with incomplete records submitted by private attorneys.[6]

At that time, a Scripps Howard Texas Poll indicated that 64 percent of Texans favored the state's $15.3 billion settlement, but 71 percent were opposed to paying the $2.3 billion in private lawyers' fees. Morales defended the amount set aside for lawyers fees, saying that this money was separate from the settlement, because it would be paid directly by the tobacco companies, as the terms of the settlement agreement stipulated. U.S. District Judge David Folsum, whose court was scheduled to hear the Texas case, had from the inception of the settlement declared that lawyer fees were reasonable.[7]

Public knowledge that plaintiffs lawyers representing the state were generous contributors to the campaign funds of Democratic party candidates and that tort reform lawyers who strongly opposed the announced legal fees were large contributors to campaign coffers of Republican party candidates provided added controversy. Texans tended to line up on one side or the other according to their politics regardless of the contractual obligations involved.[8]

The Local Government Complication

In March 1998, Harris County, the Harris County Hospital District, and numerous other local governments announced opposition to a provision in the settlement that they believed would prohibit them from obtaining damages from tobacco firms in lawsuits they might initiate. They contended that counties, hospital districts, and other units of local government spend millions of local tax dollars each year treating poor people for health care problems related to smoking and that Attorney General Morales lacked the constitutional authority to bind them to any settlement.[9]

Tobacco companies responded by asking District Judge Folsum to rule that the Texas attorney general acted with authority to resolve all state and local government claims for health care costs allegedly related to smoking. If the judge refused, the company lawyers maintained that the cause should be put back on the court's calendar and set for trial. This would amount to yet another delaying tactic employed by the tobacco industry.[10]

Thereafter, the attorney general's office, the governor, and key state legislators began negotiating with counties and hospital districts, trying to assure them that their needs would be addressed. Not deterred by those tactics, however, local government spokesmen continued to maintain that their governments had not been involved in this issue and that the attorney general does not have authority to represent them.

The Minnesota Settlement

In late May, a new development added yet another complication to the settlement of Texas tobacco suit. Minnesota settled its own lawsuit after a trial that lasted some four months. That state's deal involved payments totaling $6.1 billion over the next 25 years and was proportionally better per capita than Texas's because Minnesota is a smaller state; moreover, Minnesota will receive a larger percentage of its payments early.

Attorney General Morales promptly pressured the tobacco industry to increase its record $15.3 billion agreement with the Lone Star State by at least $2 billion and make one-third of its payments during the first five years. He also wanted cigarette makers to guarantee the total deal for Texas regardless of any conflicting tobacco legislation that Congress might enact.

Morales based his demands on a "most favored state" provision in the Texas settlement that allows it to match higher tobacco concessions won by other states. He also announced that he would seek tougher limits on tobacco advertising and additional restrictions on marketing cigarettes to children. The revised agreement, he promised, would be presented to U.S. District Judge Folsoum in June.

Morales Enters Another Suit

The political/legal disagreement between Morales and Governor Bush and a group of state legislators also entered a new phase in late May when the attorney general asked Judge Folsum to fine Bush and seven state lawmakers $25 million for alleged interference with the state's tobacco settlement. Named in the new court actions were Senators Troy Fraser, D-Horseshoe Bay; Ken Armbrister, D-Victoria; and Jane Nelson, R-Flower Mound; and Representatives Dianne Delisi, R-Temple; Tom Craddick, R-Midland; Kyle Janek, R-Houston; and Dan Kubiak, D-Rockdale.

The Republican governor and lawmakers from both parties had filed separate legal challenges against the settlement, particularly questioning the $2.3 billion in fees for private attorneys who represented the state in its lawsuit. Bush and the seven legislators contended that under the terms of the agreement Texas taxpayers will be required to pay a part of those lawyers' fees.

Thus, after more than three months of delay featuring major political battles between Democrats and Republicans, the attorney general and lawmakers, and plaintiff-oriented and defense-oriented attorneys, a final agreement had not been reached. U.S. District Judge David Folsum of Texarkana repeatedly postponed announcing his decision until some accord could be reached among the battling parties, the agreement abrogated, or the suit withdrawn.

End of the Trail

Progress toward a resolution of the Texas tobacco lawsuit emerged in mid-July with a tentative agreement between negotiators for local governments and state lawmakers. The tobacco industry agreed to pay $2.2 billion to Texas's 254 counties for health care costs in addition to the settlement won earlier by the state. The county settlement would be divided among all Texas counties that operate public hospitals. In addition, the new agreement would permit an arbitration panel to determine the question of legal fees.

Final approval to a newly revised $17.3 billion settlement of Texas's lawsuit against the tobacco industry was announced in late July. Attorney General Morales agreed to a reduction of the state's share of the record deal from $15.3 billion to $15 billion. In their turn, cigarette makers agreed to add almost $2.5 billion to the settlement for counties and hospital districts. The payments to counties and hospital districts was designated to reimburse them from their smoking-related health care costs.

In addition, Morales negotiated an understanding with Governor George Bush and seven legislators concerning legal fees. The long-standing dispute over payments to private lawyers who assisted with the suit was separated from the remainder of the settlement. A three-member arbitration panel was given the task of determining the amount of compensation to be awarded for legal fees.[11]

1. Michael Kay, "The Deal: $15 Billion for Texas," *Austin American-Stateman,* January 17, 1998.
2. Milo Geyelin, "Tobacco Firms to Pay Texas $15.3 Billion," *Wall Street Journal,* January 19, 1998.
3. Richard A. Oppel, Jr., and Mark Curriden, "$15.3 Billion Tobacco Deal Reached," *Dallas Morning News,* January 17, 1998.
4. Fred Bonavita, "Where There's Smoke, There's Politics," *San Antonio Express-News,* January 25, 1998.
5. *Ibid.*
6. Clay Robison, "Morales Tells Governor No in Fee Inquiry," *Houston Chronicle,* March 7, 1998; Stuart Eskenazi, "Bush to Get Tobacco Fee Records," *Austin American-Statesman,* March 10, 1998.
7. Ann M. Tinsley, "Poll Finds Texans Support Settlement," *Abilene Reporter News,* March 7, 1998.

8. Gregory Curtis, "Smoke Detectors," *Texas Monthly,* March 1998, pp. 9, 12–14.
9. Clay Robison, "Tobacco Firms Threaten to Nullify State Settlement," *Houston Chronicle,* March 10, 1998; Clay Robinson, "Impasse Hits Tobacco Accord," *Houston Chronicle,* March 11, 1998.
10. Ibid.
11. "Counties to Receive Their Money," *Amarillo Daily News*, July 2, 1998.

Selected Sources
for Research and Reading

Colleges and universities offer students and faculty members a growing number of electronic sources that complement traditional library collections of books, scholarly journals, magazines, public documents, newspapers, and other printed materials. Web sites and printed sources for each chapter are included below. Asterisks (*) appear before the names of specially recommended authors. A list of Texas-based think tanks that engage in public policy research is provided at the end of this section (page 316).

Chapter 1 The Environment of Texas Politics

Web Sites

Agriculture, Texas Department of <http://www.agr.state.tx.us>
　Marketing services, pesticide programs, consumer tips, agribusiness, producer services.
Economic Development, Texas Department of <http://www.tded.state.tx.us>
　Economic development, business services, tourism, community assistance, community profiles.
Electronic Library, Texas State <http://link.tsi.texas.gov>
　State agencies, councils of government, libraries, counties, cities, newspapers, and information by subject, including books and journal articles.

Books and Articles

Bakum, Dale, *The Shattering of Texas Unionism: Politics in the Lone Star State During the Civil War Era*. Baton Rouge: Louisiana State University Press, 1998.

Barnes, Marian E. *Black Texans: They Overcame*. Austin: Eakin Press, 1996.

*Barr, Elwyn. *Black Texans: A History of African Americans in Texas*. 2d ed. Norman, Okla.: University of Oklahoma Press, 1996.

Bean, Frank D., Rodolfo O. de la Garza, Bryan R. Roberts, and Sidney Weintraub. *At the Crossroads: Mexico and U.S. Immigration Policy*. Latham, Md.: Rowan & Littlefield, 1997.

Bordering the Future: Challenge and Opportunity in the Texas Border Region (Austin: Research Division, Office of the Comptroller of Public Accounts, July 1998), pp. 155–168.

*Calvert, Robert A., and Arnoldo De León. *The History of Texas*. 2d ed. Arlington Heights, Ill.: Harlan Davidson, 1996.

Chipman, Donald E. *Spanish Texas, 1519–1821*. Austin: University of Texas Press, 1992.

*Crimmins, Julie, and Greg Mt. Joy. "Lone Star Asians: Small But Growing Community, Wields Influence in Texas." *Fiscal Notes* (November 1997): 3–5.

Davis, William C. *Three Roads to the Alamo: Lives and Fortunes of David Crockett, James Bowie, and William Barret Travis.* New York: HarperCollins, 1998

Davies, Erin. "The Biggest Ranches." *Texas Monthly* (August 1998): 118–125. Sketches of the 20 largest cattle ranches in Texas.

De León, Arnoldo. *Mexican Americans in Texas: A Brief History.* Arlington Heights, Ill.: Harlan Davidson, 1993.

Dietz, Robert. "50 Most Powerful Texans." *Texans Business* (October 1997): 61–78.

Fehrenbach, T. R. *Lone Star: A History of Texas and the Texans.* New York: Macmillan, 1968.

———. *Seven Keys to Texas.* Rev. ed. El Paso: Texas Western Press, 1986.

*Foley, Neil. *The White Scourge: Mexicans, Blacks, and Poor Whites in Texas Cotton Culture.* Berkeley: University of California Press, 1998.

Forces of Change: Shaping the Future of Texas. 3 vols. Austin: Office of the Comptroller of Public Accounts, 1993–1994.

Friend, Janice. "Guerrilla Recruiting." *Texas Business* (November/December 1997): 37–49. How companies compete for high-tech talent in Texas.

Hollandsworth, Skip, "When We Were Kings," *Texas Monthly* (August 1998): 112–117, 140–144.

Hollandsworth, Skip, and Pamela Colloff. "How the West Was Won." *Texas Monthly* (March 1998): 100–103, 118–120. Oprah Winfrey's trial in Amarillo.

Hood, III, M. V., and Irwin L. Morris. "Amigo o Enemigo? Context, Attitudes, and Anglo Public Opinion toward Immigration." *Social Science Quarterly* 78 (June 1997): 109–123.

Hoyte, Don, Fran Sawyer, and Michelle Spoonemore. "Economic Destiny." *Fiscal Notes* (October 1997): 10–12. The future of the Texas economy.

The Impact of Global Warming on Texas: A Report of the Task Force on Climate Change in Texas. Edited by George North, Jurgen Schmandt, and Judith Clarkson. Austin: University of Texas Press, 1995.

Isern, Kevin A. "When Is Speech No Longer Protected by the First Amendment: A Plaintiff's Perspective of Agricultural Disparagement Laws" *De Paul Business Law Journal* 10 (Spring/Summer 1998): 233–257.

*Jordan, Terry G., with John L. Bean, Jr., and William M. Holmes. *Texas: A Geography.* Boulder, Colo.: Westview Press, 1984.

King, Michael. "Who's Poisoning Texas?" *Texas Observer* (24 April 1998): 8–12; and (8 May 1998): 8–13. Environmental pollution in the Lone Star State.

Kovin, Stephen G., Mack K. Shelley, II, and Bert E. Swanson. "Intermestic Politics." Chapter 11 in *American Public Policy.* Boston: Houghton Mifflin, 1998. Attention is given to NAFTA and Mexico.

*Montejano, David. *Anglos and Mexicans in the Making of Texas: 1836–1986.* Austin: University of Texas Press, 1987.

"Most Industries Do Better in Texas than Nationwide—But Some Do Worse." *Texas Economic Quarterly* (May 1997): 1–9.

Olsson, Karen. "In Search of the Tigua." *Texas Observer* (3 July 1998): 8–12. Controversy over casino gambling at "Speaking Rock."

———. "Mad Cows and Cattlemen." *Texas Observer* (13 February 1998): 8–11. Oprah Winfrey's trial in Amarillo.

Plaut, Tamara, Gary Preuss, and Don Ferguson. "Economic Texas—No Longer 'A Whole Other Country.'" *Texas Economic Quarterly* (September 1997): 1–37. In the 1990s, the Texas economy and the U.S. economy began following the same path.

*Rich, Paul, and Guillermo Do Los Reyes, eds. "NAFTA Revisited: Expectations and Realities." *Annals of the American Academy of Political and Social Science* 550 (March 1997). Eleven articles.

*Richardson, Rupert, Ernest Wallace, and Adrian N. Anderson. *Texas: The Lone Star State.* 7th ed. Upper Saddle River, N.J.: Prentice-Hall, 1997.

Simon, Joel. *Endangered Mexico: An Environment on the Edge.* Pasadena, Calif: Sierra Books, 1997. Consequences of erosion, deforestation, and desertification in the United States–Mexico border area and throughout the country.

*Suro, Roberto. *Strangers Among Us: How Latino Immigration Is Transforming America.* New York: Knopf, 1998.

Tejano Journey, 1770–1850. Edited by Gerald E. Poyo. Austin: University of Texas Press, 1996. Political, economic, and social changes in the lives of Spanish-Mexican Texans in a frontier environment.

Teutsch, Austin. *Barbara Jordan: The Biography.* Austin: Golden Touch Press, 1998. Includes her service as head of the National Commission for Immigration Reform.

Thacker-Kumar, Leena, and Joel R. Campbell. "The Political Animal and the Economic Animal: A Comparative Analysis of the European Union and North American Free Trade Agreement." *Texas Journal of Political Studies* 20 (June 1998): 31–51.

The Texians and the Texans. San Antonio: University of Texas Institute of Texan Cultures, 1970–. A series of more than 20 booklets and books, each dealing with an ethnic group (Anglo Americans, African Americans, Chinese Americans, Mexican Americans, and so on).

Thorpe, Helen. "Boom Is a Four-letter Word." *Texas Monthly* (July 1997): 82, 109, 111–113. Mid-1997 finds Texas experiencing low unemployment and increased productivity; Austin is the epicenter of this boom, and high technology leads the way.

———. "Historical Friction." *Texas Monthly* (October 1997): 74, 76, 78, 80, 85. The history behind the Comfort monument for Hill Country Germans killed by Texas Confederates during the Civil War.

———. "Wafer Madness." *Texas Monthly* (April 1996): 128–131, 145–146, 166–168. Making computer chips at Motorola's MOS 11 factory near Austin.

Tijerina, Andrés. *Tejanos and Texas Under the Mexican Flag, 1821–1836.* College Station: Texas A&M University Press, 1994.

Trueba, Enrique T. *Latinos Unidos: Ethnic Solidarity in Linguistic, Social, and Cultural Diversity.* Lanham, Md.: Rowman & Littlefield, 1998.

Vigil, James Diego. *From Indians to Chicanos: The Dynamics of Mexican-American Culture,* 2d ed. Prospect Heights, Ill.: Waveland Press, 1998.

Wallace, Ernest, David M. Vigness, and George B. Ward, eds. *Documents of Texas History.* 2d ed. Austin: State House Press, 1994. Includes many political documents.

*Williams, David A. *Bricks without Straw: A Comprehensive History of African Americans in Texas.* Austin: Eakin Press, 1997.

*Wright, Bill. *The Tiguas: Pueblo Indians of Texas.* El Paso: Texas Western Press, 1993.

———, and John Gesick. *The Texas Kickapoo: Keepers of Tradition.* El Paso: Texas Western Press, 1997.

Chapter 2 Federalism and the Texas Constitution

Web Sites

National Governors Association <http://www.nga.org>
Information about individual governors and issues that concern them. Among the most important of these issues is the relationship between the states and the federal government, including how power and money should be shared by these two levels of government.

Texas Constitution <http://www.capitol.state.ts.us/txconst/toc.html>
Text of each article, frequently asked questions, index of the document, search method using words and phrases.

Books and Articles

Braden, George D. *Citizen's Guide to the Proposed New Texas Constitution.* Institute of Urban Studies, University of Houston. Austin: Sterling Swift, 1975.

——, et al. *The Constitution of the State of Texas: An Annotated Comparative Analysis.* 2 vols. Austin: Texas Advisory Commission on Intergovernmental Relations, 1977.

*Brock, Ralph H. "'The Republic of Texas Is No More': An Answer to the Claim that Texas Was Unconstitutionally Annexed to the United States." *Texas Tech Law Review* 28:3 (1997): 679–751. Addresses the claim of Richard Lance McLaren and others who support the militia-influenced "Republic of Texas" (R.O.T.) actions of the 1990s.

Bruff, Harold H. "Separation of Powers Under the Texas Constitution." *Texas Law Review* 68 (June 1990): 1337–1367.

Chaloupka, William. "The County Supremacy and Militia Movements: Federalism as an Issue on the Radical Right." *Publius* 26 (Summer 1996): 161–175.

*Cornyn, John. "The Roots of the Texas Constitution: Settlement to Statehood." *Texas Tech Law Review* 26:4 (1995): 1089–1218.

Deaton, Charles. *A Voter's Guide to the 1974 Texas Constitutional Convention: A Description of the Most Important Votes Taken During the 1974 Constitutional Convention, with the Voting Records of the 181 Legislator Delegates Fully Shown.* Austin: Texas Government Newsletter, 1975.

*Halbrook, Stephen P. "The Right to Bear Arms in Texas: The Intent of the Framers of the Bill of Rights." *Baylor Law Review* 41 (December 1989): 629–688.

*Harrington, James C. *The Texas Bill of Rights: In the Mainstream of the Movement to Protect Individual Rights—A Commentary and Litigation Manual.* 2d ed. Carlsbad, Calif.: Butterworth Legal Publishers, 1994.

King, Sondrea Joy. "Ya'll Can't Do That Here: Will Texas Recognize Same-Sex Marriages Validly Contracted in Other States?" *Texas Wesleyan Law Review* 2 (Spring 1996): 515–558.

McKay, Seth S. *Debates in the Texas Constitutional Convention of 1875.* Austin: University of Texas Press, 1930.

*——. *Making the Texas Constitution of 1876.* Philadelphia: University of Pennsylvania Press, 1924.

——. *Seven Decades of the Texas Constitution of 1876.* Lubbock: Printed by the author, 1942.

*May, Janice C. *The Texas Constitutional Revision Experience in the '70s.* Austin: Sterling Swift, 1975.

*——. "Texas Constitutional Revision: Lessons and Laments." *National Civic Review* 66 (February 1977): 64–69.

*——. *The Texas State Constitution: A Reference Guide.* Greenwood, Conn.: Greenwood Press, 1996.

Peterson, Paul E. *The Price of Federalism.* Washington, D.C.: Brookings Institution, 1995.

Posner, Paul L., and Margaret T. Wrightson. "Bloc Grants: A Perennial but Unstable Tool of Government." *Publius* 26 (Summer 1996): 87–108.

Texas Constitutional Convention. *Record of Proceedings: Official Journals. 8 January–30 July 1974.* 2 vols. Austin, 1974.

——. *Record of Proceedings: Official Proceedings. 8 January–30 July 1974.* 2 vols. Austin, 1974.

Texas Constitutional Revision Commission. *A New Constitution for Texas: Text, Explanation, Commentary.* Austin, November 1973.

Tubbesing, Carl. "The Dual Personality of Federalism." *State Legislatures* (April 1998): 14–18.

Vernon's Annotated Constitution of the State of Texas. 3 vols. St. Paul, Minn.: West, 1955. Vol. 3 contains texts of the early constitutions and organic laws of Texas.

Chapter 3 Local Governments

Web Sites

Government, State and Local <http://www.piperinfo.com/state/states.html>
Information on use of electronic media by governmental entities and links to government-sponsored Internet sites, with sites for each state, multistate sites, federal resources, national organizations of state officials and institutions; other links include the Local Government Institute and state-based think tanks.

Government Information, State of Texas <http://www.state.tx.us>
Travel, jobs, and business opportunities; election information; state agencies; counties and cities; information from other states and from the federal government.

Government Information—Cities, State of Texas <http://www.state.tx.us/cities.html>
General Information about Texas, including a site which includes more than 60 Texas cities—some large, some small—from Abilene to White Oak, and links to other American cities.

Books and Articles

Bickerstaff, Steve. "Voting Rights Challenges to School Boards in Texas." *Baylor Law Review* 49 (Fall 1997): 1017–1056.

Blodgett, Terrell. "Municipal Home Rule Charters in Texas." *Public Affairs Comment* 41:2 (1996): 1–7.

*Bryce, Robert. "Eminent Disdain." *Texas Observer* (6 June 1997): 18–19. How the power of eminent domain has been used in the city of Hurst to force homeowners to give up their homes to allow expansion of a shopping mall, which is that city's biggest taxpayer.

———. "Freeport Gives Something Back." *Texas Observer* (24 October 1997): 18–20. Settlement of Freeport-McMoRan's tax suit against Culberson County.

Burka, Paul. "Breakdown!" *Texas Monthly* (December 1993): 156–157, 229–230. Politics in Eagle Pass.

———. "Stealing Home." *Texas Observer* (2 May 1997): 6–12. About the city of Arlington, the Texas Rangers' Ballpark, and George W. Bush.

"Buses and Beyond: Cities' Tactics Vary in Traffic Reduction and Clean Air Efforts." *Fiscal Notes* (June 1997): 1, 3–4.

Cagan, Joanna, and Neil deMause. *Field of Schemes: How the Great Stadium Swindle Turns Public Money into Private Profit.* Monroe, Me.: Common Courage Press, 1998. The economics of professional sports franchises and stadium construction.

*Clark, John E. *The Fall of the Duke of Duval: A Prosecutor's Journal.* Austin: Eakin Press, 1995. How George Parr, a corrupt Duval County politician, was brought to justice.

*Cole, Thomas R. *No Color Is My Kind: The Life of Eldrewey Stearns and the Integration of Houston.* Austin: University of Texas Press, 1997.

Colloff, Pamela. "Copout." *Texas Monthly* (October 1997): 114, 116, 118–119. Big cities in Texas and elsewhere are hiring outsiders as police chiefs.

———. "Not-So-Loving County." *Texas Monthly* (October 1997): 138–139, 156, 158. About the people and politics of Texas' least populated county.

*Dickson, James G. *Politics of the Texas Sheriff: From Frontier to Bureaucracy.* Boston: American Press, 1983.

*Fisher, Lewis. *Saving San Antonio: The Precarious Preservation of a Heritage.* Lubbock: Texas Tech University Press, 1996. Chronicles the politics of preservation conflicts in the Alamo city.

Goad, Kimberly. "The Pink Mafia." *D* (November 1996): 58–67. Upper-class, conservative, homosexual insiders give Dallas's gay community real clout.

Goodson, John J. *Annexation Vexation.* Session Focus No. 75-3. Austin: House Research Organization, Texas House of Representatives, January 13, 1997.

Gournay, Luke. *Texas Boundaries: Evolution of the State's Counties.* College Station: Texas A&M University Press, 1995.

Herzog, Richard J., and Ronald G. Claunch. "Stories Citizens Tell and How Administrators Use Types of Knowledge. *Public Administration Review* 57 (September-October 1997): 374–379. Based on interviews with citizens in two mid-sized Texas cities.

*Hill, Patricia Evridge. *Dallas: The Making of a Modern City.* Austin: University of Texas Press, 1996.

*Hoffman, Marvin. *Chasing Hellhounds: A Teacher Learns from His Students.* Minneapolis, Minn.: Milkweed Editions, 1996. This account of the author's experience teaching at Jones High, one of Houston's inner city schools, should be required reading for officials who make education policies.

Johnson, Seth. "In the Zone: Sorting out Texas' Economic Development Districts." *Fiscal Notes* (January/February 1998): 6–7.

Jones, Laurence F., Edward C. Olson, and Delbert A. Taebel. "Change in African-American Representation on Texas City Councils: 1880–1993." *Texas Journal of Political Studies* 18 (Spring/Summer 1996): 57–76.

Jones, Lawrence F., Nirmal Goswami, and Ralph Warren. "An Assessment of Capital Budgeting in Texas Cities: A Research Note." *Texas Journal of Political Studies* 19 (Spring/Summer 1997): 51–64.

Jordan, Larry. "Ten Things That Every Councilmember Should Know About Municipal Bonds." *Texas Town & City* 85:3 (1998): 36, 38

Kirk, Ron. "Empowering Local Communities." *Fiscal Notes* (August 1995): 12–13.

*Ladd, Jerold. *Out of Madness.* New York: Warner Books, 1994. How an African American grew up in a West Dallas housing project but escaped from poverty.

McDonald, John F. "Houston Remains Unzoned." *Land Economics* 71 (February 1995): 137–140.

Miller, Char, and Heywood T. Sanders, eds. *Urban Texas: Politics and Development.* College Station: Texas A&M University Press, 1990.

Mintrom, Michael, and Sandra Vergari. "Charter Schools as a State Policy Innovation: Assessing Recent Developments." *State and Local Government Review* 29 (Winter 1997): 43–49.

Neu, Carl H., Jr. "10 Habits of Highly Effective Councils." *Texas Town & City* 84:6 (1997): 16–19.

Olson, Edward C., and Laurence Jones. "Change in Hispanic Representation on Texas City Councils between 1980–1993." *Texas Journal of Political Studies* 18 (Fall/Winter 1995/96): 53–74.

Patoski, Joe Nick. "Wowtown!" *Texas Monthly* (April 1998): 122–125, 159, 162. The Bass brothers and the rebuidling of downtown Fort Worth.

Reavis, Dick. "Sun City." *Texas Business* (February/March 1998): 26, 28–29. Big business comes to Georgetown, a small city in central Texas.

Rocha, Gregory G. "The Ongoing Problem of Education Funding in Texas: Historical Perspectives Prior to *San Antonio ISD* v. *Rodriguez*." *Texas Journal of Political Studies* 16 (Spring/Summer 1994): 22–38.

*Siciliano, Cathy. *On Deck: Financing Sports Facilities in Texas.* Session Focus No. 75-10. Austin: House Research Organization, Texas House of Representatives, 12 March 1997.

Somma, Mark. "Institutions, Ideology, and the Tragedy of the Commons: West Texas Groundwater Policy." *Publius* 27 (Winter 1997): 1–13.

*Spagnolly, Darvyn. "Street 'Crime' in Palestine." *Texas Observer* (14 October 1994): 13–14. How Reverend Dexton Shores, a white Baptist preacher, exposed discriminatory law enforcement in an East Texas town.

Taylor, Elizabeth. "Tax Increment Financing: One Way of Funding Tourism Development." *Texas Town & City* 85:4 (1998): 24–26.

Tees, David W., Richard L. Cole, and Seth Searcy. *Durable Partnership in Texas: The Interlocal Contract at Mid-Decade.* Arlington, Va.: School of Urban and Public Affairs and Institute of Urban Studies, University of Texas at Arlington, 1995.

"Theory of Devolution." *Fiscal Notes* (July 1996): 3–5.

*Thomas, Robert D., and Richard W. Murray. *Progrowth Politics: Change and Governance in Houston.* Berkeley, Calif.: Institute of Governmental Studies, University of California, 1991.

*Thorpe, Helen. "The Fall of the Last Patrón." *Texas Monthly* (June 1998): 116–119, 129–130, 132, and 134. Corruption in Starr County.

Wilson, David, ed. "Globalization and the Changing U.S. City." *Annals of the American Academy of Political and Social Science* 551 (May 1997). Nine general articles and seven case studies.

*Wolff, Nelson W. *Mayor: An Inside View of San Antonio Politics, 1981–1995.* San Antonio: San Antonio Express-News, 1997. The author served as mayor of San Antonio from 1991 to 1995.

Chapter 4 The Politics of Elections and Parties

Web Sites

Jefferson Project <http://www.voxpop.org/jefferson>
Provides a directory of on-line political information; through hypertext links users can access data from political parties and bureaucratic agencies or explore topics of interest such as the identity and possible motives of big-dollar donors to political campaigns. Sites for all state governments can be accessed. This web site is sponsored by Stardot Consulting, a group that specializes in providing Internet advice and services to politicians and special interest groups.

Secretary of State, Texas <http://www.sos.state.tx.us>
Information about upcoming elections, as well as historical data on voter registration, election results, and voter turnout; also includes information concerning election procedure, voter registration, and applications for voter registration.

Books and Articles

Alfaro, Kim. "How to Elect Christian Republicans." *Campaigns and Elections* (October/November 1997): 36, 53.

Baker, Ray J. *I Wouldn't Do It Any Other Way: Lessons I Learned from Vote Gettin' Texas Style for the High and Mighty.* Wilsonville, Ore.: BookPartners, 1998.

Beinart, Peter. "New Bedfellows: The New Latino-Jewish Alliance." *New Republic* (11 and 18 August 1997): 22–26. Includes important information on Mexican-American voters in Houston.

Birnbaum, Jeffrey H. "Here Comes the Son." *Fortune* (22 June 1998): 114–115, 118. Texas governor George W. Bush's prospects for nomination as the Republican presidential candidate in 2000.

*Brichetto, Robert. "The Rise of Cumulative Voting." *Texas Observer* (28 July 1995): 6–10, 18. Cumulative voting helps minority candidates win some city and school district elections.

Bryson, Conrey. *Dr. Lawrence A. Nixon and the White Primary.* Rev. ed. El Paso: Texas Western Press, 1992.

Burka, Paul. "President Bush?" *Texas Monthly* (July 1998): 72–75, 100, 102, 104. How Governor George W. Bush can become the next U.S. president.

———. "Primary Color." *Texas Monthly* (March 1998): 24–26. Republican primary contests in 1998.

*Caldwell, Christopher. "The Southern Capitivity of the GOP." *Altantic Monthly* (June 1998): 55–57, 60, 62–64, 66, 68, and 70–72.

Carleton, Don E. *A Breed So Rare: The Life of J.R. Parten, Liberal Texas Oil Man (1896–1992).* Austin: Texas State Historical Association in cooperation with the Center for American History, University of Texas at Austin, 1998.

Citizens at Last! The Women's Suffrage Movement in Texas. Austin: Alice C. Temple, 1987. Includes introduction and an essay by A. Elizabeth Taylor, photographs, and documents.

Coopersmith, Jonathan. "Texas Politics and the Fax Revolution." *Information Systems Research* 7 (March 1996): 37–51.

Curtis, Gregory. "The Last Whimper." *Texas Monthly* (January 1998): 7–8. The decline of Texas Democrats.

*Davidson, Chandler. *Race and Class in Texas Politics.* Princeton, N.J.: Princeton University Press, 1990.

———, and Bernard Grofman, eds. *Quiet Revolution in the South: The Impact of the Voting Rights Act, 1965–1990.* Princeton, N.J.: Princeton University Press, 1994.

*De la Garza, Rodolfo O., et al. *Latino Voices: Mexican, Puerto Rican, and Cuban Perspectives on American Politics.* Boulder, Colo.: Westview Press, 1992.

*Dorsey, Matt, and Ben Green. "Spinning the Web: How Campaigns Will Use the World Wide Web in 1998 . . . and Beyond." *Campaigns and Elections* (September 1997): 62–66 and 68.

Dubose, Louis, *et al.* "Colorless Primaries." *Texas Observer* (27 February 1998): 4–8. Critical comments on Texas' 1998 party primaries.

———. "Val Verde Voting: GOP or KKK?" *Texas Observer* (31 January 1997): 6–7. Voting rights dispute linked to a move to cut federal funds for Texas Rural Legal Aid.

Dworaczyk, Kellie. *Can Voting by Mail Deliver Results?* Session Focus No. 74-21. Austin: House Research Organization, Texas House of Representatives, May 21, 1996.

*Fisch, Louise Ann. *All Rise: Reynaldo G. Garcia, the First Mexican American Federal Judge.* College Station: Texas A&M University Press, 1996. Biography of a South Texan who rose to the top in Texas Democratic and legal circles.

*García, Ignacio M. *Chicanismo: The Forging of a Militant Ethos Among Mexican Americans.* Tucson: University of Arizona Press, 1997.

———. *United We Win: The Rise and Fall of La Raza Unida Party.* Tucson: Mexican American Studies and Research Center at the University of Arizona, 1989.

Gómez Quiñones, Juan. *Chicano Politics: Reality and Promise, 1940–1990.* Albuquerque: University of New Mexico Press, 1990.

*Green, George Norris. *The Establishment in Texas Politics: The Primitive Years, 1938–1957.* Westport, Conn.: Greenwood Press, 1979.

Hadley, Charles D., and Lewis Bowman. *Party Activists in Southern Politics: Mirrors and Making of Change.* Knoxville: University of Tennessee Press, 1998.

Hightower, Jim. *There's Nothing in the Middle of the Road But Yellow Stripes and Dead Armadillos.* New York: HarperCollins, 1997.

*Hine, Darlene Clark. *Black Victory: The Rise and Fall of the White Primary in Texas.* Millwood, N.Y.: KTO Press, 1979.

Ivins, Molly. "Anti-Politics in Fort Worth." *Texas Observer* (3 July 1998): 23–24. A critical view of the 1998 Republican state convention in Fort Worth.

*Kingston, Mike, Sam Attlesey, and Mary G. Crawford. *The Texas Almanac's Political History of Texas.* Austin: Eakin Press, 1992. Includes county voting results for all primaries and general elections from 1845 to 1990.

Knaggs, John R. *Two Party Texas: The John Tower Era, 1961–1984.* Austin: Eakin Press, 1986.

Mauro, Garry. "Pulling No Punches: Garry Mauro on Policy and Politics." *Texas Observer* (14 August 1998): 14–16. Edited transcript of a conversation involving the Democratic party's 1998 gubernatorial candidate and editors Louis Dubois and Michael King.

*Morris, Celia. *Storming the Statehouse: Running for Governor with Ann Richards and Dianne Feinstein.* New York: Charles Scribner's Sons, 1992.

Nelson, Albert J. *Democrats Under Siege in the Sunbelt Megastates: California, Florida, and Texas.* New York: Praeger, 1996.

*Olien, Roger M. *From Token to Triumph: The Texas Republicans Since 1920.* Dallas: SMU Press, 1982.

Olsson, Karen, and Louis Dubose. "Uncovering the Vote in Val Verde." *Texas Observer* (14 February 1997): 8–12, 14–15. Absentee ballots elect Anglo Republicans in a West Texas county.

Patoski, Joe Nick. "What's Left?" *Texas Monthly* (January 1998): 92, 94, 96. Jim Hightower and the state of Texas liberalism.

Quinn, Tony, and Pat Reddy. "Tale of Two Sunbelt States." *Campaigns and Elections* (May 1998): 38–39, 59, 63. Comparison of political trends in Texas and California.

Richards, Ann. *Straight from the Heart: My Life in Politics and Other Places.* New York: Simon and Schuster, 1989.

Stanley-Coleman, Jeanie R., and Candace Windel. "Gender Politics in the 1994 Elections." *Texas Journal of Political Studies* 18 (Fall/Winter 1995/96): 5–31.

Steed, Robert P., Lawrence W. Moreland, and Tod A. Baker, eds. *Southern Politics and Elections: Studies in Regional Political Change.* Tuscaloosa: University of Alabama Press, 1997.

Stein, Robert M., and Patricia A. Garcia-Monet. "Voting Early but Not Often." *Social Science Quarterly* 78 (September 1997): 657–671.

*Swartz, Mimi. "'Truckin.'" *Texas Monthly* (June 1996): 96–100, 118, 120. Profile of Victor Morales, the schoolteacher who drove his white pickup throughout Texas in his campaign for a seat in the U.S. Senate.

Taebel, Delbert A. "Minority Voting and Special Elections: A Research Note." *Texas Journal of Political Studies* 19 (Fall/Winter 1997): 50–52.

*Thomas, Robert D., and Richard W. Murray. *Progressive Politics: Change and Governance in Houston.* Berkeley, Calif.: University of California, Institute of Governmental Studies, 1991.

*Tolleson-Rinehart, Sue, and Jeanie R. Stanley. *Claytie and the Lady: Ann Richards, Gender, and Politics in Texas.* Austin: University of Texas Press, 1994.

*Tower, John G. *Consequences: A Personal and Political Memoir.* New York: Little, Brown, 1991.

*Tucker, Chris. "Give Till It Hurts." *Texas Business* (February/March 1998): 30, 32–33. Tips for businesspeople who want to buy political influence.

*"Willie Velasquez, 1944–1988." *Texas Observer* (29 July 1988): 1, 3, 6, 13. Cover, editorial, and articles by eight authors concerning the life and work of Texas's most successful political organizer.

Chapter 5 The Politics of Interest Groups

Web Sites

Ethics Commission, Texas <http://www.ethics.state.tx.us>
  Commissioners and what the commission does; forms, rules, advisory opinions, PAC lists, lobby lists, lists of delinquent filers, commission meetings and agendas.
Teachers Association, Texas State <http://www.tsta.org>
  Includes "Advocates for Public Education," which provides information about TSTA positions on bills being considered by the Texas Legislature, political candidates that TSTA endorses, and effective lobbying techniques.

Books and Articles

Allsup, Carl. *The American G.I. Forum: Origin and Evolution.* Austin: Center for Mexican American Studies, University of Texas at Austin, 1982.

Blakeslee, Nate. "Dispatch from the Holy War." *Texas Observer* (10 April 1998): 8–9. Meeting of conservative Christians in San Antonio sponsored by the *San Antonio Voice* to discuss public education.

Bryce, Robert. "Access through the Lobby." *Texas Observer* (24 February 1995): 14–17.

*———. "Looking Back at the Lobby." *Texas Observer* (16 June 1995): 15, 17. Lobbying in the Texas Legislature's 74th regular session.

Burch, Alan Robert. "Charles Hamilton Houston, the Texas White Primary, and Centralization of the NAACP's Litigation Strategy." *Thurgood Marshall Law Review* 21 (Fall 1995): 95–153.

Dirty Air, Dirty Money: Grandfathered Pollution Pays Dividends Downwind in Austin. Austin: Texans for Public Justice, June 1998. PACs for polluting industries make big contributions to Governor George W. Bush and legislators.

Dubose, Louis. "Deschooling Society: Who's Paying for Public School Vouchers?" *Texas Observer* (27 March 1998): 4–7, 29.

———. "Had Enough Tort Reform?" *Texas Observer* (11 April 1997): 4–5. Texans for Lawsuit Reform pressure the 75th Legislature.

*———. "Realpolitics in the Valley." *Texas Observer* (20 December 1996): 12–13. Report on Valley Interfaith's "Action Issues Conference" at Pharr-San Juan-Alamo High School.

"Forget Legislative Ethics." *Texas Business* (September 1997): 20. Former state representative Dick Slack, chair of the Texas Ethics Commission, says, "We do issue opinions, but they don't carry much weight."

*Fowler, Sheri. "I'm a Believer." *Texas Monthly* (September 1995): 66, 68, 77–79. A former *Texas Monthly* assistant editor defends the Religious Right.

*Goodwyn, Lawrence R. *Texas Oil, American Dreams: A Study of the Texas Independent Producers and Royalty Owners Association.* Austin: Texas State Historical Association, 1996.

Henderson, Jim. "Texas F.O.B.s." *Texas Business* (August 1995): 29–31. How friends of business dominated the 74th Legislature and passed tort reform legislation.

Lacy, Jim. "Doing the Lord's Work in Austin." *Texas Observer* (24 October 1997): 10–12. About Cecile Richards and the Texas Freedom Network.

*Marquez, Benjamin. *LULAC: The Evolution of a Mexican American Political Organization.* Austin: University of Texas Press, 1993.

———. "Organizing Mexican-American Women in the Garment Industry: La Mujer Obrera." *Women & Politics* 15:1 (1995): 65-87.

*Navarro, Armando. *Mexican American Youth Organization: Avant Garde of the Chicano Movement in Texas.* Austin: University of Texas Press, 1995.

Newman, J. Nownes, and Patricia Freeman. "Interest Group Activity in the States." *Journal of Politics* 60 (February 1998): 86–112.

*Pittman, H. C. *Inside the Third House: A Veteran Lobbyist Takes a 50-Year Frolic through Texas Politics.* Austin: Eakin Press, 1992.

Pycior, Julie Leininger. *LBJ and Mexican Americans: The Paradox of Power.* Austin: University of Texas Press, 1997.

Robey, John S. "Transportation, Interest Groups, and the Texas State Legislature." *Texas Journal of Political Studies* 20 (June 1998): 53–75.

Rogers, Mary Beth. *Cold Anger: A Story of Faith and Power Politics.* Denton: University of North Texas Press, 1990. About the work of community organizer Ernesto Cortes, the Industrial Areas Foundation, and COPS.

*Tran, Lynn, and Andrew Wheat. *Mortgaged House: Campaign Contributions to Texas Representatives.* Published in January 1998 and sponsored by Public Citizen's Texas Office (Austin), Texans for Public Justice (Austin), and U.S. PIRG Education Fund (Washington, D.C.).

Vining, Karla. "What Is TML?" *Texas Town & City* 84:5 (1997): 12–14. A sketch of the Texas Municipal League, which lobbies for Texas cities.

*Watson, Justin. *The Christian Coalition: Dreams of Recognition, Demands for Recognition.* New York: St. Martin's Press, 1997.

Wiggins, Charles W., Keith E. Hamm, and Charles G. Bell. "Interest Group and Party Influence in the Legislative Process: A Comparative State Analysis." *Journal of Politics* 54 (February 1992): 82–100.

Chapter 6 The Legislature

Web Sites

House of Representatives, Texas <http://www.house.state.tx.us>
    Membership, committees, calendars, how a bill becomes a law (available in Spanish).
Legislature Online, Texas <http://www.capitol.state.tx.us>
    Bill history, bill text, dates of legislative actions, committee members and schedules, calendars, districts.
Legislative Reference Library <http://www.lrl.state.tx.us>
    Library board members and staff, resources, chief elected officials of state government, statistics on the legislature, bill text.
Senate, Texas <http://www.senate.state.tx.us>
    Lieutenant Governor, membership, committees, schedules, link to *Texas Legislature Online.*

Books and Articles

Alofsin, Patricia Tierney. *Redistricting: Courts Say Try Again before Next Census.* Focus No. 74–27. Austin: House Research Organization, Texas House of Representatives, October 15, 1996.

Bickerstaff, Steve. "State Legislative and Congressional Reapportionment in Texas: A Historical Perspective." *Public Affairs Comment* 37 (Winter 1991): 1–13.

Borreson, Susan. "State Reps' Continuances Irk Opponents." *Texas Lawyer* (12 May 1997): 1, 15–16.

*Deaton, Charles. *The Year They Threw the Rascals Out.* Austin: Shoal Creek Press, 1973. Political results of the Sharpstown scandal.

*"Do You Know Who I Am?" *Texas Observer* (7 November 1997): 32. Concerning Senator Drew Nixon's crimes and punishments.

Dubose, Louis. "The Regressive Caucus." *Texas Observer* (9 May 1997): 13–15. A report on House activities of April 23, 1997.

*Elliott, Janet. "Power Outage." *Texas Lawyer* (23 December 1996): 1, 19–21. Profile of Senator Rodney Ellis.

*Hamm, Keith, and Robert Harmel. "Legislative Party Development and the Speaker System: The Case of the Texas House." *Journal of Politics* 55 (November 1993): 1140–1151.

Hanna, Betty Elliott. *Ladies of the House: How to Survive as the Wife of a Texas Legislator.* Austin: Eakin Press, 1993.

Herskowitz, Mickey. *Sharpstown Revisited: Frank Sharp and a Tale of Dirty Politics in Texas.* Austin: Eakin Press, 1994.

How a Bill Becomes a Law: Rules for the . . . [Texas] Legislature. Austin: House Research Organization, Texas House of Representatives. Published early in each regular session.

*Ivins, Molly. *Molly Ivins Can't Say That, Can She?* New York: Random House, 1991. The author, formerly a liberal columnist with the defunct *Dallas Times Herald* and currently with the *Fort Worth Star-Telegram,* is the state's most outspoken critic of the Texas Legislature.

*———. *Nothin But Good Times Ahead.* New York: Random House, 1993.

———. *You Got to Dance with Them What Brung You.* New York: Random House, 1998.

King, Michael. "Austin Hot Sausage to Go." *Texas Observer* (20 June 1997): 4–13. An overview, with emphasis on the events of the last days of the 75th regular session of the Texas Legislature.

Kubin, Jeffrey C. "The Case for Redistricting Commissions." *Texas Law Review* 75 (March 1997): 837–872.

Leatherby, Drew. "The Truth about Term Limits." *State and Local Government News* (December 1997): 14–18. What legislators, staff, and lobbyists think about term limits for legislators.

Major Issues of the . . . [Texas] Legislature. Austin: House Research Organization, Texas House of Representatives. Prepared biennially by the House Research Organization staff, this publication provides a summary of many major issues—including important bills that did not pass—in each regular session and subsequent special sessions.

Presiding Officers of the Texas Legislature, 1846–1995. Rev. ed. Austin: Texas Legislative Council, 1995. Provides a brief account of the life and work of each Speaker and each lieutenant governor during this period.

Silby, Joel H., editor-in-chief. *Encyclopedia of the American Legislative System: Studies of the Principal Structures, Procedures, and Politics of Congress and the State Legislatures Since the Colonial Era.* 3 vols. New York: Charles Scribner's Sons, 1994.

Spaw, Patsy, ed. *The Texas Senate.* Vol. 1: *Republic to Civil War, 1836–1861.* College Station: Texas A&M University Press, 1990.

Texas Monthly staff. "The Ten Best and the Ten Worst Legislators." *Texas Monthly.* Biennial feature following each regular session, beginning with the 63rd in 1973.

Vega, Arturo. "Gender and Ethnicity Effects on the Legislative Behavior and Substantive Representation of the Texas Legislature." *Texas Journal of Political Studies* 19 (Spring/Summer 1997): 1–20.

Weberg, Brian. "New Age Dawns for Legislative Staff." *State Legislatures* (January 1997): 26, 29–31.

Chapter 7 The Executive and the State Bureaucratic System

Web Sites

Agencies, Texas State <http://www.state.tx.us/agency/agencies.html>
  Provides a range of information about Texas, including addresses, phone numbers, and electronic resources (where available) for more than 200 Texas agencies (executive departments, boards, commissions, universities, courts).
Employee Retirement System, Texas State <http://www.ers.texas.gov>
  Mission statement, benefit programs, publications, employment information.
Governor's Office <http://www.governor.state.tx.us>
  Welcome message, office functions, press releases, speeches, initiatives, accomplishments, and list of available appointments to state boards and commissions.
Higher Education Coordinating Board, Texas <http://www.thecb.state.tx.us>
  For and about students, parents, counselors, institutions, and board members.

Books and Articles

Belfiglio, Valentine. *Honor, Pride, Duty: A History of the Texas State Guard.* Austin: Eakin Press, 1995.

Blakeslee, Nate. "Dumping on West Texas." *Texas Observer* (27 March 1998): 11–12. Waste disposal at Sierra Blanca.

———. "George Bush's Radioactive Plot." *Nation* (9 March 1998): 18–21. Controversy over nuclear waste disposal in West Texas.

Bloom, Lackland H., Jr. "*Hopwood, Bakke* and the Future of Diversity Justification," *Texas Tech Law Review* 29:1 (1998): 1–73.

Bryce, Robert. "God's Steward at the TNRCC." *Texas Observer* (5 December 1997): 6–11. About Barry McBee and the Texas Natural Resource Conservation Commission.

———. "The Governor's Sweetheart Deal." *Texas Observer* (30 January 1998): 7. Politics, economics, and big-league baseball in Dallas.

Carman, Neil. *Grandfathered Air Pollution: The Dirty Secret of Texas Industries.* Austin: Lone Star Chapter of the Sierra Club and the Galveston-Houston Association for Smog Prevention, 1998.

*Connally, John, with Mickey Herskowitz. *In History's Shadow: An American Odyssey.* New York: Hyperion, 1993. Autobiography of a Texas governor.

De Boer, Marvin E., ed. *Destiny by Choice: The Inaugural Addresses of the Governors of Texas.* Fayetteville, Ark.: University of Arkansas Press, 1992.

Dickson, James D. *Law and Politics: The Office of Attorney General in Texas.* Austin: Sterling Swift, 1976.

Dubose, Louis. "Smoke Gets in Your Eyes." *Texas Observer* (12 September 1997): 4. TNRCC and a controversial incinerator in Lubbock.

Elder, Bob. "Texas to Teachers: Shut Up!" *Texas Observer* (10 October 1997): 14–15. Concerning the Texas law that "allows the state to withhold part or all of the salary of any state employee who is an expert witness or consultant to 'litigation against the state.'"

*Hendrickson, Kenneth E. *The Chief Executive of Texas: From Stephen F. Austin to John B. Connally, Jr.* College Station: Texas A&M University Press, 1995.

Land. Austin: Texas General Land Office, 1993.

*The Land Commissioners of Texas. Austin: Texas General Land Office, 1986.

Lurie, Irene. "Temporary Assistance for Needy Families: A Green Light for the States." *Publius* 27 (Spring 1997): 73–87.

*Mauro, Garry. *Beaches, Bureaucrats, and Big Oil.* Austin: Look Away Books, 1997.

McKenzie, William. "The Son Also Rises." *Ripon Forum* (Summer 1996): 7–9. George W. Bush emerges as a national political figure.

McLaughlin, Laure, and Greg Mt. Joy. "Thunder Roads: Texas Highways Take a Pounding as Mounting Traffic Tests Capacity of System." *Fiscal Notes* (May 1998): 1, 10–11.

Moorehead, Richard. *DeWitt C. Greer: King of the Highway Builders.* Austin: Eakin Press, 1984.

Murray, Mark. "De-Commissioning Labor." *Texas Observer* (23 May 1997): 18–20. Politics and the Texas Workforce Commission.

Olsson, Karen. "On the Line at IBP: Why One Hand Every Five Years Is No Big Deal." *Texas Observer* (22 May 1998): 8–14. Worker safety in a meatpacking plant in Amarillo.

*Paulissen, May Nelson, and Carl McQueary. *Miriam: The Southern Belle Who Became the First Woman Governor of Texas.* Austin: Eakin Press, 1995.

Potts, Susan E., and Frank M. Reilly. "A Rat's Nest of Regulation." *Texas Lawyer* (26 January 1998): 32–33. Concerning the proliferation of state regulations and administrative appeals.

Prindle, David F. *Petroleum Politics and the Texas Railroad Commission.* Austin: University of Texas Press, 1981.

*Shropshire, Mike, and Frank Schaeffer. *The Thorny Rose of Texas: An Intimate Portrait of Governor Ann Richards.* New York: Birch Lane Press, 1994.

Szurek, Marion. "The New Texas Department of Economic Development." *Texas Town & City* 85:4 (1998): 14–15. Special attention is given to the Tourism Division.

Thorpe, Helen. "The War for the Colorado." *Texas Monthly* (May 1997): 98–101, 128–130, 146–150. A case study in water politics.

Walther, Ann. *Texas at a Watershed: Planning Now for Future Needs.* Session Focus No. 75-13. Austin: House Research Organization, Texas House of Representatives, April 15, 1997.

*"Whistleblower's Vindication: George Green Wins One Fight, Begins Another." *Texas Observer* (8 December 1995): 10–12. Excerpts from a post-settlement interview with the former Department of Human Services employee who received a damage award of $13.7 million from the state.

*Wilson Robert H., ed. *Public Policy and Community Activism and Governance in Texas.* Austin: University of Texas Press, 1997. Case studies that describe how low-income Texans have affected public policies concerning education finance and reform, envrionmental protection, local infrastructure, and indigent health care.

Chapter 8 Law, Courts, and Justice

Web Sites

Attorney General, Texas <http://www.oag.state.tx.us>
About the attorney general, administrative law, consumer protection, *colonias* database, crime victims' compensation, juvenile justice, press releases, and opinions.

Court Administration, Office of <http://www.courts.state.tx.us>
Courts of the state, special organizations (e.g., State Law Library, Municipal Courts Education Center), special information (e.g., Judicial Annual Report, State Bar exam results, judicial directory), additional information (e.g., overview of the Texas judicial system).

People's Lawyer <http://www.law.uh.edu>
University of Houston Law Center with links to Professor Richard Aldeman's "People's Lawyer," which includes common questions and answers, the people's law school, information on common problems (e.g., suing in small claims court, living wills, and durable powers of attorney), references to legal texts.

Books and Articles

*Adams, Randall, with William Hoffer and Marilyn Mona Hoffer. *Adams v. Texas.* New York: St. Martin's Press, 1991. The personal account of a former inmate who spent a dozen years in the Texas prison system after conviction for a murder he did not commit.

Alderman, Richard. *Know Your Rights: Answers to Texans' Everyday Legal Questions.* 4th ed. Houston: Gulf Publishing Company, 1995.

*Anderson, Ken. *Crime in Texas: Your Complete Guide to the Criminal Justice System.* Austin: University of Texas Press, 1997. Written by the district attorney for Williamson County.

Borreson, Susan. "Docket Police Issue More Transfer Orders." *Texas Lawyer* (May 11, 1998): 1, 22–23. The Supreme Court of Texas is transferring more cases from courts with heavily backlogged dockets.

*Brown, Joyce Ann, with Jay Gaines. *Joyce Ann Brown: Justice Denied.* Chicago: Noble Press, 1990. An autobiographical account by a Texan who served more than nine years of a prison sentence for an aggravated robbery she did not commit.

Cayce, John Hill, Jr., and Felicia Harris Kyle. "Civil Appeals in Texas: Practicing Under the New Rules of Appellate Procedure." *Baylor Law Review* 49 (Fall 1997): 867–1015.

*Colloff, Pamela. "The Wrong Man." *Texas Monthly* (December 1997): 18–20. Kevin Byrd's twelve years in a Texas prison for a crime he did not commit.

Connelly, Richard. "How Judges Discipline Their Own." *Texas Lawyer* (May 1997): 1, 33–34. Describes the functions of the Texas State Commission on Judicial Conduct.

Cooper, Lance A. "An Historical Overview of Judicial Selection in Texas." *Texas Wesleyan Law Review* 2 (Fall 1995): 317–333.

*Dietz, Elly del Prado. "The Texas Crime Victims' Compensation Act." *Texas Bar Journal* 60 (April 1997): 320–322, 324.

Dow, David R. "The Humanity of Karla Faye Tucker." *Texas Observer* (13 February 1998): 4–5. Convicted of capital murder, she was the first woman to be executed under Texas law in more than a century.

*Dubose, Louis. "A Poster Boy for Reform." *Texas Observer* (9 December 1994): 3–4. About Steve Mansfield, who was elected to the Texas Court of Criminal Appeals despite his shortcomings.

Dworaczyk, Kellie. *Mandatory Supervision Reform: Safety, Cost and Legal Issues.* Session Focus No. 75-6. Austin: House Research Organization, Texas House of Representatives, February 17, 1997.

Elliott, Janet. "Democratic Judges: An Endangered Species." *Texas Lawyer* (12 January 1998): 1, 20–21.

———. "Mansfield's Masquerade: A Most Unlikely Jurist Continues to Surprise." *Texas Lawyer* (15 December 1997): 1, 14–15. Criticism of Texas Court of Criminal Appeals Judge Stephen W. Mansfield.

Garza, Patrick. "The New Juvenile Progressive Sanctions Guidelines: 'Just When You Thought You Knew the Game, They Changed the Rules.'" *Texas Bar Journal* 59 (May 1996): 428–435.

Goodson, John J. *Judicial Selection: Options for Choosing Judges in Texas.* Session Focus No. 75-9. Austin: House Research Organization, Texas House of Representatives, February 17, 1997.

Governance of the Texas Judiciary: Independence and Accountability. 2 vols. Austin: Report of the Texas Commission on Judicial Efficiency, November 1996 and January 1997. Another study of the state's judicial system and recommendations for a major overhaul (but no action was taken by the 75th Legislature in its regular session).

Griffin, Barbara. *When Can the State Be Taken to Court?* Session Focus No. 74-22. Austin: House Research Organization, Texas House of Representatives, June 29, 1996.

Heimlich, Janet. "Brute Causes." *Texas Monthly* (November 1997): 20–22. Violence in the Texas penal system.

Hollandsworth, Skip. "Michael Irvin: The Ringmaster of the Media Circus." *Texas Monthly* (September 1996): 111, 176, 178. Big crime and a small punishment for a Dallas Cowboy.

*———. "The Lawsuit from Hell." *Texas Monthly* (June 1996): 106–111, 140–147. Thousands of Lone Star Steel employees sue hundreds of companies for injuries described as "chemical AIDS."

Jeffreys, Brenda Sapino. "Plaintiff Firms Bow out as Big Campaign Donors." *Texas Lawyer* (9 March 1998): 1, 27–28. Trend toward reduced campaign spending by law firms that represent plaintiffs in civil suits.

Johnson, Coyt Randal. "Death Takes Center Stage." *Texas Lawyer* (19 January 1998): 38, 41. An attorney witnesses the execution of his client.

Jones, Gene A. *The Seduction of Black Criminality: A Psychopolitical Analysis of Black Crime in America.* Merritt Island, Fla.: GSC Books, 1997. The author is a Fort Worth police officer.

Lawrence, George Noel. "What Everyone Should Know About Sexual Harassment, But Was Afraid to Ask." *Texas Bar Journal* 60 (November 1997): 1024, 1026–1028, 1030–1031, 1033–1035.

*Lott, John. *More Guns, Less Crime: Understanding Crime and Gun Control Laws.* Chicago: University of Chicago Press, 1998.

*Medaille, Bill, and Andrew Wheat. *Payola Justice: How Texas Supreme Court Justices Raise Money from Court Litigants.* Austin: Texans for Public Justice, February 1998.

Mitchell, Ellen Bloomer. "Appellate Review of Criminal Cases in Texas." *St. Mary's Law Journal* 26:4 (1995): 941–1050.

Munn, Michele. "Crossing the Bar." *Texas Monthly* (February 1995): 52, 54, 56. One lawyer's experience with the Texas bar exam.

*Patoski, Joe Nick. "The Sweet Song of Justice." *Texas Monthly* (December 1995): 102, 105, 132, 134–136. A detailed account of the trial and conviction of Yolanda Saldivar for the murder of superstar Selena Quintanilla Perez, queen of Tejana music.

Thompson, Helen. "Best-Case Scenario." *Texas Monthly* (December 1994): 44–45, 48, 52, 61–62. Profile of Robert Hirschhorn, the Galveston lawyer who helps other lawyers pick jurors.

Trichter, J. Gary. "DWI: What Every Client Should Know." *Texas Bar Journal* 56 (March 1993): 268–270, 274–275.

*Turner, Charles, and Ralph Walton. *Texas Law in Layman's Language.* 5th ed. Houston: Gulf Publishing Company, 1995.

Vaught, James A. "Internal Procedures in the Texas Supreme Court." *Texas Tech Law Review* 26:3 (1995): 935–958.

*Wallace, L. Jean. *What Every 18-Year-Old Needs to Know about Texas Law.* Austin: University of Texas Press, 1992.

Winslade, William, T. Howard Stone, Michell Smith-Bell, and Denise M. Webb. "Castrating Pedophiles Convicted of Sex Offenses Against Children: New Treatment or Old Punishment?" *SMU Law Review* 51 (January-February 1998): 349–411.

Chapter 9 Revenues, Expenditures, and Fiscal Policy

Web Sites

Auditor's Office, Texas State <http://www.sao.state.tx.us>
Mission, goal, objective, and statement of values of the office; key points of reports since September 1994; human resources information; reports of fraud, waste, or abuse at state agencies, colleges, or universities.

Budget Board, Legislative <http://www.lbb.state.tx.us>
Description of the board, members past and present, calendar for hearings, synopses of reports, on-line copies of the most recent General Appropriations Act, and the *Texas Fact Book.*

Texas Marketplace <http://www.texas-one.org>
General procurement information on Texas state agency purchases in excess of $25,000; web site required by state law to be operational on or before June 1, 1998.

Window on State Government <http://www.window.state.tx.us>
Maintained by the Office of the Comptroller of Public Accounts; information on Texas state taxes, performance of state agencies, the state's economy, and many related subjects; links with other economic and fiscal sites.

Books and Articles

Berasley, Ann. "Lawmakers Set Spending Priorities." *Fiscal Notes* (September 1997): 3–4. Texas' state budget for the 1998-1999 biennium.

*Bunch, Beverly S., and Thomas M. Keel. "Texas State Debt Management in the 1990s." *Public Affairs Comment* 42:1 (1996): 1–7.

*Burka, Paul. "You Lose Again." *Texas Monthly* (March 1998): 108–109, 114–117. How politics ruined the Texas lottery.

*Curtis, Gregory, and Paul Burka. "For an Income Tax." *Texas Monthly* (May 1997): 9, 12, 14.

Golembiewski, Robert T., and Jack Rabin, eds. *Public Budgeting and Finance,* 4th ed. New York: Marcel Dekker, 1997.

Hacker, Stanley. "Funding Primer: Transportation Dollars Take Many Routes." *Fiscal Notes* (May 1998): 3–4.

*Howe, Edward T., and Donald J. Reeb. "The Historical Evolution of State and Local Tax Systems." *Social Science Quarterly* 78 (March 1997): 109–121.

Khan, Aman, ed. *Budgeting in Texas: Process, Problems, Prospects.* New York: University Press of America, 1991.

Miller, Donald F., and Patrick A. Pierce. "Lotteries for Education: Windfall or Hoax?" *State and Local Government Review* 29 (Winter 1997): 34–42.

Mt. Joy, Greg. "Open for Enrollment." *Fiscal Notes* (October 1997): 3. Revision of the Texas Tomorrow Fund, the state's prepaid tuition contract program.

Reichenstein, Bill. "Prepaid Tuition." *Texas Business* (September 1997): 26–27. Advantages and disadvantages of the Texas Tomorrow Fund.

Sharp, John. *Biennial Revenue Estimates, 1998–1999.* Austin: Office of the Comptroller of Public Accounts, 1997.

Texas Performance Review. *Against the Grain: High Quality, Low-Cost Government for Texas.* 2 vols. Austin: Office of the Comptroller of Public Accounts, January 1993.

———. *Breaking the Mold: New Ways to Govern Texas.* 2 vols in 3. Austin: Office of the Comptroller of Public Accounts, July 1991.

———. *Disturbing the Peace: The Challenge of Change in Texas Government.* 2 vols. Austin: Comptroller of Public Accounts, December 1996.

———. *Gaining Ground: Progress and Reform in Texas Government.* 2 vols. Austin: Office of the Comptroller of Public Accounts, November 1994.

Tweedie, Jack. "Welfare Spending: More for Less." *State Legislatures* (April 1998): 12–18.

Wallin, Bruce A. "Federal Cutbacks and the Fiscal Condition of the States." *Publius* 26 (Summer 1996): 140–159.

*"Who Pays Texas Taxes?" *Fiscal Notes* (August 1996): 3–8.

Zamrazil, Kristie. *Fiscal 1998–99 Budget—House Appropriations Committee Version.* State Finance Report No. 75-2. Austin: House Research Organization, Texas House of Representatives, March 18, 1997.

*———. *Writing the State Budget.* State Finance Report No. 75-1. Austin: House Research Organization, Texas House of Representatives, February 7, 1997.

Texas-Based Think Tanks for Public Policy Research

Included among materials on public affairs in the Lone Star State is a growing number of reports produced by Texas-based research centers (commonly called think tanks) established by special interests to influence policymakers and the general public. Names and missions of six think tanks follow. More information concerning their research activities may be obtained through use of the mailing addresses and telephone numbers provided below.

Center for Public Policy Priorities. 900 Lydia Street, Austin, TX 78702-2625. An office of the Benedictine Research Center, San Antonio, that concerns itself with public policy research and analysis, seeking sound solutions to the challenges faced by low- and moderate-income families in Texas. (Ph. 512-320-0222)

Free Market Foundation. Nathaniel Barrett Building, 903 E. 18th St., Suite 230, Plano, TX 75074. Through research and education, this foundation seeks to strengthen and protect the individual and family. It supports principles that promote responsible citizenship, limited government, free enterprise, private property ownership, and Judeo-Christian values. (Ph. 972-680-9171)

National Center for Policy Analysis. 12655 North Central Expressway, Suite 720, Dallas, TX 75243-1739. Engages in research on free market issues at national and state levels. (Ph. 972-386-6272)

Texas Center for Policy Studies. P.O. Box 2618, Austin, TX 78768. Emphasizes research on environmental and economic development issues. (Ph. 512-474-0811)

Texas Citizens for a Sound Economy. 1005 Congress, Suite 910, Austin, TX 78701. Engages in research and lobbying efforts involving free market issues at state and national levels of government. (Ph. 512-476-5905)

Texas Public Policy Foundation. 8122 Datapoint Drive, Suite 816, San Antonio, TX 78229. Research is guided by concern for limited government, free enterprise, private property rights, and individual responsibility. The foundation seeks to influence Texas government by generating research and data and by recommending its findings to group leaders, policymakers, media persons, and the general public. (Ph. 210-614-0080)

Glossary

adjudication hearing A trial in a juvenile court.

advice and consent The power of the Texas Senate to review and approve major appointments by the governor.

alternative dispute resolution Use of mediation, conciliation, or arbitration to resolve disputes among individuals without resorting to a regular court trial.

appeal A formal request to a higher court to review the actions of a lower court.

appellate court A court whose primary function is to review the judgments of other courts and of administrative agencies.

appellate jurisdiction The power of a court to review cases after they have been tried elsewhere.

at-large system A system in which members of a policymaking body, such as some city councils, are elected on a citywide basis rather than from single-member districts.

audit The final phase of the government budgetary process, which reviews the operations of an agency, especially its financial transactions, to determine whether the agency has spent its money lawfully, efficiently, and with the desired results.

Avery* v. *Midland County Resulted in the U.S. Supreme Court ruling that commissioners court precincts in Texas must be of substantially equal population.

the bar The legal profession; a jurisdiction's community of licensed lawyers (e.g., the State Bar of Texas).

bicameral Term describing a legislature with two houses, or chambers (e.g., Texas's House of Representatives and Senate).

bill A proposed law or statute.

board-commission system Texas's weak executive model; which features an administrative system with many boards and commissions that are largely outside the control of the governor.

bond A certificate of indebtedness issued by a borrower to a lender that constitutes a legal obligation to repay the principal of the loan plus accrued interest. In Texas, both state and local governments issue bonds under restrictions imposed by state law.

bracket bill A bill, local in intent, that is presented as a general bill to avoid constitutional limitations; usually bracket bills specify a population bracket that applies to only one unit of local government.

bribery The giving or offering of anything of value with intent to unlawfully influence public officials in the discharge of their duties; public officials' receipt or request of anything of value with intent to be unlawfully influenced.

bureaucracy The totality of government offices that constitute the permanent government of a state; that is, those personnel and functions that continue regardless of changes in political leadership.

capital felony A crime punishable by death or life imprisonment.

caption The first part of a bill or resolution; states briefly the purpose of the legislation.

challenge for cause A reasoned objection to a prospective jury member.

civil commitment Mandatory placement of offenders identified as sexual predators in mental institutions after they have completed their prison terms.

closed primary A primary in which voters must declare their support for the party before they are permitted to participate in the selection of its candidates.

coalition A joining of political actors or organizations to advance legislation or to elect candidates; a prominent example is the Texas Conservative Coalition, an alliance of Republicans and conservative Democrats in the Texas House of Representatives.

code A comprehensive collection of statutory laws, organized by topics for easy reference (e.g., the Texas Election Code).

commission form A type of municipal government in which each elected commissioner is a member of the city's policymaking body but also heads an administrative department (e.g., public safety with police and fire divisions).

commissioners court A Texas county's policymaking body, with five members: the county judge, who presides, and four commissioners representing single-member districts.

commission-manager form Term sometimes used for the council-manager form of municipal government.

community supervision Formerly called *probation,* this form of punishment does not require confinement in a jail or prison. Such a sentence is commonly given to a first offender guilty of a misdemeanor or lesser felony. Failure to comply with rules enforced by supervising personnel may result in incarceration.

concurrent jurisdiction Authority of more than one court to try a case (e.g., a civil dispute involving more than $500 but less than $5,000 may be heard in either a justice of the peace court or a county court).

concurrent resolution A resolution adopted by majorities present in the House and Senate and then approved by the governor (e.g., request for action by Congress or authorization for someone to sue the state).

conference committee A committee composed of members of the House and Senate who are appointed for the purpose of reaching agreement on a disputed bill and then recommending changes that will be acceptable to both chambers.

consolidated metropolitan statistical area Composed of two or more primary metropolitan statistical areas and a total population of 1 million or more.

constitutional amendment A constitutional provision added by actions of the legislature and the voters since adoption of the original constitution.

convention A political meeting of the members or delegates of one party; precinct, county, district, state, and national conventions are parts of the temporary organizational structures of the Democratic and Republican parties.

coroner Role of a justice of the peace in determining the cause of a death occurring under violent, unusual, or suspicious circumstances.

council-manager system A system in which an elected city council hires a manager to coordinate budgetary matters and supervise administrative departments.

council of governments Representatives of local governments in Texas constitute 24 regional planning bodies that evaluate grant proposals by member governments.

court of record Has a court reporter to record testimony and proceedings.

crossover voting Participating in the primary of one party, then voting for one or more candidates of another party in the general election.

cumulative voting When multiple vacancies occur in 40 at-large city councils in Texas, voters cast one or more of the specified number of votes for one or more candidates in any combination. It is designed to increase representation of minorities.

dealignment Citizens abandon allegiance to a political party and become independent voters.

decree of the court (See **judgment.**)

defendant The person who is sued in a civil proceeding or prosecuted in a criminal proceeding.

deficit The amount by which a government's expenditures exceed its revenues.

deregulation Elimination of government restrictions to allow free-market competition to determine the actions of individuals and corporations.

devolution Financial and administrative responsibilities of the federal government are shifted to state and local governments, especially in the area of social services.

direct primary A nominating system that allows voters to participate directly in the selection of candidates for public office.

disposition hearing A juvenile justice proceeding whereby a court decides whether to dismiss the case, commit the juvenile delinquent to a Texas Youth Commission facility, or place the youth on probation.

dual budgeting system The compilation of separate budgets by a legislative budget board and an executive budget office.

early voting Conducted at the county courthouse and selected polling places before the designated primary, special, or general election day.

election judge Appointed by the county commissioners court to administer an election in a voting precinct.

electioneering Campaigning actively on behalf of a candidate; the total efforts made to win an election.

engrossment Preparation of an officially prescribed copy of a bill, with the text as amended by floor action in either the House or the Senate on the third reading.

enhanced punishment Repeat offenders convicted of felonies or class A and B misdemeanors are given more severe punishment than first offenders.

enrollment Preparation of an officially prescribed copy of a bill, with text as amended and approved by both the House and the Senate.

exclusive jurisdiction Authority of only one court to hear a particular type of case.

executive branch In a government with separation of powers, the branch with responsibility for enforcing or administering the law.

executive clemency Power of the the governor to set aside or reduce a court-imposed penalty through pardon, reprieve, or commutation of sentence.

executive committee A committee that heads a permanent party organization at the county, district, or state level.

federalism A system of government with powers divided between a national government and associated regional (state) governments.

filibuster A tactic to delay floor action whereby a senator may speak as long as physical endurance permits.

fiscal Having to do with taxation, public revenues, or public debt.

foreman (or presiding juror) The person who chairs and speaks for a jury.

franchise fee A fee collected by cities and based on gross receipts of public utilities (e.g., telephone and cable TV companies).

freeport amendment A constitutional provision that allows tax exemption for items that may not be located within Texas for more than 175 days in a year (e.g., aircraft).

functional representation Representation provided by an interest group for its members.

general bill A bill that applies to all people or property in the state and becomes a public law if passed.

general election Held in November of even-numbered years to elect county and state officials from among candidates nominated in primaries.

general law city Municipality with a charter prescribed by the legislature.

gerrymander To draw the boundaries of a district (e.g., state senatorial district) to include or exclude certain groups of voters and thus affect the election outcome.

graded penalties A range of punishments providing higher fines and/or longer sentences for increasingly serious offenses.

grant-in-aid Money, goods, or services given by one government to another (e.g., federal grants-in-aid to states for financing social welfare programs).

grassroots governments Governments for cities, counties, and special districts.

Harper v. *Virginia State Board of Education* Resulted in the U.S. Supreme Court invalidating payment of a poll tax as a prerequisite for voting.

hazardous waste Any by-product that poses a substantial present or potential threat to plants, animals, and humans because it is harmful to their health and welfare.

high-level radioactive waste Waste derived largely from nuclear energy generation and the manufacture of nuclear weapons; it is potentially toxic for thousands of years.

high technology Technology that applies to research, development, manufacturing, and marketing of computers and other electronic products.

home rule city Municipality with a locally drafted charter.

hung jury Occurs when a minimum number of jurors cannot agree on a verdict.

impeachment Process in which the Texas House of Representatives, by a simple majority vote, initiates action (brings charges) leading to possible removal of certain judicial and executive officials (e.g., the governor) by the Senate.

indictment Action by a grand jury charging a person with commission of a crime.

initiative A citizen-drafted measure introduced by a petition signed by a certain number or percentage of qualified voters.

interest group (or pressure group) An organization that seeks to influence government officials and their policies on behalf of members sharing common views and objectives (e.g., labor union or trade association).

joint resolution Must pass by a simple majority vote in each house when used to ratify an amendment to the U.S. Constitution. As a proposal for an amendment to the Texas Constitution, a joint resolution requires a two-thirds majority vote in each house. Gubernatorial approval is not required.

judgment (or decree of the court) A judge's written opinion based on a verdict.

jurisdiction A court's authority to hear a particular case.

juror A person selected to determine matters of fact based on evidence presented at a trial and to render a verdict.

Kilgarlin v. *Martin* The federal district court case of 1965 that first applied the "one person, one vote" principle in Texas.

legislative caucus A group of like-minded legislators organized to influence the House and Senate (e.g., House Republican Caucus, Legislative Black Caucus).

legislative committee A subdivision of the House or Senate that prepares bills and resolutions for floor action or that makes investigations as directed by the respective house.

legislative immunity A constitutional exemption from ordinary legal culpability while engaged in legislative work.

legislature The lawmaking branch of state government.

lobbyist A person who communicates with legislators or other government officials on behalf of an interest group or a corporation for the purpose of influencing the decision-making process.

local bill A bill that affects only a single unit of local government (e.g., a city, county, or special district).

Lone Star Card A plastic card that has replaced government-issued stamps for the purpose of authorizing certain welfare recipients to obtain food without personal payment.

magistrate A minor official with limited judicial authority (e.g., a justice of the peace or the judge of a municipal court).

martial law Temporary rule by military authorities when civil authorities are unable to handle a riot or other civil disorder.

master The judge who hears evidence and reports on alleged judicial misconduct.

mayor-council form A form of city government with a separately elected executive head (the mayor) and an urban legislative body (the council). It is called a *strong mayor-council form* if the office of mayor is filled in a citywide election and has veto, appointment, and removal powers; when a mayor lacks such powers, that government is identified as a *weak mayor-council form.*

metro government Consolidation of units of local government within an urban area under a single authority.

metropolitan area An urban area composed of one or more large cities and surrounding suburban communities; although socially and economically integrated, a metropolitan area is composed of separate units of local government, including counties, cities, and special districts.

metropolitan statistical area (MSA) A freestanding urban area with a minimum total population of 50,000.

metropolitanization Concentration of people in urban centers that become linked.

motor-voter law Legislation requiring certain government offices (e.g., motor vehicle licensing agencies) to offer voter registration applications to clients.

municipal annexation law A law that allows Texas cities to annex territory beyond their corporate limits, with some restrictions.

NAACP v. Alabama By recognizing the right of association, this U.S. Supreme Court decision facilitated the development of the National Association for the Advancement of Colored People and other interest groups.

North American Free Trade Agreement (NAFTA) An agreement among the United States, Mexico, and Canada that was designed to expand trade among the three countries by reducing and then eliminating tariffs over a 15-year period.

off-year election A general election held in the even-numbered year following a presidential election.

Ogallala Aquifer The world's largest underground water-bearing rock formation, extending from Texas to North Dakota.

open primary A primary in which voters are not required to declare party identification.

ordinance A local law enacted by a city council or approved by popular vote in a referendum election.

organized labor Unions that serve as bargaining agents for members and promote their interests through lobbying activities.

original jurisdiction The power of a court to hear a case first.

pardon An act of clemency releasing a person from the legal consequences of a criminal act.

parole Release from prison before completion of a sentence; the release is conditioned by good behavior of the parolee and other requirements that may not be imposed.

party-column ballot A ballot that lists candidates under their party designation; this makes it easy to vote for all candidates of one party (straight-ticket voting) by pulling a single lever on a voting machine or writing a single X at the top of a party column.

penal code A compilation of laws that regulate individual conduct and spell out punishments for violations.

per diem allowance Daily allowance for living expenses (e.g., $95 per day for Texas legislators during the 75th regular session in 1997).

peremptory challenge An attorney's objection, without having to give a reason, to the selection of a juror.

place system A system in which city council candidates file for numerically designated places and all voters in the city vote in each place contest.

plaintiff The injured party who initiates a civil suit.

platform The political document that sets forth a party's position on current issues.

plea bargain Occurs when the accused agrees to plead guilty in return for a prosecutor's promise to ask for a shorter period of confinement, smaller fine, or community supervision.

plural executive The governor and elected department heads as provided by the Texas Constitution and statutes.

police power The authority of a government to protect the health, morals, safety, and welfare of citizens.

political action committee (PAC) An organizational device used by corporations, labor unions, and other organizations to raise money for campaign contributions.

political culture Attitudes, habits, and general behavior patterns that develop over time and affect the political life of a state or region.

politics The process employed by individuals and political parties to nominate and elect public officials and to formulate public policy.

postadjournment veto Rejection by the governor of a pending bill or concurrent resolution during the 20 days following a legislative session.

power linkage A triangular relationship connecting interest group, bureaucracy, and legislature.

precinct chair The party official responsible for the interests of a political party in a voting precinct; typical duties include supervising party volunteer workers, encouraging voter registration, and getting out the vote on election day.

president of the Senate Title of the lieutenant governor in his or her role as presiding officer for the Texas Senate.

president pro tempore The person elected by the Senate to preside in the absence of the president of the Senate (lieutenant governor).

presidential primary A primary in which the voters indicate their preference for a person seeking nomination as the party's presidential candidate.

presiding juror See **foreman**.

pressure group See **interest group**.

primary election A preliminary election conducted within the party to select candidates who will run for public office in a subsequent general election.

primary metropolitan statistical area (PMSA) Composed of two or more metropolitan statistical areas (MSAs) with a total population of 100,000 or more.

progressive taxation A tax policy whereby people in each successively higher income bracket pay a progressively higher tax rate.

proposition An issue, printed on the ballot, to be voted on in a referendum election.

prosecutor An attorney who initiates and maintains criminal proceedings on behalf of the government against people accused of committing offenses.

public interest group An organization claiming to represent a broad public interest (environmental, consumer, civil rights) rather than a narrow private interest.

public opinion polling Private and informal surveys of public opinion or of the opinions of any group.

Puerto Rico v. *Brandstadt* Ruling by the U.S. Supreme Court requiring a state governor to comply with a valid extradition request.

radioactive waste The by-product of military and civilian use of nuclear materials.

readings of a bill The traditional requirement that a bill be read three times before it can be passed in one legislative chamber.

realignment Occurs when members of one party shift their affiliation to another party.

recall A procedure that allows citizens to vote officeholders out of office between regularly scheduled elections.

recess appointment An appointment made by the governor when the Texas Legislature is not in session.

recidivism Criminal behavior that results in reincarceration after a person has been released from confinement for a prior offense.

redistricting Redrawing of boundaries following the federal decennial census to create districts with approximately equal population (e.g., legislative, congressional, and commissioners court districts in Texas).

referendum A procedure for submitting proposed citizen-drafted municipal ordinances or proposed state constitutional amendments to the voters for ratification.

regressive taxation A tax policy whereby the effective tax rate falls as the tax base (e.g., individual income, corporate profits) increases.

regulation Government intervention in the workings of business markets to promote a socially, economically, or politically desirable goal.

reprieve An act of executive clemency that temporarily suspends the execution of a sentence.

Reynolds v. *Sims* The U.S. Supreme Court case that established the criterion of "one person, one vote" for state legislative apportionment.

right A legally enforceable power or privilege.

right-to-work law A Texas law that prohibits collective bargaining agreements containing maintenance of membership, preferential hiring, union shop, or any other clauses calling for compulsory union membership.

road user tax State tax on motor vehicles, motor vehicle fuels, and motor vehicle registration; provides revenue for building and maintaining state highways.

Ruiz v. *Estelle* A 1980 case in which U.S. district court judge William Wayne Justice condemned an overcrowded, understaffed Texas prison system and ordered sweeping changes in its policies and operations.

sales tax A tax on consumption rather than income. It is levied in most states for a fixed rate, usually ranging from 2 to 9 percent, to be charged on most purchases. The state sales tax in Texas is 6.25 percent, with exemptions for groceries and prescription drugs; additional sales taxes may be levied by cities and some other local governments.

school district A special district providing local public education for all children in its service area; a nonsalaried elected board, the typical governing body, hires a superintendent to administer the system.

senatorial courtesy Before making an appointment, the governor is expected to obtain approval from the state senator in whose district the prospective appointee resides; failure to obtain such approval will probably cause the appointee to be "busted" by the Senate.

separation of powers The assignment of lawmaking, law-enforcing, and law-interpreting functions to separate branches of government.

service industry The most rapidly growing sector of the Texas economy in the 1990s; includes the services of hospitals, hotels, bowling alleys, data processing companies, and management consultants.

simple resolution A resolution that requires action by one legislative chamber only and is not acted on by the governor.

sin tax A selective sales tax on items such as cigarettes, other forms of tobacco, and alcoholic beverages.

single-member district An area that elects only one representative to serve on a policy-making body (e.g., city council, county commissioners court, state House and Senate).

Smith v. *Allwright* U.S. Supreme Court case in which the Court outlawed the white primary for nominating public officials in Texas.

speaker The state representative who is elected by House members to serve as the presiding officer for that chamber.

special bill A bill that makes an exception to general laws for the benefit of a specific individual, class, or corporation.

special district A unit of local government that serves a specific group of people within a particular geographic area (e.g., hospital district, water district, soil conservation district).

special election An election called by the governor to fill a vacancy (e.g., U.S. congressional or state legislative office) or vote on a proposed state constitutional amendment or local bond issue.

special session A legislative session called by the governor and limited to not more than 30 days.

Spring Branch Independent School District v. *Stamos* Resulted in the Supreme Court of Texas upholding the "no pass, no play" provision concerning academic eligibility to participate in extracurricular activities (e.g., high school football).

state jail felony A so-called "fourth-degree felony" punishable by fine and confinement in a state felony jail; such an offense typically involves drug and/or alcohol abuse.

state of the state address Delivered by the governor early in a regular legislative session; typically, it covers important issues and the general condition of the State of Texas.

state ombudsman Provides advice and assistance to persons regarding their dealings with the Texas bureaucracy.

suburb A relatively small town or city, usually incorporated but outside the corporate limits of a central city.

suffrage The right to vote.

sunset laws Statutes that fix termination dates on agencies; implemented to force evaluation and encourage legislative inquiry, these laws require formal review and subsequent affirmative legislation if an agency is to continue.

tax A compulsory contribution exacted by a government for a public purpose.

tax appraisal district board The governing body established to appraise all real estate and income-producing property for taxation by the county and other units of local government functioning within its boundaries; each Texas county is required to operate with a single appraisal district.

tax reinvestment zone (TRZ) Municipal tax incentives are offered to encourage businesses to locate in and contribute to the development of a blighted urban area. Commercial and residential property taxes are frozen for a specific period.

Temporary Assistance for Needy Families (TANF) Replaced Aid to Families with Dependent Children (AFDC) in an attempt to help some poor people move from welfare to the workforce.

temporary party organization Primaries and conventions that function briefly to nominate candidates, pass resolutions, adopt a party platform, and select delegates to party conventions at higher levels.

Texas* v. *White U.S. Supreme Court case in which the Court ruled that states do not have a right to secede from the Union.

Third House A term for the many lobbyists who seek to influence policymaking by the Texas Legislature.

tort reform Legislation limiting the liability of employers and physicians for injuries and damage caused by their actions, capping punitive damage awards by juries, and prescribing monetary punishment for persons filing frivolous lawsuits.

trade association A business organization that lobbies on behalf of an industry (e.g., Texas Association of Builders, Texas Wine and Grape Growers Association).

trial court A court with the primary functions of initially hearing and deciding cases.

trial jury A statutorily defined number of persons selected to determine matters of fact based on evidence presented at a trial and to render a verdict.

umbrella organization An interest group that unites a variety of concerns under one overarching umbrella, the organization itself (e.g., Texas Association of Business and Chambers of Commerce).

unicameral The term that describes a one-house legislature (e.g., the Nebraska Legislature).

user fee A charge levied for services performed (e.g., charges for sewage disposal, garbage collection, and use of some municipal swimming pools).

venire A panel of prospective jurors drawn by random selection.

voting precinct The basic geographic area for conducting primaries and elections; Texas is divided into almost 9,000 voting precincts.

whistleblower law The statute that allows state employees to sue the State of Texas if they are dismissed unjustly as a result of their attempts to report fraud and corruption.

witness A person who has knowledge of the circumstances of a case and may present such knowledge as evidence in a trial.

writ A document issued by a judicial officer ordering or forbidding the performance of a specified act.

Index